# New Histories of Pre-Columbian Florida

FLORIDA MUSEUM OF NATURAL HISTORY: RIPLEY P. BULLEN SERIES

FLORIDA MUSEUM
OF NATURAL HISTORY

UNIVERSITY PRESS OF FLORIDA

Florida A&M University, Tallahassee
Florida Atlantic University, Boca Raton
Florida Gulf Coast University, Ft. Myers
Florida International University, Miami
Florida State University, Tallahassee
New College of Florida, Sarasota
University of Central Florida, Orlando
University of Florida, Gainesville
University of North Florida, Jacksonville
University of South Florida, Tampa
University of West Florida, Pensacola

# New Histories
# of Pre-Columbian Florida

Edited by Neill J. Wallis and Asa R. Randall

University Press of Florida
Gainesville / Tallahassee / Tampa / Boca Raton
Pensacola / Orlando / Miami / Jacksonville / Ft. Myers / Sarasota

21 20 19 18 17 16    6 5 4 3 2 1

First cloth printing, 2014
First paperback printing, 2016

Library of Congress Cataloging-in-Publication Data
New histories of Pre-Columbian Florida / edited by Neill J. Wallis and Asa R. Randall.
pages cm
Includes bibliographical references and index.
ISBN 978-0-8130-4936-6 (cloth: alk. paper)
ISBN 978-0-8130-6209-9 (pbk.)
1. Indians of North America—Florida—Antiquities. 2. Mississippian culture—Florida.
3. Woodland Indians—Florida. 4. Excavations (Archaeology)—Florida. 5. Kitchen-
middens—Florida. 6. Florida—Antiquities. I. Wallis, Neill J. II. Randall, Asa R.
E78.F6N45 2014
975.9'01—dc23      2013044109

The University Press of Florida is the scholarly publishing agency for the State University System of Florida, comprising Florida A&M University, Florida Atlantic University,
Florida Gulf Coast University, Florida International University, Florida State University,
New College of Florida, University of Central Florida, University of Florida, University
of North Florida, University of South Florida, and University of West Florida.

University Press of Florida
15 Northwest 15th Street
Gainesville, FL 32611-2079
http://www.upf.com

# Contents

# Figures

# Tables

# Introduction

## New Approaches to Ancient Florida

NEILL J. WALLIS AND ASA R. RANDALL

Florida inhabits a peculiar spot in our national narrative. As a vacation destination, it is a place to be celebrated, visited, and recorded in photographs. These experiences are materialized in pieces of the state. Painted seashells, postcards, and other kitsch are redistributed globally as mnemonics of this particular paradise. Largely because of its striking beauty, the state is also upheld as one of the last great vestiges of primordial nature to be enjoyed in the United States. The more ecologically conscious can delight in the environment for its own sake or for sport. The prospect of engaging with either of these Floridas has drawn many outsiders into the region (Mohl and Pozzetta 1996), reinforcing these conceptions. These two Floridas are, not surprisingly, often at odds. The tension between environmental preservation and development for recreation helps drive contemporary political agendas (Colburn 1996; Mohl and Mormino 1996). Despite their differences, these Floridas share a common origin. They have been crafted by environmentalists, land speculators, and inhabitants who have objectified the region as either timeless and pristine or full of potential for future economic success (e.g., Grunwald 2006; Noll and Tegeder 2009; Standiford 2002).

There is a third, much more ancient Florida. This is a place that is often forgotten, downplayed, or actively denied in recent grand narratives (Weisman 2003). The archaeology of ancient Florida has revealed vibrant cultures and communities filled with diverse persons who engaged with the world in various and at times competing ways. Human settlement of the region can be traced back to at least 12,000 years ago, and perhaps even earlier. Over successive millennia, inhabitants made histories of their own by modifying the landscape and through social interaction. These processes are materialized in well-preserved Paleoindian sites and wet sites laden with organic matter, represented by early and grandiose traditions of mound building, and evidenced by repeated moments of cultural contact, extralocal connections, and by practicing distinctive traditions.

While our understanding of this ancient Florida continues to grow through ar-chaeological field research and laboratory analyses, the richness of Florida's aborigi-nal past is too often appreciated by only a small group of practitioners working in the state. Several factors have impeded regional, national, or international consider-ation of Florida's significance, each leading to the creation of erroneous notions that continue to impede interpretations of the past. Foremost among these factors is that Florida has been maintained as a geographically peripheral appendage to southeast-ern North America. Sociopolitical developments in the ancient Southeast are regu-larly conceived as centered in places far from the Florida peninsula, often in various parts of the Mississippi Valley. For instance, Poverty Point in northeast Louisiana looms large as a Late Archaic center of nascent sociopolitical complexity (Kidder 2010; Sassaman 2005). Similarly, the well-known Hopewell Interaction Sphere of the Middle Woodland period is conceived as originating in the Midwest in areas of Ohio and Illinois (Carr and Case 2006; Charles 2006), and the "Big Bang" of Cahokia in southern Illinois set in motion a history of Mississippianization that would reach far into the deep south (Anderson 1994; Pauketat 2007). Although Florida communities were implicated in all of these broad-scale cultural and histori-cal phenomena to some degree, their role has inevitably been interpreted as that of receivers rather than generators of grand traditions and social change. Florida is un-questionably unique in its archaeology and geography, and much of the state is far more proximate to the Caribbean than to the Southeast, as traditionally conceived. But the view that Florida is located on the geographical and cultural periphery tends to neglect the formative role of ancient Floridians in large-scale regional processes. Consider, for example, the remarkable abundance of Florida-made St. Johns pot-tery at Poverty Point (Hays and Weinstein 2004) or the widespread distribution of *Busycon* shells thousands of miles across the Midwest in the Archaic, Woodland, and Mississippi periods (Carr 2006; Claassen 1996, 2008). Indeed, when one con-siders the fact that many well-known and widespread phenomena (e.g., Hopewell, Mississippianization) originated on the edges of the Southeast, Florida's geographic remoteness would seem to be of little consequence in terms of engagement with or influence of regional politics and ritual processes.

Another factor that has diminished Florida's archaeological significance has been the tacit acceptance of our national narrative about the state's natural beauty and the assumption that Florida's inhabitants are best understood in purely ecological terms. "Adaptation," a long-standing legacy of the intersections of Steward's (1955) cultural ecology, various "New Archaeologies" (Binford 1962), and the environ-mental movement that burgeoned in the 1960s (e.g., Carson 1962), is a buzzword whose popularity can be traced throughout Americanist archaeology until very re-cently. Although research in many regions of the hemisphere has recently embraced holistic concepts of history and process that are informed by social theory, research

on Florida has often held fast to a somewhat narrow focus on ecology (e.g., Marquardt 2010a; Marquardt 2010b). This tendency is probably due, at least in part, to
the formidable legacy of Elizabeth Wing's environmental archaeology program at
the Florida Museum of Natural History. Study of the natural environment holds an
important place in archaeological research, as it should, but the place of humans
in the natural world must be considered in the context of a holistic view of social
practices and institutions that enhances the relevance of archaeological work.

Finally, Florida's ancient past has been projected as a slow, long-term process that
was separated from the modern world by the European encounters that began in the
sixteenth century. Indeed, the pace of ancient Florida history appears insufferably
sluggish at certain times and in certain places. For instance, from some long-term
perspectives, the adoption of pottery could be considered the most exciting development over a period of more than a thousand years. This focus on technology
can be seen as the counterpart to ecological determinism. These two frameworks
of analysis work together to identify the histories of native groups as *developmental*
(i.e., gradual) rather than *eventful* (i.e., punctuated or rapid) (Fogelson 1989). The
resulting characterizations are especially problematic because they define the ancient past using Western post-industrialist notions of history that inevitably serve
to separate, romanticize, and naturalize ancient communities as inherently different
from modern and technologically advanced peoples. This separation of past and
present worlds is not unique to Florida investigations (e.g., Cobb 2005; Harvey
1989), but they make an artificial separation between the dynamism of the present
and the (presumed) stasis of the past.

This book brings together recent archaeological research in Florida that provides detailed and nuanced interpretations of the pre-Columbian past. The contributions to this volume cover much of the Florida panhandle and peninsula (figure
Intro.1) and consider time periods between 7,500 and 500 years ago. While the
archaeology of Florida has been the focus of several widely cited syntheses (e.g.,
Milanich 1994; Milanich and Fairbanks 1980), these broad treatments entrenched
certain notions that are no longer tenable. In particular, data from fieldwork, the
use of new techniques, and reconsideration of work by earlier preeminent archaeologists (e.g., Wyman, Moore, Bullen, Goggin, Sears, Fairbanks, and Milanich)
has revealed considerable variation in how societies were organized across the
state that was unanticipated and is often at odds with previous models that emphasize long-term continuities, environmental determinism, and localized social
interaction. Recent work in Florida features significant contributions to several
overarching anthropological themes that include the construction of monuments
and meaningful places, the dynamics of how humans interacted with the environment, and how ritual is constituted through materiality. The archaeological record
of Florida offers unsurpassed opportunities for investigating these questions, but

long-standing taxonomies, chronologies, and concepts have often hindered realization of this potential.

Each chapter in this volume reassesses long-held notions of the past, but the volume does not represent the definitive statement on pre-Columbian archaeology in Florida and is not the only recent evaluation of Florida as central to regional-scale ancient histories. Indeed, recent journal articles and chapters in books are steadily revising portions of the histories of ancient Florida. A recently published volume, *Late Prehistoric Florida* (Ashley and White 2012), showcases some of the most recent research pertaining to Mississippi period contexts across most of the state. While this volume partially overlaps with Ashley and White's work in terms of time and space, this volume offers more significant time depth and deeply diachronic perspectives and is primarily focused on explicating themes derived from theory that have broad significance beyond Florida.

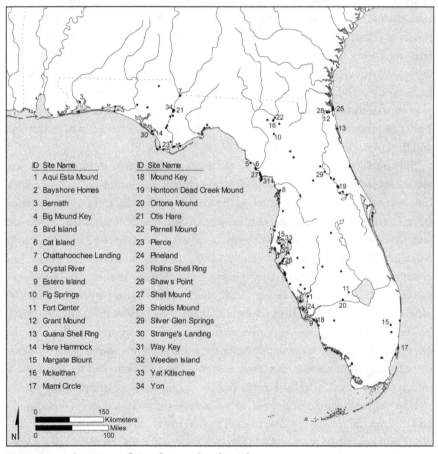

| ID | Site Name | ID | Site Name |
|----|-----------|----|-----------|
| 1 | Aqui Esta Mound | 18 | Mound Key |
| 2 | Bayshore Homes | 19 | Hontoon Dead Creek Mound |
| 3 | Bernath | 20 | Ortona Mound |
| 4 | Big Mound Key | 21 | Otis Hare |
| 5 | Bird Island | 22 | Parnell Mound |
| 6 | Cat Island | 23 | Pierce |
| 7 | Chattahoochee Landing | 24 | Pineland |
| 8 | Crystal River | 25 | Rollins Shell Ring |
| 9 | Estero Island | 26 | Shaws Point |
| 10 | Fig Springs | 27 | Shell Mound |
| 11 | Fort Center | 28 | Shields Mound |
| 12 | Grant Mound | 29 | Silver Glen Springs |
| 13 | Guana Shell Ring | 30 | Strange's Landing |
| 14 | Hare Hammock | 31 | Way Key |
| 15 | Margate Blount | 32 | Weeden Island |
| 16 | Mckeithen | 33 | Yat Kitischee |
| 17 | Miami Circle | 34 | Yon |

Figure Intro.1. Locations of sites discussed in this volume.

Our task in this volume is to rethink how the practices and worldviews of Florida's ancient communities can contribute to the study of the past at different scales. In this chapter, we highlight what we consider to be important themes and trends that link Florida both conceptually and historically with the greater Southeast: 1) monumentality and modified landscapes; 2) the materiality of ritualization; and 3) the environment and history. Although we separate these concepts and practices in this chapter, they are inherently relational and mutually reinforcing.

## Monuments and Modified Landscapes

Our first theme centers on one of the most enduring—and controversial—hallmarks of ancient Florida communities: the transformation of natural landscapes into cultured spaces through the deposition of earth, shellfish remains, objects, and the deceased. These practices are materialized in a variable constellation of places that includes lithic scatters, reused sinkholes, low-visibility mortuary ponds, singular earthen or shell mounds, and vast and elaborate centers. Florida communities created such places early and often: Paleoindians encultured now-inundated sites through hunting and dwelling, dedicated mortuaries are almost equal in their antiquity, the deposition of shell began as early as 7,500 years ago, and formal centers were constructed and dwelled in throughout the interior and coastal zones for much of the Middle and Late Holocene.

The diversity and intensity of place-making in Florida makes it a location unparalleled for documenting and rethinking the significance of monuments in nonwestern societies. Until recently, materialist perspectives and unilineal evolutionary thought have precluded researchers from seeing all but the most recent and structurally complex places as intentional—that is, *monumental*—constructions. This viewpoint is summed up by Bruce Trigger's oft-cited definition of monumental architecture that links monumentality with institutionalized leadership. According to Trigger, a monument's "principal defining feature is that its scale and elaboration exceed the requirements of any practical functions that a building is intended to perform"; in addition, it "expresses in a public and enduring manner the ability of an authority to control the materials, specialized skills, and labor required to create and maintain such structures" (Trigger 1990, 119, 127). A number of obfuscating corollaries and categories follow from this definition: the function of any particular construction is singular and self-evident, hierarchically stratified society is required for labor organization, the final form of a place was more significant than the *process* of construction, and finally, that food production or provisioning was a necessary precondition. Because many ancient Floridian societies effectively lack one or more of these attributes, many researchers have essentialized them as socially simple, have assumed that their histories reflect gradual process, and have reduced the places they created to comfortable and anemic western categories such as middens, trash heaps, or villages (Randall and Sassaman 2010).

*New Histories of Pre-Columbian Florida* provides a much-needed critique of this perspective. Indeed, no one definition of monumentality is sufficient to explain the preponderance and diversity of constructions across Florida or indeed throughout the world (Rosenswig and Burger 2012). Using a trait-based approach to distinguish monuments from non-monumental spaces has the potential to obscure the actual practices of ancient communities. An alternative and inclusive perspective on monumentality explores how the construction of place is inherently contextual and historical (Barrett 1999; Basso 1996). Context in this sense refers to the cosmologies, ecologies, worldviews, and interactions of potentially diverse practitioners. History here has a dual meaning: it is both the ever-emergent and contingent practices of people and the recognition of a past through commemoration and social memory (Trouillot 1995). Such an open-ended definition allows us to consider the alternative social realities that were referenced and transformed during place-making as a process. Similarly, it allows us to investigate how making places was one of several means by which past societies composed their own histories (e.g., Bradley 2002; Randall 2011).

Seeing monumentality as a process that is decoupled from particular modes of social organization, subsistence pursuits, or building materials requires us to interrogate the archaeological record and critique long-held assumptions. A particularly relevant example is the Fort Center site, a Woodland period earthen mound and mortuary complex in the Okeechobee region where W. H. Sears (1982) reported the presence of maize pollen. This find prompted Sears to explain the elaborate earthworks and the apparent complexity of their builders as a consequence of agriculture (ibid., 197–198). As Victor Thompson and Thomas Pluckhahn detail in this volume, the evidence from recent field investigations shows that this interpretation is no longer tenable. Not only were they unable to identify maize, but there was no evidence for any other cultigens. The implication is that the construction of Fort Center and indeed the modifications to the greater Okeechobee basin were done by hunter-gatherers. This new interpretation is one of many in this volume that open up the possibility of discussing the social histories of hunter-gatherers (e.g., Sassaman and Holly 2011). In a related vein, Thomas Pluckhahn and Victor Thompson address which criteria define constructed places as monumental. Using Trigger's definition as a starting point, they consider whether scale is the most informative attribute when comparing mound construction, community organization, and hierarchy across the region. Drawing on the shell and sand mound complex at the Crystal River site as an example, they argue that the degree of planning, the presence of authorities, and the organization of labor may be assessed from the arrangement of architectural features. They suggest that construction at Crystal River may have presented a context through which local authorities expressed social control, but more importantly, this context could have provided a venue at which diverse regional communities were incorporated in large-scale building projects.

Several contributors explore multiple spatial scales of analysis to understand how sites of different histories and configurations were ultimately linked through practice and significance (Luer; Randall et al.; White). These chapters demonstrate that much of Florida's "natural landscape" actually has a deep anthropogenic history. As recorded in the data in the Florida Master Site File, over 2,000 sites from all 67 counties are classified as prehistoric burial grounds or "mounds" or have the word "mound" in their name. The density of constructed spaces is often at odds with ecological narratives of Florida: seemingly neutral toponyms such as Ten Thousand Islands or "chain of lakes" obscure largely anthropogenic constructions. The widespread use of aerial remote sensing technologies such as multispectral imagery and LiDAR are adding to our understanding of the complexities of landscape generation across Florida.

Monuments and cultural landscapes are significant only in the contexts of their construction and inhabitation. We must consider the *tempo*, or pace, of depositional practices; the *temporality*, or situatedness and cyclicity, of deposition; and the *history*, or biography, of places. As many contributors to this volume note, the pace of mound construction in Florida—particularly shell mounds—has long been presumed to have been gradual and accretional. The implications of this gradualist view are that mounds were constructed by small scale-communities and likely reflect the accumulation of domestic refuse. However, radiocarbon assays have the potential to revolutionize how we think about ancient social change (e.g., Rosenswig and Burger 2012; Whittle et al. 2011). In this book, Theresa Schober reviews arguments that shell mounds reflect long-term processes. Through an analysis of radiocarbon assays from the Estero Mound site and others in southwest Florida, she demonstrates that at least some were constructed over short-term (likely generational) time scales. Furthermore, she finds that the bulk of the mound fill was acquired by mining preexisting shell sites, indicating that zooarchaeological studies of mound fill would be wise to incorporate the social and historical context of sample deposition in their analysis. The reuse of ancient places reminds us that it is not just absolute time that matters and that biographies of site abandonment, reuse, and transformation can provide key insights into the historical consciousness of ancient communities. For example, Randall and colleagues track changing Archaic period strategies of commemoration through detailed considerations of shell deposition, hydrological change, mortuary mound construction, and object circulation in the Silver Glen Springs watershed in the St. Johns River valley. Their data indicate that although this locale was repeatedly occupied over the course of many millennia, communities actively incorporated the past as places, and even pieces of those places, in the construction of later ceremonial mounds and residential spaces.

## The Materiality of Ritualization

We call a second important theme the materiality of ritualization. According to Catherine Bell (1997) and others, the term "ritualization" refers to a process whereby practices are imbued with symbolic importance in order to transform and reproduce social structures. When the analytical focus is on social practice, virtually all domains of culture have the potential to become ritualized, not just the domains traditionally relegated to ritual, such as mortuary ceremonialism and other specific aspects of culture that make little sense using functionalist explanations. An inclusive view of ritual may be particularly appropriate in studies of pre-Columbian southeastern natives, for whom "ritual" or "religion" or the "symbolic" were not always isolated from the practices of day-to-day life. Ritual is potentially everywhere, and the challenge for archaeologists is to follow the connections, continuities, disjunctures, and transformations evident in materiality. The process of signification is historical and unpredictable. We would therefore do well to abandon our preconceived categories, such as sacred and secular, and instead trace histories of material practice. When we take this view, our traditional categories become blurred as we find that a variety of practices and materials shift from the unmarked background of human experience to the marked foreground of ritual importance (Keane 2005). Significantly, in Florida (as in other locales), these ritualities can be seen to inflect both local legacies and more distant and widespread trends across the Southeast and beyond.

Many researchers have moved away from the received wisdom of traditional approaches to Florida archaeology by looking for ritualization where there was supposed to have been none. For example, several authors in this volume consider ritualized practices outside the context of mortuary ceremony and mounds. Neill Wallis examines evidence in the Middle Suwannee River valley for grandiose feasting events adjacent to modest Late Woodland and Mississippi period burial mounds in areas that are normally characterized as ephemeral villages. After his recent excavation of a large pit feature near the Parnell Mound, Neill J. Wallis argues that the smaller scale of mounding and apparently diminished density and size of sites following the abandonment of the well-known McKeithen site reflect shifting emphases in practice and the temporality of ceremonial gatherings more than the attenuation of ritual.

Another example of evidence of ritual in places that earlier archeological theories overlooked comes from Late Archaic shell rings, where consistent patterns in the deposition of shell, other fauna, and pottery may be the traces of ritualized practices, such as feasts, that are implicated in the reworking of social structures (e.g.,

Russo 2004). In this context, Rebecca Saunders and Margaret Wrenn consider the technological and stylistic characteristics of fiber-tempered pottery distributed at Atlantic coastal shell rings, and they assess the possibilities for craft specialization and the scale of social interaction. Comparing assemblages from Guana and Rollins, two contemporaneous shell rings located in separate river drainages in northeast Florida, they conclude that vessel attributes and the execution of incised designs denote distinctive local practices by potters, perhaps specialists, in each community. This conclusion does not necessarily invalidate the idea that rings served as loci of gathering among distant communities because hosts may have routinely provided the vessels used in these events.

Michael Russo, Craig Dengel, and Jeffrey Shanks consider how the material culture of shell rings is implicated in ritual in Woodland period contexts on the northwest coast of Florida's panhandle. They deconstruct Sears's (1973) dichotomy of sacred and secular by emphasizing the commensurability of mound and shell-ring pottery assemblages. They find that the pottery assemblages appear more similar than anticipated and that other categories of material culture that one would expect to find mostly in burial mounds are often found in rings. Indeed, exotica and mortuary paraphernalia such as ochre, mica, polished stone, and quartz crystal are found at most shell rings. These data indicate that shell rings are not simply "secular" habitation locales but are the loci of ceremony, especially those that led to the deposit of some of these objects in the adjacent burial mounds.

Ryan Wheeler and Bob Carr contextualize the archaeological manifestations of ritual in South Florida, taking as a point of departure the Miami Circle and popular interpretations of the site that have tended to sensationalize its ritual function. One dimension that has been debated is the status of animal interments that some have interpreted as sacrifices. Wheeler and Carr provide a wide-ranging discussion of ritual and sacrifice in Florida's ancient communities and conclude that there is not enough data to state specifically what these deposits may represent. However, they argue that anyone interpreting these or similar finds would be well advised to start thinking about animals as other (non-human) persons. In all cases, seeing such finds as evidence of ritualization tends to expand a system of meaningful references that emerge from practices that can be linked to other times and other places.

Closely related to the process of ritualization are patterns of movement: the travels of people, things, and ideas. Quite obviously, the convergence of people from different places often provides opportunities for ritualized performances of social distinction: place of origin becomes the basis for differentiation. As pieces of places (Bradley 2000; Thomas 1999), or at least as things that bear marks of those places, material things are also important testimony to conceptions of difference, hegemony, solidarity, or dissonance that play out in ritualized practices. Through the study of the life histories of objects (how they were produced and distributed, the trajectories of their use, and shifts in context), we can follow the paths of ritualization. Such an approach avoids assumptions about what is symbolically important. For example, detailed materials analysis sometimes demonstrates that commonplace and heavily used artifacts (for example, Swift Creek cooking vessels) were transported long distances and ritually buried in mounds, thus demonstrating that many and sundry objects can hold the symbolic capacity to be repurposed as ceremonial material in certain contexts (Wallis 2011). Technological refinements in recent years have improved our ability to study object histories. Artifact provenance research is growing with the increased use of portable X-ray fluorescence (pXRF), neutron activation analysis (NAA), and inductively coupled plasma mass spectrometry (ICP-MS). Although residue analysis techniques such as gas chromatography have been used less frequently in Florida, such techniques would also benefit research programs focused on object histories. Radiocarbon assays can also identify when mound fill has been extracted from earlier places (see Randall et al. this volume; Schober this volume). Finally, the widespread use of GIS and the digitization of state site file data have significantly increased the speed and complexity of our analyses of spatial distributions of sites and artifacts.

Several contributors to this book consider the movement of people and things within ritualities centered in various areas of Florida. Nancy White explains that persistent long-distance exchange connections are evidence that the Apalachicola/ Lower Chattahoochee Valley was not peripheral to the Southeast during the Woodland and Mississippi periods but was actually a central player in larger-scale developments. She finds that the frequency of nonlocal materials such as mica, copper, and exotic cherts, especially during the Middle Woodland period, reflect the importance of pieces of other places for important rites of passage that were necessary for social reproduction. There is notable continuity in the occupation of sites through time and in much of the material culture, implicating locally long-lived communities within the Apalachicola Valley whose participation in extralocal networks was an enduring part of local identity.

In contrast, Keith Ashley and Vicki Rolland showcase the strategies of social reproduction among St. Johns II communities who were immigrants with comparatively short-lived histories of occupation. Lacking the physical resources of an ancient constructed landscape, St. Johns II communities emplaced dense feasting deposits on which to construct burial mounds and acquired ancestral objects from Woodland and Archaic deposits, thereby invoking connections to a sacred mythical past. Sacred objects were also acquired as gifts from long distances, particularly nonlocal stone, metal, and mineral artifacts from the major monumental centers at Cahokia and Macon Plateau. These signs of distant connection and alliance were essential for St. Johns II social reproduction in rites of passage negotiated at Mill Cove.

## Environment and History

Our final theme considers the significance of the environment in the histories and historicities of pre-Columbian Florida. The study of paleoenvironment and subsistence has been a mainstay of archaeological research in Florida for decades. Guided by processualist thought, researchers have tended to place the balance of interpretive weight on external environmental processes as agents of change. Increasingly, and throughout the world, archaeologists are becoming concerned with the recursive relationship of human-environment interactions, infusing dynamism and relevancy into tired models of ecological functionalism (e.g., Braje and Rick 2011; Marquardt 1994; Reitz, Newsom, and Scudder 1996; Rick and Erlandson 2008). Indeed, a focus on the intersection of communities, culture, and environment is perhaps one of the most effective ways to make archaeology relevant today in the midst of potentially rapid climate change and displaced populations (Sabloff 2008). Florida, with its more than 1200 miles of coastline, is particularly well positioned to contribute to understandings of the human response to changes in sea level. Furthermore, the emphasis by Florida researchers on subsistence and environment provides a massive database that can be used to track community responses to climatic variability.

From the perspectives of traditional developmental and evolutionary archaeology, perhaps the differences perceived between the deep past and the present in terms of technology, population density, and permanent infrastructure preclude serious consideration of lessons from the past. However, as George Luer summarizes for the coast of west peninsular Florida, native populations were not hapless denizens of an untamed wilderness; instead, they modified the landscape substantially. They built mounds to elevate living surfaces, dug canals to facilitate travel, and probably altered landscapes in other ways to cultivate plants. We thus have a record of ancient environmental engineering that belies characterizations of pre-Columbian peoples as more directly impacted by the inevitable forces of nature than present-day communities. Thus, the archaeological record of some coastal communities that showcases an extensive history of experience with flooded and newly exposed coastlines in the context of compulsory displacement and resettlement is in fact highly relevant to current circumstances. What is more, some communities, such as those in the Big Bend region of Florida that Kenneth Sassaman and colleagues describe, demonstrate social and economic resilience in the midst of perpetual change that closely parallels more recent experiences in the region. Specifically, the recent history of the Cedar Key community mirrors histories of resilience in the deep past. The community has repeatedly reconstituted itself in the midst of natural forces and circumstances (e.g., hurricanes and shallow bathymetry) and sociopolitical factors (e.g., fisheries regulation) but has avoided the expansion and development that characterize nearby coastal metropolises such as Tampa.

Using a detailed chronology made possible by a robust database of radiometric assays, Robert Austin, Jeffrey Mitchem, and Brent Weisman investigate variable human responses to changes in sea level. Their work shows that settlements in the Tampa Bay region confronted the presumably lower sea levels of the Vandal Minimum (ca. AD 600 to 800) and the Little Ice Age (ca. AD 1200 to 1700) according to local parameters and sensibilities. The record of site abandonment, continual occupation, or population relocation during these periods of sea regression were evidently influenced by the nuances of local environmental, political, and demographic factors that cannot be anticipated at region-wide scales. Sometimes chronologies such as these can be coupled with fine-grained ecological studies that incorporate the systematic use of stable isotopes, schlerochronology, and other seasonal or climatological indicators to reveal transformative histories. For example, Randall and colleagues demonstrate that shell mounds on the middle St. Johns River are not the vestiges of accumulated waste that are simple and interchangeable environmental proxies. Instead, while particular environments certainly facilitated shell-fishing, the actions of transporting, depositing, excavating, and reworking shell (at mounds and other sites) were part of dynamic and various historical strategies of place making.

## Strategies and the Future of Florida's Ancient Past

Although distant in time, Florida's ancient histories are pertinent to contemporary and future Floridas. As we have outlined briefly, the pre-Columbian archaeology of Florida presents unique opportunities for investigating questions of broad anthropological significance. Furthermore, there are important lessons to be learned about past responses to social and climatic upheavals. Yet the promise of Florida's ancient past has yet to be fully realized. We offer three strategies that can help move archaeological research in the direction of fulfilling more of Florida archaeology's latent potential.

First, we need to emphasize temporality and the multiple horizons of human experience. Gaining ever-better understandings of absolute chronologies in various regions of the state through more radiocarbon dating is obviously helpful, but we need to consider more often the different implications of rapid, eventful histories and longer-term trajectories. The deep time scales that have been the basis for observing cultural conservatism in ancient Florida and for tracing a slow, incremental social evolution are belied by archaeological evidence at finer scales. As examples such as large shell mounds that were sometimes constructed in decades rather than over centuries and the short periodicity of climate changes that caused significant oscillations in sea level within the lifetimes of individuals demonstrate, the arc of pre-Columbian history was punctuated by events that presented opportunities to radically alter historical trajectories. These realizations force us to investigate the intersections of histories of practice and events that, at least in part, constituted longer-term trends.

Second, we emphasize that Florida's current political boundaries are irrelevant to Florida's ancient past. While these boundaries have conveniently circumscribed research areas in previous studies, the view of Florida as an appendage that is dismembered from its continental body and separate from adjacent Caribbean archipelagoes obscures the histories of connection to the greater Southeast and beyond and emphasize the region's liminality (e.g., Milanich 1994, xiv). Florida need not be excised from the Southeast or the Caribbean to be considered a legitimate primary research area. Since Ford's diffusionist explanations in 1969, Caribbean connections with Florida rarely have been considered, but those who dismiss such connections out of hand are premature (Altes 2011). Florida's disciplinary and cultural (both ancient and recent) connections to the Southeast are more evident. Although Florida is geographically peripheral to the Southeast, it was historically and socially peripheral only during particular times and an in certain places. In other contexts, for example the "Shell Mound Archaic" or Weeden Island rituality, Florida was at the heart of emergent social practices that had broad implications across the Southeast. By erasing today's boundaries, we can refocus on how the arrangement of places and different landscapes influenced the pace and character of social interaction. For example, can we recognize spatial boundaries in past traditions and did persistent nodes of intercultural contact exist?

A third strategy involves giving serious reflection to Florida's place in our national narrative. The allure of Florida's natural resources has resonated with interpretations of the state's aboriginal inhabitants as ecological savages who were largely devoid of history and agency. There is still much to be written in critique of these pervasive perspectives that would move toward a more historical, contextual, and social account of the past that more fairly represents the diverse lives of past inhabitants. We must also consider how the archaeological record can influence policy, including policies to manage regional heritage and strategies to engage in broader discourses concerned with cultural diversity, historical preservation, and repatriation. The contemporary political climate of and economic conditions in Florida are increasingly unfavorable to anthropology and stewardship of cultural resources. In 2011 and 2012, budget and space for the Florida Division of Historical Resources was significantly reduced and Governor Rick Scott repeatedly disparaged anthropology as esoteric and irrelevant to economic recovery from recession (Gibbons 2012). Now more than ever we are obliged to justify the value of doing archaeological research and preserving archaeological sites. Public archaeology, because of its potential economic impact and its capacity to inform the public, certainly has an important role to play. But how we perceive these problems is equally important. A historical and contextual perspective that moves away from ecological determinism and traditional evolutionary models of culture change will serve us well. Why save archaeological sites or devote resources to studying them if we already know the answers to the questions that frame our research (e.g., Pauketat 2007)? And yet, in the present political climate of economic austerity, unabated land development, and anti-intellectualism, a successful strategy for pursuing Florida's past must be situated in the context of discussions that have regional and global significance, such as the major contributions our research makes to the themes that orient this book. Thus, the future of Florida's ancient past must be written using a strategy that is multiscalar: it must be simultaneously historically situated, contextually detailed, and broadly relevant. The chapters in this book represent some of the most compelling archaeological research being conducted in Florida today. They use detailed descriptions of data compiled from previous excavations, draw upon new fieldwork and new analysis of materials, and offer fresh perspectives on the ancient histories of the state. These contributions indicate that the past is not merely prologue but continues to offer new and valuable insights that often have broad relevance to the present.

## References

Altes, Christopher F.

2011    A Brief Note on Currents, Current Archaeologists, and Ancient Fiber-Tempered Pots. *Florida Anthropologist* 64: 113–18.

Anderson, David G.

1994    Factional Competition and the Political Evolution of Mississippian Chiefdoms in the Southeastern United States. In *Factional Competition and Political Development in the New World*, edited by E. M. Brumfiel and J. W. Fox, 61–76. Cambridge University Press, Cambridge, UK.

Ashley, Keith H., and Nancy Marie White (editors)

2012    *Late Prehistoric Florida: Archaeology at the Edge of the Mississippian World*. University Press of Florida, Gainesville.

Barrett, John C.

1999    The Mythical Landscapes of the British Iron Age. In *Archaeologies of Landscape: Contemporary Perspectives*, edited by Wendy Ashmore and A. Bernard Knapp, 253–65. Blackwell Publishing, Malden, MA.

Basso, Keith H.

1996    Wisdom Sits in Places: Notes on a Western Apache Landscape. In *Senses of Places*, edited by Steven Feld and Keith H. Basso, 53–90. School of American Research, Santa Fe, NM.

Bell, Catherine M.

1997    *Ritual: Perspectives and Dimensions*. Oxford University Press, New York.

Binford, Lewis R.

1962    Archaeology as Anthropology. *American Antiquity* 28: 217–25.

Bradley, Richard

2000    *An Archaeology of Natural Places*. Routledge, New York.

2002    *The Past in Prehistoric Societies*. Routledge, New York.

Braje, Todd J., and Torben C. Rick (editors)

2011    *Human Impacts on Seals, Sea Lions, and Sea Otters: Integrating Archaeology and Ecology in the Northeast Pacific.* University of California Press, Berkeley.

Carr, Christopher

2006    Rethinking Interregional Hopewellian "Interaction." In *Gathering Hopewell: Society, Ritual, and Ritual Interaction,* edited by Christopher Carr and D. Troy Case, 575–623. Springer, New York.

Carr, Christopher, and D. Troy Case (editors)

2006    *Gathering Hopewell: Society, Ritual, and Ritual Interaction.* Kluwer Academic/Plenum Publishers, New York.

Carson, Rachel L.

1962    *Silent Spring.* Houghton Mifflin, Boston.

Charles, Douglas K., and Jane E. Buikstra (editors)

2006    *Recreating Hopewell.* University Press of Florida, Gainesville.

Claassen, Cheryl

1996    A Consideration of the Social Organization of the Shell Mound Archaic. In *Archaeology of the Mid-Holocene Southeast,* edited by Kenneth E. Sassaman and David G. Anderson, 235–58. University Press of Florida, Gainesville.

2008    Shell Symbolism in Pre-Columbian North America. In *Early Human Impact on Megamolluscs,* edited by Andrzej Antczak and Roberto Cipriani, 231–36. Archaeopress, Oxford.

Cobb, Charles R.

2005    Archaeology and the "Savage Slot": Displacement and Emplacement in the Premodern World. *American Anthropologist* 107: 563–74.

Colburn, David R.

1996    Florida Politics in the Twentieth Century. In *The New History of Florida,* edited by Michael Gannon, 344–72. University Press of Florida, Gainesville.

Fogelson, Raymond D.

1989    The Ethnohistory of Events and Nonevents. *Ethnohistory* 36: 133–47.

Ford, James A.

1969    *A Comparison of Formative Cultures in the Americas: Diffusion or the Psychic Unity of Man.* Smithsonian Contributions to Anthropology no. 11. Smithsonian Institution Press, Washington, DC.

Gibbons, Ann

2012    An Annus Horribilis for Anthropology? *Science* 338: 1520.

Grunwald, Michael

2006    *The Swamp: The Everglades, Florida, and the Politics of Paradise.* Simon and Schuster, New York.

Harvey, David

1989    *The Condition of Postmodernity: An Enquiry into the Origins of Cultural Change.* Blackwell, Oxford, UK.

Hays, Christopher T., and Richard A. Weinstein

2004    Early Pottery at Poverty Point. In *Early Pottery: Technology, Function, Style, and Interaction in the Lower Southeast,* edited by Rebecca Saunders and Christopher T. Hays, 150–68. University of Alabama Press, Tuscaloosa.

Keane, Webb

2005    Signs Are Not the Garb of Meaning: On the Social Analysis of Material Things. In *Material-*

*ity: Politics, History, and Culture*, edited by Daniel Miller, 182–205. Duke University Press, Durham, NC.

Kidder, Tristam R.

2010    Hunter-Gatherer Ritual and Complexity: New Evidence from Poverty Point, Louisiana. In *Ancient Complexities: New Perspectives in Precolumbian North America*, edited by Susan M. Alt, 32–51. University of Utah Press, Salt Lake City.

Marquardt, William H.

1994    The Role of Archaeology in Raising Environmental Consciousness: An Example from Southwest Florida. In *Historical Ecology: Cultural Knowledge and Changing Landscapes*, edited by C. L. Crumley, 203–21. School of American Research, Santa Fe, New Mexico.

2010a    Mounds, Middens, and Rapid Climate Change During the Archaic-Woodland Transition in the Southeastern United States. In *Trend, Tradition, and Turmoil: What Happened to the Southeastern Archaic?* edited by David Hurst Thomas and Matthew C. Sanger, 253–71. Anthropological Papers of the American Museum of Natural History no. 93. American Museum of Natural History, New York.

2010b    Shell Mounds in the Southeast: Middens, Monuments, Temple Mounds, Rings, or Works? *American Antiquity* 75: 551–70.

Milanich, Jerald T.

1994    *Archaeology of Precolumbian Florida*. University Press of Florida, Gainesville.

Milanich, Jerald T., and Charles Herron Fairbanks

1980    *Florida Archaeology*. New World Archaeological Record. Academic Press, New York.

Mohl, Raymond A., and Gary R. Mormino

1996    The Big Change in the Sunshine State: A Social History of Modern Florida. In *The New Florida History*, edited by Michael Gannon, 418–47. University Press of Florida, Gainesville.

Mohl, Raymond A., and George E. Pozzetta

1996    From Migration to Mutliculturalism: A History of Florida Immigration. In *The New History of Florida*, edited by Michael Gannon, 391–417. University Press of Florida, Gainesville.

Noll, Steven, and David Tegeder

2009    *Ditch of Dreams: The Cross Florida Barge Canal and the Struggle for Florida's Future*. University Press of Florida, Gainesville.

Pauketat, Timothy R.

2007    *Chiefdoms and Other Archaeological Delusions*. Issues in Eastern Woodlands Archaeology. AltaMira Press, Lanham, MD.

Randall, Asa R.

2011    Remapping Archaic Social Histories Along the St. Johns River in Florida. In *Hunter-Gatherer Archaeology as Historical Process*, edited by Kenneth E. Sassaman and Donald H. Holly Jr., 120–42. University of Arizona Press, Tucson.

Randall, Asa R., and Kenneth E. Sassaman

2010    (E)Mergent Complexities During the Archaic in Northeast Florida. In *Ancient Complexities: New Perspectives in Precolumbian North America*, edited by Susan M. Alt, 8–31. University of Utah Press, Salt Lake City.

Reitz, Elizabeth J., Lee A. Newsom, and Sylvia J. Scudder (editors)

1996    *Case Studies in Environmental Archaeology*. Plenum, New York.

Rick, Torben C., and Jon M. Erlandson (editors)

2008    *Human Impacts on Ancient Marine Ecosystems: A Global Perspective*. University of California Press, Berkeley.

Rosenswig, Robert M., and Richard L. Burger

2012    Considering Early New World Monumentality. In *Early New World Monumentality*, edited by Richard L. Burger and Robert M. Rosenswig, 3–22. University Press of Florida, Gainesville.

Russo, Michael

2004    Measuring Shell Rings for Social Inequality. In *Signs of Power: The Rise of Cultural Complexity in the Southeast*, edited by Jon L. Gibson and Philip J. Carr, 26–70. University of Alabama Press, Tuscaloosa.

Sabloff, Jeremy

2008    *Archaeology Matters: Action Archaeology in the Modern World*. Left Coast Press, Walnut Creek, CA.

Sassaman, Kenneth E.

2005    Poverty Point as Structure, Event, Process. *Journal of Archaeological Method and Theory* 12: 335–64.

Sassaman, Kenneth E., and Donald H. Holly Jr.

2011    Transformative Hunter-Gatherer Archaeology in North America. In *Hunter-Gatherer Archaeology as Historical Process*, edited by Kenneth E. Sassaman and Donald H. Holly Jr., 1–13. University of Arizona Press, Tucson.

Sears, William H.

1973    The Sacred and the Secular in Prehistoric Ceramics. In *Variations in Anthropology: Essays in Honor of John McGregor*, edited by J. Douglas and D. Lathrap, 31–42. Illinois Archaeological Survey, Urbana.

1982    *Fort Center: An Archaeological Site in the Lake Okeechobee Basin*. University Press of Florida, Gainesville.

Standiford, Les

2002    *Last Train to Paradise: Henry Flagler and the Spectacular Rise and Fall of the Railroad That Crossed the Ocean*. Crown Publishers, New York.

Steward, Julian H.

1955    *Theory of Culture Change: The Methodology of Multilinear Evolution*. University of Illinois Press, Urbana.

Thomas, Julian

1999    An Economy of Substances in Earlier Neolithic Britain. In *Material Symbols: Culture and Economy in Prehistory*, edited by John E. Robb, 70–89. Center for Archaeological Investigations, Southern Illinois University Press, Carbondale.

Trigger, Bruce G.

1990    Monumental Architecture: A Thermodynamic Explanation of Symbolic Behavior. *World Archaeology* 22: 119–32.

Trouillot, Michel-Rolph

1995    *Silencing the Past: Power and the Production of History*. Beacon Press, Boston, MA.

Wallis, Neill J.

2011    *The Swift Creek Gift: Vessel Exchange on the Atlantic Coast*. University of Alabama Press, Tuscaloosa.

Weisman, Brent R.

2003    Why Florida Archaeology Matters. *Southeastern Archaeology* 22: 210–26.

Whittle, Alasdair, Frances Healy, Alex Bayliss, and Michael J. Allen (editors)

2011    *Gathering Time: Dating the Early Neolithic Enclosures of Southern Britain and Ireland*. 2 vols. Oxbow Books, Oxford.

# 1

## Archaic Histories beyond the Shell "Heap" on the St. Johns River

ASA R. RANDALL, KENNETH E. SASSAMAN, ZACKARY I. GILMORE,
MEGGAN E. BLESSING, AND JASON M. O'DONOUGHUE

Freshwater shell mounds have shaped the course of culture history on the middle St. Johns River Basin in northeast Florida for seven millennia. For the Archaic (ca. 7300–3600 cal BP) communities who initiated their construction, they were places of residence and ceremony. The fact that they deposited diverse objects, materials, and ancestors on mound surfaces and incorporated these items within them attests to the ongoing importance of shell mounds in Archaic lives. Subsequent St. Johns period (ca. 3600–500 cal BP) communities also engaged with them, often constructing mortuary facilities on mounds of great antiquity. Although they were largely ignored in the immediate post-Colombian era, they were rediscovered in the nineteenth century by archaeologists such as Jeffries Wyman (1875), who were interested in determining their origins. Their contents were distributed among museums and insights garnered from investigating them inspired archaeological research throughout the United States. In Florida, shell mound research formed the basis for the delineation of archaeological culture histories (e.g., Goggin 1952) and later provided the basis for advances in subsistence and settlement studies focused on middle Holocene hunter-gatherers (e.g., Russo et al. 1992). The monetary incentive of shell mounds did not escape curio seekers, land speculators, hoteliers, and shell miners either. Their collective exploitative actions resulted in the destruction or near-destruction of all but a handful of the mounds by the 1970s. The few that remain intact today are but a fraction of the scores of mounds that once dominated the otherwise flat, watery terrain of the St. Johns (figure 1.1).

Shell mounds persist today at the center of popular and intellectual histories. But what of the histories of Archaic communities encased within these places? Ironically, for such an enduring object of inquiry, shell mounds continue to be interpreted using nineteenth-century principles of archaeological knowledge. The

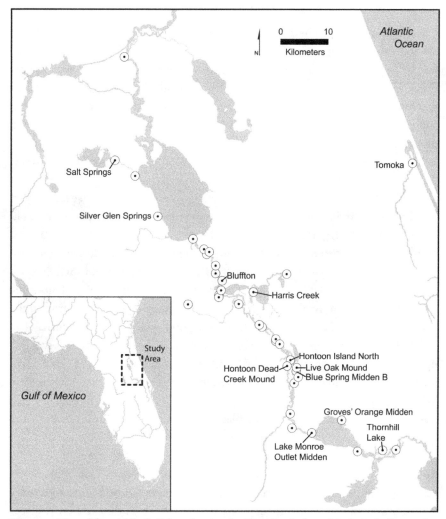

Figure 1.1. Map of the middle St. Johns showing the location of selected Archaic shell mounds.

standard model of shell mound formation and significance is informed by three themes or assumptions. One theme is that shell mounds are best understood as trash heaps—or kitchen middens, to use Wyman's borrowing of the Danish term *kjökkenmödding*—that were created when the remains of innumerable small meals extracted from local resource patches were discarded. Another theme has to do with the duration or tempo of mound use: shell mounds emerged gradually and the continued deposition of shell throughout the ages is evidence of continuities in "basic lifeways" (Milanich 1994, 86). A final assumption is that shell mounds are inherently interchangeable and that the history of each mound reflects the local resource structure (e.g., Cumbaa 1976). In this tradition of thought, environmental processes are emphasized at the expense of social histories (e.g., Miller 1998). In part, this tradition developed because of processes particular to Florida. For example, in the era of shell mining, individual mounds became anonymized as a composite culture history was assembled from their fragmented remains to create a regional synthesis. However, the standard view also follows trends in anthropological thought that downplayed the long-term significance of aquatic resources (Erlandson 2001), and reduced past social change among hunter-gatherer communities to general processes of social evolution.

Despite the elegant rationality of the standard model, there is good reason to suspect that it tells us more about contemporary concerns and assumptions than about the world views and histories of Archaic mound dwellers. The more we learn about the chronology and composition of shell mounds, the less these mounds are explicable in purely local, gradual, or ecological terms. Some mounds were constructed rapidly out of shellfish remains while others were established as dedicated mortuaries (Aten 1999; Sassaman and Randall 2012). In some cases, old shell deposits were mined for mound fill (see also Schober this volume). The balance of inorganic Archaic material culture was decidedly nonlocal in origin, derived either from the coasts or the interior of peninsular Florida and points farther afield (Wheeler et al. 2000). Just like contemporary "snowbirds," Archaic Floridians may have descended upon the peninsula from points north. As Quinn and colleagues (2008) have documented, at least some individuals interred in preceramic St. Johns mounds were born elsewhere, possibly as far away as present-day Tennessee or Virginia. In short, the middle St. Johns was a dynamic place that was made significant through the construction of mortuary monuments and encounters among diverse persons.

These facts necessitate a fundamental reassessment of the presumed sameness and insignificance of shell mounds in Archaic societies. Our approach in this chapter is to decenter Archaic mounds as singularities and instead privilege the variations among depositional practices through which they and other places emerged as historical processes. We focus on the results of recent investigations in the Silver Glen Springs watershed (SGSW), a landscape that was extensively transformed by pre-Columbian Floridians (detailed below). The SGSW provides a bounded context in which to explore variability in depositional practices that resulted from the dispositions of specific communities. The significance of these practices cannot be reduced to regional environmental change. Although there is evidence of at least 10,000 years of occupation within the SGSW, we will restrict our discussion to the preceramic Mount Taylor period (which is subdivided into the Early Mount Taylor phase [ca. 7300–5600 cal BP] and Thornhill Lake phase [ca. 5600–4700 cal BP]) and the ceramic Orange period (ca. 4700–3600 cal BP). Using this landscape as a point of departure, we first consider the extent to which all mounds were created equal by investigating occupational histories through a review of the tempo and context of shell deposition. The results of this discussion lead us to briefly address a second issue: if shell mounds were not simply places of residence composed of mundane, gradually accumulating trash, then to what extent were experiences at mounds informed by practices outside mounded contexts? Our perspective is inspired by recent insights in social theory that sidestep a sacred-secular dichotomy and related oppositions such as "midden" and "monument" that form the basis of contemporary debate (e.g., Marquardt 2010; see also Russo et al. this volume). We are interested in how Archaic practices—and the objects, persons, materials, and places involved—not only were significant within local temporalities and social contexts but also refer to other times, places, and peoples. Communities constructed their own histories through particular combinations and assemblies of places and things, and these assemblies and combinations are what provided opportunities for transformation (Randall 2011). The past in the form of ancient places or ancestors thus provided important resources for local inhabitants. Moreover, far from excluding the environment as a factor in social change through time, this perspective requires that we consider how past communities experienced and incorporated ecological processes into their worldviews.

## The Silver Glen Springs Watershed in Context

Ongoing research by the University of Florida's Laboratory of Southeastern Archaeology (LSA) in the SGSW is providing the fine-grained spatial and chronological details that are necessary for reconstructing daily and commemorative traditions within and away from mounded spaces. This research area encompasses a spring run one kilometer long that emerges from the first-magnitude Silver Glen Springs pool and debouches into Lake George, Florida's second-largest body of water (figure 1.2). Since 2007, the LSA, through its St. Johns Archaeological Field School, has investigated the privately owned southern half of the run with a multifaceted strategy of shovel testing, bucket augering, test unit excavation, and surface collection (Sassaman, Gilmore, and Randall 2011). In 2010 and 2011, the LSA executed a participating agreement with the U.S. Forest Service to document cultural resources within the Silver Glen Springs Recreational Area, which forms the northern half of the watershed (Randall et al. 2011). This work expanded on earlier excavations by Florida State University (Marrinan et al. 1990).

    Along the St. Johns, Archaic culture history cannot be divorced from recent events. The SGSW is no different; the current disposition of cultural resources there reflects a complex history of ancient deposition and more recent land development. Probate court documents, oral histories, and post-mining aerial photographs demonstrate that shell removal commenced as early as 1922. Although they are difficult to analyze, the records indicate that upward of 91,000 cubic meters

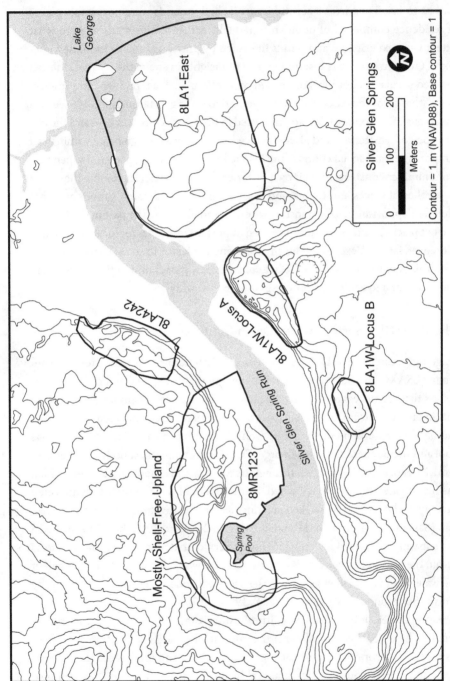

Figure 1.2. Archaic shell-bearing and shell-free loci in the Silver Glen Springs watershed.

of shell were scheduled for removal by the Lake George Shell Corporation (Lake County Probate Court, Misc. Book 6, 315). In the ensuing decade, shell-mining operations involved clear-cutting, terrestrial shell removal, and channel dredging. Fortunately, pre- and peri-mining descriptions allow us to characterize the scale and diversity of ancient deposits within the SGSW. We know that at least four large shell mounds were emplaced in the watershed (figure 1.2). The largest was the U-shaped mound at the mouth of the run referred to as 8LA1-East. This mound was described by Jeffries Wyman (1875) as up to eight meters high at the northeast summit and 300 meters on a side. Wyman described a second mound, now recorded as 8MR123, as an "amphitheater" of shell. This mound was sketched by Civilian Conservation Corps archaeologists in 1932 as shell was being removed (Potter 1935).

The remainder of this landscape has been documented during recent fieldwork. Two shell mounds situated midway down the run were never described historically but were identified during pedestrian surveys based on post-mining hallmarks of shell escarpments and dug-out pits. On the south side of the run, 8LA1W-Locus A is a 200-meter-long shell ridge of which up to three meters of basal and lateral deposits are intact. This ridge has been subject to stratigraphic excavations. Site 8LA4242 is directly across the run to the north but remains untested. Finally, a wide array of nonmounded shell and shell-free buried contexts has been documented along the upland terraces of the run. Locus B, for example, is a stratified but minimally mounded locality south of the spring pool. A large assemblage of lithics and ceramics was also encountered in predominately shell-free contexts north of the spring, highlighting how Archaic land-use practices extended beyond shell deposition. This landscape's final configuration reflects a long and complex history of inhabitation and terraforming.

## The Diversity of Shell Deposition

Studies of shell mounds in Florida (Endonino 2010; Randall 2010; Russo 2004; Schwadron 2010) suggest that the scale and arrangement of a mound can provide important insights into community planning. This evidence can be combined with detailed chronologies to reveal the sequence and tempo of shell mound construction, which help us understand how ancient communities incorporated social and environmental change into land-use practices and even their social histories (Randall 2010). Mound size means nothing if the site's chronology is unknown: gradual or rapid rates of accumulation have different implications for social process. Indeed, a long-held assumption about the history of shell mounds is that their large size was attained gradually, over long stretches of time, particularly in areas of high ecological productivity (Milanich 1994, 89). Models of human settlement in the St.

Johns River basin have emphasized the apparent relationship between the onset of riverine exploitation and a near-modern hydrological regime (Miller 1998). In this model, Paleoindian and Early Archaic populations would be restricted to well-watered locations such as first-magnitude springs (Thulman 2009). The middle Holocene increase in surface water elevation, which was made possible in part by higher flow from springs connected to the Floridan aquifer, aided the development of lakes, sloughs, and wetlands. Once well-watered environments were available, Middle Archaic communities began exploiting shellfish and other aquatic resources intensively. Traditional thought predicts that the SGSW attracted shell fishers early and often. Not only is it centered on a first-magnitude spring in proximity to a large lake but the watershed is also bounded by uplands (including several interior wetlands) that would have provided numerous opportunities for hunting and foraging.

## The Onset of Shell Fishing

In order to document the chronology and tempo of occupation in the watershed, we have amassed radiocarbon assays from Archaic period terrestrial shell deposits, subaqueous components, and sooted sherds (figure 1.3). Although there are extensive post-Archaic components within the SGSW, we have excluded them from our present discussion. If we took the age determinations at face value we would estimate that shell fishing commenced as early as 7,100 years ago and continued well past 4,000 years ago. This interval conforms roughly to the known range of Archaic shell fishing in the region, and it spans the preceramic Mount Taylor and Thornhill Lake phases as well as the ceramic Orange period. Although one might characterize these assays as indicative of continuity, it is important to note that portions of the watershed were differentially occupied during this interval. Moreover, there is good reason to suspect that the two earliest dates are not from primary contexts. One was derived from a surface exposure, while another was recovered from a mortuary deposit of demonstrably later age. We will return to the significance of these assays in a later section.

Once the two early assays are removed from consideration, it becomes apparent that shell was intensively deposited after 6,500 years ago. We have to travel outside the SGSW to characterize earlier shell fishing in the region. Along the St. Johns, the earliest age estimates on shell-bearing deposits come from two sites, Hontoon Dead Creek Mound and Live Oak Mound, both situated near present-day Deland in Volusia County (Sassaman and Randall 2012). Basal dates place initial shellfish exploitation at these sites as early as 7300 cal BP. This date is roughly coeval with a significant shift in atmospheric water availability: the St. Johns would have experienced a rapid change in hydrology associated with increased availability of surface water (Randall 2010). Neither of these sites is situated on a spring; they are located up to 200 meters away from present-day channel segments. In the case of the Hon-

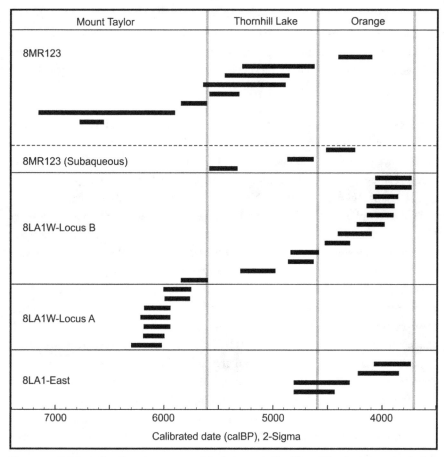

Figure 1.3. Calibrated radiocarbon assays of Archaic age in the Silver Glen Springs watershed.

toon Dead Creek Mound, the site may have been situated on a lagoon that has since filled in with sediment (Sassaman 2005).

Radiocarbon assays from throughout these two mounds (each roughly 100 meters long, 70 meters wide, and 5 meters high) demonstrate that they emerged in as little as 200 and no more than 500 years. Sequences with similar tempos have been identified for younger mounds (see below). Based on their staged sequences, we have argued elsewhere that these places register the purposeful construction of commemorative platforms whose surfaces were renewed repeatedly, possibly during feasting events that included regional populations (Sassaman and Randall 2012). Furthermore, assays from spring-side deposits at Salt Springs and Groves' Orange Midden highlight the variability in the onset of shell fishing adjacent to springs. For example, at Groves' Orange Midden, shell deposition definitively began at roughly 6900 cal BP, although the deposits may date as early as 7300 cal BP (McGee and

Wheeler 1994). At Salt Springs, shell deposits date to roughly 6300 cal BP, although the LSA's excavations may not have encountered earlier facies (O'Donoughue et al. 2011). From the onset, the timing and tempo of shell deposition cannot be assumed to have been gradual or regionally synchronous.

## Ridges and Mortuaries

The most surprising result of testing in the SGSW has been the limited evidence of shell deposition before 6500 cal BP. Regional histories indicate that the cessation of intensive shell deposition at Hontoon Dead Creek and Live Oak mounds after 6,600 years ago, possibly due to local infilling of nearby lagoons, precipitated a reorganization of regional settlement. New linear ridges were established at the Thornhill Lake complex south of Hontoon Island (Endonino 2010), at Locus A at Silver Glen Springs, and likely elsewhere. The mortuary mound at Harris Creek may have also been established at this time (Aten 1999). Details from the Locus A ridge suggest that the process of establishing new contexts for living was ritualized and may have made reference to prior traditions or places (Sassaman, Gilmore, and Randall 2011). Over the course of 600 years (ca. 6300–5700 cal BP), a 200-meter-long, three-meter-high ridge was emplaced through the deposition of shell and earth (Sassaman, Gilmore, and Randall 2011). The earliest occupation is represented by depositional events of shell and other materials, perhaps associated in part with the digging and use of pits. Beginning 6,300 years ago, the ridge was fundamentally transformed as a mantle of brown sand was emplaced across the preexisting surface. This sand was identified in three excavation units spread 80 meters apart. The elevation of this surface above the floodplain precludes the possibility that the sand came from a river. Instead, the community appears to have opened up this space for a fundamentally different use by capping the old surface and possibly cleansing it with extensive fires. Thereafter, a structured settlement composed of discrete household and habitation areas was established and reproduced over the course of no more than 400 years. The fact that this ridge was located along the run and away from the main spring pool is intriguing. There is a seep spring in the linear embayment just to the east of the ridge. Whether or not this spring experienced higher flow 6,000 years ago remains to be determined. Regardless, the location of the Locus A ridge may have had more to do with the placement and siting of 8LA4242, a similarly configured linear mound situated directly across the run (figure 1.2). Furthermore, there is circumstantial evidence that the north ridge of 8LA1-East was constructed during the Mount Taylor period (Sassaman, Gilmore, and Randall 2011).

By 5,800 years ago there were dramatic changes within the watershed, as there were throughout the St. Johns basin. This was the beginning of the Thornhill Lake phase (Endonino 2008), which was characterized by a new program of mortuary sand and shell mounds and widespread extraregional exchange networks. This was

also a time of hydrological change, evidenced primarily by the initiation of peat formation at wet sites on the St. Johns. Peat forms as vegetation accumulates in stand-
ing water and is not subsequently subjected to extended drawdowns that would
oxidize or wash away organic matter. Peat formation may have been made possible
by elevated sea levels or by increased atmospheric moisture. Either way, long hy-
droperiods made possible the development of bottomland swamps and fostered
emergent vegetation growth in shallow bodies of water (Randall 2010). Within the
SGSW, peat deposition occurred sometime during the Thornhill Lake phase. The
saturated shell encountered in near-shore deposits at 8MR123 dates to ca. 5600
cal BP; it was subsequently capped by a deposit of fibrous peat and sand. This date
places peat formation well after the onset of shell fishing at 8MR123, implying that
the new mortuary program and extensive social interaction of the Thornhill Lake
phase cannot be reduced to ecological change alone.

The details of these transformations suggest that new relationships between the
living, the dead, and other people were enabled through the reconfiguration of the
landscape that involved widespread terraforming. At the SGSW, the Locus A shell
ridge was apparently abandoned. Elsewhere on the south side of the run, shell deposition was initiated on the upland terrace at Locus B, where stacked sequences
attest to repeated events of a residential nature (Gilmore 2011). Microlithic tools
consistent with Thornhill Lake phase occupation were found in shell-free contexts
at the base of 8LA1-East, suggesting occupation there as well. The bulk of evidence
for shell deposition comes from the north side of the run at 8MR123. Florida State
University's excavations in a remnant shell ridge documented up to three meters of
Thornhill Lake phase deposits. Excluding one anomalously early date, the three assays from this sequence all overlap at 2-sigma, implying that deposition was rapid.
Moreover, age estimates from basal and near-basal shell lenses acquired during
bucket augering attest to the outward growth of the mound beginning 5,600 years
ago in a ridge abutting the terrace edge and continuing south and west to the current
spring pool margin. That these deposits were initially made within a persistently
saturated context is demonstrated by well-preserved uncarbonized organic matter (nutshells, seeds, and other plant remains) and the virtual absence of terrestrial
gastropods. Over the course of 1,000 years, the site's margins were expanded by at
least 60 meters along a segment of the shoreline 250 meters long. This figure should
be considered a minimum, however, as the possibility remains that shell extended
much further into the spring run but was dredged in the 1920s. The volumetric rate
of accumulation is hard to estimate because we do not know the height of shell in
this area. We also note that because of the properties of the spring water, the bulk of
shellfish found at this site was likely not available in the spring run itself and instead
came from Lake George or other localities (O'Donoughue 2010).

Although shell deposition was prominent at 8MR123, it referenced decidedly nondaily aspects of Archaic community life. Indeed, the earliest Thornhill Lake phase practices apparently involved the construction of a mortuary sand and shell mound. Our excavation of the mining escarpment north of the spring pool intercepted the remnants of a brown and yellow sand and shell mortuary deposit that was subsequently capped with shell. An AMS assay on charcoal from the sand suggests it was deposited a century or two before the onset of significant shell fishing. Although we cannot state with certainty how large this mortuary mound may have been, it is likely that it was extensive and had multiple interments. For example, Potter (1935) noted that several skeletons were encountered in this area. His descriptions imply that the burials were predominantly located below shell deposits, further indicating that the mortuary predated significant shell deposition to the north of the spring. The photographs Norman (2010) presented suggest that multiple interments were present in stacked sand and shell lenses. Whether or not the mortuary directly preceded or was contemporaneous with shell deposition cannot be stated with certainty. Regardless, it is in this context that the anomalously early dates on shell-bearing contexts we noted above are relevant. We intercepted an amorphous pit of shell and other materials in the lower brown sand that predates the mortuary by up to 900 years. One plausible explanation is that the pit represents an early deposit upon which a sand mound was later constructed. Given the lack of early deposition elsewhere, however, the possibility remains that the pit fill was excavated from a preexisting component in antiquity and emplaced as a mortuary offering. When we consider this evidence in conjunction with the early estimate from the investigations by Florida State University, it would appear that old shell midden was being extracted and circulated during Thornhill Lake times. Such practices are evident at the coeval and similarly composed Bluffton Burial Mound (Sears 1960) and the roughly coeval Tomoka Mound complex (Piatek 1994).

## Pots, Pits, and Mounds

The onset of local pottery production around 4,700 years ago is traditionally thought to have involved little more than the addition of technology with no impact on the daily or commemorative lives of Archaic communities (Milanich 1994, 88). However, there is increasing evidence that pottery was deeply implicated in a revolution in the structure, location, and organization of the ritual and daily lives of Archaic persons (see also Saunders and Wrenn this volume). Within the SGSW, we have identified a number of transformations in how and where communities amassed shell. The intensive deposition of shell during the Thornhill Lake period was continued into the Orange period and arguably resulted in the two U-shaped mounds observed by Wyman that enclose that watershed. At 8MR123, the focus of shell deposition was the spring pool and run. This inference is based solely on radiocarbon assays, as few diagnostic ceramics were recovered during the LSA's investigations.

We do know that approximately 2.5 meters of shell was deposited at the current edge of the spring pool around 4520–4080 cal BP. An equally impressive amount of shell was deposited at the mouth of the spring run (8LA1-East). Subsurface testing there has produced mixed results, mostly due to extensive shell mining. However, there is abundant evidence that shell was laid down at the northeast point of the mound during the Orange period, perhaps upon a preexisting Mount Taylor period shell ridge. Construction of the south ridge was also begun during the Orange period, a process that may have involved clear-cutting and preparing the ground surface before shell deposition (Sassaman, Gilmore, and Randall 2011).

In addition to shell, many Orange period fiber-tempered vessels were deposited in the watershed. Sherds of thick and technologically distinct Orange Incised vessels were found at 8LA1-East and 8MR123. This particular ware was produced early in the Orange period and appears to have been restricted to only a few large shell mounds in the St. Johns basin (Randall and Sassaman 2010). The fact that these vessels are typically restricted to large shell deposits indicates they may have been deposited during feasting events involving diverse communities who gathered at mounds. Slightly later, shellfish were also processed and deposited in large pits in the uplands, away from mounds. The most significant example of this practice is on the south side of the run at Locus B, where scores of Orange-era pits have been documented. As Gilmore has demonstrated (2011), these pits were used to process large quantities of shellfish that were likely destined for deposition at the two U-shaped mounds. At least one Orange period pit was documented on the north side of the run, and there may be others. Interestingly, Locus B itself was capped off with shell during late Orange times, an apparent use of an earlier Mount Taylor tradition for transforming places during moments of social change (Gilmore 2011).

## Community Organization beyond the Mounds

Within the SGSW and indeed across the region, shell mounds had multiple roles for Archaic period societies. Some were apparently places where people lived, some were mortuary mounds, and some were ceremonial platforms. These roles were neither static nor mutually exclusive in time and space; a shell mound likely had multiple, often overlapping identities during its life history. If these places were not simply refuse heaps, what can be said about nonmounded localities where residence or other activities may have taken place? Investigations into St. Johns communities have tended to focus on shell-bearing components. Not only are they ideal contexts for recovering organic assemblages but these loci have also been most in need of mitigative efforts because of shell mining. However, the recognition that at least some of these larger shell sites were not places of daily living (Aten 1999; Endonino 2010; Randall 2010; Sassaman 2005) has brought the limited extent of off-mound archaeology into stark relief. Comprehensive surveys of landforms in the St. Johns basin are few and far between. However, where off-mound reconnaissance has been conducted, a wide array of shell-bearing and shell-free sites has been documented. For example, surveys of Hontoon Island near present-day Deland, which occupies 400 hectares, identified no fewer than 10 sites, ranging from small scatters to multi-ridge shell mounds (Randall 2007). Similar diversity has been recorded for the Thornhill Lake locality (Endonino 2008).

Living Locally

One of the most significant results produced by testing areas away from mound localities in the SGSW has been the discovery of stratified and horizontally differentiated occupation in the upland terrace located north and west of the spring pool that did not involve the widespread deposition of shell. A less dense but still pervasive shell-free component is present on the south side as well. Evidence for Late Paleoindian or Early Archaic occupation is present across the landform. Although no diagnostic hafted bifaces were encountered, several formal sidescrapers and endscrapers, each heavily patinated, were recovered. The visible evidence of occupation of the upland terrace increases significantly during the Middle and Late Archaic. Of the 21 whole and fragmentary hafted bifaces recovered during testing north of the spring pool, 95 percent are examples of the Florida Archaic Stemmed type. This form dates to the Mount Taylor period, although stemmed hafted bifaces were produced through the later Orange period as well. In addition to hafted bifaces, the assemblage includes a variety of tools such as late-stage bifaces and preforms, expanded-base microliths, and informal flake tools. Analysis of the waste flake assemblage determined that lithic reduction was geared primarily toward late-stage tool production and maintenance. The diversity of these tool classes implies that preceramic Archaic groups engaged in a wide array of practices at this locality. In the absence of more expansive stratigraphic testing, it is unclear whether these depositional patterns simply resulted from different activity areas away from living areas during the Mount Taylor period or if they represent a residential encampment. A shell-free lithic reduction area was documented on the upland terrace at the Lake Monroe Outlet Midden to the south (Archaeological Consultants, Inc. and Janus Research 2001), suggesting that the use of space beyond mounds was equally structured.

Significant changes in the organization of community planning and practice are evident at the onset of the Orange period. Although shell deposition is widespread throughout the watershed, actual evidence for habitation structures is restricted to the mostly shell-free uplands north of the spring pool where close-interval shovel testing was done (figure 1.4). The bulk of the plain and incised wares are consistent with the post-4600 cal BP assemblage documented at Locus B on the south side of the run by Gilmore (2011). Unlike the evidence that suggests structured deposition during the preceding Mount Taylor period, the Orange period occupation may represent an arcuate or circular village. This village has been inferred from the distribution of diagnostic Orange pottery from shovel tests and from stratigraphic excavations (Test Unit 6). In general, Orange sherds were clustered in the western two-thirds of the survey area. When Orange sherds were separated by size (greater or less than 0.5 inch), it became apparent that large sherds were concentrated in an arc with an interior diameter of about 70 meters and an exterior diameter of about 160 meters. The interior of the arc is characterized by small crumb sherds only, implying that this area may have been a plaza that was purposefully kept clean.

A closer examination of the Orange component also revealed highly suggestive evidence of architecture (figure 1.4C). Within the arc there were at least three voids approximately 25 to 30 meters in diameter. Excavation of TU6, located outside one

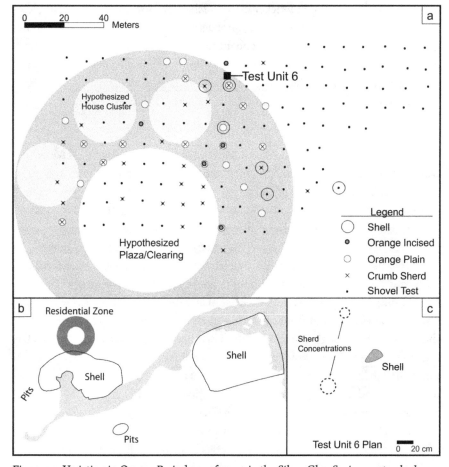

Figure 1.4. Variation in Orange Period use of space in the Silver Glen Springs watershed.

of these voids, revealed large, flat-lying, fiber-tempered sherds that were clustered on one side of the test unit. A small shell-filled pit around 20 centimeters wide and 5 centimeters deep was discovered nearby and at a slightly lower elevation. The matrix and character of the pit contents were consistent with shell-bearing matrices documented elsewhere. The shell may have been gathered from a preexisting deposit and emplaced in a posthole. A similar shell deposit was encountered in a shovel test just two meters to the south of Test Unit 6. The implication is that Test Unit 6 intercepted an Orange period structure of unknown dimensions. The presence of voids (that lack large sherds) that were around 30 meters wide may indicate that multiple structures were arranged around small plazas, which were further organized around one large plaza. Although this scenario may seem overly elaborate, precedent exists for such spatial patterning in affiliated Orange communities along the St. Johns (Sassaman 2003) and at Late Archaic shell rings on the coast (Russo 2004; Saunders and Wrenn this volume). Indeed, one need look no further than the two U-shaped mounds that bracket the watershed. As discussed previously, radiocarbon assays from around the spring pool demonstrate that Orange communities gathered and deposited shell in great quantities during relatively brief spans of time. Moreover, the U-shaped shell mound at the mouth of the Silver Glen Springs run was likely erected during the Orange period. It remains to be determined whether an Orange village was present on the south ridge of 8LA1-East.

Beyond the St. Johns

Within the SGSW we have little direct evidence for the wide-ranging exchange networks involving objects that are present at other sites in the region, such as groundstone beads from the mid-South or bannerstones from the lower coastal plain (Randall and Sassaman 2010). Nevertheless, objects recovered from the SGSW highlight how Archaic community practices incorporated other places. The chipped-stone tools recovered from the shell-free upland terraces are instructive in this regard. This lithic assemblage included Florida Archaic stemmed hafted bifaces, microlithic tools, and abundant debitage. Jon Endonino determined the provenance of raw materials using the quarry cluster method (see Upchurch et al. 1982). The majority of raw material was derived from the Ocala and Santa Fe quarries 125 kilometers to the northwest, although a portion of the assemblage was derived from Tampa Bay quarries 150 kilometers to the southwest. When this evidence is considered in conjunction with lithic provenance studies of coeval assemblages at Lake Monroe Outlet Midden and Thornhill Lake, it becomes apparent that communities along the St. Johns either traveled to sources and extracted the materials themselves or were embedded in a larger network that circulated raw material. Although the dynamics of this system currently elude us, communities along the St. Johns had knowledge of and experience with other peoples throughout Florida. There are also hints of production for exchange. In addition to hafted bifaces, the lithic assemblage includes a large number of expanded-base microliths. These tools likely date to the Thornhill Lake phase occupation, based on their associations at the Lake Monroe Outlet Midden. Without detailed use-wear analysis it is impossible to know what these tools were used to produce. One possibility suggested by the width of their working edge is that they were involved in the production of marine shell beads. Similar marine shell beads were used by communities in the interior Southeast (Claassen 1996), and perhaps groups on the St. Johns River were embedded in the exchange network.

Objects recovered from 8MR123 also highlight Archaic community practices beyond daily subsistence tasks. Marine shell was encountered in the LSA's investigations and included celts and axes. This sample also included three *Busycon contrarium* vessels, one of which was found in mortuary mound fill and another at Locus B. Sassaman, O'Donoughue, and Byrd (2011) have argued that these vessels likely had special significance and may have been used to brew medicinal beverages. Other insights are to be gained from future analysis of Orange vessels, whose production, use, and deposition were likely embedded in daily and ceremonial events (see Saunders and Wrenn this volume). In this regard, the large steaming pits at Locus B and at least one shell-filled pit in the confines of 8MR123 have considerable significance. One plausible explanation is that such pits were excavated and used to process shellfish during feasting events (Gilmore 2011). In this case, shell and associated pottery were intentionally deposited as mound fill. One potential avenue of research is to explore whether the proposed upland village was inhabited for extended periods of time by a large community or reflects a short-term aggregation of households from throughout the St. Johns basin.

## Heaps and Histories

We began this discussion by arguing that shell mounds should not be treated as interchangeable isolates and that Archaic communities were neither local nor ahistorical in their outlook. On a practical level, this requires archaeologists to adopt a broader landscape perspective. In suggesting that shell mounds should be decentered, however, we are not simply arguing for a shift from looking at trees to looking at forests. As seen at Silver Glen Springs, Archaic communities had complex relationships with shellfish that preclude interpreting shell mounds as incidental. Indeed, numerous places existed in which shell and earth deposition, object production and acquisition, and veneration of the dead were inextricably coupled. Each depositional event was structured by social and ecological contexts and varied in intensity, duration, and character. For example, some alterations in settlement, such as the onset of shell fishing locally, were no doubt influenced by broader environmental trends. As seen at Locus A, however, even the seemingly benign act of creating new spaces for residential occupation involved significant ritual effort. Other mounds and nonmounded spaces were brought about through sustained and perhaps unanticipated contacts with other communities during the Thornhill Lake and Orange periods. Shell mounds were thus constructed under a variety of social and ecological conditions and no doubt had shifting and potentially competing meanings through time. Importantly, however, the social lives of mounds and their constituent parts were not complete when they were deposited in place. While the data on this topic are limited, Archaic communities appear to have incorporated the plan of and even pieces of old places in the course of making new histories. In moving forward, we must recognize that just like Archaic communities and objects, shell mounds too were constantly on the move.

## Acknowledgments

We are indebted to the Juniper Club, whose generosity has made our continued investigation of the Silver Glen Springs watershed possible. Rhonda Kimbrough and Ray Willis of the United States Forest Service also deserve many thanks for facilitating the participating agreement. Finally, this chapter benefited greatly from comments by Chris Rodning and an anonymous reviewer.

## References

Archaeological Consultants, Inc., and Janus Research
2001    Phase III Mitigative Excavations at Lake Monroe Outlet Midden (8VO53), Volusia County, Florida. Report Submitted to the U.S. Department of Transportation Federal Highway Administration and Florida Department of Transportation District Five.

Aten, Lawrence E.
1999    Middle Archaic Ceremonialism at Tick Island, Florida: Ripley P. Bullen's 1961 Excavations at the Harris Creek Site. *Florida Anthropologist* 52: 131–200.

Claassen, Cheryl
1996    A Consideration of the Social Organization of the Shell Mound Archaic. In *Archaeology of the Mid-Holocene Southeast*, edited by Kenneth E. Sassaman and David G. Anderson, 235–58. University Press of Florida, Gainesville.

Cumbaa, Stephen L.
1976    A Reconsideration of Freshwater Shellfish Exploitation in the Florida Archaic. *Florida Anthropologist* 29: 49–59.

Endonino, Jon C.
2008    The Thornhill Lake Archaeological Research Project: 2005–2008. *Florida Anthropologist* 61: 149–65.
2010    Thornhill Lake: Hunter-Gatherers, Monuments, and Memory. PhD dissertation, Department of Anthropology, University of Florida, Gainesville.

Erlandson, Jon M.
2001    The Archaeology of Aquatic Adaptations: Paradigms for a New Millennium. *Journal of Archaeological Research* 9: 287–350.

Gilmore, Zackary I.

2011    Locus B. In *St. Johns Archaeological Field School 2007–2009: Silver Glen Run*, edited by Kenneth E. Sassaman, Zackary Gilmore, and Asa R. Randall. Technical Report 12. Laboratory of Southeastern Archaeology, Department of Anthropology, University of Florida, Gainesville.

Goggin, John M.

1952    *Space and Time Perspectives in Northern St. Johns Archaeology, Florida*. Yale University Publications in Anthropology no. 47. Yale University Press, New Haven, CT.

Marquardt, William H.

2010    Shell Mounds in the Southeast: Middens, Monuments, Temple Mounds, Rings, or Works? *American Antiquity* 75: 551–70.

Marrinan, Rochelle A., H. Stephen Hale, and William M. Stanton

1990    Test Excavations at Silver Glen Springs, Florida (8MR123). Miscellaneous Report Series no. 2. Department of Anthropology, Florida State University, Tallahassee.

McGee, Ray M., and Ryan J. Wheeler

1994    Stratigraphic Excavations at Groves' Orange Midden, Lake Monroe, Volusia County, Florida: Methodology and Results. *Florida Anthropologist* 47: 333–49.

Milanich, Jerald T.

1994    *Archaeology of Precolumbian Florida*. University Press of Florida, Gainesville.

Miller, James J.

1998    *An Environmental History of Northeast Florida*. University Press of Florida, Gainesville.

Norman, Robert

2010    *Images of America: Ocala National Forest*. Arcadia Publishing, Charleston, NC.

O'Donoughue, Jason M.

2010    Shell Springs Eternal. Paper presented at the 67th Annual Meeting of the Southeastern Archaeological Conference, Lexington, KY.

O'Donoughue, Jason M., Kenneth E. Sassaman, Meggan E. Blessing, Johanna B. Talcott, and Julie Byrd

2011    Archaeological Investigations at Salt Springs (8MR2322), Marion County, Florida. Technical Report 11. Laboratory of Southeastern Archaeology, Department of Anthropology, University of Florida, Gainesville.

Piatek, Bruce John

1994    The Tomoka Mound Complex in Northeast Florida. *Southeastern Archaeology* 13: 109–18.

Potter, Alden L.

1935    The Remains at Silver Glenn Springs. In *Some Further Papers on Aboriginal Man in the Neighborhood of the Ocala National Forest*, edited by A. E. Abshire, Alden L. Potter, Allen R. Taylor, Clyde H. Neil, Walter H. Anderson, John I. Rutledge, and Stevenson B. Johnson, 13–14. Civilian Conservation Corps, Company 1420, Ocala Camp, Florida.

Quinn, Rhonda L., Bryan D. Tucker, and John Krigbaum

2008    Diet and Mobility in Middle Archaic Florida: Stable Isotopic and Faunal Data from the Harris Creek Archaeological Site (8VO24), Tick Island. *Journal of Archaeological Science* 35: 2346–56.

Randall, Asa R.

2007    St. Johns Archaeological Field School 2005: Hontoon Island State Park. Technical Report no. 7. Laboratory of Southeastern Archaeology, Department of Anthropology, University of Florida, Gainesville.

2010    Remapping Histories: Archaic Period Community Construction Along the St. Johns River, Florida. PhD dissertation, Department of Anthropology, University of Florida, Gainesville.

2011    Remapping Archaic Social Histories Along the St. Johns River in Florida. In *Hunter-Gatherer Archaeology as Historical Process*, edited by Kenneth E. Sassaman and Donald H. Holly Jr., 120–42. University of Arizona Press, Tucson.

Randall, Asa R., Meggan E. Blessing, and Jon C. Endonino

2011    *Cultural Resource Assessment Survey of Silver Glen Springs Recreational Area in the Ocala National Forest, Florida*. Technical Report 13. Laboratory of Southeastern Archaeology, Department of Anthropology, University of Florida, Gainesville.

Randall, Asa R., and Kenneth E. Sassaman

2010    (E)Mergent Complexities During the Archaic in Northeast Florida. In *Ancient Complexities: New Perspectives in Precolumbian North America*, edited by Susan M. Alt, 8–31. University of Utah Press, Salt Lake City.

Russo, Michael

2004    Measuring Shell Rings for Social Inequality. In *Signs of Power: The Rise of Cultural Complexity in the Southeast*, edited by Jon L. Gibson, and Philip J. Carr, 26–70. University of Alabama Press, Tuscaloosa.

Russo, Michael, Barbara Purdy, Lee A. Newsom, and Ray M. McGee

1992    A Reinterpretation of Late Archaic Adaptations in Central-East Florida: Grove's Orange Midden (8VO2601). *Southeastern Archaeology* 11: 95–108.

Sassaman, Kenneth E.

2003    St. Johns Archaeological Field School 2000–2001: Blue Spring and Hontoon Island State Parks. Technical Report 4. Laboratory of Southeastern Archaeology, Department of Anthropology, University of Florida, Gainesville.

2005    Hontoon Dead Creek Mound (8VO214). In *St. Johns Archaeological Field School 2003–2004: Hontoon Island State Park*, edited by Asa R. Randall, and Kenneth E. Sassaman, 83–106. Technical Report 6. Laboratory of Southeastern Archaeology, Department of Anthropology, University of Florida, Gainesville.

Sassaman, Kenneth E., Zackary I. Gilmore, and Asa R. Randall

2011    St. Johns Archaeological Field School 2007–2010: Silver Glen Run (8LA1). Technical Report 12. Laboratory of Southeastern Archaeology, Department of Anthropology, University of Florida, Gainesville.

Sassaman, Kenneth E., Jason M. O'Donoughue, and Julie Byrd

2011    Material Culture. In *Archaeological Investigations at Salt Springs (8MR2322), Marion County, Florida*, edited by Jason M. O'Donoughue, Kenneth E. Sassaman, Meggan E. Blessing, Johanna B. Talcott, and Julie Byrd, 49–64. Technical Report 11. Laboratory of Southeastern Archaeology, Department of Anthropology, University of Florida, Gainesville.

Sassaman, Kenneth E., and Asa R. Randall

2012    Shell Mounds of the Middle St. Johns Basin, Northeast Florida. In *Early New World Monumentality*, edited by Richard L. Burger, and Robert M. Rosenswig, 53–72. University Press of Florida, Gainesville.

Schwadron, Margo

2010    Prehistoric Landscapes of Complexity: Archaic and Woodland Period Shell Works, Shell Rings, and Tree Islands of the Everglades, South Florida. In *Trend, Tradition, and Turmoil: What Happened to the Southeastern Archaic*, edited by David Hurst Thomas, and Matthew C. Sanger, 113–46. American Museum of Natural History, New York.

Sears, W. H.

1960    Bluffton Burial Mound. *Florida Anthropologist* 13(2–3): 55–60.

Thulman, David K.

2009    Freshwater Availability as the Constraining Factor in the Middle Paleoindian Occupation of North-Central Florida. *Geoarchaeology* 24: 243–76.

Upchurch, Sam B., Richard N. Strom, and Mark G. Nuckels

1982    Methods of Chert Provenance: Determination of Florida Cherts. Report prepared for the Florida Division of Archives, History, and Records Management, Bureau of Historic Sites and Properties, Tallahassee, FL.

Wheeler, Ryan J., Christine L. Newman, and Ray M. McGee

2000    A New Look at the Mount Taylor and Bluffton Sites, Volusia County, with an Outline of the Mount Taylor Culture. *Florida Anthropologist* 53: 133–57.

Wyman, Jeffries

1875    *Fresh Water Shell Mounds of the St. John's River, Florida.* Memoirs of the Peabody Academy of Science no. 1. Peabody Academy of Science, Salem, MA.

## 2

## Deconstructing and Reconstructing Caloosahatchee Shell Mound Building

THERESA SCHOBER

Remnants of elevated mounds and ridges, sculpted canals, and watercourts are a visible yet subtle reminder of the once-thriving Calusa chiefdom in today's southwest Florida landscape. The Calusa heartland was centered on the Greater Charlotte Harbor watershed from the Peace River to the north and the Cocohatchee River to the south, encompassing the large estuaries of Charlotte Harbor proper, Pine Island Sound, and San Carlos and Estero Bays while spreading inland along the Caloosahatchee River (figure 2.1). The Calusa and their predecessors exploited and intensified the natural abundance of coastal and estuarine systems to establish a highly stratified, politically complex tributary chiefdom. Its sphere of influence and alliances incorporated the southern third of the Florida peninsula by the sixteenth century (Fontaneda 1944; Laudonnière 1975; Solís de Merás 1923; Zubillaga 1946; Goggin and Sturtevant 1964; Hann 1991, 2003; Marquardt 1988; Milanich and Fairbanks 1980).

Models devised to explain the characteristics of maritime hunting and gathering societies repeatedly acknowledge that marine environments provide an abundant and stable resource base (Murdock 1968; Yesner 1980) and that subsistence stress in such societies is buffered by resource scheduling (Arnold 1992) and food storage (Schalk 1981; Testart 1982). Where documentation exists, both ethnohistoric and archaeological data demonstrate that these societies are represented to greater or lesser degrees by the presence of semi-sedentary to sedentary village sites, high population densities, social and political hierarchies, hereditary chiefs, exchange networks between villages, occupational specialization, and warfare (Fiedel 1992). Not surprisingly then, interpretations of the Calusa archaeological record and discussions of the development of social formations are heavily interwoven with an understanding of resource availability and stability across time and space.

This partiality to environmental explanations of social change is reinforced by the

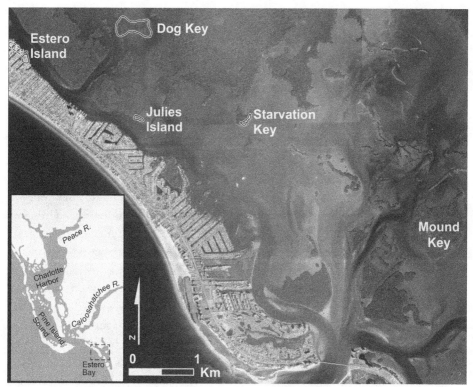

Figure 2.1. Locations of Estero Bay archaeological sites mentioned in text with inset of study region. Map inset courtesy of Asa Randall.

nature of the archaeological record in the Caloosahatchee region. Torrence (2001) argued that archaeological sites composed predominantly of shell "manipulate the mind." In contrast to the earthen architecture among Hopewellian and Mississippian sites in northern Florida and beyond, the piling of food refuse into elevated mounds and ridges lends itself to mundane interpretations of accumulation rather than intentional construction.

If shell-bearing sites are gradual accumulations, detailed studies of the specific dietary, seasonal, and environmental characteristics of these sites directly explore human-environmental interactions through time in the Caloosahatchee region (e.g., Marquardt 1992; Walker 1992) and can be extrapolated as proxies for environmental change (e.g., Walker et al. 1995). However, if shell-matrix sites are the product of landscape shaping and reshaping at monumental scales (Cushing 2000; Hrdlicka 1922; Torrence 1999; Torrence and Schober 2008), the relationship of site composition to subsistence and settlement patterns becomes more complex.

Instead of integrative studies that focus on identifying depositional characteristics of shell-bearing deposits to test both cultural and natural processes, a polarizing debate has developed across the Southeast among researchers who explore the purposeful use of shell for cosmological, ritual, or sociopolitical reasons and those who focus on the functional and ecological consequences of collecting, consuming, and discarding shellfish (see summaries by Thompson and Worth 2011; Randall 2010). Essentially, where some see platforms for elite structures, others see midden accumulations on storm surges (e.g., the Wightman site; see Widmer 1988, 93–94 and Walker et al. 1994 for contrasting perspectives), and where some see intentional construction, others see the opening of ocean passes (e.g., Useppa's Collier Ridge; see Milanich et al. 1984 and Marquardt 1999, 89–91 for contrasting perspectives).

The contrast in paradigms is also borne out in debates about the development of Calusa complexity. Marquardt (1988, 1987) interpreted the intensified tributary characteristics of the Calusa chiefdom as a by-product of heightened economic interaction and the influx of Spanish goods in the late contact period (Marquardt 2004, 210). Viewing the variety of Caloosahatchee site types, including mound complexes such as Pineland, as representative of gradual accumulation (Marquardt 2010a, 2010b) is consistent with this model. Widmer (1988) viewed the complex Calusa chiefdom as a cultural phenomenon of deeper time that emerged by AD 800. Both researchers correlate site distribution with fluctuations in sea level. However, despite the environmental causation embedded in Widmer's model, he attributes the construction of shellworks, changes in burial patterns, and the development of regional trade networks to solidification of social hierarchies for resource regulation. More recently, a number of economic models have focused on craft specialization, transportation, and trade as catalysts for changes in social formation (Dietler 2008; Patton 2001; Torrence and Schober 2008).

Ultimately, answers to questions of how and when inequality and hierarchy develop and the meanings of shell-matrix sites rely on our ability to interpret the cultural landscape at any one point in time. Although chronological assessment of shell-bearing sites is fundamental, it remains elusive (Claassen 1998, 15; Marquardt 1992; Patton 2001; Schwadron 2010, 123; Torrence 1999; Torrence and Schober 2008). This chapter seeks to contribute a deeper understanding of the depositional sequences at one shell-matrix site. This complexity challenges conceptualizations of shell mounds as slowly accumulating midden deposits and offers new insights into previously identified relationships between the Calusa heartland and interior Florida.

## Case Study

The Estero Island site is an unassuming shell ridge located along the bay side of Estero Island, now the municipality of Fort Myers Beach. The site fronts Matanzas

Pass, providing an entrance into Estero Bay proper. The Calusa capital of Mound Key is located to the south and the confluence of the Caloosahatchee River and San Carlos Bay are to the north (figure 2.1). As with many archaeological sites on barrier islands in south Florida, the elevated portions of the site were incorporated into the earliest homestead on Estero Island (figure 2.2). Residential development in the 1950s reduced the archaeological deposits from approximately 14 acres to the 2.7 acres remaining today. In an effort to protect the site from further destruction, the Florida Communities Trust provided the funds that purchased the property for the local community in 2000.

Despite its prominent position along the route from Mound Key to Pine Island Sound, the Estero Island site was not occupied during the early contact era. Archaeological excavations initiated in 2002 established that the remaining site area includes a 4.3-meter-high platform that is relatively undisturbed. These elevated deposits once formed the southern apex of a longer shell ridge. Stereoscopic analysis of 1944 aerial photographs of the site indicates that in addition to the prominent elevation of the current shell mass, the site included a series of lower platforms and basins (Schober and Torrence 2002, 41). Small finger-like projections into the mangroves and bay may have served as fish weirs or ponds to support the site's population (Torrence and Schober 2008).

As with many shell-matrix sites in the Caloosahatchee region (e.g., Bullen and Bullen 1956; Marquardt 1992; Torrence 1999) and elsewhere (e.g., Russo 2004; Sassaman 2003; Thompson 2007), the Estero Island site is constructed of alternat-

Figure 2.2. Circa 1906 photograph of the southern portion of the Estero Island site along Matanzas Pass. Courtesy of the William H. Grace Collection.

ing layers with greater amounts of shell and earthen sediments, respectively. The interpretation of these contrasting deposits has been central to debates about the meanings of shell mounds (see Randall 2010; Thompson and Worth 2011). Excavations at the Estero Island site have revealed that the sediment-rich layers demonstrate domestic occupation of the site based on the presence of post molds and associated house floors. These layers exhibit higher artifact density relative to the quantity of food refuse (Schober and Torrence 2002). Shell-bearing deposits are typically characterized by high shellfish diversity and the inclusion of non-edible aquatic creatures such as slipper shells and barnacles (Peres et al. 2009). Many strata exhibit low numbers of vertebrates and low concentrations of artifacts. This pattern has been interpreted as the result of secondary deposition where smaller fish bones and other debris are lost in transport.

Certain shell-bearing deposits in the site show resource collection strategies focused on particular foods, specifically fighting conch and surf clam. Dense shell deposits with disproportionate numbers of certain taxa may reflect primary deposition of preferred foods, increased availability of particular resources at certain times of the year (both surf clam and fighting conch are species adapted to high salinity), deposits from feasting or event-based meal preparation (Schober and Torrence 2002, 158), or trade-related shellfish processing.

Macroscopic analysis of aboriginal pottery revealed that 98 percent by count and weight of the overall assemblage consisted of the sand-tempered plain ware (Schober and Torrence 2002) that dominates southwest Florida ceramic assemblages from 500 BC to contact (Bullen and Bullen 1956; Cordell 1992; Luer and Almy 1980; Sears 1967; Widmer 1988). Most of the Estero Island site was initially interpreted as having accumulated prior to AD 600 during the Caloosahatchee I (ca. 500 BC–AD 500) and Caloosahatchee IIA early (ca. AD 500–650) periods. The evidence for this interpretation was limited amounts of Belle Glade Plain pottery in the upper 30 centimeters of intact cultural deposits. Radiocarbon results on food shell from four units excavated in 2002 corroborated these results (table 2.1).[1] Only radiocarbon dates on shell from the southernmost knoll on the site (cal AD 680–820) and the elevated area adjacent to the historic home approximately 40 centimeters below the surface (cal AD 830–985) demonstrated that the site was occupied during the Caloosahatchee IIA late (ca. AD 650–800) and IIB (ca. AD 800–1200) periods but had been abandoned by approximately AD 1000 (Schober and Torrence 2002).

Nonlocal Belle Glade Plain pottery in appreciable frequency and a single St. Johns Check Stamped sherd were found in only one test unit along the site's northern periphery near the water's edge (Schober and Torrence 2002, 119–20). An AMS date on unidentified wood charcoal from the lowest excavated layer in this unit yielded calibrated dates between AD 1035 and 1210 (table 2.1) that support

Figure 2.3. Circa 1958 aerial photograph taken during the development of the Shell Mound Park subdivision. Remaining portion of the Estero Island site is located in the foreground along the water's edge. Courtesy of the Florence Long Estate.

the interpretation that site use in the Caloosahatchee IIB and III periods (ca. AD 1200–1350) was limited. A pavement of 223 net weights and one fragment of a net mesh gauge in the same unit are evidence of net repair activities but not necessarily habitation. In 2004, monitoring and excavation associated with underground utility upgrades confirmed these results. Because of the destruction of the northern 11 acres of the site in the 1950s (figure 2.3), it is not possible to determine whether Caloosahatchee III occupation of the site was more pervasive.

## Radiocarbon Ages of Shell-Bearing Strata

Subsequent archaeological investigations at the Estero Island site were performed to monitor or mitigate site development that consisted of installing underground utilities, rehabilitating the historic structures, and installing a permanent archaeological exhibit at the site of an in-ground swimming pool that was constructed in 1958. The latter project, which was conducted from 2005 to 2007, presented the opportunity to evaluate site stratification and mound construction over a larger area than previous investigations.

Table 2.1. Radiocarbon dates from the Estero Island site

| Provenience | Beta Number | Analysis | Material | Measured Radiocarbon Age | $^{13}C/^{12}C$ Ratio | Conventional Radiocarbon Age | Calibration 1 sigma | Calibration 2 sigma |
|---|---|---|---|---|---|---|---|---|
| **SCHOBER AND TORRENCE 2002** | | | | | | | | |
| N256 E181, Stratum 4 | 170836 | AMS | Charcoal | 880±60 | -23.8 | 900±60 | AD1035–1210 | AD1010–1260 |
| N232 E197, Stratum 10 | 170835 | Radiometric | Fighting conch | 1930±70 | +1.1 | 2360±70 | BC130–AD50 | BC200–AD120 |
| N231 E162 Stratum 2a | 170834 | Radiometric | Fighting conch | 1510±60 | -0.4 | 1910±60 | AD420–560 | AD350–620 |
| N199 E188, Stratum 5a | 170833 | Radiometric | Quahog clam | 1100±60 | -1.2 | 1490±60 | AD830–985 | AD775–1025 |
| N177 E204, Stratum 4 | 170831 | Radiometric | Fighting conch | 1410±60 | +0.4 | 1830±70 | AD490–650 | AD425–690 |
| N177 E204, Stratum 7c | 170832 | Radiometric | Fighting conch | 1680±70 | +0.5 | 2100±70 | AD170–350 | AD90–430 |
| N176 E177, Stratum 4 | 170830 | Radiometric | Fighting conch | 1560±60 | +1.0 | 1980±60 | AD345–460 | AD260–545 |
| N156 E202, Stratum 3 | 170829 | Radiometric | Quahog clam | 1230±60 | -0.7 | 1630±70 | AD680–820 | AD640–900 |
| **MOUND EXHIBIT PROFILE: SHELL-BEARING STRATA** | | | | | | | | |
| 1, East Profile | 234645 | Radiometric | Fighting conch | 1660±50 | +0.4 | 2080±60 | AD220–360 | AD140–430 |
| 2, East Profile | 234646 | Radiometric | Fighting conch | 1340±60 | +1.2 | 1770±60 | AD580–680 | AD510–710 |
| 3, East Profile | 234647 | Radiometric | Fighting conch | 1450±50 | +0.5 | 1870±50 | AD460–590 | AD420–640 |
| 4, East Profile | 234648 | Radiometric | Quahog clam | 1460±50 | -1.8 | 1840±60 | AD480–630 | AD430–670 |
| 5, East Profile | 234649 | Radiometric | Quahog clam | 1360±50 | -1.0 | 1750±50 | AD610–680 | AD560–710 |
| 6, East Profile | 234650 | Radiometric | Fighting conch | 1850±50 | +0.8 | 2280±50 | BC10–AD100 | BC60–AD150 |
| 1, South Profile | 234651 | Radiometric | Fighting conch | 1470±50 | +0.2 | 1890±50 | AD440–570 | AD400–620 |
| 2, South Profile | 234652 | Radiometric | Fighting conch | 1530±60 | +0.5 | 1950±60 | AD370–510 | AD280–580 |
| 3, South Profile | 234653 | Radiometric | Fighting conch | 1670±50 | +0.3 | 2090±50 | AD220–340 | AD140–400 |

| | | | | | | | | |
|---|---|---|---|---|---|---|---|---|
| 4, South Profile | 234654 | Radiometric | Fighting conch | 1550±60 | +1.1 | 1980±70 | AD330–470 | AD240–570 |
| 5, South Profile | 234655 | Radiometric | Fighting conch | 1520±60 | +0.6 | 1940±60 | AD390–540 | AD300–590 |
| 6, South Profile | 234656 | Radiometric | Fighting conch | 1490±50 | 0.0 | 1900±60 | AD430–570 | AD360–630 |
| 7, South Profile | 234657 | Radiometric | Quahog clam | 1480±50 | -1.5 | 1860±50 | AD470–600 | AD430–650 |
| 8, South Profile | 234658 | Radiometric | Quahog clam | 1560±50 | -0.8 | 1960±60 | AD360–480 | AD270–570 |
| 9, South Profile | 234659 | Radiometric | Fighting conch | 1680±50 | +0.6 | 2110±50 | AD180–300 | AD130–370 |
| 10, N5 E9, Zone 10 | 234660 | Radiometric | Fighting conch | 1850±50 | +0.7 | 2270±50 | AD10–120 | BC40–AD160 |

**SHELL MOUND PROFILE: EARTHEN STRATA**

| | | | | | | | | |
|---|---|---|---|---|---|---|---|---|
| E1, South Profile | 258369 | AMS | Pine wood | 1220±40 | -25.8 | 1210±40 | AD770–880 | AD690–900 |
| E2, South Profile | 258370 | AMS | Red mangrove | 1120±40 | -24.0 | 1140±40 | AD880–970 | AD780–990 |
| E3, South Profile | 258371 | AMS | Red mangrove | 1250±40 | -25.8 | 1240±40 | AD690–810 | AD670–890 |
| E5, South Profile | 258372 | AMS | Black mangrove | 1070±40 | -22.6 | 1110±40 | AD890–980 | AD870–1010 |
| E6, South Profile | 258373 | AMS | Acorn nutshell and nutmeat | 1100±40 | -25.4 | 1090±40 | AD900–1000 | AD880–1020 |
| E7, South Profile | 258374 | AMS | Acorn nutmeat | 1510±40 | -15.4 | 1670±40 | AD340–420 | AD260–300, AD310–430 |
| E8, N2 E13, 9.34–9.36mbd | 258375 | AMS | Acorn nutshell and nutmeat | 1450±40 | -28.9 | 1390±40 | AD640–660 | AD600–680 |
| E9, N4 E13, 9.17–9.20mbd | 258368 | AMS | Black mangrove | 1350±40 | -22.9 | 1380±40 | AD640–660 | AD610–680 |
| E10, N4 E12, 9.40–9.44mbd | 258376 | AMS | Acorn nutshell and nutmeat | 1370±40 | -24.2 | 1380±40 | AD640–660 | AD610–680 |
| N4 E14, 9.50mbd | 240990 | AMS | Loose residue in pipe | 1310±40 | -23.2 | 1340±40 | AD650–680 | AD 640–720, AD740–770 |
| N4 E14, 9.50mbd | 257655 | AMS | Scraped residue in pipe | 1630±40 | -23.5 | 1650±40 | AD380–420 | AD260–280, AD330–450, AD450–460, AD480–530 |

Fifteen one-by-two-meter units were hand excavated below the base of the swimming pool, revealing a 65-foot-long profile that extended from culturally sterile beach sand to the current mound summit. Although the archaeological excavation was constrained to the western (back) slope of the mound that was damaged by the swimming pool, substantial data could be drawn to address questions of how and when this shell-matrix site accumulated.

Temporally diagnostic Belle Glade ceramics or other nonlocal wares are conspicuously absent from the artifact assemblage of the 2005–2007 excavations. This result was not unexpected because of the previously inferred age of the site and because the swimming pool damaged the upper four to seven feet of the archaeological deposits in the area of excavation.

Construction disturbance was limited to the immediate area of the swimming pool. Alternating stratification of intact mixed-species shell deposits, thin earthen matrix layers, occasional homogenous shell layers, and burned and fragmented shell layers were encountered behind a construction trench of 35 to 40 centimeters that was filled with clean sand. To facilitate meaningful interpretation of the visible mound profile for visitors, shell samples were selected from 15 observable layers from the east and south profiles for radiocarbon analysis (figure 2.4). Unmodified food shells of fighting conch (*Strombus alatus*) and quahog clam (*Mercenaria campechiensis*) were sampled from dense strata with clear boundaries to reduce the likelihood of intrusion from other deposits.

Along the east profile, the upper three strata targeted for radiocarbon dating were composed of predominantly shell matrices that are roughly horizontal in orientation (East Profile samples 1–3). Three additional samples were recovered from layers of pen shell hash that appear to cap underlying shell deposits (East Profile samples 4–6), a practice also reported at Key Marco (Widmer 1996, 24). Along the south profile, seven samples were selected from variable shell matrix layers in the upper two-thirds of the mound profile, including those that are interpreted to be mound-building layers (South Profile samples 2–4) and feasting deposits (South Profile samples 1, 7). Two additional samples were selected from the lower profile (South Profile samples 8 and 9) where layers of earth and pen shell hash, respectively, capped a discrete elevated area. One additional shell sample was taken from 15 to 20 centimeters above culturally sterile sands located three meters north of the south profile wall (sample 10).

Composition of basal deposits at the site varies across space. In this location, a layer of whole and broken surf clam and degraded pen shell, oyster, crown conch, fighting conch, and quahog clams was mixed with fine pale brown sands, sand-tempered plain pottery, and manufactured shell tools. A calibrated date of AD 10 to 120 is consistent with radiocarbon results from the 2002 excavations and provides additional evidence that the earliest site occupation was approximately 2,000 years

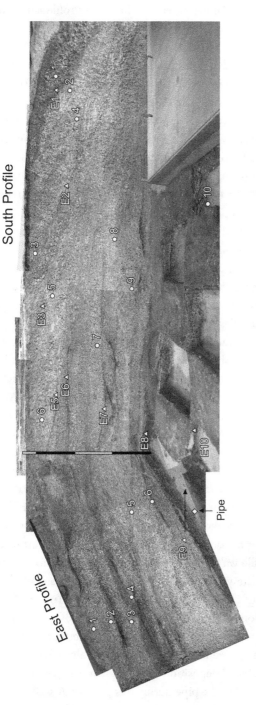

Figure 2.4. East and south stratigraphic profiles of the 2005–2007 excavations at the Estero Island site illustrating locations of radiocarbon samples discussed in the text. Samples labeled 1–6 on the east profile and samples labeled 1–10 on the south profile derive from shell-bearing strata. Samples labeled "E1–3 and E5–10" are from predominantly earthen matrix layers. Photo compilation includes images by the author and images courtesy of White Hawk Communications.

ago. A contemporaneous calibrated date of 10 BC to AD 100 was also obtained from deposits that cap a small mound along the east profile (East Profile sample 6; figure 2.4; table 2.1).

In general, radiocarbon dates on shell from deposits in these small low mounds that are visible on the south and east profiles are consistent with Caloosahatchee I period occupation (East Profile sample 6, South Profile samples 8–10). It appears that this portion of the site was originally a series of discrete shell elevations; this is also demonstrated by the north profile (not shown). This site pattern has been observed elsewhere in the Caloosahatchee region (e.g., Batty Mound) and may represent separate but clustered habitation areas for extended kin groups or lineages.

The observed stratification and shell radiocarbon dates appear to indicate that substantial building activity occurred at the junction of the Caloosahatchee I and Caloosahatchee IIA early periods, when at least 2.7 meters of deposits were added to the mound. Seven calibrated radiocarbon samples yielded dates between AD 390 and 680 (East Profile samples 2–5, South Profile samples 5–7). The deposition pattern first filled in lower-lying areas between the smaller discrete mounds, resulting in one larger and higher elevated feature that was then expanded in an easterly direction toward Matanzas Pass. Layers of burned and fragmented shell appear to have capped deposition episodes.

Mound construction continued with the addition of thick building layers separated by microstrata of burned shell, charcoal, and pottery. These strata exhibit less non-shell matrix and contain non-edible aquatic colonizers such as barnacles. Four shell samples yielded calibrated radiocarbon dates ranging in age from AD 220 to 510 (East Profile sample 1, South Profile samples 2–4), indicating that increased elevation of the mound was achieved by relocating older midden from elsewhere. A final layer of fighting conch and oyster that is observable in the extreme upper right-hand corner of figure 2.4 (South Profile sample 1) yielded a calibrated radiocarbon date of AD 440 to 570, which is consistent with results from deeper strata.

Loose carbonized residue from the bowl of a ceramic pipe recovered near the base of excavation in an area where bone meal and dense charcoal overlaid sterile sands was submitted for radiocarbon analysis. The depth of the artifact and its proximity to the east profile wall suggested deposition prior to mound construction. However, an AMS date yielded a calibrated radiocarbon age of AD 650 to 680. While following stratification across space can be particularly challenging in shell-matrix sites, excavation records reveal that this portion of the site was where the discrete low mounds evident in the east and north profiles intersected. The filling in of the low-lying area between small mounds in the Caloosahatchee I and IIA early periods may have included deposition of the pipe or may have contaminated the loose carbonized material in the pipe during this process. A second AMS date from scrapings inside the bowl yielded a result of AD 380 to 420, suggesting that the artifact may have been passed down over many generations (table 2.1).

## Radiocarbon Ages of Earthen Strata

Many researchers have interpreted the thinner earthen surfaces between shell-rich strata as representing stable periods of mound occupation, or "living surfaces" (Goggin 1949, 67; Russo 2004; Thompson 2007; Schober and Torrence 2002). Additional radiocarbon analyses have focused on these strata to provide finer chronological control for episodes of mound occupation and to temporally bracket construction-related deposition.

Following identification of wood charcoal and macrobotanical analysis of sediment samples (Leone 2009), seven samples from visible earthen strata in the south profile (samples E1–3, E5–8) and two samples from the lower excavation area (samples E9–10) were selected for radiocarbon assay (figure 2.4). Charred annual plant remains were preferentially analyzed, such as nutshell and nutmeat or wood charcoal samples from shorter-lived taxa. Unlike radiocarbon results from shell, two AMS dates on acorn nutshell and nutmeat and one from black mangrove charcoal (samples E8–10) in the dense series of midden layers underlying the elevated shell deposits demonstrate rapid site accumulation between AD 640 and 660. This result is consistent with the loose carbonized material recovered from the pipe.

Upper mound layers also appear to have been deposited more rapidly and more recently than the shell dates would suggest. Five calibrated AMS dates on charcoal from pine, red and black mangrove, or acorn nutshell and nutmeat from observable earthen lenses on the south profile (samples E1–3, E5–6) yielded calibrated ages ranging from AD 690 to 1000. All calibrated age ranges overlapped between AD 880 to 890 at the 95 percent confidence interval. One earthen layer (sample E7) yielded an anomalous radiocarbon age of AD 340 to 420. This date is more similar to surrounding shell dates, suggesting primary deposition. In addition to small amounts of wood charcoal (0.58 g) and nutmeat (0.27 g), two seeds from the nettle genus suggest a high nitrogen context, such as that containing human or animal waste (Leone 2009).

As can be seen in figure 2.5, the mound summit was leveled during the installation of a swimming pool deck, leaving open the possibility that more recent deposits were destroyed during construction. However, the absence of artifacts that are diagnostic of a later period across the site and rapid deposition of upper mound layers during the Caloosahatchee IIB period support the interpretation that the site was abandoned relatively quickly after intensive mound-building efforts.

## AD 900

A straightforward understanding of intrasite chronology and intersite contemporaneity in the Caloosahatchee region is not disclosed by this analysis of the Estero Island site because of the complexity of site formation processes in shell-bearing sites. However, these data complement a growing body of research that attest to

Figure 2.5. Excavation photo illustrating leveled mound deposits from swimming pool deck. Photo by T. Schober.

a significant transformation in the Caloosahatchee cultural landscape around AD 900.

Based on the variety of sites in close proximity to Estero Island and what was perceived as contemporaneous deposition, Torrence and Schober (2005) have argued that clusters of sites in the Estero Bay watershed comprised petty chiefdoms between AD 600 and 900. In this scenario, the Estero Island site served as a large settlement with facilities for resource management and storage. Smaller shell middens at Julies Island and Starvation Key served as limited-use procurement areas (figure 2.1). Dog Key was interpreted as a community center that served both domestic and ceremonial functions because of its large shell mound, which has a deep circular depression in the summit, a sand burial mound, and a low shell ridge (Torrence and Schober 2005). A similar cluster of site types, although smaller in volume and less elaborate, has been recorded in Hurricane Bay.

This model draws in part on earlier research by Torrence (1999) that established a preliminary site typology that correlated mound volume with architectural design and temporal context when such data was available. The radiocarbon dates and pottery assemblage from the 2002 excavations at the Estero Island site fit well with the prevailing interpretation that long linear shell-ridge features were an early Caloosahatchee I/IIA architectural form throughout the region. The linear orientation of the sites paralleling the shoreline is consistent with resource exploitation in many societies that focus on aquatic resources (Waselkov 1987). Finger ridges and partially enclosed lagoons projecting into the estuary at many of these sites have been interpreted as weirs or semi-enclosed fish/conch ponds (Cushing 2000; Luer and Archibald 1988; Torrence and Schober 2008; Schwadron 2010) and may also have supported habitation areas for lower-status members of society (Torrence and Schober 2008).

Detailed sea-level curves for Charlotte Harbor demonstrate that AD 850 marks the transition between cooler, drier conditions and low sea levels of the Buck Key Low and the Neo-Atlantic La Costa High warming trend (Stapor et al. 1991; Tanner 2000; Walker et al. 1995). While this warming trend is equated with higher sea levels and increased resource availability, it also correlates with the apparent abandonment of many Caloosahatchee IIA/B sites in smaller inland bays and on barrier islands, such as the petty chiefdom mentioned above. Larger centers such as Mound Key and Pineland then underwent significant construction. The rapid construction of upper deposits at the Estero Island site reported here indicates this structural reorganization was widespread, not restricted to the largest villages, and because of recycled shell deposits for purposes of construction may not be readily apparent from superficial radiocarbon dates on shell.

That vertical mound construction among sites in the Caloosahatchee region accelerated after AD 800 in the Caloosahatchee IIB period is not a new observation. Adelaide and Ripley Bullens's (1956, 33–52) excavations on the most elevated ridge feature at the John Quiet Mound in northern Charlotte Harbor identified a 1.5-meter-thick layer of clean shell dated to AD 900 located over more organic-rich strata with possible post molds and burned shell. Similarly rapid depositional episodes after AD 800 have been observed at Big Mound Key (Luer et al. 1986, 103), Useppa's Collier Ridge (Milanich et al. 1984), and, after AD 900, at Josslyn and Pineland, where approximately 3.6 meters of shell-bearing deposits were added to the Randall Mound around AD 906 to 1257 (Marquardt 1992). Intensive accumulations are also observed on the Brown's Mound at Pineland, where shell-bearing strata dated to AD 762 to 956 were placed over deposits dated to AD 1235 to 1424. Based on this stratigraphic reversal, Marquardt and Walker (2001, 55–56) suggest intentional mound building in the Caloosahatchee III period (AD 1200–1350) but not before. Redeposited material is also observed in Randell Complex Mound 1 stratification dating to the Caloosahatchee IIB period (Wallace 2013, 758).

From topographic mapping of multiple sites in Charlotte Harbor, Torrence (1999, 2013) demonstrated the synergy between layouts of shell-bearing deposits and sand mounds at the largest sites in the Caloosahatchee region, particularly Pineland and Mound Key. Using a symbolic and structuralist approach, Torrence separated Caloosahatchee site forms into a culturally determined architectural grammar that offered primary elements of paired frontal mounds, a central canal and water court, and segregation of domestic and mortuary areas by geography and matrix. Mound complexes such as Mound Key, the sixteenth-century Calusa capital (Goggin and Sturtevant 1964, 182; Griffin 1974, 342; Lewis 1978, 19, 36–43; Wheeler 2000), express hierarchical social organization through conscious selection of building materials and vertical differentiation of site uses. The accentuation of shell mound construction after AD 800 further separated elite and commoner spaces and demonstrates increasingly hierarchical organization and control of labor. Perhaps the simplest expression of Mound Key's social dominance is that it includes the tallest mound in the Caloosahatchee region (Torrence et al. 1994).

Other archaeological correlates of hierarchical organization were established around AD 900, including mortuary differentiation and ceremonialism (Luer 1999, this volume; Marquardt 2001). The frequency of Belle Glade wares increased as peoples from the Okeechobee Basin interacted (e.g., Luer 1989, 116–21; Luer and Almy 1980, 212; Sears 1967, 101; Sears 1982, 22; Widmer 1988, 84–85). The shallow and unrestricted rims of Belle Glade Plain sherds have been interpreted as allowing for "stacking or nesting" of vessels during the transfer of commodities (Cordell 1992, 161).

Increased trade with the interior necessitated effective routes and means of transportation and enhanced social differences. Patton (1994) argues for specialized production of canoes based on an increase in the frequency of shell cutting-edged tools in the Caloosahatchee IIB period and a decrease in tool richness through time at Pineland. Shell cutting-edged tool production also becomes more standardized during Caloosahatchee IIB (Dietler 2008). Luer (1989) suggests that tributary relationships between the Lake Okeechobee Basin peoples and the Calusa heartland became institutionalized by AD 1000, as evidenced by canal construction, Belle Glade "trade wares," and the presence of shell artifacts that included lightning whelk (*Busycon sinistrum*) dippers, cutting-edged tools, and shell adzes in the habitation deposits associated with mortuary processing on Mound A at Fort Center (Luer 1989, 116, 119–21; Sears 1982). Skeletal evidence of deep-water diving, possibly to procure large marine shells, dates to AD 640–770 (Hutchinson 1999, 143). Other manufactured shell objects such as beads and plummets are found in greater proportion in the interior. For example, Willey (1949, 51) reports 750 seed beads and 750 disk beads from the Belle Glade site, while only two shell beads have been recovered from the Estero Island site (Schober and Torrence 2002).

*Busycon* drinking vessels are also found more widely in ceremonial contexts after AD 800 (e.g., Spiro; see Brown 1976, 20), and other lightning whelk products are well-represented exotica at many Mississippian sites across the Southeast. Galena and ground stone appear in deposits at Pineland in Caloosahatchee IIB/III contexts (Marquardt 2001). Because the Gulf coast was the primary source of *Busycon*, interpretations of change in the Caloosahatchee landscape must consider the impacts of supply and demand in core Mississippian markets. Deep-rooted competition with other Gulf coast groups that is described in ethnohistoric accounts, particularly accounts of the Tocobaga in Tampa Bay, may explain the pattern of ceramic wares from the St. Johns region in Caloosahatchee III sites (Torrence and Schober 2008).

Taken together, these multiple lines of evidence corroborate a significant transition in the Calusa heartland around AD 900 that points to an expanding sphere of interaction. Rapidly increased site volume and elaboration reflects more conspicuous inequality as production and exchange became centralized. Torrence and Schober (2008) hypothesized that the realignment of population toward larger settlements with imposing frontal mounds and shell ridges enclosing water courts is coincident with resource intensification. Aquaculture would have had many benefits, including surplus for chiefly redistribution, occupational specialization (i.e., adornment or production of tools), and interior trade, and it would have ameliorated the stress of overcrowding from higher population densities at major centers. Shellfish harvests from conch ponds could have provided the raw material for the thick, homogenous "clean" shell layers observed at certain sites (e.g., Brown's Mound at Pineland). The management of this new system required decision makers, an increasing division of labor, and more pronounced social boundaries (Paynter 1989). These divisions are then reflected in changes in site architecture (Torrence 1999, 2013).

When the chronological reconstruction and zooarchaeological analysis of the Estero Island site is placed in the context of broad regional change, interpretations of shell deposits as monument construction are no longer unsubstantiated, even if the deposits are also midden (contra Marquardt 2010a, 557–59).

## One Step Forward, Two Steps Back?

Careful consideration of the results generated by this analysis offers a detailed view of the stratification of one portion of the Estero Island site. These data reflect the complexity inherent in shell mound construction that supports idiosyncratic variability among areas of the same site and, potentially, between sites and regions (see also Randall et al. this volume for similar patterns in northeast Florida; and Austin et al. this volume for similar patterns in the Tampa Bay area). At the site level, the interpretation that the majority of deposits at the Estero Island site were attributable to the late Caloosahatchee I/IIA early period with limited Caloosahatchee IIB occupation followed by abandonment around AD 1000 is not supported. While the overall era of site occupation remains unchanged, more refined chronological data demonstrate that most of the shell accumulation occurred in two brief episodes—first around AD 600 and then at about AD 900, before the population reorganized elsewhere on the Calusa landscape. The discrepancies between radiocarbon results from the shell deposits and the organic-rich earthen layers offer compelling evidence of monumental construction and support a revised approach to assessing the contemporaneity of sites in the Caloosahatchee region.

Inverted stratigraphic sequences provide clear evidence that middens were reused for mound construction. However, many inverted sequences may be missed when radiocarbon analysis is restricted to food shell. These data would only establish when resources were harvested and not when they were recycled for mound building. Given the myriad ways that discarded shell can accumulate (see Claassen 1998, 10–11) and the degree of secondary deposition seen at the Estero Island site, it is imperative that models for distinguishing primary context midden from other shell-bearing deposits be developed and employed. This is equally true when stratified midden deposits are examined to assess changes in environmental availability, seasonality studies, and paleoclimatic inferences or to investigate changes in technology through time, particularly after AD 800.

Perhaps most definitively, this research demonstrates the need for detailed radiocarbon profiles for sequences of site occupation at a greater number of sites across the Caloosahatchee region and for assessment of the zooarchaeological and artifact profiles of well-dated deposits. Many researchers have noted the absence of intersite chronological control that is fundamental to understanding Calusa social development (Marquardt 1992; Milanich and Fairbanks 1980, 245; Patton 2001, 5; Widmer 1988, 34), but the absence of correlation between the accepted ceramic chronology and the dramatic construction at the Estero Island site also opens the question of how exotic wares entered the region and were distributed. The need to test the existing southwest Florida pottery chronology with independently dated samples from other sites has been previously acknowledged (Widmer 1988; Cordell 1992).

Our collective understanding of regional chronology and exchange would benefit from a fine-grained technological analyses of pottery such as those conducted by Cordell at the Pineland site (1992, 2013) at sites that represent different levels of settlement hierarchy and in both core and periphery areas. In conjunction with additional radiocarbon dating, more intensive study of pottery assemblages at sites across the region would allow for more accurate identification of trade wares so that patterns of exchange can be better understood. Comprehensive analyses may also reveal the degree of standardization and specialization in pottery production through time and its correlation with architectural transformations.

The fact that monumentality increased at the Estero Island site but was not accompanied by an increase in exotic wares or by elaboration in architecture (see Pluckhahn and Thompson this volume) may suggest a response to competition for authority over local resources that was later extended to control over exchange networks among regions. Did the occupants of Estero Island lose a battle for control of resource extraction that ultimately led to a reorientation of its population to Mound

Key? Did this earlier phase of monumentality necessitate monumentality at an even greater scale by Calusa chiefs during subsequent periods, thus contributing to the heightened hierarchical organization observed in the sixteenth century?

•

The patterns of behavior represented archaeologically through material remains and features are implemented every day, every season, and in each generation and are influenced by the full spectrum of behavioral processes, from idiosyncratic variation to cultural norms. However our ability to extract chronological information from these remains is limited by our methodology and the natural and cultural processes that follow from collection and/or modification of an object to its deposition and redeposition.

We may see considerable discrepancy in radiocarbon ages of shell-building layers and earthen occupation surfaces, such as at the Estero Island site, only in deposits that accumulated in and around AD 900. As regional competition intensified and vertical differentiation of status became paramount, the need for building material also increased. The possible inclusion of conch ponds in major centers for high-status food and building material after Caloosahatchee IIB may obscure this pattern. Gradual accumulation from discarded refuse or large-scale harvests from conch ponds or feasting deposits would provide for similar radiocarbon sequences from shell and intermittent earthen surfaces because harvest and building dates are in closer alignment. In these cases, identifying the origin of the shell accumulation would play a greater role in discerning cultural patterns.

In summary, radiocarbon ages of alternating shell and earthen strata in a complete mound profile demonstrate that monumental construction at the Estero Island site was conducted on the human scale of generations rather than over multiple centuries. This monumentality also occurred considerably earlier in the Caloosahatchee archaeological record than was previously accepted and at a site with only a single shell mass. In combination with regional data on site settlement patterns and architectural forms, these data suggest that no one explanation or interpretation will address the social and environmental context of Calusa mound building at all sites. In order to move beyond the dichotomous debate about construction or accumulation, we need to evaluate both the environmental variability and the sociopolitical challenges past inhabitants faced to generate testable hypotheses for evaluating shell-bearing deposits.

## Acknowledgments

An earlier version of this chapter was presented at the 68th annual meeting of the Southeastern Archaeological Conference in Jacksonville, Florida. Ann Cordell,

Chris Rodning, and one anonymous reviewer provided valuable comments and suggestions. The composite image of Estero Bay in figure 2.1 was created by Scott Goodwin and is used with permission. Archaeological fieldwork at the Estero Island site was conducted under the direction of the author and Corbett Torrence for the town of Fort Myers Beach and was funded by the Florida Department of State, Division of Historical Resources. Thank you to the many volunteers and student interns that helped make this research possible and to Asa Randall and Neill Wallis for the opportunity to contribute to this volume.

## Notes

1. Radiocarbon dates in the text are reported at 1-sigma. Assays on marine shell were calibrated with the MARINE04 curve and corrected for the global reservoir, with a local $\Delta R$ of -5 ± 20 applied. Carbonized samples were calibrated with the INTCAL04 curve.

## References

Arnold, Jeanne E.

1992    Complex Hunter-Gatherer-Fishers of Prehistoric California: Chiefs, Specialists, and Maritime Adaptations of the Channel Islands. *American Antiquity* 57: 60–84.

Brown, James

1976    *The Artifacts*. Spiro Studies vol. 4. Stovall Museum of Science and History, University of Oklahoma Research Institute. Norman.

Bullen, Ripley P., and Adelaide K. Bullen

1956    *Excavations on the Cape Haze Peninsula, Florida*. Contribution of the Florida State Museum no. 1. University of Florida, Gainesville.

Claassen, Cheryl

1998    *Shells*. Cambridge Manuals in Archaeology. Cambridge University Press, Cambridge, UK.

Cordell, Ann

1992    Technological Investigation of Pottery Variability in Southwest Florida. In *Culture and Environment in the Domain of the Calusa*, edited by W. H. Marquardt, 105–89. Institute of Archaeology and Paleoenvironmental Studies Monograph 1. University Press of Florida, Gainesville.

2013    Technological Investigation of Pottery Variability at the Pineland Site Complex. In *The Archaeology of Pineland: A Coastal Southwest Florida Village Complex, A.D. 50–1710*, edited by W. H. Marquardt and Karen J. Walker, 383–543. Institute of Archaeology and Paleoenvironmental Studies Monograph 4. University Press of Florida, Gainesville.

Cushing, Frank Hamilton

2000    *Exploration of Ancient Key-Dweller Remains on the Gulf Coast of Florida*. University Press of Florida, Gainesville.

Dietler, John E.

2008    Craft Specialization and the Emergence of Political Complexity in Southwest Florida. PhD dissertation, University of California, Los Angeles.

Fiedel, Stuart J.

1992    *Prehistory of the Americas*. 2nd ed. Cambridge University Press, Cambridge, UK.

Fontaneda, Do. D'Escalante

1944   *Memoir of Do. D'Escalante Fontaneda Respecting Florida.* Translated by B. Smith with editorial comments by D. O. True. Glades House, Coral Gables, FL.

Goggin, John M

1949   Cultural Occupation at Goodland Point, Florida. *Florida Anthropologist* 2(3–4): 65–91.

Goggin, J. M., and W. C. Sturtevant

1964   The Calusa: A Stratified Nonagricultural Society (with Notes on Sibling Marriage). In *Exploration in Cultural Anthropology: Essays in Honor of George Peter Murdock,* edited by W. H. Goodenough, 179–219. McGraw-Hill, New York.

Griffin, John W.

1974   Archaeology and Environment in South Florida. In *Environments of South Florida: Present and Past,* edited by P. J. Gleason, 342–46. Miami Geological Society Memoir 2. Miami Geological Society, Miami, FL.

Hann, John H.

1991   *Missions to the Calusa.* University Press of Florida, Gainesville.

1993   *Indians of Central and South Florida, 1513–1763.* University Press of Florida, Gainesville.

Hrdlicka, A.

1922   *The Anthropology of Florida.* Publications of the Florida State Historical Society no. 1. Florida State Historical Society, Deland, FL.

Hutchinson, Dale L.

1999   Precolumbian Human Skeletal Remains from Useppa Island. In *The Archaeology of Useppa Island,* edited by W. Marquardt, 139–47. Institute of Archaeology and Paleoenvironmental Studies Monograph no. 3. University of Florida, Gainesville.

Laudonnière, René de.

1975   *Three Voyages.* Translated and edited by C. E. Bennett. University Press of Florida, Gainesville.

Leone, Karen

2009   Archaeobotanical Analysis of the Estero Island Site (8LL4), Pool Exhibit, in Lee County, Florida. Report submitted to the Town of Fort Myers Beach by Ohio Valley Archaeology, Inc.

Lewis, Clifford M.

1978   The Calusa. In *Tacachale: Essays on the Indians of Florida and Southeastern Georgia during the Historic Period,* edited by J. T. Milanich and S. Proctor, 19–49. University Press of Florida, Gainesville.

Luer, George M.

1989   Calusa Canals in Southwestern Florida: Routes of Tribute and Exchange. *Florida Anthropologist* 42: 89–130.

1999   An Introduction to the Archaeology of the Lemon Bay Area. In *Maritime Archaeology of Lemon Bay, Florida,* edited by G. M. Luer, 1–22. Florida Anthropological Society Publications no.14. Florida Anthropological Society, Tampa.

Luer, George M., David Allerton, Dan Hazeltine, Ron Hatfield, and Darden Hood

1986   Whelk Shell Tool Blanks from Big Mound Key (8CH10), Charlotte County, Florida: With Notes on Certain Whelk Shell Tools. In *Shells and Archaeology in Southern Florida,* edited by G. M. Luer, 92–124. Florida Anthropological Society Publication no. 12. Florida Anthropological Society, Tallahassee.

Luer, George M., and Marion M. Almy

1980   The Development of Some Aboriginal Pottery of the Central Peninsular Gulf Coast of Florida. *Florida Anthropologist* 33: 207–25.

Luer, George M. and Lauren C. Archibald

1988    An Assessment of Known Archaeological Sites in Charlotte Harbor State Reserve. Archaeological and Historical Conservancy Technical Report no. 6. Miami.

Marquardt, William H.

1987    The Calusa Social Formation in Protohistoric South Florida. In *Power Relations and State Formation*, edited by T. C. Patterson and C. W. Gailey, 98–116. American Anthropological Association, Washington, DC.

1988    Politics and Production among the Calusa of South Florida. In *Hunters and Gatherers: 1. History, Evolution, and Social Change*, edited by T. Ingold, D. Riches and J. Woodburn, 161–88. Berg Publishers, London.

1992    Recent Archaeological and Paleoenvironmental Investigations in Southwest Florida. In *Culture and Environment in the Domain of the Calusa*, edited by W. H. Marquardt, 9–57. Institute of Archaeology and Paleoenvironmental Studies Monograph no. 1. University of Florida, Gainesville.

1999    Useppa Island in the Archaic and Caloosahatchee Periods. In *The Archaeology of Useppa Island*, edited by W. Marquardt, 77–98. Institute of Archaeology and Paleoenvironmental Studies Monograph no. 3, University of Florida, Gainesville.

2001    The Emergence and Demise of the Calusa. In *Societies in Eclipse: Archaeology of the Eastern Woodlands Indians, A. D. 1400–1700*, edited by D. Brose, C. W. Cowan, and R. Mainfort, 157–71. Smithsonian Institution Press, Washington, DC.

2004    Calusa. In *Handbook of North American Indians, Volume 14, Southeast*, edited by R. D. Fogelson, 204–12. Smithsonian Institution Press, Washington, DC.

2010a   Shell Mounds in the Southeast: Middens, Monuments, Temple Mounds, Rings, or Works? *American Antiquity* 75(3): 551–70.

2010b   Mounds, Middens, and Rapid Climate Change During the Archaic-Woodland Transition in the Southeastern United States. In *Trend, Tradition, and Turmoil: What Happened to the Southeastern Archaic?* edited by D. H. Thomas and M. C. Sanger, 253–72. Anthropological Papers no. 93. American Museum of Natural History, New York.

Marquardt, William H., and Karen J. Walker

2001    Pineland: A Coastal West Site in Southwest Florida. In *Enduring Records: The Environmental and Cultural Heritage of Wetlands*, edited by Barbara Purdy, 48–60. Oxbow Books, Oxford.

Milanich, Jerald T., Jefferson Chapman, Ann S. Cordell, Stephen Hale, and Rochelle A. Marrinan

1984    Prehistoric Development of Calusa Society in Southwest Florida: Excavations on Useppa Island. In *Perspectives on Gulf Coast Prehistory*, edited by D. D. Davis, 258–314. University Press of Florida, Gainesville.

Milanich, Jerald T., and Charles H. Fairbanks

1980    *Florida Archaeology*. Academic Press, New York.

Murdock, George P.

1968    The Current Status of the World's Hunting and Gathering Peoples. In *Man the Hunter*, edited by R. B. Lee and I. DeVore, 13–22. Aldine, Chicago.

Patton, Robert B.

1994    The Temporal Contexts of Prehistoric Shell Artifacts from Southwest Florida: A Case Study of the Pineland Site Complex. MA thesis, University of Florida, Gainesville.

2001    Spatial Structure and Process of Nonagricultural Production: Settlement Patterns and Political Development in Precolumbian Southwest Florida. PhD dissertation, Department of Anthropology, University of Florida, Gainesville.

Paynter, Robert

1989    The Archaeology of Equality and Inequality. *Annual Review of Anthropology* 18: 369–99.

Peres, Tanya M., Theresa M. Schober, and Corbett McP. Torrence

2009    Semantics of a Shell Mound: Analysis and Interpretation of the Estero Island Site. Paper presented at the 66th annual meeting of the Southeastern Archaeological Conference, Mobile, AL.

Randall, Asa R.

2010    Something is Rotten in the State of Shell Site Studies. Paper presented at the 67th annual meeting of the Southeastern Archaeological Conference, Lexington, KY.

Russo, Michael

2004    Measuring Shell Rings for Social Inequality. In *Signs of Power: The Rise of Cultural Complexity in the Southeast*, edited by J. L. Gibson and P. J. Carr, 26–70. University of Alabama Press, Tuscaloosa.

Sassaman, Kenneth E.

2003    St. Johns Archaeological Field School 2000–2001: Blue Spring and Hontoon Island State Parks. Laboratory of Southeastern Archaeology Technical Report 4. Department of Anthropology, University of Florida, Gainesville.

Schalk, Randall F.

1981    Land Use and Organizational Complexity Among Foragers of Northwestern North America. In *Affluent Foragers*, edited by S. Koyama and D. H. Thomas, 53–75. Senri Ethnological Studies no. 9. National Museum of Ethnology, Osaka, Japan.

Schober, Theresa M., and Corbett McP. Torrence

2002    Archaeological Investigations and Topographic Mapping of the Estero Island Site (8LL4), Lee County, Florida. Cultural Resource Management Program Report 1, Florida Gulf Coast University, Fort Myers.

Schwadron, Margo

2010    Prehistoric Landscapes of Complexity: Archaic and Woodland Period Shell Works, Shell Rings, and Tree Islands of the Everglades, South Florida. In *Trend, Tradition, and Turmoil: What Happened to the Southeastern Archaic?*, edited by David Hurst Thomas and Matthew C. Sanger, 113–46. American Museum of Natural History, New York.

Sears, William H.

1967    Archeological Survey in the Cape Coral Area at the Mouth of the Caloosahatchee River. *Florida Anthropologist* 20: 93–102.

1982    *Fort Center: An Archaeological Site in the Lake Okeechobee Basin.* University of Florida Press, Gainesville.

Solís de Merás, Gonzalo

1923    *Pedro Menéndez de Avilés, Adelantado, Governor, and Captain-General of Florida: A. Memorial.* Translated and notated by J. T. Conner. Florida State Historical Society, Deland.

Stapor, Frank W., Jr., Thomas D. Mathews, and Fonda E. Lindfors-Kearns

1991    Barrier-Island Progradation and Holocene Sea-Level History in Southwest Florida. *Journal of Coastal Research* 7(3): 815–38.

Tanner, William F.

2000    Beach Ridge History, Sea Level Change, and the A.D. 536 Event. In *The Years Without Summer: Tracing A.D. 536 and Its Aftermath*, edited by J. D. Gunn, 89–97. David Brown Book Company, Oakville, CT.

Testart, Alain

1982    The Significance of Food Storage Among Hunter-Gatherers: Residence Patterns, Population Densities, and Social Inequalities. *Current Anthropology* 23: 523–37.

Thompson, Victor D.

2007    Articulating Activity Areas and Formation Processes at the Sapelo Island Ring Complex. *Southeastern Archaeology* 26: 91–107.

Thompson, Victor D., and John E. Worth

2011    Dwellers by the Sea: Native American Adaptations along the Southern Coasts of Eastern North America. *Journal of Archaeological Research* 19(1): 51–101.

Torrence, Corbett McP.

1999    Caloosahatchee Landscapes: An Architectural Analysis of Precolumbian Social Structure in Southwest Florida. Paper presented at the 56th Annual Meeting of the Southeastern Archaeological Conference, Pensacola, FL.

2001    Middens, Mounds, or Monuments: How the Matrix Manipulates the Mind. Paper presented at the 66th annual meeting of the Society for American Archaeology, New Orleans, LA.

2013    A Topographic Reconstruction of the Pineland Site Complex as It Appeared in 1896. In *The Archaeology of Pineland: A Coastal Southwest Florida Village Complex, A.D. 50–1710*, edited by W. H. Marquardt and Karen J. Walker, 155–73. Institute of Archaeology and Paleoenvironmental Studies Monograph no. 4. University of Florida, Gainesville.

Torrence, Corbett McP., Samuel J. Chapman, and William H. Marquardt

1994    Topographic Mapping and Archaeological Reconnaissance of Mound Key State Archaeological Site (8LL2), Estero Bay, Florida. Report submitted to the Koreshan Unity Alliance Inc., Institute of Archaeology and Paleoenvironmental Studies, Florida Museum of Natural History, University of Florida, Gainesville.

Torrence, Corbett McP. and Theresa M. Schober

2005    Topographic Mapping and Preliminary Archaeological Assessment of the Dog Key Site (8LL726), Lee County, Florida. A report submitted to the Department of Environmental Protection and the Division of Historical Resources, Florida Department of State.

2008    An Economic Frontier: Evolution of Settlement Patterns in Coastal Southwest Florida. Paper presented at the 73rd annual meeting of the Society for American Archaeology. Vancouver, Canada.

Walker, Karen J.

1992    The Zooarchaeology of Charlotte Harbor's Prehistoric Maritime Adaptation: Spatial and Temporal Perspectives. In *Culture and Environment in the Domain of the Calusa*, edited by W. H. Marquardt, 265–366. Institute of Archaeology and Paleoenvironmental Studies Monograph no. 1. University of Florida, Gainesville.

Walker, Karen J., Frank W. Stapor Jr., and William H. Marquardt

1994    Episodic Sea Levels and Human Occupation at Southwest Florida's Wightman Site. *Florida Anthropologist* 47: 161–79.

1995    Archaeological Evidence for a 1750–1450 B.P. Higher-Than-Present Sea Level Along Florida's Gulf Coast. In Holocene Cycles: Climate, Sea Levels, and Sedimentation, *Journal of Coastal Research*, Special Issue 17: 205–18.

Wallace, Jennifer A.

2013    The 1995 Excavations of Calooshatachee II Deposits at Pineland's Old Mound and Randell Complex Mound 1. In *The Archaeology of Pineland: A Coastal Southwest Florida Village Complex, A.D. 50–1710*, edited by W. H. Marquardt and Karen J. Walker, 741–766. Institute of Archaeology and Paleoenvironmental Studies Monograph 4. University Press of Florida, Gainesville.

Waselkov, Gregory A.

1987    Shellfish Gathering and Shell Midden Archaeology. *Advances in Archaeological Method and Theory* 10: 93–210.

Wheeler, Ryan J.

2000    *Treasure of the Calusa: The Johnson/Willcox Collection from Mound Key.* Rose Printing, Tallahassee, FL.

Widmer, Randolph

1988    *The Evolution of the Calusa: A Non-Agricultural Chiefdom on the Southwest Florida Coast.* University of Alabama Press, Tuscaloosa.

1996    Recent Excavations at the Key Marco Site, 8CR48, Collier County, Florida. *Florida Anthropologist* 49: 10–25.

Willey, Gordon R.

1949    *Archaeology of the Florida Gulf Coast.* Smithsonian Miscellaneous Collections no. 113. Smithsonian Institution Press, Washington, DC.

Yesner, David R.

1980    Maritime Hunter-Gatherers: Ecology and Prehistory. *Current Anthropology* 21: 727–50.

Zubillaga, Felix

1946    *Monumenta Antiquae Floridae (1566–72).* Missionum Societatis Iesu 3. Monumenta Historical Society, Rome.

# 3

## Monumentality beyond Scale

### The Elaboration of Mounded Architecture at Crystal River

THOMAS J. PLUCKHAHN AND VICTOR D. THOMPSON

*Monumental* is a term that archaeologists often use but often use uncritically. The phrase has been evoked widely in archaeology, from Childe's (1950) urban revolution in Mesopotamia, to Flannery's (1976, 58, 66, 159) early Mesoamerican village, to Pauketat's (1994) "Big Bang" at Cahokia and many points between and beyond. In most of these works, the term is never formally defined, although we suspect that the general understanding of monumental architecture is aptly expressed by Flannery's Real Mesoamerican Archaeologist (RMA): "you couldn't miss it if you tried" (Flannery 1976, 9). (Some might also subscribe to the RMA's even less formal definition: "those mounds which require four-wheel drive to get over.")

Trigger (1990) is one of the few archaeologists to provide a more explicit definition; he defines monumental architecture as architecture that exhibits scale or elaboration that exceeds the practical requirements of the intended purpose of its construction. This definition is widely cited (see, for example, the introduction to this volume by Wallis and Randall) but usually only in reference to scale. The second component of monumentality Trigger described—elaboration—is usually neglected (Smith 2007; for examples, see contributors to Burger and Rosenwig 2012).

There are good reasons for emphasizing scale when discussing the monumental architecture of ancient societies. Size clearly does matter when it comes to monumental architecture. Larger monuments can accommodate more people at political or ceremonial events. Greater size generally indicates a greater investment of labor and greater power in its appropriation. In addition, monuments of greater scale probably communicate these properties more effectively. We suspect that archaeologists also emphasize scale for practical reasons: size is more easily quantified than elaboration.

Size alone does not equal monumentality, however, as the recent debate about Florida's shell mounds clearly illustrates. As Marquardt (2010) argues, the combination of the quotidian deposition of shell waste and taphonomic processes may produce archaeological deposits that mimic those of intentional monument construction (see also Thompson and Andrus 2011 and Thompson and Worth 2011; for arguments to the contrary, see Sassaman 2010, Sassaman et al. 2011, and the contributions to this volume by Randall et al. and Sassaman et al.). This argument, while clearly applicable to the more amorphous shell mounds common in Florida, cannot be extended to architectural features that demonstrate greater care in construction and thus are more than simple refuse disposal. In this case, elaboration rather than scale may be the key to differentiating between the incidental accumulation of midden and purposeful monument construction. As Thompson and Andrus (2011, 319) point out, when compared to other architecture, shell monuments are defined as much by their quality of construction as they are by their scale.

Furthermore, like size, the degree of elaboration is important to considerations of labor and its appropriation and the understanding of how these are represented symbolically. Indeed, according to Trigger's definition, monumental architecture entails elaboration that requires an expenditure of labor that is conspicuous in its excess.

We assert the need for archaeologists to grant greater consideration to elaboration in their consideration of monumental architecture. First, we discuss what we mean by elaboration. Drawing largely on Michael Smith's (2007) work on the principles of ancient urban planning, we define attributes that might be used to evaluate greater or lesser elaboration and thus monumentality. The debate is more than semantic; as Smith and many others note (e.g., Benfer 2012; Haas and Creamer 2012; Pozorski and Pozorski 2012) and as we have alluded to above, monumental architecture has multiple layers of meaning but often serves as an expression of power and authority. Thus, the terms and concepts with which we regard the constitution of monumentality have implications for our understanding of the organization of ancient societies.

We use the site of Crystal River (8CI1) as an example of these principles of elaboration. This site is located on Florida's west-central Gulf coast (figure 3.1) and dates to the Woodland period, around 1000 BC to AD 1050 (Milanich 1999; Pluckhahn et al. 2010; Weisman 1995). Crystal River is famous for two reasons. First, it marks the southernmost major expression of the Hopewell Interaction Sphere. Excavations by Moore (1903, 1907, 1918) and Bullen (1951, 1953, 1999 [1965], 1966) recovered Hopewellian artifacts, including copper panpipes and gorgets and various other ornaments of bone, stone, and shell, in greater numbers and diversity than at any other site in Florida (Ruhl 1981; Seeman 1979). Next, Crystal River is famous as one of the largest and most complex of Florida's mound sites. The site includes two burial mounds and at least three platform mounds, one of which (Mound A) rises about 9 meters above the surrounding ground surface.

Recently, Sassaman and colleagues and Randall and colleagues have questioned

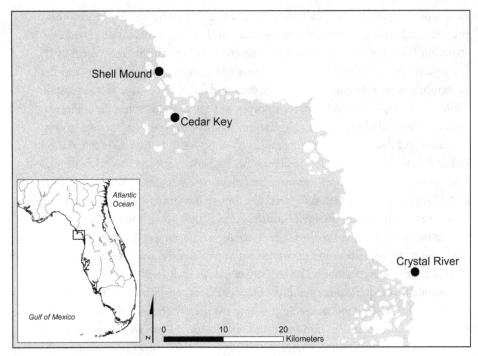

Figure 3.1. Locations of Cedar Key, Shell Mound, and Crystal River.

whether Crystal River's mantle as one of the largest Woodland mound centers in Florida, pointing to the equivalent or greater scale of roughly contemporaneous mound complexes in the Big Bend region just to the north (Randall et al. 2010; Sassaman et al. 2011, 56). We take their comments as a challenge to more clearly articulate what differentiates Crystal River in terms of its monumental architecture. Specifically, we suggest that the greater elaboration of monumental construction helped distinguish Crystal River from its peers and was both the cause and consequence of its seemingly disproportionate representation of prestige goods.

## Elaboration as a Component of Monumentality

While Trigger (1990) offers us a definition of monumental architecture that is eloquent in its simplicity, he does not clearly describe what he means by either scale or elaboration. The former is self-explanatory, the latter less so. Fortunately, others have conceptualized the concept of architectural elaboration, albeit in slightly different terms. We have found Michael Smith's (2007) archaeological take on the concept of ancient urban planning most useful. Among the basic components Smith sees as indicative of a greater degree of planning are axiality, orthogonality, symmetry, and the use of plazas, formal entrances, and walls (ibid., 12). Planning and elaboration, we would argue, are two sides of the same coin, and thus Smith's principles are relevant to our discussion of the elaboration of monumental architecture.

At first glance, it might seem ethnocentric to associate properties such as symmetry, orthogonality, and axiality with greater monumentality, given that these are generally valued in western societies but are arguably less important in other cultures. There is logic here, however. At the core of the concept of monumentality as employed by most archaeologists is the ability to mobilize and direct labor, whether through elite control or broader-based, less hierarchical social institutions. It requires more labor and more direction to produce mounds that adhere to principles of symmetry, orthogonality, and axiality, and thus it makes sense to include these in our discussions of monumental architecture. We can illustrate this with an example with which most of us are familiar: an archaeological field school. It is relatively easy to mobilize and direct field school students to dig holes through the granting of credit hours and the implicit or explicit threat of grades. It requires a great deal more labor and considerably more direction to get students to excavate and record a good test unit; the methods include (in various measures) threats, promises, charisma, and appeals to professional standards and ethics.

## The Elaboration of Mounded Architecture at Crystal River

Having defined elaboration with regard to monumental architecture, we now illustrate these concepts with the example of Crystal River. Specifically, we discuss how axiality, orthogonality, symmetry, and the use of plazas, formal entrances, and walls are manifested in the mounded architecture of Crystal River. Before beginning, we note that we do not assume that these elements were necessarily planned from the outset of construction; indeed, in some cases, it is clear that the qualities we describe developed over time. Nevertheless, we argue that the patterns were the result of deliberate attempts at elaboration.

### Axiality

Smith (2007, 12) uses the term axiality to refer to the use of straight avenues. We take a slightly broader perspective, defining the term to include the use of straight lines, specifically in regard to the placement of mounds and other architectural features relative to one another. When thus defined, axiality is represented in the mounded architecture at Crystal River. As we have previously noted, Mounds A and K and the western edge of Mound J align on an azimuth of 142° (Pluckhahn and Thompson 2009; Pluckhahn et al. 2009) (figure 3.2). The same approximate azimuth of orientation is apparent in the axis between Mounds F and G. Thus, although the site lacks a single central axis, parallel axes link many of its most important features. This clearly indicates a concern with planning in the layout of the

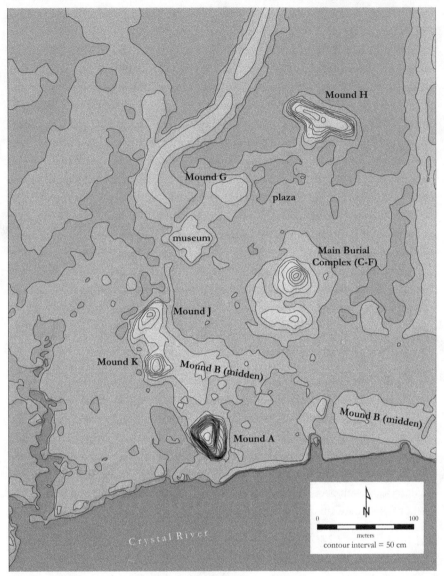

Figure 3.2. Topographic map of the Crystal River site.

monumental landscape at Crystal River, even if it also suggests that the landscape developed over a long term.

Orthogonality

Orthogonality refers to the use of right angles in the design of individual architectural features and in their layout relative to one another (Smith 2007,12). The dual axes at Crystal River are placed in parallel by a right angle between Mounds K and the Mound C–F Burial Complex (Pluckhahn and Thompson 2009; Pluckhahn et al. 2009) (see figure 3.2). Mounds G and H exhibit another right angle relative to these axes.

At the level of individual architectural features, we believe that several of the mounds at Crystal River display a degree of orthogonality virtually without parallel among sites in Florida. This is perhaps most evident in the surviving portions of Mound A; in figure 3.2, note the right angles in the contour lines of the northern corners of the mound. Similarly, albeit slightly less dramatically, orthogonality is apparent in the contours of Mounds H and K.

We suggest that the concept of orthogonality can also be applied in a vertical dimension, as what we usually discuss in terms of steepness of slope. In this sense too, the surviving portions of Mound A are exemplary; the western slope rises 8.5 meters over a distance of just 14 meters, for a slope angle of about 57°, not quite a right angle but about as close as one is likely to find in the vertical dimensions of the prehistoric architecture of eastern North America. Mounds H and K slope less steeply, but the former exhibits slopes of as much as 40–50° in places and the latter has slopes of 30–40°.

## Symmetry

To symmetry in the form of parallel axes, we would add the placement of the two burial complexes—Mound G and the Main Burial Complex—on complementary positions on either side of the plaza (Pluckhahn and Thompson 2009; Pluckhahn et al. 2009). A concern with symmetry is also apparent at the level of individual mounds at Crystal River, specifically with regard to the three platform mounds. Mound H is the best example of this, thanks to its excellent state of preservation. The mound measures 77 meters long at its base. This long axis is almost perfectly bisected by a line up the ramp on the southern face of the mound. The ramp thus emphasizes the bilateral symmetry of the mound, a visual effect that we suspect was intentional. We add that this is an additional example of orthogonality.

Although it is no longer apparent because of the borrowing of its eastern half, Mound A appears to have exhibited similar bilateral symmetry. Moore's (1903, figure 16) map of the site, which we have found remarkably accurate in most of its details, shows Mound A as having a ramp placed centrally along its east face. Bullen's (1966) later sketch of the mound shows the same configuration. It is worth noting that Bullen also depicted a ramp projecting from the east face of Mound K. Our mapping and visual inspection supports the possibility that a ramp was present, although it appears in our contour map to have been positioned less centrally than Bullen suggested. Mound K was damaged by trees felled during a tornado about twenty years ago, however, so it is possible that the current shape of the mound is not indicative of its former state.

Plazas, Formal Entrances, and Walls

Discussion of the bilateral symmetry of the platform mounds at Crystal River leads naturally to the observation that at least two of these mounds, and possibly the third as well, had formal entrances defined by ramps. Mound H is, again, the best-preserved example. In this case the formality of the entrance is accentuated by the long gradual slope of the ramp and its termination on the northern edge of a plaza (see figure 3.2). The ramp to Mound A as mapped by Moore and Bullen terminated in what appears to have been a shallow lagoon, a feature potentially akin to a plaza in the watery world of central Florida.

There is also evidence of the use of walls to define spaces at Crystal River. Bullen (1966) noted the presence of a shell causeway linking Mounds G and H. While this indeed may have been a formal route of procession between the two mounds, a more immediate visual effect of the feature is the definition of the edge of the plaza in an area where the elevation dips gradually to the surrounding swamp.

A more compelling example of the use of a wall to formally define an area is provided by the circular embankment (Mound C) of the Main Burial Complex. Although poorly preserved today due to past excavations, Moore (1903, 379) described the embankment as a nearly perfect circle of earth about 2 meters high and 23 meters wide. The embankment, which contained a number of burials, encloses a level area (Feature D) and small platform mound (Mound E) topped by a small burial mound (Mound F).

## Monumentality Beyond Scale: The Uniqueness of Crystal River

If, as we have argued, there is evidence for the elaboration of monumental architecture at Crystal River, how unique is the site in this regard? Sassaman and colleagues (2011, 147) have suggested that the scale of mound construction in the Big Bend area, particularly at Cedar Key, may have surpassed that of Crystal River. Their comparison, to our minds, raises the question of how the two areas compare in terms of the elaboration of monuments.

Unfortunately, many of the larger sites in the Big Bend, including Cedar Key, were partially or completely destroyed before they could be adequately mapped, making relative comparison of the elaboration of monuments difficult. However, we can form some impressions from a comparison of Crystal River and the Shell Mound site (8LV42), which Sassaman and colleagues (2011, 41) describe as the largest extant example of monumental architecture in their study area (see figure 3.1). The principal architectural feature at Shell Mound consists of a ring-shaped mound measuring about 120 × 160 meters in extent and about 6 meters tall with a central hollow that opens to the southeast. Although the hollow was presumed to be the result of mining, recent testing suggests this was not the case; instead, it appears that the mound was deliberately constructed in a circular form around a central plaza, possibly with habitation around the perimeter (Sassaman 2012).

Compared to Crystal River, Shell Mound displays relatively little concern with axiality, although the circular pattern may represent an alternative form of spatial order. The architecture at the Shell Mound site displays a certain degree of orthogonality: the northwestern and southwestern corners of the mound approach right angles, but most of the other corners are more rounded. We estimate from the map provided by Sassaman and colleagues (2011, figure 2-8) that the better preserved north face of the mound rises about 6 meters over a horizontal interval of 20 meters, for a slope of 30°. This is relatively steep, but compared to some of the mounds at Crystal River, less elaboration is apparent. We see little regard for symmetry in the monumental architecture at the Shell Mound site, apart from the circular feature that possibly represents a plaza.

Obviously, we have used the Shell Mound site as something of a foil. But we think the comparison—however simplistic—illustrates the uniqueness of Crystal River among its peers along the west-central Gulf coast (if not the Florida peninsula at large) for its combination of scale *and* elaboration. Indeed, straying beyond peninsular Florida for a moment to put Crystal River in a larger perspective, it is striking to us that the sites in the Southeast that archaeologists commonly regard as best exemplifying monumentality are considered as such not simply because of the scale of their monumental constructions but also because of the elaboration evident in the form and layout of monuments. This is true regardless of period, from Archaic period Poverty Point (Gibson 2001, Kidder 2002; Sassaman 2003), to Woodland period Newark Earthworks (Byers 2004; Lepper 2010), to Mississippian period Cahokia (Collins 1997; Fowler 1975; Pauketat 2007).

This uniqueness in monumental architecture, in turn, suggests to us an unprecedented ability to not only mobilize labor but also to direct it to very specific purposes. As Smith (2007, 35) notes, among the messages that monumental architecture communicates is an ability "to carry out large projects, convert disorder to order, and convince or force individuals to conform to societal needs." A great deal of research clearly indicates that this ability need not have been limited to a few powerful individuals (e.g., Gibson 2001; Pluckhahn 2003; Sassaman and Randall 2012; Saunders 2012) but that the power and authority needed to create monuments of such scale and elaboration, wherever and however these were vested, were reinforced for both visitors and inhabitants through the architecture itself.

More than simply a reflection of authority, however, the act of monument building bound builders to leaders and the community as a whole (Smith 2007, 36). Recent scholarship (e.g., Pauketat 2003; Sassaman 2005) suggests that monument building was, at least in the case of major monumental centers such as Poverty Point and Cahokia, a process of pluralistic community formation among formerly disparate peoples. We cannot yet make the case for this at Crystal River, but the scale and elaboration of architecture suggests the bringing together of people and ideas from long distances. Indeed, we suggest that the elaboration of monuments may have fostered this pluralism by creating spaces that combined diverse elements in new and unusual ways while remaining rooted in earlier architectural traditions. This blending of the colloquial and the familiar with the formal and the exotic would have been instrumental to the production of pluralistic communities.

It is difficult for us to imagine that the uniqueness of scale and elaboration of monumental architecture at Crystal River is unrelated to the seemingly disproportionate representation of exotic artifacts at the site compared to others in the region. Specifically, the authority to mobilize and direct labor for monument construction is no doubt related to the ability to acquire—through manufacture, tribute, offering, or exchange—symbolically charged objects such as copper cutouts and quartz crystals. Such items would have been the media through which social relations were reinforced, expressed, and reimagined during the construction and use of many of the monuments at Crystal River. It is conspicuous to us that as at Crystal River, the people who resided at elaborate monumental centers such as Poverty Point, Newark, and Cahokia displayed similar propensities for unusual and exotic objects.

A richer conceptualization of monumentality, both in general and specifically as it relates to Crystal River, moves us a small step closer to the goal of understanding the nature of architectural variability in the past. From our perspective, an approach that incorporates some of the key themes we describe in this chapter provides us with the necessary methodological tools to explore more complex ideas regarding the nature of monumentality than are currently employed by archaeologists. Such an understanding is key to exploring the wide variety of human behaviors and social histories that such constructions enabled.

## Acknowledgments

An earlier version of this paper was presented at the 68th annual meeting of the Southeastern Archaeological Conference, Jacksonville, Florida, 2011. We thank Asa Randall and Neill Wallis for their invitation to participate both at that session and in this volume. T. R. Kidder and Tony Ortmann provided helpful comments on an early version of the paper. This chapter benefited greatly from additional suggestions from Chris Rodning and an anonymous reviewer.

## References

Benfer, Robert A., Jr.
2012    Monumental Architecture Arising from an Early Astronomical Religious Complex in Peru, 2200–1750 B.C. In *Early New World Monumentality*, edited by Richard L. Burger and Robert M. Rosenswig, 313–63. University Press of Florida, Gainesville.

Bullen, Ripley P.

1951    The Enigmatic Crystal River Site. *American Antiquity* 17: 142–43.

1953    The Famous Crystal River Site. *Florida Anthropologist* 6: 9–37.

1966    Stelae at the Crystal River Site, Florida. *American Antiquity* 31: 861–65.

1999 [1965]    Recent Additional Information. An addendum to a brochure from the Crystal River Indian Mound Museum. Reproduced in *Famous Florida Sites: Crystal River and Mount Royal*, edited by Jerald T. Milanich, pp. 225–26. University Press of Florida, Gainesville.

Burger, Richard L., and Robert M. Rosenswig (editors)

2012    *Early New World Monumentality*. University Press of Florida, Gainesville.

Byers, A. Martin

2004    *The Ohio Hopewell Episode: Paradigm Lost, Paradigm Gained*. University of Akron Press, Akron, OH.

Childe, V. Gordon

1950    The Urban Revolution. *Town Planning Review* 21: 3–17.

Collins, James M.

1997    Cahokia Settlement and Social Structure as Viewed from the ICT–II. In *Cahokia: Domination and Ideology in the Mississippian World*, edited by T. R. Pauketat and T. E. Emerson, 124–40. University of Nebraska Press, Lincoln.

Flannery, Kent V.

1976    *The Early Mesoamerican Village*. Academic Press, Orlando, FL.

Fowler, Melvin L.

1975    A Precolumbian Urban Center on the Mississippi. *Scientific American* 23(2): 92–101.

Gibson, Jon L.

2001    *The Ancient Mounds of Poverty Point: Place of Rings*. University Press of Florida, Gainesville.

Hass, Jonathan, and Winifred Creamer

2012    Why Do People Build Monuments? Late Archaic Platform Mounds in Norte Chico. In *Early New World Monumentality*, edited by Richard L. Burger and Robert M. Rosenswig, 298–312. University Press of Florida, Gainesville.

Kidder, Tristram R.

2002    Mapping Poverty Point. *American Antiquity* 67: 89–101.

Lepper, Bradley T.

2010    The Ceremonial Landscape of the Newark Earthworks and the Raccoon Creek Valley. In *Hopewell Settlement Patterns, Subsistence, and Sacred Landscapes*, edited by A. Martin Byers and DeeAnne Wymer, 95–125. University Press of Florida, Gainesville.

Marquardt, William H.

2010    Shell Mounds in the Southeast: Middens, Monuments, Temple Mounds, Rings, or Works? *American Antiquity* 75: 551–70.

Milanich, Jerald T.

1999    Introduction. In *Famous Florida Sites: Crystal River and Mount Royal*, edited by Jerald T. Milanich, 1–27. University Press of Florida, Gainesville.

Moore, Clarence Bloomfield

1903    Certain Aboriginal Mounds of the Central Florida West-Coast. *Journal of the Academy of Natural Sciences of Philadelphia* 12: 361–438.

1907    Crystal River Revisited. *Journal of the Academy of Natural Sciences of Philadelphia*, second series 13(3): 406–25.

1918    The Northwestern Florida Coast Revisited. *Journal of the Academy of Natural Sciences of Philadelphia*, second series 16(4): 514–81.

Pauketat, Timothy R.

1994    *The Ascent of Chiefs: Cahokia and Mississippian Politics in Native North America*. University of Alabama Press, Tuscaloosa.

2003    Resettled Farmers and the Making of a Mississippian Polity. *American Antiquity* 68(1): 39–66.

2007    *Chiefdoms and Other Archaeological Delusions*. AltaMira Press, Lanham, MD.

Pluckhahn, Thomas J.

2003    *Kolomoki: Settlement, Ceremony, and Status in the Deep South, A.D. 350 to 750*. University of Alabama Press, Tuscaloosa.

Pluckhahn, Thomas J., and Victor D. Thompson

2009    Mapping Crystal River: Past, Present, Future. *Florida Anthropologist* 62: 3–22.

Pluckhahn, Thomas J., Victor D. Thompson, Nicolas Laracuente, Sarah Mitchell, Amanda Roberts, and Adrianne Sams

2009    Archaeological Investigations at the Famous Crystal River Site (8CI1) (2008 Field Season), Citrus County, Florida. Department of Anthropology, University of South Florida, Tampa. Submitted to Bureau of Natural and Cultural Resources, Division of Recreation and Parks, Florida Department of Environmental Protection, Tallahassee.

Pluckhahn, Thomas J., Victor D. Thompson, and Brent R. Weisman

2010    Towards a New View of History and Process at Crystal River (8CI1). *Southeastern Archaeology* 29: 164–81.

Pozorski, Thomas, and Shelia Pozorski

2012    Preceramic and Initial Period Monumentality within the Casma Valley of Peru. In *Early New World Monumentality*, edited by Richard L. Burger and Robert M. Rosenswig, 364–98. University Press of Florida, Gainesville.

Randall, Asa R., Micah P. Mones, and Kenneth E. Sassaman

2010    Visit Shell City: Another Coastside Attraction. Paper presented at the 67th annual meeting of the Southeastern Archaeological Conference, Lexington, KY.

Rosenswig, Robert M., and Richard L. Burger

2012    Considering New World Monumentality. In *Early New World Monumentality*, edited by Richard L. Burger and Robert M. Rosenswig, 3–24. University Press of Florida, Gainesville.

Ruhl, Donna

1981    An Investigation into the Relationships Between Midwestern Hopewell and Southeastern Prehistory. MA thesis, Department of Anthropology, Florida Atlantic University, Boca Raton.

Sassaman, Kenneth

2012    Preliminary Report on Archaeological Investigations at Shell Mound (8LV42), Levy County, Florida. Laboratory of Southeastern Archaeology, Department of Anthropology, University of Florida, Gainesville. Submitted to U.S. Fish and Wildlife Service.

2005    Poverty Point as Structure, Event, Process. *Journal of Archaeological Method and Theory* 12(4): 335–64.

2010    *The Eastern Archaic, Historicized*. AltaMira, Lanham, MD.

Sassaman, Kenneth E., Paulette S. McFadden, and Micah P. Monés

2011    Lower Suwannee Archaeological Survey 2009–10: Investigations at Cat Island (8DI29), Little Bradford Island (8DI32), and Richards Island (8LV137). Technical Report no. 10. Laboratory of Southeastern Archaeology, Department of Anthropology, University of Florida, Gainesville.

Sassaman, Kenneth E., and Asa Randall

2012    Shell Mounds of the Middle St. Johns Basin, Northeast Florida. In *Early New World Monumentality*, edited by Richard L. Burger and Robert M. Rosenswig, 53–77. University Press of Florida, Gainesville.

Saunders, Joe

2012    Early Mounds in the Lower Mississippi Valley. In *Early New World Monumentality*, edited by Richard L. Burger and Robert M. Rosenswig, 25–52. University Press of Florida, Gainesville.

Seeman, Mark F.

1979    The Hopewell Interaction Sphere: The Evidence for Inter-Regional Trade and Structural Complexity. PhD dissertation, Department of Anthropology, University of Indiana, Bloomington. University Microfilms, Ann Arbor.

Sherwood, Sarah C., and Tristram R. Kidder

2011    The DaVincis of Dirt: Geoarchaeological Perspectives on Native American Mound Building in the Mississippi River Basin. *Journal of Anthropological Archaeology* 30: 69–87.

Smith, Michael E.

2007    Form and Meaning in the Earliest Cities: A New Approach to Ancient Urban Planning. *Journal of Planning History* 6(1): 3–47.

Thompson, Victor D., and C. F. T. Andrus

2011    Evaluating Mobility, Monumentality, and Feasting at the Sapelo Island Shell Ring Complex. *American Antiquity* 76: 315–43.

Thompson, Victor D., and Thomas J. Pluckhahn

2010    History, Complex Hunter-Gatherers, and the Mounds and Monuments of Crystal River, Florida, USA: A Geophyiscal Perspective. *Journal of Island and Coastal Archaeology* 5: 33–51.

Thompson, Victor D., and John Worth

2011    Dwellers by the Sea: Native American Coastal Adaptations along the Southern Coasts of Eastern North America. *Journal of Archaeological Research* 19: 51–101.

Trigger, Bruce G.

1990    Monumental Architecture: A Thermodynamic Explanation of Symbolic Behavior. *World Archaeology* 22(2):119–32.

Weisman, Brent R.

1995    *Crystal River: A Ceremonial Mound Center on the Florida Gulf Coast.* Florida Archaeology Series no. 8. Florida Department of State, Division of Historical Resources, Tallahassee.

# 4

## New Insights on the Woodland and Mississippi Periods of West-Peninsular Florida

GEORGE M. LUER

I will discuss four themes that offer new insights in Florida archaeology: 1) monumentality; 2) exchange, migration, and mobility; 3) human-landscape interactions; and 4) symbolism and ritualization. I draw mostly from the Manasota (ca. 500 BC to AD 700), late peninsular Weeden Island (ca. AD 700 to 1000), and Safety Harbor (ca. AD 1000 to 1700) cultures of the Tampa Bay to Charlotte Harbor area, citing primarily burial mounds, shell middens, shell artifacts, and ceramics. I also bring together data from throughout west-peninsular Florida, the wider region stretching along the Gulf coast from just north of Crystal River to just south of Naples and extending inland to Lake Okeechobee and the central ridges and lakes (figure 4.1).

The typology of the Weeden Island and Safety Harbor cultures was first defined in detail by Willey (1949). Safety Harbor is a Mississippian culture known for large mounds. Weeden Island is a Woodland culture famous for decorated pottery. Manasota is an early and middle Woodland culture (defined typologically by Luer and Almy 1979, 1982) that is best known for plain sand-tempered pottery and flexed burials. Early Manasota is coeval with the Deptford period of north Florida (ca. 500 BC to AD 300), while late Manasota includes early Weeden Island–influenced times (ca. AD 300 to 700). It is followed by late Weeden Island culture, extending to Charlotte Harbor.

During these Woodland and Mississippian times, west-peninsular Florida supported growing populations and increasing sociopolitical organization, leading to the simple and complex chiefdoms the Spanish encountered in the 1500s, such as the Mocozo, Tocobaga, and Calusa (Bullen 1978; Lewis 1978). I include the Caloosahatchee Region as part of west-peninsular Florida, as it shares many similar developments with the Sarasota and Tampa Bay areas, including shell tools, burial rituals, and symbolism.

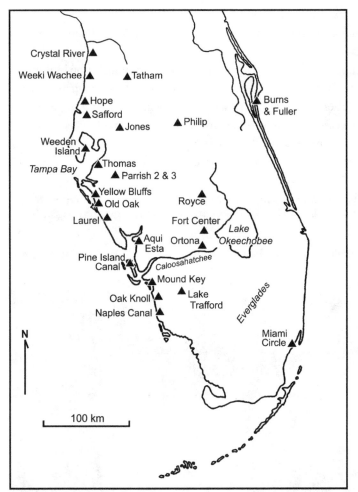

Figure 4.1. Selected sites in west peninsular Florida and nearby. Many of these important sites are now destroyed. Map created by George M. Luer and Tesa R. Norman; used by permission of George M. Luer, Sarasota, Florida.

## Monumentality

Peoples of the past used "the past" to validate their belief systems and reinforce their social organization. An example is the commemoration of the dead through building burial mounds. These monuments persisted for generations and often involved large numbers of people in their construction and use.

### Burial Mounds as Monuments

In west-peninsular Florida, Native Americans built large burial mounds in significant locations to serve as monuments where often relatively small numbers of individuals were interred. These mounds were sacred places. They served to integrate the general community and to separate the individuals buried in them from other members of society.

New research shows that burial monuments were beginning to be built in the region during early Woodland times, earlier than was previously thought. In Sarasota, new radiocarbon research shows that the Yellow Bluffs Mound (figure 4.2) is more than 2,000 years old, dating to the early mid-Manasota period (ca. 200 to 50 BC). This impressive mound was 2.5 meters high and was built on a rare piece of high ground, providing a wide view over Sarasota Bay (Luer 2011; Luer and Hughes 2011).

Farther north, radiocarbon dates from the Crystal River site also support the beginning of burial mounds during the mid-Deptford period (ca. 100 BC). They include Mound G and basal portions of the nearby mortuary precinct (Mounds C, E, F). The central burial tumulus (Mound F) continued to be used into Weeden Island times,

Figure 4.2. Sarasota's 2,000-year-old Yellow Bluffs Mound, now destroyed, at the start of salvage excavations in 1969. Courtesy of Sarasota County History Center, Sarasota, Florida.

growing to an imposing height of 3.3 meters. Equally impressive was the precinct's encircling embankment (Mound C) (Pluckhahn et al. 2010).

Early mound-building also took place at the Fort Center site, near Lake Okeechobee (see Thompson and Pluckhahn this volume). In middle Woodland times, around AD 200, construction was under way at Fort Center's Mound B. In addition to containing Crystal River–related pottery sherds, Mound B had an encircling embankment resembling the one at Crystal River. The embankment enclosed a mortuary precinct, including a pond with remains of a charnel structure (Sears 1982, 186–88, figure 9.5).

Embankments need more attention. Near Tampa, the Jones Mound had a horseshoe-shaped embankment (Bullen 1952, 43, figure 12), as did Parrish Mound 3 (Willey 1949, 152) and the Stanley Mound in eastern Manatee County. Farther inland, an embankment accompanied the Philip Mound in Polk County (Benson 1967), the burial mound at the Myakkahatchee Site in eastern Sarasota County (Luer et al. 1987), and (reportedly) a mound near Ona in Hardee County. Such embankments indicate greater monumental complexity than just mounds.

Perhaps embankments enclosed charnel areas. Charnel structures are poorly known in Florida, with a Woodland example at Fort Center (Sears 1982, 165–68) and a Safety Harbor example at Parrish Mound 2 (Willey 1949, 146–52). Some ramped, steep-sided, flat-topped "temple mounds" in the Tampa Bay area (dating to Safety Harbor and probably as early as Weeden Island times) might have supported temple ossuaries, but this is not known (Luer and Almy 1981).

Another imposing burial mound is the Pineland Burial Mound, also known as Smith Mound. It has yielded sherds from late Woodland and Mississippian times (the local Caloosahatchee II through IV periods). It overlooked other earthworks, including a large artificial pond with a lateral canal leading to the even larger Pine Island Canal (Luer 1991, figures 4 and 5). I have interpreted the mound to reflect "social power in the landscape" and to be "testimony to the care and labor spent to memorialize the life and death of important persons" (Luer 1991, 71).

## Burial Mounds and Later Reuse

Many mounds were revisited by Native American people of later times. They recognized burial mounds as monuments to the deceased and they interred some of their own dead in them. They treated them as sacred monuments, even though they could not have known how old some mounds really were.

For example, near Tampa Bay, the Thomas Mound was originally built during the Weeden Island and precontact Safety Harbor periods, but early postcontact Native Americans placed burials in the mound accompanied by glass trade beads, mirror fragments, and two ceremonial metal tablets (Bullen 1952). At Lake Weir in north-central Florida, Sears (1959) found an intrusive burial with a blue glass trade bead in a Weeden Island burial mound. In south Florida, postcontact period goods of European and Native American manufacture were placed with intrusive burials in preexisting sand burial mounds (Allerton et al. 1984, 10, 22; Hughes and Hardin 2003; Sears 1982, 162). A cache of large shells in the Yellow Bluffs Mound appears to reflect reuse of a 2,000-year-old mound by postcontact Safety Harbor people (Luer and Hughes 2011, 39–43). Clearly, burial mounds were enduring, meaningful monuments in the Native American landscape and cultural geography of Florida.

### Age of Monuments

New radiocarbon dates from west-peninsular Florida push back the beginning of burial mound construction to more than 2,000 years ago. In a similar way, radiocarbon dates from the Aqui Esta Mound, near Punta Gorda, pushed back the beginning of the Safety Harbor period to around AD 900 to 1000, which was corroborated by dates from Cemochechobee in Georgia and the lower Tatham Mound in Florida (Luer 2002a, 115, 168–69, table 6, Appendix II; Luer and Almy 1982, 53). This long tradition of burial mounds supports the notion that they were important as monuments.

## Exchange, Migration, and Mobility

Native American people in west-peninsular Florida consumed exotic goods and ideas for local uses. People, goods, and ideas moved via footpaths and dugout canoes. Future research will benefit from sourcing studies, especially of ceramics.

### Exotic Goods

Native American groups in west-peninsular Florida interred exotic goods with some of their dead. The practice began at least in the Late Archaic or Orange period (ca. 2000 to 1000 BC). An example is a perforated serpentine-like (greenstone) pendant, probably from northern Georgia or Alabama, found at the Republic Groves site near Zolfo Springs (Wharton et al. 1981, 65, 77–78, figure 8).

Exotic goods are known from Woodland period burial mounds across west-peninsular Florida. Around 200 to 50 BC, pottery vessels from north Florida are evidenced by Deptford Linear Check Stamped sherds with mica inclusions at the Yellow Bluffs Mound (Luer 2011, 18). Later, during Hopewell-influenced times (ca. AD 1 to 350), imported Deptford Check Stamped (and/or Gulf Check Stamped) vessels (some with tetrapod bases) and large, chipped-stone bifaces were interred in the Safford Mound at Tarpon Springs (Bullen et al. 1970), the Royce Mound near Sebring (Austin 1993), the mound-pond complex at Fort Center (Sears 1982, 28–31, 80), and the Oak Knoll Mound between Fort Myers and Naples (Dickel and Carr 1991). These grave goods resemble Deptford-related vessels with tetrapods and stone bifaces in Crystal River's central burial area (Mounds E and F) (Moore 1903, 387–93, 397).

North-to-south Hopewellian contacts appear to reflect down-the-line trade of prestige goods, which brought some famous artifacts to Crystal River, such as copper earspools, copper panpipes, and plummet pendants of quartz, stone, and copper (Moore 1903; Pluckhahn and Thompson this volume). Similar southward trade brought copper, quartz, galena, mica, and other stone artifacts to Safford Mound (Bullen et al. 1970) and galena, mica, and exotic stone plummet pendants to the Royce Mound (Austin 1993). Not all of the Middle Woodland contacts of this period were with other Native American groups to the north (indirectly as far as the Ohio Valley), as is commonly thought. My research also supports interaction in the opposite direction, based on the fact that Crystal River and a number of southern Florida sites share the same kind of carved-shell symbolic pendants and gorgets in the late Deptford or early Weeden Island period (figure 4.3).

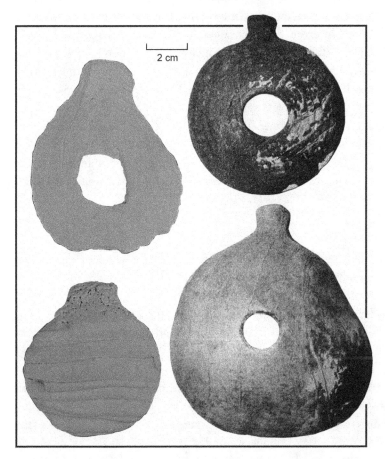

Figure 4.3. Carved shell gorgets of tabbed circle form of the Middle Woodland period. *Top left*: from Manatee County; *bottom left*: from Sarasota County (from Luer 2013, by permission of George M. Luer, Sarasota, Florida). *Top and bottom right*: from Crystal River (from Moore 1907, figures 13, 15).

During Weeden Island times, decorated ceramics were placed in west-peninsular Florida burial mounds, many apparently representing vessels imported from north Florida. They include Weeden Island Incised and Punctated, Carrabelle Incised and Punctated, Keith Incised, Wakulla Check Stamped, and Swift Creek–style complicated stamped varieties. Such pottery was notable at the Safford, Weeden Island, Thomas, Prine, and Pillsbury Mounds (Bullen et al. 1970; Luer and Almy 1982, table 2; Willey 1949) and at a mound in Charlotte County. At the latter site, I have seen complicated stamped sherds with a stamped circle and cross design, similar to motifs in Georgia and at the Block-Sterns site near Tallahassee (Jones et al. 1998, figure 13.7; Williams 1977, figure 38). The same Charlotte County site yielded a small plain bowl with a wide, outward-flaring lip, very similar to vessels from Crystal River and Hope Mound (Moore 1903, figures 25, 33; Smith 1971, figure 3f). Other Weeden Island ceramics apparently obtained through trade with north Florida include micaceous-paste bird-effigy vessels from sites near Tampa Bay.

Southward trade of exotic goods continued in the Safety Harbor period. Ceramics of possible northwest Florida origin include Fort Walton Incised varieties, Marsh Island Incised, Point Washington Incised, Lake Jackson Plain and Incised, and perhaps Pinellas Incised and Safety Harbor Incised (Cordell 2005a, 2005b, 2005c; Luer 2002a, 2005). Notable exotic goods are known from Tatham Mound, such as a copper earspool, a copper effigy plume, two elk teeth, galena, quartz pendants, ground stone celts, and valves of freshwater clams from Georgia (Mitchem 1989, 406–33, 533–36). Red ocher also might have been traded southward. In the opposite direction, pieces of queen conch shells were traded northward from south Florida, apparently as bead blanks (Luer 1992a, 271–74).

## Migrations

Archaeologists have not detected intrusions of foreign cultures into west-peninsular Florida during the Woodland and Mississippi periods. However, it is possible that "outsiders" occasionally arrived and melded with local inhabitants. The continuation of many local traditions through time, such as making and using certain kinds of shell tools and plain ceramics, supports the notion of the persistence of local peoples.

One possible arrival may involve Fort Walton immigrants to the Tampa Bay area, around AD 1000 to 1300. Sherds of diverse Fort Walton ceramic types from Snead Island, located at the mouth of the Manatee River, suggest that Fort Walton immigrants or potters resided there. Many of these sherds are known from an area to the southwest of the Snead Island Temple Mound, also known as the Portavant Mound (Luer and Almy 1981; Mitchem 1989, 167–68). Immigration of early Fort Walton potters to one or more large sites in west-peninsular Florida could explain the origin of Safety Harbor Incised pottery, if it was made in the region.

## Mobility

Peninsular peoples interacted with one another. In south Florida, Hopewell-style ceramic platform pipes occur at Pineland on the Gulf coast, at Fort Center and Ortona in the interior, and at the Miami Circle near Biscayne Bay (Carr 2006; Luer 1986, 1995a; Sears 1982). They were made of Belle Glade paste, suggesting they were carried to both coasts from the Lake Okeechobee region, perhaps by dugout canoe via the Caloosahatchee River and the Everglades. Such travel routes eventually were aided by canoe canals that probably date to the Mississippi period. Two Ortona canals were located near headwaters of the Caloosahatchee, and the Naples and Pine Island Canals were on the Gulf coast (Carr et al. 2002; Luer 1998; Luer and Wheeler 1997, 2001). No canal existed at Cape Coral (Luer 1999a).

In the Mississippi period, burial mounds containing radial burials appear on both coasts and between, suggesting contacts among peoples of these areas. Atlantic coast examples include the Burns and Fuller Mounds near Cape Canaveral and reports from the Miami area. On the Gulf coast, reports include the Laurel Mound near Venice, the Sarasota Bay Mound, a mound on Longboat Key, and the Pithlochascootie Mound north of Tarpon Springs. Between the two coasts, the Woodward and Henderson Mounds in north-central Florida, near Gainesville, are other examples (Luer 2005, 15, 30; Luer and Almy 1987).

Evidence of mobility during the early postcontact period is easier to detect. Florida's Atlantic coast was a source of shipwrecked and salvaged metal, especially silver. Native people carried it into the interior, especially the Kissimmee and Okeechobee regions, and some reached the Gulf coast. It was reworked into ornaments used by the Ais, Tisime, Tocobaga, Mayaimi, Calusa, and other groups (Luer 2000, 2010).

## Regional Exchange

Similarities in style and paste indicate that Safety Harbor pottery was traded throughout west-peninsular Florida. Examples include Lake Jackson Plain sherds with loop handles from at least 19 different mounds in nine counties (Luer 1996, 185; Luer 2005, 26–27). Other coeval pottery that was widely dispersed includes human face medallions from at least eight burial mounds in six counties (Luer 1986; Luer 1991, 70–71) and ceramic popeyed bird-head effigy adornos from more than nine sites in six counties (Luer 1992b). The occurrence of such pottery (a few large sites have more than many small sites) can perhaps be explained using a model of prestige goods exchange, with dispersal from more powerful to lesser chiefs (Luer 2002d, 105–6).

Certain villages probably specialized in making utilitarian ceramic vessels, such as those used in everyday cooking (judging by decreasing sherd frequencies as one moves from apparent source areas). Villages on the west side of Lake Okeechobee apparently produced Belle Glade Plain bowls, which appear to have been dispersed

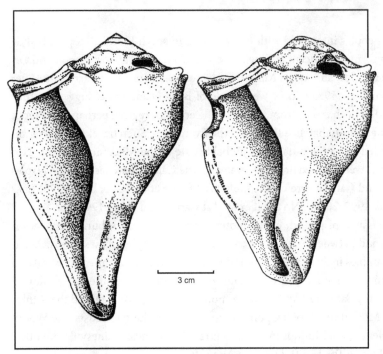

Figure 4.4. Whelk shell artifacts of progressive reduction and exchange. *Left*: Tool blank from outer estuary source site; *right*: cutting-edged tool with bevel on reduced tip from an inner estuary use site on the lower Myakka River. Both artifacts are from Charlotte County, Florida. *Source*: Luer et al. 1986. Illustrations by George M. Luer; used by permission of George M. Luer, Sarasota, Florida.

outward, including to the greater Charlotte Harbor and Sarasota areas (Luer 1989, 119–21, figure 11, table 2; Luer 2002b, 77). Abundant sherds of Pinellas Plain lip-notched bowls suggest such vessels originated at several large Tampa Bay village sites; some were transported southward along the coast (Luer 1992a, 270; Luer 1999b, 53).

## Local Mobility and Exchange

Fishing economies supplemented by hunting and gathering required mobility within catchment areas. In the Sarasota area, food remains show that Native Americans exploited both coastal and inland zones. For example, remains of saltwater fish and mollusk shells at inland sites, such as Nineteen Owner Midden in North Port, support the idea that native groups trekked inland from estuarine sites near upper Charlotte Harbor (Luer 2002b). Conversely, remains of freshwater siren, bowfin, and pond turtles at bayside sites, such as the Old Oak Site on Sarasota Bay and the Midnight Pass Midden on Siesta Key, support shoreward transport of foods by Native Americans who exploited inland areas (Luer 1995b).

Where estuaries were large and productive, such as the outer Charlotte Harbor area, inshore fishing was predominant and surpluses could be redistributed. This led to the growth of complex societies and large, centrally located sites with probable year-round or sedentary occupation, surrounded by smaller satellite sites. Large coastal sites appear to have been provisioned by their own inhabitants, plus those of surrounding smaller sites (Luer 2007, 309–19, 354–63).

That was the situation on Big Mound Key, near Charlotte Harbor, based on my detailed analyses of a large, multilayered pit feature dating to approximately cal AD 1115, or early in the Mississippi period. I used patterns in the pit feature's cultural assemblage of food remains to interpret "common" foods, such as abundant kinds of fish and shellfish (including saltwater catfish, pinfish, pigfish, king's crown mollusks, and others), and "favored" foods, such as animals of less frequency, large size, and young age (including ducks, green sea turtle, large snook, large black drum, and large goliath grouper from estuaries and siren, snapping turtle, pond turtles, sandhill crane, and deer [especially meaty hindquarters] from landward areas, including freshwater wetlands) (Luer 2007, 354–80). From a perspective of theory, this and other evidence from the pit feature supports "elite private food consumption" (Jackson and Scott 1995, 107–8, table 1) that can be classified as "patron-role feasting," a type of feasting that reflected unequal social power between the patron (chief) and clients and reinforced chiefly and client reciprocal relationships in the political structure and economy (Dietler 1996, 96–97; Luer 2007, 364–80).

This same pit feature sheds light on human-animal relations, or how possible beliefs of native peoples might have affected their uses of animals. The absence or great scarcity of remains of some kinds of animals, such as alligator, snake, gopher tortoise, opossum, pelicans, and birds of prey, suggests that people avoided them as food in that context (Luer 2007, 380–88). Plus, in this case and at sites throughout the region, I have not observed manatee remains, again suggesting avoidance.

Our discovery of whelk shell tool blanks (figure 4.4) and their occurrence in caches support the notion that valued tool materials were hoarded. These could be controlled and exchanged with members of a community, who then shaped them into finished tools for needs that probably included canoe manufacture (Luer 2008, 73; Luer et al. 1986). Whelk shell tool blanks comprising known caches vary in number from five to fourteen. Most come from recently disturbed shell midden deposits, so feature details are few. They apparently were buried intentionally for storage and protection instead of being burial goods. Varied stages of fabrication suggest that some caches represent tool blanks in production, whereas caches of finished blanks may represent items ready for exchange and further modification into working tools.

I also have seen single, finished whelk shell tool blanks in contexts suggesting that they were obtained through exchange. For example, a large robust specimen came from a shell midden on the lower Myakka River. Whelks do not live in the lower Myakka, which is characterized by fluctuating salinity. Whelk and quahog

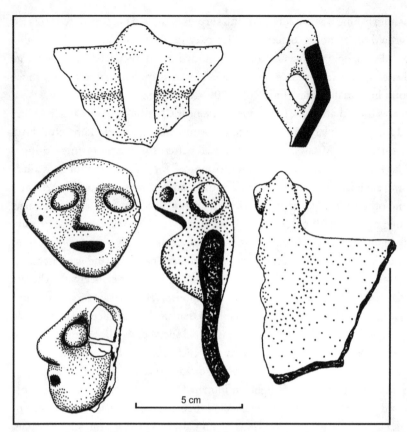

Figure 4.5. Safety Harbor pottery traded widely. *Top*: Front and side views of a loop handle broken from the rim of a collared vessel at the Sarasota Bay Mound. *Left*: Front and side views of a human face medallion removed from the shoulder of a bottle. *Right*: Side and rear views of a popeyed bird-head effigy adorno from a vessel rim. Left and right artifacts are from the Lake Trafford Mound, Collier County. *Sources*: *Top*: Luer 2005; *right*: Luer 1992b; *left*: Luer 1986. Illustrations by George M. Luer; used by permission of George M. Luer, Sarasota, Florida.

shells were needed for tools in such upper estuarine and landward areas, and they had to be obtained from high-salinity, outer estuaries through mobility and/or exchange (Luer 2002c, 65; Luer 2008, 73, notes 3 and 4). Similarly, coastal resources such as shark teeth and shell vessels were transported landward to these upper estuarine and inland areas.

## Human-Landscape Interactions

Along islands, rivers, sloughs, and bays, native people lived in strategic places where they built high ground to raise their habitations above floods, tides, and storm surges and to provide visibility and a breeze (Luer 2007, 31–40). At Big Mound

Key, stratigraphic profiles and radiocarbon dates support the interpretation that the site grew steadily from around AD 200 to AD 1700. Native people created Big Mound Key by using sand and shells to build a series of middens, mounds, and elevated habitation surfaces throughout the site's 1,500-year history (Luer 2007, 40–131; Luer et al. 2010). Part of the site displays bilateral spatial arrangement, including a partially bisecting tidal trough or "canal," an attribute shared with some other shell mound sites in the region. These constructed bilateral landscapes may reflect social organization, but they are not yet understood. The explanatory hypotheses range from separate residence areas for different clans or moieties to perhaps separate residence areas for males and females.

Native people also modified their environment by building ramps and linear ridges, including walkways and causeways. Ramps served for ascending the steep sides of elevated middens, such as at the Roberts Bay site in Sarasota (Luer 1977) and on the steep flanks of platform mounds such as those around Tampa Bay (Luer and Almy 1981). Causeways were large, such as at Maximo Point in St. Petersburg (Moore 1900, 353–54), Boots Point on Terra Ceia Island (Bullen 1951, 10–11), and at the Ortona site near Lake Okeechobee (Carr et al. 1995), whereas walkways were smaller. Probably the last remaining intact walkway is at Sarasota's Old Oak Site, where it runs inland and connects several small shell middens along the north side of Spring Creek. Built of sand and discarded food shells, this narrow ridge is an important feature but it is not of monumental size or elaboration. Apparently it served everyday utilitarian purposes by providing an elevated connection between habitation loci. Similarly, narrow ridges of midden shells in tidal areas at some sites, such as those that bracket the entrance to a canoe canal at Indian Field, do not appear to be monumental; they instead served utilitarian purposes as breakwaters (Luer 1989, 103–5, figure 6).

Another landscape intervention was the building of lengthy canoe canals. These features were not crude drainage ditches that bled water from the land. On the contrary, Native American canoe canals needed to retain water. They were linked to the natural landscape and were charged by shallow ground water and rainfall runoff. Some apparently functioned as series of stepped impoundments. Besides being feats of engineering, canals required labor to build and maintain and they probably aided in the delivery of tribute and the projection of political and military power. Thus, they (like mounds) reflect social power in the landscape (Luer 1998, 34).

Native American people in west-peninsular Florida used a variety of plants. Gourds and squashes appear as rind and seed remains and in ceramic effigies that reflect uses of real ones (Luer 1996; Luer 2002a, 131–36; Mitchem 1989, 464). Bushes and trees bearing edible fruits or nuts, such as tropical cocoplum, false mastic, and sea grape and temperate pignut hickory, occur in the archaeobotanical record and might have been spread and encouraged by Native Americans (Luer 2007, 255–64; Luer 2011, 26; Newsom 1998; Scarry and Newsom 1992). Even today, some plants that had economic uses, such as gumbo limbo and wild cotton, thrive better on shell middens than anywhere else in the region. Native people probably grew or actively encouraged many of these plants, including trees.

## Symbolism and Ritual

My analyses of Safety Harbor and Weeden Island pottery are yielding new insights on symbolism and ritual practices. In west-peninsular Florida, decorated ceramics occur primarily in burial mounds and are rare in shell middens, where plain wares predominate. Ceramic vessel forms and iconography and their associations (such as in burial mound assemblages) provide clues to their uses and meanings.

Several Safety Harbor ceramic types display vessel shapes shared with Mississippian forms elsewhere in the Southeast. They include bottles, beakers, and bowls with effigy rim adornos and collared jars and collared bowls with rim lugs and loop handles. Each of these vessel forms includes variants that also occur elsewhere in the Southeast.

Bottles of Safety Harbor Incised pottery display a variety of shapes and sizes. A few show composite forms, a terraced shoulder, or effigy ropes and medallions. Point Washington Incised bowls with effigy rim adornos often depict popeyed birds. Lake Jackson Plain collared jars and bowls vary in size, usually consist of simple forms (though a composite vessel is known), and display variable lugs and loop handles that often project above the vessel orifice (figure 4.5).

Safety Harbor Incised decoration shows Mississippian influence, including appliqué and incised symbols. Some of these, such as human hands, batons, bird feet, human heads, and zigzags (apparent lightning) might have been associated with warfare and high military ranks (Luer 1996, 188–89; Luer 2002d, 101). Other symbols on Safety Harbor Incised pottery include barred ovals, scrolls, volutes, figure eights, circles, semicircles, and chevrons (Luer 1993, 2002a, 2002d). Furthermore, Sarasota Incised beakers display encircling bands of incised and punctated triangles like those on Andrews Decorated beakers of Georgia's Rood phase (Luer 2002a). Likewise, Safety Harbor Incised bottles have analogs among Nunnally Incised and Nunnally Plain vessels of the Rood phase (Luer 2002a; Schnell et al. 1981, 175–87).

Even double rim effigies are reported rarely in west-peninsular Florida, recalling double portrayals in other Mississippian ceramics. Examples are Point Washington Incised bird-tail handles and dog-like heads from the Weeki Wachee Mound (Mitchem et al. 1985, 187, figure 3) and a 1930s report of an apparent Point Washington Incised vessel with two flat handles and two opposing rim projections from the Laurel Mound in Sarasota County. Outside the region, a Pensacola Incised bowl from the Fort Walton site displays a pair of human head rim adornos (Willey 1949, 214, figure 60d), and a Mound Place Incised bowl from Arkansas has twin tails and twin bird heads (Hathcock 1976, 122, figure 314).

While a number of vessel forms and iconographic symbols are clearly Mississippian, other aspects of Safety Harbor culture show strong local roots. Many kinds of shell tools continued in use (though they too were dynamic and changing), and local symbols persisted, such as ornaments shaped like scallop shells or shark teeth. The contextual associations of Safety Harbor decorated vessels show that many were broken and interred in burial mounds in ways similar to late Weeden Island vessels in west-peninsular Florida burial mounds (Luer 2002a, 162, 169–70). Furthermore, decorated vessels of both periods were used with other wares of local and imported origins. At the Aqui Esta Mound, such other pottery included large Belle Glade Plain bowls, various St. Johns Plain and Check Stamped vessels, bottle gourd effigy dippers, and numerous whelk shell vessels of local forms. All these apparently had a use-life before being ritually perforated or broken and eventually interred in the burial mound (Luer 2002a).

My studies of both Safety Harbor and peninsular Weeden Island burial mounds have led me to interpret two stages of ritual behavior involving the perforating and breaking of vessels. In the first stage, a vessel's base was either perforated (by drilling, tapping out, or grinding a hole while keeping the rest of the vessel intact) or the entire vessel bottom was knocked out (often breaking the rest of a ceramic vessel into several large fragments). After this initial treatment, perforated and fragmentary vessels were stored for a period of time (judging by eroded breaks and missing pieces), perhaps in a charnel house. In the second stage, thusly "killed" ceramic vessels and vessel fragments apparently were taken to the burial area and broken again. Before being covered with sand and buried, the resulting sherds were strewn across the surface and sometimes intentionally cupped and piled in neat stacks. My crossmending studies of such sherds have produced vessel portions with missing bottoms, apparently owing to initial breakage elsewhere. I have viewed such evidence of mortuary ritual from a theoretical perspective of "rites of passage" (Van Gannep 1960) because it has a tripartite, sequential structure that can be interpreted in terms of separation, transition, and reincorporation (Luer 2002a, 169–70).

But how were intact vessels used? Their forms suggest that many were used together. A dipper could dispense liquid from a large open bowl, and a funnel could direct liquid or seeds into a container. More intriguing is the pre-fired basal hole, large or small, which is a feature of many Weeden Island and Safety Harbor vessels, including bottles and beakers. These basal holes suggest that some vessels were used in a stacked or compound arrangement, perhaps so that liquid or steam could pass through them.

A possible example dating to the Safety Harbor period consists of three vessels: 1) an uppermost funnel incorporating an effigy of a fluted ovifera gourd with a large pre-fired hole and coupling ring in its base; 2) a globular vessel (itself perhaps an effigy of a carved bottle gourd) having an orifice that could accommodate the funnel, plus its own incised human hand symbols and its own pre-fired basal hole; and 3)

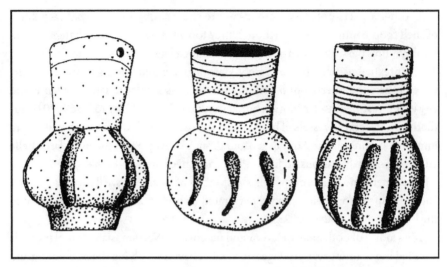

Figure 4.6. Safety Harbor Incised vessels incorporating effigies of fluted gourds. *Source*: Luer 1996. Illustration by George M. Luer; used by permission of George M. Luer, Sarasota, Florida.

a loop-handled collared jar in which the globular vessel might have rested. Similar stacked arrangements are depicted by composite effigy vessels in Alabama and Arkansas (Luer 1996). Some composite vessels of Weeden Island types also appear to depict nested or stacked vessels (Moore 1902, 1903, figure 5; Willey 1949, 291, 303, 307, 504, figure 71b–d).

Several Safety Harbor Incised vessels incorporate effigies of fluted gourds or squashes (figure 4.6). I have interpreted such pottery in light of an historic period Apalachee myth that describes a culture-hero warrior, tells how to achieve high warrior rank, and explains why squash and a deceased chief's body parts should be boiled in pots during mortuary ritual. This is a Mississippian myth linking horticultural fertility with chiefs, warfare, and mortuary activities and it suggests why such symbols as human hands and heads, batons, zigzags (cf. lightning), and gourds appear together in Safety Harbor Incised pottery found in burial mounds (Luer 1996, 188–89).

## Conclusion

Dynamic Woodland and Mississippian societies flourished across west-peninsular Florida, which was an integral region of the Southeast. The bountiful coastal, terrestrial, and wetland region supported simple and complex chiefdoms based largely on fishing, augmented by hunting, gathering, and probably some encouragement of economically useful plants, including bushes and trees. In Woodland times, the Florida Gulf coast played a central role in the birth and subsequent unfolding of

Weeden Island culture, including the Tampa Bay and Charlotte Harbor areas. Similarly, the region's Safety Harbor culture was deeply involved in the Mississippian ceramic tradition; it had close ties to north Florida's Fort Walton culture and Georgia's and Alabama's Rood phase of the Chattahoochee River valley. Across west-peninsular Florida, there were commonalities among diverse sites, including Crystal River, in terms of age, mounds, embankments, and artifacts, such as ceramics and symbolic shell gorgets and pendants. Crystal River is not an enigma, as some researchers have thought.

In west-peninsular Florida, native people actively modified their landscape in a variety of ways. They constructed spaces and used them to project political and social dimensions of their societies. During Woodland and precontact Mississippian times, they built monumental burial mounds, which later postcontact native people continued to view as sacred places where they interred some of their own dead. Native people improved their physical living conditions by using sand and shells to build elevated living surfaces, ramps, walkways, causeways, breakwaters, and other site features. At some sites, bilateral arrangements of midden-mounds may reflect social organization and differentiated residence patterns. Lengthy canoe canals not only represent feats of hydrological engineering and labor in their construction and maintenance, but they probably also facilitated the delivery of tribute and aided in the projection of political and military power by complex chiefdoms, such as the Calusa and Mayaimi.

Native people exploited the environment according to social roles and cultural values. At one site, a large pit feature on the spacious summit of a high, flat-topped shell mound reveals provisioning of foods, elite private consumption, and a type of feasting that reinforced reciprocal chiefly and client relationships in the economic and political structure of the early Mississippi period. In this context, some foods apparently had a favored status while others apparently were avoided, reflecting human-animal relations and dietary ritual. At two other sites, a Weeden Island burial mound and an early Safety Harbor (Englewood) burial mound, a three-stage process of ritualization in mortuary activity is evidenced among assemblages of intentionally broken pottery vessels.

Finally, it must be stressed that the region's sites have suffered from twentieth-century land development, and many cited in this chapter are now destroyed. Important sites, such as the Old Oak Site in Sarasota, continue to be severely endangered. The region's sites desperately need better preservation and more appreciation.

## References

Allerton, David, George M. Luer, and Robert S. Carr
1984   Ceremonial Tablets and Related Objects from Florida. *Florida Anthropologist* 37: 5–54.

Austin, Robert J.

1993    The Royce Mound: Middle Woodland Exchange and Mortuary Customs in South Florida. *Florida Anthropologist* 46: 291–309.

Benson, Carl A.

1967    The Philip Mound: A Historic Site. *Florida Anthropologist* 20: 118–32.

Bullen, Ripley P.

1951    *The Terra Ceia Site, Manatee County, Florida.* Florida Anthropological Society Publication no. 3. University of Florida, Gainesville.

1952    *Eleven Archaeological Sites in Hillsborough County, Florida.* Florida Geological Survey, Report of Investigations no. 8. Florida Geological Survey, Tallahassee.

1978    Tocobaga Indians and the Safety Harbor Culture. In *Tacachale: Essays on the Indians of Florida and Southeastern Georgia during the Historic Period,* edited by Jerald T. Milanich and Samuel Proctor, 50–58. University Presses of Florida, Gainesville.

Bullen, Ripley P., William L. Partridge, and Donald A. Harris

1970    The Safford Burial Mound, Tarpon Springs, Florida. *Florida Anthropologist* 23: 81–118.

Carr, Robert S.

2006    Analysis of Ceramics from Brickell Point, 8DA12. *Florida Anthropologist* 59: 133–59.

Carr, Robert S., David Dickel, and Marilyn Masson

1995    Archaeological Investigations at the Ortona Earthworks and Mounds. *Florida Anthropologist* 48: 227–63.

Carr, Robert S., Jorge Zamanillo, and Jim Pepe

2002    Archaeological Profiling and Radiocarbon Dating of the Ortona Canal (8GL4), Glades County, Florida. *Florida Anthropologist* 55: 3–22.

Cordell, Ann S.

2005a    Variability in the Sarasota Bay Mound (8SO44) Pottery Assemblage. *Florida Anthropologist* 58: 75–90.

2005b    Notes on Pottery from the Myakka Valley Ranches Mound (8SO401). *Florida Anthropologist* 58: 99–104.

2005c    Revisiting the Aqui Esta Mound (8CH68): Paste Variability in the Pottery Assemblage. *Florida Anthropologist* 58: 105–20.

Dickel, David, and Robert S. Carr

1991    Archaeological Investigations at the Oak Knoll Mound, 8LL729, Lee County, Florida. Archaeological and Historical Conservancy Technical Report no. 21, Miami.

Dietler, Michael

1996    Feasts and Commensal Politics in the Political Economy: Food, Power, and Status in Prehistoric Europe. In *Food and the Status Quest,* edited by Polly Wiessner and Wulf Schiefenhovel, 87–125. Berghahn Books, Providence, RI.

Hathcock, Ray

1976    *Ancient Indian Pottery of the Mississippi River Valley.* Hurley Press Inc., Camden, AR.

Hughes, Daniel, and Kenneth Hardin

2003    Beehive Hill: Another Pre- and Post–First Contact Period Site in Central Florida. *Florida Anthropologist* 56: 267–75.

Jackson, H. Edwin, and Susan L. Scott

1995    The Faunal Record of the Southeastern Elite: The Implications of Economy, Social Relations, and Ideology. *Southeastern Archaeology* 14: 103–19.

Jones, B. Calvin, Daniel T. Penton, and Louis D. Tesar

1998    Excavations at the Block-Sterns Site, Leon County, Florida. In *A World Engraved: Archaeology of the Swift Creek Culture,* edited by Mark Williams and Daniel T. Elliott, 222–46. University of Alabama Press, Tuscaloosa.

Lewis, Clifford M.

1978    The Calusa. In *Tacachale: Essays on the Indians of Florida and Southeastern Georgia during the Historic Period,* edited by Jerald T. Milanich and Samuel Proctor, 19–49. University Presses of Florida, Gainesville.

Luer, George M.

1977    The Roberts Bay Site, Sarasota, Florida. *Florida Anthropologist* 30: 121–33.

1986    Ceramic Faces and a Pipe Fragment from South Florida, with Notes on the Pineland Site, Lee County. *Florida Anthropologist* 39: 281–86.

1989    Calusa Canals in Southwestern Florida: Routes of Tribute and Exchange. *Florida Anthropologist* 42: 89–130.

1991    Historic Resources at the Pineland Site, Lee County, Florida. *Florida Anthropologist* 44: 59–75.

1992a   The Boylston Mound: A Safety Harbor Period Shell Midden, with Notes on the Paleoenvironment of Southern Sarasota Bay. *Florida Anthropologist* 45: 266–79.

1992b   Mississippian Period Popeyed Bird-Head Effigies from West-Central and Southwest Florida. *Florida Anthropologist* 45: 52–62.

1993    A Safety Harbor Incised Bottle with Effigy Bird Feet and Human Hands from a Possible Headman Burial, Sarasota County, Florida. *Florida Anthropologist* 46:238–50.

1995a   Pipe Fragments from Ortona, South Florida: Comments on Platform Pipe Styles, Functions, and Middle Woodland Exchange. *Florida Anthropologist* 48: 301–8.

1995b   The Brookside Mound, Sarasota County, Florida, with Notes on Settlement Pattern, Scrub Habitat, and Isolated Burial Mounds. *Florida Anthropologist* 48: 200–216.

1996    Mississippian Ceramic Jars, Bottles, and Gourds as Compound Vessels. *Southeastern Archaeology* 15: 181–91.

1998    The Naples Canal: A Deep Indian Canoe Trail in Southwestern Florida. *Florida Anthropologist* 51: 25–36.

1999a   Surface Hydrology and an Illusory Canal in Cape Coral, Florida. *Florida Anthropologist* 52: 255–65.

1999b   Cedar Point: A Late Archaic through Safety Harbor Period Occupation on Lemon Bay, Charlotte County, Florida. In *Maritime Archaeology of Lemon Bay, Florida,* edited by George M. Luer, 43–56. Florida Anthropological Society Publication no. 14. Florida Anthropological Society, Clearwater.

2000    Three Metal Ceremonial Tablets, with Comments on the Tampa Bay Area. *Florida Anthropologist* 53: 2–11.

2002a   The Aqui Esta Mound: Ceramic and Shell Vessels of the Early Mississippian-Influenced Englewood Phase. In *Archaeology of Upper Charlotte Harbor, Florida,* edited by George M. Luer, 111–81. Florida Anthropological Society Publication no. 15. Florida Anthropological Society, Tallahassee.

2002b   Settlement and Subsistence at a Late Weeden Island-Safety Harbor Period Inland Midden in North Port. In *Archaeology of Upper Charlotte Harbor, Florida,* edited by George M. Luer, 73–93. Florida Anthropological Society Publication no. 15. Florida Anthropological Society, Tallahassee.

2002c   Archaeology and Faunal Analysis at Tippecanoe Bay. In *Archaeology of Upper Charlotte Harbor, Florida,* edited by George M. Luer, 49–71. Florida Anthropological Society Publication no. 15. Florida Anthropological Society, Tallahassee.

2002d   Ceramic Bottles, Globular Vessels, and Safety Harbor Culture. In *Archaeology of Upper Char-*

*lotte Harbor, Florida*, edited by George M. Luer, 95–110. Florida Anthropological Society Publication no. 15. Florida Anthropological Society, Tallahassee.

2005    Sarasota Bay Mound: A Safety Harbor Period Burial Mound, with Notes on Additional Sites in the City of Sarasota. *Florida Anthropologist* 58: 7–55.

2007    Mound Building and Subsistence during the Late Weeden Island Period (ca. A.D. 700–1000) at Big Mound Key (8CH10), Florida. PhD dissertation, Department of Anthropology, University of Florida, Gainesville.

2008    Notes on Florida Shell Artifacts, Including Specimens from Hooker Key and Mason Island. *Florida Anthropologist* 61: 73–83.

2010    Ceremonial Metal Tablet #60: Stylistic and Compositional Analyses of a Lead-Iron Tablet from the Blueberry Site, Highlands County, Florida. *Florida Anthropologist* 63: 35–45.

2011    The Yellow Bluffs Mound Revisited: A Manasota Period Burial Mound in Sarasota. *Florida Anthropologist* 64: 5–32.

2013    Tabbed Circle Artifacts in Florida: An Intriguing Type of Gorget and Pendant. *Florida Anthropologist* 66: 103–27.

Luer, George, David Allerton, Dan Hazeltine, Ron Hatfield, and Darden Hood

1986    Whelk Shell Tool Blanks from Big Mound Key (8Ch10), Charlotte County, Florida: With Notes on Certain Whelk Shell Tools. In *Shells and Archaeology in Southern Florida*, edited by George M. Luer, 92–124. Florida Anthropological Society Publication no.12. Florida Anthropological Society, Tallahassee.

Luer, George M., and Marion M. Almy

1979    Three Aboriginal Shell Middens on Longboat Key, Florida: Manasota Period Sites of Barrier Island Exploitation. *Florida Anthropologist* 32: 34–45.

1981    Temple Mounds of the Tampa Bay Area. *Florida Anthropologist* 34: 127–55.

1982    A Definition of the Manasota Culture. *Florida Anthropologist* 35: 34–58.

1987    The Laurel Mound (8SO98) and Radial Burials, with Notes on the Safety Harbor Period. *Florida Anthropologist* 40: 301–20.

Luer, George, Marion Almy, Dana Ste. Claire, and Robert Austin

1987    The Myakkahatchee Site (8So397), A Large Multi-Period Inland from the Shore Site in Sarasota County, Florida. *Florida Anthropologist* 40: 137–53.

Luer, George, Michele Cotty, Lisa Surdam, Sarah Bourget, Ben Apperson, Bill Godek, Tesa Norman, Ben Bilgri, and Felicia Silpa

2010    Big Mound Key (8CH10) Special Category Grant Report. Survey #16156. On file, Florida Master Site File, Tallahassee.

Luer, George M., and Daniel Hughes

2011    Radiocarbon Dating the Yellow Bluffs Mound (8SO4), Sarasota, Florida. *Florida Anthropologist* 64: 33–45.

Luer, George M., and Ryan J. Wheeler

1997    How the Pine Island Canal Worked: Topography, Hydraulics, and Engineering. *Florida Anthropologist* 50: 115–31.

2001    An Experiment at Dating the Pine Island Canal. *Florida Anthropologist* 54: 87–89.

Mitchem, Jeffrey M.

1989    Redefining Safety Harbor: Late Prehistoric/Protohistoric Archaeology in West Peninsular Florida. PhD dissertation, Department of Anthropology, University of Florida, Gainesville.

Mitchem, Jeffrey M., Marvin T. Smith, Albert C. Goodyear, and Robert R. Allen

1985    Early Spanish Contact on the Florida Gulf Coast: The Weeki Wachee and Ruth Smith Mounds. In *Indians, Colonists, and Slaves: Essays in Memory of Charles H. Fairbanks*, edited by Kenneth W. Johnson, Jonathan M. Leader, and Robert C. Wilson, 179–219. Florida Journal of Anthropology Special Publication no. 4. Florida Anthropology Student Association of the University of Florida, Gainesville.

Moore, Clarence B.

1900    Certain Antiquities of the Florida West-Coast. *Journal of the Academy of Natural Sciences of Philadelphia* 11: 350–94.

1902    Certain Aboriginal Remains of the Northwest Florida Coast, Part 2. *Journal of the Academy of Natural Sciences of Philadelphia* 12: 128–358.

1903    Certain Aboriginal Mounds of the Central Florida West-Coast. *Journal of the Academy of Natural Sciences of Philadelphia* 12: 361–438.

1907    Crystal River Revisited. *Journal of the Academy of Natural Sciences of Philadelphia* 13: 406–25.

Newsom, Lee

1998    Archaeobotanical Research at Shell Ridge Midden, Palmer Site (8SO2), Sarasota County, Florida. *Florida Anthropologist* 51: 207–22.

Pluckhahn, Thomas J., Victor D. Thompson, and Brent R. Weisman

2010    Toward a New View of History and Process at Crystal River (8CI1). *Southeastern Archaeology* 29: 164–81.

Scarry, C. Margaret, and Lee A. Newsom

1992    Archaeobotanical Research in the Calusa Heartland. In *Culture and Environment in the Domain of the Calusa*, edited by William H. Marquardt, 375–401. Institute of Archaeology and Paleoenvironmental Studies Monograph no. 1. Institute of Archaeology and Paleoenvironmental Studies, Gainesville.

Sears, William H.

1959    *Two Weeden Island Period Burial Mounds, Florida*. Contributions of the Florida State Museum no. 5. University of Florida, Gainesville.

1982    *Fort Center: An Archaeological Site in the Lake Okeechobee Basin*. University Press of Florida, Gainesville.

Schnell, Frank T., Vernon J. Knight Jr., and Gail S. Schnell

1981    *Cemochechobee: Archaeology of a Mississippian Ceremonial Center on the Chattahoochee River*. University Presses of Florida, Gainesville.

Smith, Daniel D.

1971    Excavations at the Hope Mound, Tarpon Springs, Florida. *Florida Anthropologist* 24: 107–34.

Van Gennep, Arnold

1960    *The Rites of Passage*. Translated by Monika B. Vizedom and Gabrielle L. Caffee. University of Chicago Press, Chicago.

Wharton, Barry R., George R. Ballo, and Mitchell E. Hope

1981    The Republic Groves Site, Hardee County, Florida. *Florida Anthropologist* 34: 59–80.

Willey, Gordon R.

1949    *Archeology of the Florida Gulf Coast*. Smithsonian Miscellaneous Collections no. 113, Washington, D.C.

Williams, Stephen (editor)

1977    *The Waring Papers: The Collected Works of Antonio J. Waring, Jr.* Papers of the Peabody Museum of Archaeology and Ethnology 58. Peabody Museum, Harvard University, Cambridge, MA.

# 5

# Radiocarbon Dates and the Late Prehistory
# of Tampa Bay

ROBERT J. AUSTIN, JEFFREY M. MITCHEM, AND BRENT R. WEISMAN

A little more than 60 years ago, in 1949, Gordon Willey published *Archeology of the Florida Gulf Coast*, in which he developed a post-Archaic, ceramic-based chronology for the state's Gulf coast, from the panhandle south to Charlotte County. This landmark of cultural-historical reconstruction formed the basic chronological framework that we continue to use today. A comparison of his sequence of culture periods with Jerald Milanich's 1994 chronology for the Central Peninsular Gulf Coast, which includes Willey's central Gulf coast and Manatee regions, shows that despite a small site sample, Willey's formulation has held up remarkably well.

The major refinement has been in resolving the pre–Weeden Island portion of the sequence. Deptford and Swift Creek ceramics were found to be rare at sites in the region and Perico Island turned out to be a non-existent culture. As George Luer and Marion Almy (1982) demonstrated, an archaeological manifestation dominated by sand-tempered plain pottery that they name Manasota followed the Archaic period. Late Manasota burial practices were influenced by Weeden Island mortuary customs that were developed farther north (Luer and Almy 1982, 47, 52; Milanich 1994, 221–22, 227). Luer and Almy's reevaluation of the archaeological data has been confirmed repeatedly by excavations throughout the region since they published their original formulation in 1982 (e.g., Austin 1995; Austin et al. 1992; Austin et al. 2008; Burger 1986; Estabrook and Newman 1984, 103–14; Schwadron 2002; Whitehurst 1988). In the area from Tampa Bay south to Charlotte Harbor, the Mississippian-influenced Safety Harbor culture appears to have developed out of Weeden Island–related Manasota (Luer and Almy 1982, 52–53; Milanich 1994, 226; Milanich 2002, 369). The subdivision of Safety Harbor into four sequential phases is the result of Jeff Mitchem's research in the 1980s (Mitchem 1989, 557–67).

Despite their successes, a weakness of both Willey's and Milanich's chronologies is a relative absence of chronometric dates with which to fix more firmly these ceramic-based sequences in time. No such dates were available for Willey and only a handful had been published for the Central Peninsular Gulf Coast when Milanich developed his chronology. Since then, several excavation projects in Pinellas, Hillsborough, and Manatee counties have contributed many new dates and associated ceramic and environmental data for the period after 500 BC. We have compiled these dates and use them here to reexamine the archaeological sequence of the Tampa Bay area.

There are several reasons why such a study is relevant. Well-dated chronologies provide the foundation on which all archaeological research is based, regardless of theoretical approach. To answer the kinds of research questions we wish to ask today requires much greater chronological refinement than has been available. For example, establishing the contemporaneity of archaeological deposits from different sites, correlating archaeological occupations with climatic events, and examining periods of transition between major cultural traditions all require precise chronometric dating. Advancements in radiocarbon research, especially the ability to date minute carbon samples using AMS, has given archaeologists an important tool for refining the timing of archaeological events and correcting earlier interpretations (see Sassaman 2003 for a recent example).

In the following pages we discuss three specific examples of research issues in the Tampa Bay region of the Central Peninsular Gulf Coast that can be addressed or refined by an expanded radiocarbon database: the relationship between settlement patterns, fluctuations in sea level, and climatic events; refinements of the region's ceramic chronology; and site formation.

## The Study Area and Data Sample

The geographic area we focus on is the greater Tampa Bay watershed, which includes Pinellas, Hillsborough, and Manatee counties. Tampa Bay is the largest estuary on Florida's west coast at more than 1,000 square kilometers, but it also is exceptionally shallow, with an average depth of only 4 meters (Brooks and Doyle 1998). The shallow bottom, differential rates and sources of sedimentation, and the "multi-lobed" nature of bay and lagoon structure immediately suggest that bay-wide generalizations will not be readily apparent. Tidal fluctuations are highly variable depending on location, and, of greater significance, fluctuations in Holocene sea levels would have had differential rather than uniform consequences for the prehistoric human inhabitants of the region.

Figure 5.1 shows the locations of 11 sites from which we have drawn our sample of 72 dates, as well as other sites mentioned in the text. The majority of our dates are from five sites: Yat Kitischee (8PI1753), Bayshore Homes (8PI41), the Kut-

tler Mound (8PI10650), the Anderson site (8PI54) in Pinellas County, and Shaw's
Point (8MA7) in Manatee County.

Our sample was drawn from a total of 136 reported radiocarbon dates for the
three counties that comprise our study area. We eliminated from consideration dates

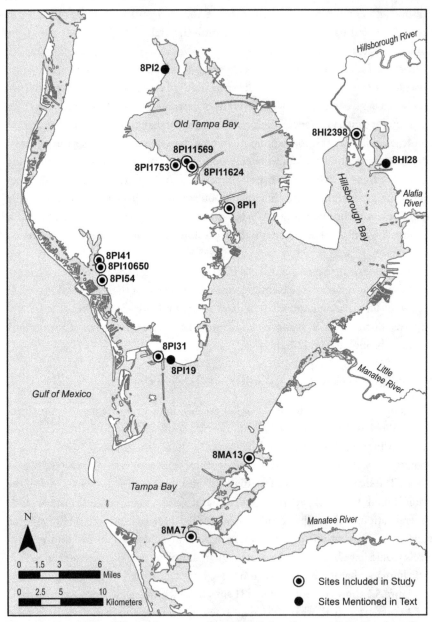

Figure 5.1. Locations of Tampa Bay area archaeological sites that contributed to the radiocarbon sample or are mentioned in the text.

before 500 BC, dates from noncoastal locations, and any dates that we considered to be questionable. These considerations caused us to discard 12 dates from five coastal sites with late prehistoric components. One radiocarbon date from Weeden Island (8PI1), collected from a soil core, is anomalously late for its context (well below the late prehistoric midden), and a second date, also from a core, falls outside our period of interest. One late prehistoric date from a "calcareous concretion" at Maximo Beach (8PI31) was discarded because the dated material was not well described and was considered problematic. All six of the dates from Delaney Creek (8HI28) were discarded because of concerns about stratigraphic mixing and possible laboratory error. Finally, three dates obtained from human bone at Bayshore Homes and Safety Harbor (8PI2) were not used because they are inconsistent with the associated artifacts.

Our decision not to include radiocarbon dates before 500 BC and dates from sites in noncoastal settings is due partly to our research focus—late prehistory—but also to the fact that dates from interior sites tend to come from deep sand deposits where the provenience and origin of the dated samples are sometimes in doubt, resulting in dates that are often interpreted as too old or too young for their corresponding archaeological components (Austin 2006, 179).

Table 5.1 provides the relevant data for our sample. Thirty-three dates are from marine shell samples, 31 are from charred wood or charcoal, six are from soot on ceramic sherds, and two are from wood. When they were available, we used published conventional ages that have been adjusted for isotopic fractionation. When no such adjustments were reported, we used the suggested mean $\Delta^{13}C$ values published by Stuiver and Polach (1977) to derive conventional ages from measured $^{14}C$ ages. CALIB 6.01 was used to calibrate all of the radiocarbon dates reported here using the INTCAL09 and MARINE09 calibration datasets. For marine shell samples a $\Delta R$ of -5 ± 20 was used to correct for local (Gulf of Mexico) reservoir effects (Queens University 2012). Unless otherwise noted in the text, all dates are presented as calibrated calendrical dates.

## Settlement Patterns, Sea Level, and Climate

Using the median dates calculated by CALIB 6.01 we have grouped the data from our sample of 11 sites in figure 5.2. The frequency distribution is bimodal, with a concentration of dates between AD 1 and AD 600 and another between AD 800 and AD 1400. These two peaks in the frequency distribution correspond respectively with the Wulfert and La Costa sea level highs posited by Stapor et al. (1991) and are consistent with sea-level proxy data from barrier islands in northwest Florida (Tanner 1991, 1992) and archaeological sites in southwest Florida (Walker et al. 1994, 1995). Walker (2013) relates these periods of higher sea level with presumed

Table 5.1. Radiocarbon dates from the Tampa Bay area

| Site # | Site Name | Lab ID | Conventional [14]C Age | Calibrated Age BP (2σ) | Calibrated Calendar Date (2σ) | Reference |
|---|---|---|---|---|---|---|
| 8HI2398 | Bay Cadillac | Beta-26741[a] | 560±60 | 511–655 | AD 1295–1439 | Austin et al. 1992 |
| 8HI2398 | Bay Cadillac | Beta-26740[a] | 1350±110 | 1002–1516 | AD 434–948 | Austin et al. 1992 |
| 8MA7 | Shaw's Point | Beta-103932[b] | 1790±70 | 1212–1515 | AD 435–738 | Schwadron 2000, 2002 |
| 8MA7 | Shaw's Point | Beta-103934[b] | 2200±70 | 1613–1979 | 30 BC–AD 337 | Schwadron 2000, 2002 |
| 8MA7 | Shaw's Point | Beta-103935[a] | 1560±50 | 1346–1546 | AD 404–604 | Schwadron 2000, 2002 |
| 8MA7 | Shaw's Point | Beta-103936[b] | 1630±60 | 1046–1306 | AD 644–904 | Schwadron 2000, 2002 |
| 8MA7 | Shaw's Point | Beta-103937[a] | 1610±70 | 1353–1692 | AD 258–597 | Schwadron 2000, 2002 |
| 8MA7 | Shaw's Point | Beta-103938[b] | 1100±60 | 541–779 | AD 1171–1409 | Schwadron 2000, 2002 |
| 8MA7 | Shaw's Point | Beta-103939[b] | 1220±60 | 661–900 | AD 1050–1289 | Schwadron 2000, 2002 |
| 8MA7 | Shaw's Point | Beta-103940[b] | 1710±60 | 1131–1395 | AD 555–819 | Schwadron 2000, 2002 |
| 8MA7 | Shaw's Point | Beta-103941[b] | 2210±60 | 1655–1978 | 29 BC–AD 295 | Schwadron 2000, 2002 |
| 8MA7 | Shaw's Point | Beta-103942[b] | 2210±60 | 1655–1978 | 29 BC–AD 295 | Schwadron 2000, 2002 |
| 8MA7 | Shaw's Point | Beta-103943[b] | 2040±60 | 1458–1794 | AD 156–492 | Schwadron 2000, 2002 |
| 8MA7 | Shaw's Point | Beta-103944[b] | 2320±70 | 1764–2134 | 185 BC–AD 186 | Schwadron 2000, 2002 |
| 8MA7 | Shaw's Point | Beta-103945[b] | 2190±70 | 1602–1969 | 20 BC–AD 348 | Schwadron 2000, 2002 |
| 8MA7 | Shaw's Point | Beta-103946[b] | 2360±60 | 1825–2149 | 200 BC–AD 125 | Schwadron 2000, 2002 |
| 8MA7 | Shaw's Point | Beta-103947[b] | 2510±60 | 2012–2324 | 375–63 BC | Schwadron 2000, 2002 |
| 8MA7 | Shaw's Point | Beta-103948[b] | 1930±70 | 1325–1671 | AD 279–625 | Schwadron 2000, 2002 |
| 8MA7 | Shaw's Point | Beta-103949[b] | 2110±60 | 1538–1852 | AD 98–412 | Schwadron 2000, 2002 |
| 8MA7 | Shaw's Point | Beta-103950[b] | 2260±70 | 1691–2060 | 111 BC–AD 259 | Schwadron 2000, 2002 |
| 8MA7 | Shaw's Point | Beta-103951[b] | 2260±60 | 1707–2033 | 84 BC–AD 243 | Schwadron 2000, 2002 |
| 8MA13 | Harbor Key | Beta-159347[a] | 1790±40 | 1575–1823 | AD 127–375 | Wheeler 2002 |
| 8MA13 | Harbor Key | Beta-159349[a] | 1940±40 | 1815–1993 | 44 BC–AD 135 | Wheeler 2002 |
| 8MA13 | Harbor Key | Beta-159348[a] | 1990±40 | 1831–2014 | 93 BC–AD 86 | Wheeler 2002 |
| 8MA13 | Harbor Key | Beta-159350[a] | 2060±40 | 1926–2133 | 184 BC–AD 24 | Wheeler 2002 |
| 8PI1 | Weeden Island | n/a[a] | 1453±40 | 1298–1400 | AD 550–652 | Lambert 2006 |

| 8Pl1 | Weeden Island | M-1598[a] | 1550±130 | 1183–1775 | AD 175–767 | Sears 1971 |
|------|---------------|-----------|----------|-----------|------------|------------|
| 8Pl31 | Maximo Beach | UM-143[a] | 976±70 | 735–1051 | AD 899–1215 | Williams 1979 |
| 8Pl41 | Bayshore Homes | Beta-243014 | 890±40 | 731–915 | AD 1035–1219 | Austin et al. 2008 |
| 8Pl41 | Bayshore Homes | Beta-244142[a] | 850±40 | 684–904 | AD 1046–1266 | Austin et al. 2008 |
| 8Pl41 | Bayshore Homes | Beta-243013[c] | 890±40 | 731–915 | AD 1035–1219 | Austin et al. 2008 |
| 8Pl41 | Bayshore Homes | Beta-244143[a] | 950±40 | 771–934 | AD 1016–1179 | Austin et al. 2008 |
| 8Pl41 | Bayshore Homes | Beta-244144[a] | 910±40 | 740–918 | AD 1032–1210 | Austin et al. 2008 |
| 8Pl41 | Bayshore Homes | Beta-243012[c] | 1080±40 | 929–1061 | AD 889–1021 | Austin et al. 2008 |
| 8Pl41 | Bayshore Homes | Beta-244141[a] | 1200±40 | 1002–1261 | AD 689–948 | Austin et al. 2008 |
| 8Pl41 | Bayshore Homes | Beta-297991[c] | 1560±30 | 1385–1526 | AD 424–565 | This study |
| 8Pl41 | Bayshore Homes | Beta-244145[a] | 1650±40 | 1416–1690 | AD 260–534 | Austin et al. 2008 |
| 8Pl41 | Bayshore Homes | Beta-243011[c] | 1730±40 | 1538–1736 | AD 224–412 | Austin et al. 2008 |
| 8Pl41 | Bayshore Homes | Beta-243015[c] | 1750±40 | 1553–1810 | AD 140–397 | Austin et al. 2008 |
| 8Pl41 | Bayshore Homes | Beta-297990[a] | 1730±30 | 1560–1710 | AD 240–390 | This study |
| 8Pl41 | Bayshore Homes | AA75729[b] | 2071±35 | 1534–1769 | AD 181–416 | Dietler, personal communication 2008 |
| 8Pl54 | Anderson | Beta-106638[b] | 790±60 | 297–517 | AD 1433–1653 | Tykot 1998 |
| 8Pl54 | Anderson | Beta-106639[b] | 880±60 | 396–627 | AD 1323–1554 | Tykot 1998 |
| 8Pl54 | Anderson | Beta-106640[a] | 690±50 | 553–722 | AD 1228–1397 | Tykot 1998 |
| 8Pl54 | Anderson | Beta-106641[b] | 880±70 | 363–635 | AD 1315–1587 | Tykot 1998 |
| 8Pl54 | Anderson | Beta-106642[b] | 800±70 | 289–536 | AD 1414–1661 | Tykot 1998 |
| 8Pl54 | Anderson | Beta-106643[a] | 540±50 | 505–650 | AD 1300–1445 | Tykot 1998 |
| 8Pl54 | Anderson | Beta-106644[b] | 1330±70 | 720–1039 | AD 911–1230 | Tykot 1998 |
| 8Pl54 | Anderson | Beta-109274[b] | 1180±70 | 625–897 | AD 1053–1325 | Tykot 1998 |
| 8Pl54 | Anderson | Beta-109275[b] | 890±60 | 412–630 | AD 1320–1538 | Tykot 1998 |
| 8Pl54 | Anderson | Beta-121300[b] | 1010±70 | 490–703 | AD 1247–1460 | Tykot 1998 |
| 8Pl54 | Anderson | Beta-121301[b] | 1070±70 | 516–764 | AD 1186–1434 | Tykot 1998 |
| 8Pl1753 | Yat Kitischee | Beta-81073[b] | 1260±70 | 667–942 | AD 1008–1283 | Austin and Woods 1995 |

(continued)

(*Continued*)

| Site # | Site Name | Lab ID | Conventional $^{14}C$ Age | Calibrated Age BP (2σ) | Calibrated Calendar Date (2σ) | Reference |
|---|---|---|---|---|---|---|
| 8PI1753 | Yat Kitischee | Beta-81074[b] | 1290±50 | 715–944 | AD 1006–1235 | Austin and Woods 1995 |
| 8PI1753 | Yat Kitischee | Beta-53533[b] | 1250±60 | 675–918 | AD 1032–1275 | Austin and Woods 1995 |
| 8PI1753 | Yat Kitischee | Beta-53534[b] | 1340±50 | 751–1010 | AD 940–1199 | Austin and Woods 1995 |
| 8PI1753 | Yat Kitischee | Beta-76963[a] | 1040±50 | 798–1062 | AD 888–1152 | Austin and Woods 1995 |
| 8PI1753 | Yat Kitischee | Beta-53535[b] | 1520±60 | 928–1225 | AD 725–1012 | Austin and Woods 1995 |
| 8PI1753 | Yat Kitischee | Beta-76969[a] | 1160±40 | 971–1175 | AD 775–979 | Austin and Woods 1995 |
| 8PI1753 | Yat Kitischee | Beta-53536[b] | 1850±60 | 1277–1536 | AD 414–673 | Austin and Woods 1995 |
| 8PI1753 | Yat Kitischee | Beta-76967[a] | 1720±70 | 1419–1820 | AD 130–531 | Austin and Woods 1995 |
| 8PI1753 | Yat Kitischee | Beta-76965[a] | 1750±110 | 1408–1918 | AD 32–542 | Austin and Woods 1995 |
| 8PI1753 | Yat Kitischee | Beta-76966[a] | 1770±90 | 1421–1915 | AD 35–529 | Austin and Woods 1995 |
| 8PI1753 | Yat Kitischee | Beta-76968[a] | 1820±120 | 1533–2112 | 163 BC–AD 417 | Austin and Woods 1995 |
| 8PI1753 | Yat Kitischee | Beta-76964[a] | 1960±70 | 1729–2107 | 158 BC–AD 221 | Austin and Woods 1995 |
| 8PI1753 | Yat Kitischee | Beta-76962[a] | 2020±130 | 1708–2326 | 377 BC–AD 242 | Austin and Woods 1995 |
| 8PI10650 | Kuttler | Beta-155218[a] | 740±50 | 563–764 | AD 1186–1387 | Austin et al. 2008 |
| 8PI10650 | Kuttler | Beta-153922[a] | 900±60 | 699–927 | AD 1023–1251 | Austin et al. 2008 |
| 8PI10650 | Kuttler | Beta-153925[a] | 1030±40 | 800–1050 | AD 895–1150 | Austin et al. 2008 |
| 8PI11569 | Shoreline Midden | Beta-241386[a] | 1560±40 | 1360–1535 | AD 415–590 | Kolianos and Estabrook 2010 |
| 8PI11624 | Shoreline Canoe | Beta-241373[d] | 1090±50 | 924–1167 | AD 783–1026 | Kolianos and Estabrook 2010 |
| 8PI11624 | Shoreline Canoe | Beta-241372[d] | 1160±60 | 956–1256 | AD 694–994 | Kolianos and Estabrook 2010 |

*Notes:* [a] Charcoal or charred wood
[b] Marine shell
[c] Soot from ceramic sherd
[d] Wood

widespread climatic events, the Roman Warm Period and the Medieval Warm Period, respectively. She also posits increased storm activity during these periods due to warmer sea surface temperatures (e.g., Keigwin 1996; Lund and Curry 2004; Lund et al. 2006) as well as evidence of storm overwash deposits on barrier islands in northwest and southwest Florida (Walker et al. 1994, 1995; see also Goodbred et al. 1998).

The 200-year interval that separates the two frequency peaks in figure 5.2 was a period of lower sea levels and cooler climate, the Buck Key Low and the Vandal Minimum climatic event, respectively (Stapor et al. 1991; Tanner 2000; Walker 2013; Wang et al. 2011). Although data on precipitation in peninsular Florida are lacking for this period, Walker (2013) indicates that there is no evidence for severe storms in southwest Florida during this time.

The effects of these events on coastal settlement patterns appear to have been variable depending on local conditions. For example, at Bayshore Homes and the associated Kuttler Mound, the radiocarbon dates suggest occupation during the Wulfert and La Costa High Stands with an apparent abandonment during the intervening Buck Key Low Stand. The sites are located on Boca Ciega Bay, a shallow estuary protected from the open gulf by a series of barrier islands. Prior to dredging of the Intracoastal Waterway, the average water depth of the estuary was about 4 feet, or 1.2 meters (Hutton et al. 1956, 12; Office of Coast Survey 1879). A drop in sea level of

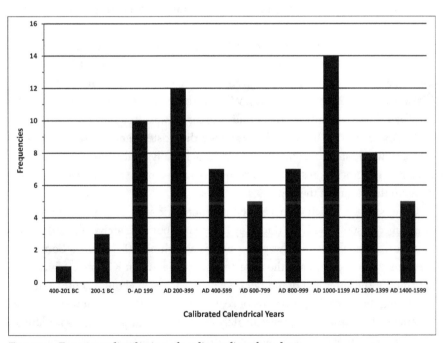

Figure 5.2. Frequency distribution of median radiocarbon dates.

one meter, which Stapor et al. (1991) have estimated to have occurred around AD 450, in combination with the drier Vandal climate, would have dramatically altered the marine ecology of Boca Ciega Bay, affecting the fish and shellfish resources on which the inhabitants of Bayshore Homes relied for subsistence. Today the barrier islands are breached by several passes, including John's Pass located directly across the bay from Bayshore Homes. However, John's Pass was created by a hurricane in 1848 (Becker 1999) and did not exist prior to this time; this eliminates the possibility that gulf waters entered the bay at this location before 1848. Occupation at Bayshore Homes resumed at around AD 950 and continued until about AD 1250, a period that corresponds with the La Costa High Stand and the Medieval Warm Period (Hughes and Diaz 1994; Lamb 1995, 155–69; Richey et al. 2007) and a likely reflooding of the estuary.

At the Anderson site, located about one mile south of Bayshore Homes, occupation began around AD 1000 and continued through the mid-sixteenth century AD. This occupation spans both the Medieval Warm Period and the following period of cool weather known as the Little Ice Age (Lamb 1995, 192–221). The archaeological record does not indicate any reduction in site activities during this period of cooler climate and lower sea levels, and this large mound complex apparently continued to thrive. It may be that the effect of lowered sea levels on local conditions was not as severe as during previous low stands. Alternatively, political mechanisms may have been in place to ameliorate any reduction in marine productivity, or perhaps the location on the landscape was important for social, religious, or political reasons.

Another possible explanation for settlement continuity at the Anderson site is territorial circumscription. Located about 12 kilometers southeast of the Anderson site at the mouth of Boca Ciega Bay is another large Safety Harbor mound complex, Maximo Point (8PI19 on figure 5.1). While we have no radiocarbon dates from this site, the ceramic assemblage there indicates that it was occupied at the same time as the Anderson site. If that is the case, then the existence of two large polities in such a relatively small area may have made it politically difficult for the people who inhabited the Anderson site to move southward to a more advantageous location closer to the mouth of the bay.

Other sites for which we have good chronometric data display gaps in occupation that correspond with the Buck Key Low Stand, but their archaeological records indicate that people did not always respond by abandoning their homes. Sometimes they simply moved closer to the retreating shoreline. At Yat Kitischee, a hiatus occurs during the latter half of the Buck Key Low, between about AD 600 and 800; but during the preceding 200 years or so, the portion of the site that was excavated experienced deposition of predominately food refuse and potsherds with little or no accumulation of sand or organic detritus and no structural features, suggesting a relatively rapid deposition of secondary refuse in an area that both previously and subsequently was occupied by small residences and was marked by dark, organic midden deposits.

Yat Kitischee is on the edge of the upland-mangrove forest transition, located along the open waters of Old Tampa Bay. A lowering of sea level by one meter would have moved the shoreline farther away, but it would not have dramatically altered the local ecology. It is possible that people simply moved their residences closer to the shoreline. The nearby Shoreline Midden (8PI11569) has produced a single radiocarbon date of cal AD 415–590, squarely within the Buck Key Low Stand, and the Shoreline Canoe (8PI11624) produced two radiocarbon dates that span the period of about AD 700–1000, at the tail end of this low stand. Both are located several hundred meters east of Yat Kitischee on the edge of a mangrove forest facing Old Tampa Bay, suggesting the location was chosen to follow retreating bay waters.

At Shaw's Point at the mouth of the Manatee River on the south side of Tampa Bay, radiocarbon dating of a series of shell midden ridges has been interpreted as reflecting a similar adjustment to sea levels through time: occupation moved shoreward during periods of low stands and landward during periods of high stands (Schwadron 2000, 2002).

These data suggest that the estuarine shoreline of Tampa Bay was not a uniform area of habitation but instead presented a host of different micro-environmental conditions that affected how people lived and how they responded to climate and sea level changes. In some locations the effects were dramatic, in others less so.

Dates from other sites in our study area (e.g., Weeden Island, Maximo Beach, Bay Cadillac, Harbor Key) are more difficult to interpret. While they seem to suggest occupation during both high and low sea-level stands, the number of dates from any one site is small, ranging from two to four, so it is difficult to arrive at any firm conclusions even when the dates are viewed in the aggregate. Perhaps the main conclusion that can be drawn here is the obvious one that the more dates from a site the better when attempting to derive temporal patterns of occupation and landscape use.

## Ceramic Chronology

Turning next to the Tampa Bay ceramic chronology, we used ceramic data from five sites in Pinellas County to arrive at the seriation shown in Figure 5.3: Anderson, Bayshore Homes, Kuttler, Yat Kitischee, and Weeden Island. Several temporal patterns are obvious. The dominance of sand-tempered plain up to around AD 400 is consistent with Luer and Almy's data related to the identification of Manasota. After this time, there is an increase in the number of auxiliary types, including St. Johns and Wakulla Check Stamped, Belle Glade Plain, and grog-tempered plain, as well as a small but significant amount of Weeden Island decorated wares. These include Ruskin Dentate Stamped, Carrabelle Punctate, Weeden Island Incised, Hillsborough Shell Stamped, West Florida Cord Marked, Swift Creek Complicated Stamped, and Pasco Complicated Stamped. While some of these ceramics might have been made locally, others were likely obtained from Weeden Island–related groups to the north, as were some of the ornately decorated Weeden Island ceramics in the burial mound at Weeden Island and in Mound C at Bayshore Homes.

What is surprising is that Weeden Island ceramics last until at least AD 1000 and perhaps as late as AD 1200 at Bayshore Homes and Yat Kitischee. Pinellas Plain, which is the dominant utilitarian pottery at the Safety Harbor–period Anderson site, appears to have a longer time depth than was previously believed, appearing as early as AD 200–300 at Bayshore Homes and Yat Kitischee.

The Anderson site is the sole representative of the latest portion of the sequence. The ceramic data there indicate that after about AD 1200, Weeden Island decorated wares were replaced by decorated Safety Harbor pottery, including Pinellas Incised and Safety Harbor Incised, as well as the Fort Walton–related Point Washington Incised. European ceramics, such as Early Style Spanish olive jars, El Morro ware, and unglazed coarse earthenwares, were introduced during the mid-sixteenth century. Because these ceramic data are from a single site, the abrupt change in the seriation to predominately Pinellas Plain may not be completely representative of the transition to Safety Harbor. On the other hand, ceramic data from Maximo Point (8PI19) to the south and the Safety Harbor site (8PI2) at the northern end of Tampa Bay, although undated, show a similar predominance of Pinellas Plain (approximately 90 percent) throughout their excavated strata (Bushnell 1962; Griffin and Bullen 1950; Sears 1958).

One of the issues that has puzzled us (and is emphasized by this seriation) is the absence of any indication of an Englewood presence in midden deposits that date to the period AD 900–1100, the period of time proposed by Mitchem (1989, 557–61 and errata sheet) as incorporating the Englewood phase of Safety Harbor. There is no Englewood Incised or Sarasota Incised pottery, the two ceramic types diagnostic of the Englewood phase. One hypothesis is that middens dating to the Englewood phase might be represented by just the type of ceramic assemblage that is present in post-AD 900 contexts at Bayshore Homes—undecorated plain wares accompanied by small amounts of decorated Weeden Island pottery—but they have not been so identified because of an absence of Englewood series ceramics. In order to test this, we tabulated ceramic data from dated middens in the larger Safety Harbor region and compared them to ceramic data from burial mounds that contain Englewood ceramics (table 5.2).

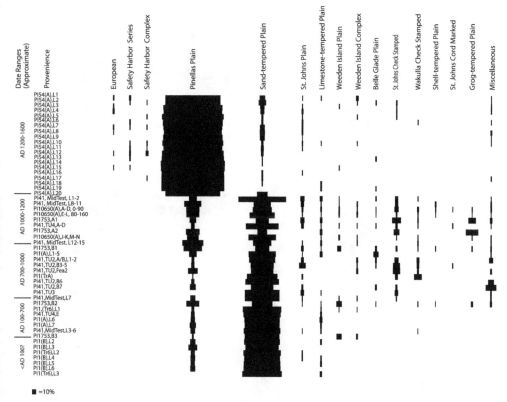

Figure 5.3. Temporal seriation of ceramics from selected sites. Following Willey (1949, 6), a ceramic *series* is one that groups together a number of types that share similar pastes and tempers. A ceramic *complex* includes types that occur together in geographic space during a specific period of time.

Middens in the Central Peninsular Gulf Coast region that have been radiocarbon dated to the Englewood phase typically fail to contain any of the diagnostic Englewood ceramic types and instead contain primarily sand-tempered plain, Pinellas Plain, and small amounts of St. Johns Plain, St. Johns Check Stamped, and occasionally Weeden Island and/or Safety Harbor decorated types. Exceptions to this pattern typically occur at sites located in Sarasota County near the southern end of the region. Ceramics collected from the surface of the Osprey site (8SO2) by Aleš Hrdlička reportedly include a mix of Weeden Island and Safety Harbor types along with a single sherd of Englewood Incised and three sherds of what Willey (1949, 474) called Englewood Plain but which in reality is simply a fine sand-tempered plain. Ripley Bullen's excavations at the Sarasota County Mound (8SO23) recovered two sherds of Englewood Incised and one sherd of Sarasota Incised, along with Weeden Island–related types such as Carrabelle Incised and Dunns Creek Red

Table 5.2. Comparison of ceramic assemblages from selected Englewood period burial mounds and middens

| Site # | Site Name | Englewood Period Dates[a] | STP | PP | WI | ENG | SH | FW | References |
|---|---|---|---|---|---|---|---|---|---|
| **BURIAL MOUNDS** | | | | | | | | | |
| 8CH68 | Aqui Esta | AD 677–921, AD 769–1062, AD 899–1192 | X | X | X | X | X | X | Luer 2002b |
| 8CH75 | Wrecked Site | No dates | | | | | | | Luer 1985 |
| 8CI203 | Tatham Mound, precontact stratum | AD 674–994, 694–997, 923–1213[b] | X | | | X | X | | Mitchem 1989 |
| 8DE2 | Keen | AD 1029–1259 | | | | X | | | Willis and Johnson 1980 |
| 8MA30 | Pillsbury | No dates | X | | X | X | X | | Mitchem 1989 |
| 8MA44 | Ellenton | No dates | | | X | X | X | X | Mitchem 1989 |
| 8MA83C | Prine | No dates | X | | X | X | X | X | Bullen 1951 |
| 8PA2 | Pithlochascootie River Mound | No dates | | | X | X | X | | Willey 1949 |
| 8PI1 | Weeden Island | No dates | X | X | X | X | X | | Willey 1949 |
| 8PI51 | Tierra Verde | No dates | X | X | X | X | X | X | Sears 1967 |
| 8PO46 | Philip Mound | No dates | | | X | X | X | | Benson 1967; Karklins 1974 |
| 8SO1 | Englewood | No dates | X | | X | X | X | | Willey 1949 |
| 8SO17 | Casey Key | No dates | | | X | X | X | | Bullen and Bullen 1976 |
| 8SO2A | Palmer | AD 667–1120 | X | X[c] | X | X | X | | Bullen and Bullen 1976 |
| 8SO44 | Sarasota Bay Mound | No dates | X | X | X | X | X | | Cordell 2005 |
| 8SO397 | Myakahatchee | No dates | X | | X | X | X | | Luer et al. 1987 |
| **MIDDENS** | | | | | | | | | |
| 8PI5 | Clearwater | No dates | X | X | X | X | X | | Willey 1949 |
| 8PI55 | Canton Street | No dates | X | X | | X[d] | | | Bullen et al. 1978 |
| 8SO2 | Osprey | No dates | X | X | X | | X | | Willey 1949 |
| 8SO23 | Sarasota County Mound | No dates | X | | X | X | | | Bullen 1971 |
| 8SO35 | Boylston | AD 884–1217; AD 1037–1299 | X | X | X | X | | | Luer 1992 |
| 8CH10 | Big Mound Key, West Mound | 16 dates: AD 687–938 thru AD 1050–1289 | X | X | X | | | | Luer 2007 |

| Site | Context | Radiocarbon dates | Ceramics / notes | Reference |
|---|---|---|---|---|
| 8CH17 | Hollenbeck Key | AD 1038–1280, AD 1041–1243, AD 1048–1252, AD 1160–1406 | X | Porter and Glowacki 2008 |
| 8CI97 | Bayonet Field | AD 774–1205; AD 895–1172 | "mixed Weeden Island-related and Safety Harbor" | Mitchem 1985, 1989 |
| 8MA7 | Shaw's Point, Ridge 3 | AD 1050–1289; AD 1171–1409 | X   X | Schwadron 2000, 2002 |
| 8PI31 | Maximo Beach, SQ9, 72 cm | AD 899–1215 | X[e]   X[e] | Williams 1979 |
| 8PI41 | Bayshore Homes, midden test, L 12–15 | AD 889–1021 | X   X | Austin et al. 2008; Sears 1960 |
| 8PI41 | Bayshore Homes, TU4, Str. A–D | AD 1032–1210, AD 1016–1179 | X   X | Austin et al. 2008 |
| 8PI41 | Bayshore Homes, midden test, L8–11 | AD 1035–1219 | X   X | Austin et al. 2008; Sears 1960 |
| 8PI54 | Anderson, TUB, L 16 | AD 911–1230 | No ceramics from this dated level. No Englewood ceramics from TUs A or B or from Bushnell's 1966 test | Bushnell 1966; Mitchem 1998 |
| 8PI10650 | Kuttler | AD 895–1150, AD 1023–1251, AD 1186–1387 | X X   X X | Austin et al. 2008 |
| 8PI1753 | Yat Kitischee, Zone A | AD 940–1199; AD 1032–1275 | X   X | Austin 1992 |
| 8PI1753 | Yat Kitischee, Zone B1 | AD 775–979; AD 725–1012 | X   X | Austin and Woods 1995; White 1995 |
| 8SO2 | Palmer, Test F, 66–72 in | AD 813–1263 | X   X | Bullen and Bullen 1976 |
| 8SO2 | Palmer, Shell Ridge, profile cleaning, 39–50 cm, 130 cm, 195 cm | AD 1016–1267, AD 948–1230, AD 948–1230 | X[f] | Bullen and Bullen 1976; Marquardt, personal communication 2012 |
| 8SO51 | Old Oak, "deeply buried lens" | AD 1016–1267 | X | Luer 1977, 2005 |
| 8SO608 | Catfish Creek | AD 997–1255 | X   X[g] | Austin and Russo 1989 |

*Notes:* KEY: STP=sand-tempered plain; PP=Pinellas Plain; WI=Weeden Island Series; ENG=Englewood Series; SH=Safety Harbor Series; FW=Fort Walton Series

[a] Calibrated, 2 σ range

[b] Sherds from three Englewood Incised and four Sarasota Incised vessels were recovered "from all strata" in the mound (Mitchem 1989, 356) and are presumed to have been curated. However, several sherds of both ceramic types were recovered from precontact strata, including all but three of the Sarasota Incised sherds. The Englewood dates are from the mound's precontact stratum.

[c] Identified as plain, contorted paste by Bullen.

[d] One Englewood Incised sherd in Level 6, considered to be out of context. Site is primarily Transitional period.

[e] No ceramics in dated level, all are from upper levels. No Englewood ceramics recovered in any of Williams's excavation or in Austin's (1988) test.

[f] Radiocarbon dates are from the 1991 cleaning of the midden profile in preparation for a "Window to the Past" exhibit. Bullen recovered only plain ceramics and no Englewood ceramics in his four tests in the Shell Ridge, and no Englewood series sherds were recovered during the profile cleaning (George Luer, personal communication 2012).

[g] Includes one "possible" Weeden Island Plain sherd.

(Bullen 1971, 7–11). At the Boylston Mound (8SO35), a rim sherd of Sarasota Incised was recovered from a shovel test in the midden (Luer 1992, 266). Outside
Sarasota County, only the Clearwater (8PI5) and Canton Street (8PI55) sites in
Pinellas County are reported to have Englewood ceramics. A single sherd of Englewood Incised was collected from the surface of 8PI5 by S. T. Walker and identified
by Willey (1949, 332), and Bullen et al. (1978, table 1) report a sherd of Englewood
Incised from a disturbed context at 8PI55.

This small collection of Englewood series sherds from midden sites is contrasted
with the occurrence of Englewood series vessels, broken and whole, in burial
mounds. At least 16 of these are known, distributed from as far north as Citrus
County to as far south as Charlotte County and inland to Polk and DeSoto counties.

Willey's original definition of Englewood emphasized the presumed transitional
nature of the ceramic assemblage; he assumed that it was intermediate between late
Weeden Island and early Safety Harbor (1949, 471). The middens datable to the
Englewood phase contain what we would expect for a period of transition between
two archaeologically visible components: a mixture of the preceding Weeden Island and the subsequent Safety Harbor ceramics (see table 5.2). The burial mounds
also reflect this transition, with the addition of Englewood Incised and Sarasota
Incised vessels. It appears, then, that Englewood represents a mortuary phenomenon similar to Weeden Island in the Tampa Bay area and that middens dating to
the Englewood phase contain little in the way of Englewood-style pottery because
it was made to be used in a mortuary context, not a secular one (Luer 1985, 239; see
also Luer this volume). Here it should be mentioned that Mitchem (1989, 257–95)
describes several middens and burial mounds that contain Englewood ceramics on
the southwest Gulf coast south of Charlotte County. This is within the Caloosahatchee archaeological region and is probably the result of interaction with Safety
Harbor groups to the north of Charlotte Harbor.[1]

Several archaeologists have offered hypotheses about what Englewood represents and where it came from. In a 1948 paper, Willey noted the Mississippian
influences evident in both Englewood and Safety Harbor pottery types. When he
published his formal definitions in 1949, he made no mention of Mississippian
influence in his Englewood period, but he did stress its importance in his Safety
Harbor period. William Sears (1967, 69–70) saw similarities in designs and vessels among Englewood, Safety Harbor, and Caddoan pottery. George Luer (2002a,
105–6; 2002b, 157, 170; this volume) has suggested influences from Fort Walton
cultures in northwest Florida and the Rood phase of west-central Georgia.

In our view, it appears likely that the Mississippian influences in Safety Harbor
pottery, including the Englewood Series, probably originated from western Georgia and eastern Alabama, with some Fort Walton influence thrown in for good
measure. The Safety Harbor culture (at least in terms of pottery) appears to have

resulted from broad Rood phase, Fort Walton, and possible Lamar influences on a local Manasota/Weeden Island–related template. That the most common central and lower Mississippi Valley pottery types are not found in the Safety Harbor area argues against any sustained direct interaction between the Mississippi Valley and the Safety Harbor region during Mississippian times, which suggests that the Mississippian traits observed in Safety Harbor pottery are from the early to middle Mississippi period (AD 1000–1350) rather than the late Mississippi period (after AD 1350). Englewood would thus reflect initial Mississippian influences on the local Weeden Island–related Manasota culture (see Mitchem 2012 for an extended discussion).

## Site Formation

Radiocarbon dates from contexts that are out of place stratigraphically or are inconsistent with the associated artifacts often are discounted or ignored in archaeological analysis. Indeed, some within the current study were discarded and others that were included in our data set are explainable as a result of prehistoric mixing, old wood, or incorrect marine reservoir corrections for the Gulf of Mexico. There are 11 dates, however, that require closer examination as they can inform us of site formation processes.

Three dates from the upper levels of Sears's test in the Bayshore Homes midden (AA5729, Beta-243011, and Beta-243015) are approximately 600–800 years older than four dates obtained from the underlying midden deposits. Two of the three upper midden dates were obtained from soot on the exterior of ceramic sherds, and the third was obtained from a marine-shell (*Busycon sinistrum*) cutting-edge tool. All three dates are statistically similar and span a period of cal AD 140–416; the underlying midden dates to cal AD 889–1219. The upper and lower midden deposits are separated by a thin (2–3 cm) layer of white sand. Ceramics recovered from the two midden components are consistent with the radiocarbon dates. The upper midden is characterized by a predominantly sand-tempered plain assemblage, and the lower midden contains both sand-tempered plain and Pinellas Plain accompanied by a small number of Weeden Island decorated sherds (Mitchem 2008, 101–9; Sears 1960, 8–12).

The radiocarbon dates, the ceramic assemblages, and a soil analysis by John Foss (2008) all indicate that the upper midden was redeposited on top of the lower midden sometime around AD 1200. We have argued elsewhere (Austin 2008, 163–65; Austin and Mitchem 2008) that the upper midden represents an intentional redeposition event related to monumental mound construction or efforts to elevate structures and protect them from flooding during periods of higher sea level and/or increased storm activity.

Four radiocarbon samples from the Harbor Key Temple Mound (8MA13) were obtained from a vandal pit profile after cleaning. Within the 2.3-meter-deep profile, various shell lenses were identified; samples from the approximate top, middle, and base of the vandal pit profile range between 184 cal BC and cal AD 375. These dates are considered much too old for the mound, which is thought to date sometime after AD 1000 (Wheeler 2002, 4). Although the dates are not in stratigraphic order, they are internally consistent. They led Wheeler (2002, 4–5) to argue that the shell used to construct the mound might have been obtained from the shell ridge component of Harbor Key (8MA15), where limestone-tempered ceramics suggest a time frame of circa 300 BC.

The use of earlier midden deposits as construction fill provides an interesting comparison to interpretations of mound construction using so-called clean shell, particularly during the Late Archaic period (e.g., Russo 2004, 61–62; Randall and Sassaman 2005, 101; Schwadron 2010, 131). The accurate identification of "clean" shell deposits notwithstanding (cf. Marquardt 2010), there would appear to be differences in the visual and compositional characteristics of the fill material used during the Late Archaic and late Woodland–early Mississippian periods. If one accepts the interpretation that the Late Archaic mounded features were intentionally constructed, then the use of visually clean shell as fill may have served as visual or symbolic markers (Sassaman 2010, 72–78), while during the later, post-Archaic period, no such visual marking appears to have been intended, at least in the Tampa Bay region (see also Schober this volume).

The other group of incongruous dates that we wish to mention briefly consists of the three dates on human bone from Bayshore Homes and Safety Harbor. Although these were not included in our data set, they require some discussion because of a number of similarities: the presence of older dates in burial mounds containing much later archaeological deposits, sample material (human bone), and possible contamination of the bone material.

Stojanowski and Johnson (2011, 166) question the early date (cal AD 778–980) of skeletal material from the Safety Harbor burial mound but note that the later end of the 2-sigma range overlaps the presumed age of the mound (AD 900–1750), which is based on ceramics and European artifacts. They do not discuss the date further, nor do they describe the condition of the bone sample, which was obtained from the Aleš Hrdlička collection curated at the Smithsonian Institution. Uncertainty about the provenience of the dated bone within the mound and the absence of any comparative dates from the mound make it difficult to determine if the date reported by Stojanowski and Johnson is truly anomalous or in fact provides an accurate dating of at least some of the mound's interments.

More problematic are the Bayshore Homes dates. The assays on skeletal material from two individuals excavated by Sears from the site's large burial mound (Mound

B) are a minimum of 1,000 years earlier than the presumed age of the mound based on ceramic content. Both individuals were interred in what Sears (1960, 19) interpreted as a mass burial near the top of the mound.

A rib bone from Burial 29 returned a calibrated age of 3728–4065 BP, or 2116–1779 cal BC (Beta 282473), which is equivalent to the Late Archaic period in the Tampa Bay region. Since St. Johns Check Stamped ceramics are present throughout the Mound B fill, mound construction could not have occurred before about AD 750–800 (Luer and Almy 1980).[2] A second assay on the same rib bone returned a similar result: cal 3482–3717 BP, or 1768–1353 cal BC (Beta 280697). According to Beta Analytic, Inc., both bones were coated with an unknown substance, probably a preservative, and contained white to opaque-colored spheroids in the bone marrow cavities. Subsequent treatment (including grinding off the outer surface to get to a clean, unaltered surface) and solvent extraction removed all traces of these materials prior to analysis, and in the absence of significant site-wide contamination (of which there is no discernible evidence), the ages of both samples were considered to be accurate (Ron Hatfield, Beta Analytic, Inc., personal communication with Robert Austin, April 20, 2011).

A second rib bone from a different Mound B burial (Burial 37) was submitted to determine if the first date was an anomaly. This sample was similarly coated with an unknown substance and similarly treated. It returned a calibrated age of 2153–2337 BP, or 380–204 cal BC. This would place the burial within the early Manasota period: better, but still much older than anticipated.

There are three ways to interpret these early dates: they accurately date the time of interment; they represent the inclusion of ancestral remains in burial mounds that date much later than the time of death; or they represent contamination or laboratory error. The first explanation is hard to reconcile with the ceramic data from Mound B, as discussed above. The second explanation is feasible for the later of the two dates (Burial 37) but seems far-fetched for the older sample (Burial 29). Burials have been identified within and near the base of the site's midden component (Drwiega 2008). All of these appear to have been disturbed prehistorically, and one hypothesis is that early burials might have been encountered by later occupants of the site during the excavation of pits or other site maintenance activities. Some of these remains might have been interred in the burial mound or perhaps placed in a charnel house for later interment with burials contemporaneous with the site's later occupation. On the other hand, while the midden burials are undated, the site's earliest midden component has been dated to between cal AD 180 and 534, still several hundred years later than Burial 37 and two millennia later than Burial 29.

The third explanation continues to remain viable. For one thing, it seems strange that two independently selected samples that were spatially separated from one another would both produce early dates. Moreover, the presence of an unknown substance on and within the bones suggests that this substance may have contaminated the bones, despite the best efforts of the laboratory to remove it from the samples.

The contamination issue becomes more salient when radiocarbon data from Crystal River (8CI1) are considered. Pluckhahn et al. (2010) report two anomalously early dates on human bone from two different contexts at Crystal River, Mound G (cal 800–420 BC) and Mound C (cal 780–420 BC). They discuss the contamination issue but conclude that the dates are acceptable and that they reflect interments during the Early Woodland period rather than the Middle Woodland period, which is indicated for Mound G by the ceramic assemblage (which includes St. Johns Check Stamped).

The skeletal collections were excavated during the late 1950s (Bayshore Homes) and early 1960s (Crystal River), were processed and have been stored at the Florida Museum of Natural History in Gainesville, and have been used in subsequent research or in classrooms. This could have caused mixing of bones from these sites with bones from other Florida skeletal collections (Pluckhahn et al. 2010, 166; Donna Ruhl, North Florida Collections Manager, Florida Museum of Natural History, personal communication with Robert Austin, 2010). Additional dating of Mound B skeletal material (perhaps using dental remains that may not have been treated with preservative) may be the only way to resolve this question.

## Conclusion

Our primary goal in this chapter has been to integrate the large number of radiocarbon dates that have been obtained over the past two decades with associated ceramic data to provide a temporal baseline for considering the interplay between culture and nature in the Tampa Bay region. It is most desirable that such studies result from a coherent and systematic research design, a circumstance rarely achieved in studies of complex urbanized estuaries like Tampa Bay. In our study we have reached back to the known archaeological record of a specific time period, the late prehistoric (500 BC–AD 1500), and have attempted what is at best a first pass in bringing cultural developments and climatic events into the same frame of reference.

As is often the case in research that seeks correlations, our efforts have resulted in new and unanticipated questions. We must now account for the unexpectedly early appearance of Pinellas Plain pottery, for example, which begins with minor frequencies at certain sites for several hundred years before becoming the dominant pottery at others. The nature and timing of the shift from Weeden Island to Safety Harbor also loom as major issues that require additional research. The continued use of Weeden Island decorated pottery well beyond the presumed end date of the

Weeden Island period at ca. AD 900 in conjunction with a sparse and irregular distribution of Englewood ceramics suggests that the arrival and acceptance of Mississippian elements may have occurred in a few concentrated areas, then spread out once they became fully developed. We also have identified issues related to site formation, monument construction, and landscape use that can be addressed profitably only from a firm chronological foundation.

In anthropological terms, we expect that shifting trends in social organization (division of labor, marriage practices, kinship organization) will be reflected in changes in pottery types and frequencies. But even as our understanding of these relationships becomes more precise, we now find larger and more significant explanations of prehistoric cultural dynamics in Tampa Bay to be unsatisfactory if they do not give a role to climatic factors. We know that human occupation of the Tampa Bay region predates the emergence of the Tampa Bay estuary that exists today. The economic focus of these first inhabitants was most probably not estuarine, although coastal and aquatic foods were likely important. As the estuary began to develop under Holocene conditions, human populations readily adapted to the biologically rich environment. Once committed to a way of life based on fishing, collecting shellfish, turtling, hunting, and gathering wild plant foods, humans found themselves embedded in a deceptively fragile web of connections tying them to the natural world. Human systems merge with natural systems and share causes and effects. Shallow water estuaries might appear to the modern eye to be relatively stable and benign features of the natural landscape, but archaeology tells us that over longer spans of time they can change in ways that have consequence for human life. That larger story is the one we eventually hope to tell.

## Acknowledgments

We wish to thank Neill Wallis and Asa Randall for asking us to participate in the 2011 Southeastern Archaeological Conference symposium that formed the basis for this book. We also wish to extend our appreciation to George Luer, Bill Marquardt, Karen Walker, Chris Rodning, and an anonymous reviewer, who read early versions of this chapter and provided valuable comments and suggestions. Curtis Diely prepared the map in Figure 5.1.

## Notes

1. Just before publication, we became aware of a Sarasota Incised beaker in a private collection that reportedly was excavated from a burial mound (Mound C) at Bayshore Homes (8PI41). This artifact is diagnostic of the Englewood phase of Safety Harbor and obliges us to reconsider our suggestion that Englewood may have been less prevalent in the Tampa Bay region than it was farther

south. However, it does not alter (and indeed it strengthens) our opinion that Englewood is a mortuary complex and therefore is difficult to identify in habitation middens.

2. Based on excavation data from several sites in the Miami area, Carr (2006, 142–51) has argued that St. Johns Check Stamped pottery may date as early as the Deptford or St. Johns I periods, or ca. 500 BC to AD 100. Of particular interest is a check-stamped sherd with a tetrapodal foot from the Brickell Point midden (Carr 2006, 151), possibly representing a copy of Deptford Check Stamped on chalky St. Johns paste (see Milanich 1994, 247). However, there is no evidence for St. Johns Check Stamped pottery in midden deposits dating earlier than AD 750–800 at Bayshore Homes or elsewhere in the Tampa Bay region.

# References

Austin, Robert J.

1988    Maximo Park Improvement Plan, Phase I: Archaeological Monitoring and Limited Testing at the Maximo Beach Site (8PI31), Pinellas County, Florida. Report prepared for the City of St. Petersburg, Florida, by Piper Archaeological Research, Inc. On file, Florida Division of Historical Resources, Tallahassee.

1992    Phase II Archaeological Testing at the Moog Midden Site (8PI1753), Pinellas County, Florida. Report prepared for the Pinellas County Board of County Commissioners by Janus Research/Piper Archaeology. On file, Florida Division of Historical Resources, Tallahassee.

2006    *Knife and Hammer: An Exercise in Positive Deconstruction. The I-75 Project and Lithic Scatter Research in Florida.* Florida Anthropological Society Publication no. 16. Florida Anthropological Society, Tallahassee.

Austin, Robert J. (compiler)

1995    Yat Kitischee: A Prehistoric Coastal Hamlet 100 B.C.–A.D. 1200. Report prepared for the Pinellas County Board of County Commissioners by Janus Research. On file, Florida Division of Historical Resources, Tallahassee.

Austin, Robert J., Kenneth W. Hardin, Harry M. Piper, and Jacquelyn G. Piper

1992    Archaeological Investigations at the Site of the Tampa Convention Center, Tampa, Florida. Vol. 1, Prehistoric Resources. Report prepared for the City of Tampa Public Works Department by Janus Research. On file, Florida Division of Historical Resources, Tallahassee.

Austin, Robert J., and Jeffrey M. Mitchem

2008    Site Formation and Chronology at Bayshore Homes: A Late Weeden Island Mound Complex on the Gulf Coast of Florida. Paper presented at the 65th annual meeting of the Southeastern Archaeological Conference, Charlotte, NC.

Austin, Robert J., Jeffrey M. Mitchem, Arlene Fradkin, John E. Foss, Shanna Drwiega, and Linda Allred

2008    Bayshore Homes Archaeological Survey and National Register Evaluation. Report prepared for the Bureau of Historic Preservation, Florida Division of Historical Resources by Central Gulf Coast Archaeological Society. On file, Florida Division of Historical Resources, Tallahassee.

Austin, Robert J., and Michael Russo

1989    Limited Excavations at the Catfish Creek Site (8SO608), Sarasota County, Florida. Report prepared for Palmer Venture, Inc. by Piper Archaeological Research, Inc. On file, Florida Division of Historical Resources, Tallahassee.

Austin, Robert J., and Alfred Woods

1995    Stratigraphy, Chronometric Dates and Site Formation. In Yat Kitischee: A Prehistoric Coastal Hamlet 100 B.C.–A.D. 1200, compiled by Robert J. Austin, 22–36. Report prepared for the Pinellas County Board of County Commissioners by Janus Research. On file, Florida Division of Historical Resources, Tallahassee.

Becker, Mary Ling

1999    Interaction of Tidal Inlets on a Microtidal Coast: A Study of Boca Ciega Bay, John's Pass, and Blind Pass. MS thesis, Department of Geology, University of South Florida, Tampa.

Benson, Carl A.

1967    The Philip Mound: An Historic Site. *Florida Anthropologist* 20: 118–32.

Brooks, Gregg R., and Larry J. Doyle

1998    Recent Sedimentary Development of Tampa Bay, Florida: A Microtidal Estuary Incised by Tertiary Platform Carbonates. *Estuaries* 21: 391–406.

Bullen, Ripley P.

1951    *The Terra Ceia Site, Manatee County, Florida.* Florida Anthropological Society Publications no. 3. University of Florida, Gainesville.

1971    The Sarasota County Mound, Englewood, Florida. *Florida Anthropologist* 24:1–30.

Bullen, Ripley P., Walter Askew, Lee M. Feder, and Richard L. McDonnell

1978    *The Canton Street Site, St. Petersburg, Florida.* Florida Anthropological Society Publications no. 9. Florida Anthropological Society, Gainesville.

Bullen, Ripley P., and Adelaide K. Bullen

1976    *The Palmer Site.* Florida Anthropological Society Publication no. 8. Florida Anthropological Society, Gainesville.

Burger, B. W.

1986    Salvage Excavations of the Bishop Harbor Archaeological Site Located in Section 31, Township 35 East, Range 18 East, Manatee County, Florida. Report on file, Florida Division of Historical Resources, Tallahassee.

Bushnell, Francis F.

1962    The Maximo Point Site. *Florida Anthropologist* 15: 89–101.

1966    A Preliminary Excavation of the Narvaez Midden, St. Petersburg, Florida. *Florida Anthropologist* 19: 115–24.

Carr, Robert S.

2006    Analysis of Ceramics from Brickell Point, 8DA12. *Florida Anthropologist* 59: 133–59.

Cordell, Ann S.

2005    Variability in the Sarasota Bay Mound (8SO44) Pottery Assemblage. *Florida Anthropologist* 58: 75–90.

Drwiega, Shanna

2008    Description of Human Skeletal Remains from Bayshore Homes. In Bayshore Homes Archaeological Survey and National Register Evaluation, 148–60. Report prepared for the Bureau of Historic Preservation, Florida Division of Historical Resources by Central Gulf Coast Archaeological Society. On file, Florida Division of Historical Resources, Tallahassee.

Estabrook, Richard W., and Christine Newman

1984    *Archaeological Investigations at the Marita and Ranch House Sites, Hillsborough County, Florida.* Archaeological Report no. 15. Department of Anthropology, University of South Florida, Tampa.

Foss, John E.

2008    Soil Morphology of Cores Retrieved from Bayshore Homes Archaeological Site. In Bayshore Homes Archaeological Survey and National Register Evaluation, 46–59. Report prepared for the Bureau of Historic Preservation, Florida Division of Historical Resources by Central Gulf Coast Archaeological Society. On file, Florida Division of Historical Resources, Tallahassee.

Goodbred, Steven L., Eric E. Wright, and Albert C. Hine

1998    Sea-Level Change and Storm-Surge Deposition in a Late Holocene Florida Salt Marsh. *Journal of Sedimentary Research* 68: 240–52.

Griffin, John W., and Ripley P. Bullen

1950    *The Safety Harbor Site, Pinellas County, Florida.* Florida Anthropological Society Publications no. 2. Florida Anthropological Society, Tallahassee.

Hughes, Malcolm K., and Henry F. Diaz

1994    Was There A "Medieval Warm Period," and If So, Where and When? *Climatic Change* 26: 109–42.

Hutton, Robert F., Bonnie Eldred, Kenneth D. Woodburn, and Robert M. Ingle

1956    The Ecology of Boca Ciega Bay with Special Reference to Dredging and Filling Operations. Technical Series no. 17, Part I. Florida State Board of Conservation Marine Laboratory, St. Petersburg.

Karklins, Karlis

1974    Additional Notes on the Philip Mound, Polk County, Florida. *Florida Anthropologist* 27: 1–8.

Keigwin, Lloyd D.

1996    The Little Ice Age and the Medieval Warm Period in the Sargasso Sea. *Science* 274: 1504–8.

Kolianos, Phyllis E., and Richard W. Estabrook

2010    Prehistoric Coastal Habitation and Early Maritime Travel on Old Tampa Bay. In *Proceedings of the Fifth Tampa Bay Area Scientific Information Symposium, Basis 5: 20–23 October, 2009,* edited by St. T. Cooper, 505–13. Tampa Bay Estuary Program, St. Petersburg.

Lamb, Hubert H.

1995    *Climate, History, and the Modern World.* Routledge, London.

Lambert, Jeanne

2006    Coastal Processes and Anthropogenic Factors Influencing the Geomorphic Evolution of Weedon Island, Florida. MA thesis, Department of Environmental Science and Policy, University of South Florida, Tampa.

Luer, George M.

1977    Excavations at the Old Oak Site, Sarasota, Florida: A Late Weeden Island-Safety Harbor Period Site. *Florida Anthropologist* 30: 37–55.

1985    Some Comments on Englewood Incised, Safety Harbor Incised, and Scarry's Proposed Ceramic Changes. *Florida Anthropologist* 38: 236–39.

1992    The Boylston Mound: A Safety Harbor Period Shell Midden; with Notes on the Paleoenvironment of Southern Sarasota Bay. *Florida Anthropologist* 45: 266–79.

2002a   Ceramic Bottles, Globular Vessels, and Safety Harbor Culture. In *Archaeology of Upper Charlotte Harbor, Florida,* edited by George M. Luer, 95–110. Florida Anthropological Society Publication no. 15. Florida Anthropological Society, Tallahassee.

2002b   The Aqui Esta Mound: Ceramic and Shell Vessels of the Early Mississippian-Influenced Englewood Phase. In *Archaeology of Upper Charlotte Harbor, Florida,* edited by George M. Luer,

111–81. Florida Anthropological Society Publication no. 15. Florida Anthropological Society, Tallahassee.

2005    Sarasota Bay Mound: A Safety Harbor Period Burial Mound, with Notes on Additional Sites in the City of Sarasota. *Florida Anthropologist* 58: 7–55.

2007    Mound Building and Subsistence during the Late Weeden Island Period (ca. A.D. 700–1000) at Big Mound Key (8CH10), Florida. PhD dissertation, Department of Anthropology, University of Florida, Gainesville.

Luer, George M., and Marion M. Almy

1980    The Development of Some Aboriginal Pottery of the Central Gulf Coast of Florida. *Florida Anthropologist* 33: 207–25.

1982    A Definition of the Manasota Culture. *Florida Anthropologist* 35: 34–58.

Luer, George, Marion Almy, Dana Ste. Claire, and Robert Austin

1987    The Myakkahatchee Site (8SO307), A Large Multi-Period Inland from the Shore Site in Sarasota County, Florida. *Florida Anthropologist* 40: 137–53.

Lund, David C., and William B. Curry

2004    Late Holocene Variability in Florida Current Surface Density: Patterns and Possible Causes. *Paleoceanography* 19: 1–17.

Lund, David C., Jean Lynch-Stieglitz, and William B. Curry

2006    Gulf Stream Density Structure and Transport during the Past Millennium. *Nature* 444: 601–4.

Marquardt, William H.

2010    Shell Mounds in the Southeast: Middens, Monuments, Temple Mounds, Rings, or Works? *American Antiquity* 75: 551–70.

Milanich, Jerald T.

1994    *The Archaeology of Precolumbian Florida.* University Press of Florida, Gainesville.

2002    Weeden Island Cultures. In *The Woodland Southeast*, edited by David G. Anderson and Robert C. Mainfort, Jr., 352–72. University of Alabama Press, Tuscaloosa.

Mitchem, Jeffrey M.

1985    New Dates from Eastern Citrus County. *Florida Anthropologist* 38: 247–48.

1989    Redefining Safety Harbor: Late Prehistoric/Protohistoric Archaeology in West Peninsular Florida. PhD dissertation, Department of Anthropology, University of Florida, Gainesville. University Microfilms, Ann Arbor.

1998    Analysis of Ceramics from the Narvaez/Anderson Site (8PI54). In *The Narvaez/Anderson Site (8PI54): A Safety Harbor Culture Shell Mound and Midden—A.D. 1000–1600*, compiled by Terrance L. Simpson, 66–84. Central Gulf Coast Archaeological Society, St. Petersburg.

2008    Preliminary Report on Bayshore Homes Site (8PI41) Ceramic Analysis. In Bayshore Homes Archaeological Survey and National Register Evaluation, 99–111. Report prepared for the Bureau of Historic Preservation, Florida Division of Historical Resources by Central Gulf Coast Archaeological Society. On file, Florida Division of Historical Resources, Tallahassee.

2012    Safety Harbor: Mississippian Influence in the Circum-Tampa Bay Region. In *Late Prehistoric Florida: Archaeology at the Edge of the Mississippian World*, edited by Keith H. Ashley and Nancy M. White, 172–85. University Press of Florida, Gainesville.

Office of Coast Survey

1879    Coast Chart No. 77, Tampa Bay, Florida. Image Archives of the Historical Map and Chart Collection, Office of Coast Survey, National Ocean Survey, National Oceanographic and Atmospheric Administration.

Pluckhahn, Thomas J., Victor D. Thompson, and Brent R. Weisman

2010    Toward a New View of History and Process at Crystal River (8CI1). *Southeastern Archaeology* 29: 164–81.

Porter, Kevin M., and Mary Glowacki

2008    Archaeological Salvage at Catfish Point (8CH9) and Hollenbeck Key (8CH17), Charlotte County, Florida. *Florida Anthropologist* 61: 95–103.

Queens University

2012    Marine Reservoir Correction. CHRONO Center, Queens University, Belfast. http://radio-carbon.pa.qub.ac.uk/.

Randall, Asa R., and Kenneth E. Sassaman

2005    St. Johns Archaeological Field School 2003–2004: Hontoon Island State Park. Technical Report no. 6. Laboratory of Southeastern Archaeology, Department of Anthropology, University of Florida, Gainesville.

Richey, J. N., R. Z. Poore, B. P. Flower, and T. M. Quinn

2007    1400 yr Multiproxy Record of Climate Variability from the Northern Gulf of Mexico. *Geology* 35: 423–26.

Russo, Michael

2004    Measuring Shell Rings for Social Inequality. In *Signs of Power: The Rise of Cultural Complexity in the Southeast,* edited by Jon L. Gibson and Phillip J. Carr, 26–70. University of Alabama Press, Tuscaloosa.

Sassaman, Kenneth E.

2003    New AMS Dates on Orange Fiber-Tempered Pottery from the Middle St. Johns Valley and Their Implications for Culture History in Northeast Florida. *Florida Anthropologist* 56: 5–13.

2010    *The Eastern Archaic Historicized.* AltaMira Press, Lanham, MD.

Schwadron, Margo

2000    Archaeological Investigations at DeSoto National Memorial: Perspectives on the Site Formation and Cultural History of the Shaw's Point Site (8MA7), Manatee County, Florida. *Florida Anthropologist* 53: 168–88.

2002    Archeological Investigation of DeSoto National Memorial. SEAC Technical Reports no. 8. National Park Service, Southeast Archaeological Center, Tallahassee.

2010    Prehistoric Landscapes of Complexity: Archaic and Woodland Period Shell Works, Shell Rings, and Tree Islands of the Everglades, South Florida. In *Trend, Tradition, and Turmoil: What Happened to the Southeastern Archaic?* edited by David Hurst Thomas and Matthew C. Sanger, 113–46. American Museum of Natural History Anthropological Papers no. 93. American Museum of Natural History, New York.

Sears, William H.

1958    The Maximo Point Site. *Florida Anthropologist* 11: 1–10.

1960    *The Bayshore Homes Site, St. Petersburg, Florida.* Contributions of the Florida State Museum, Social Sciences no. 6. University of Florida, Gainesville.

1967    The Tierra Verde Burial Mound. *Florida Anthropologist* 20: 25–73.

1971    The Weeden Island Site, St. Petersburg. *Florida Anthropologist* 24: 51–60.

Stapor, Frank W., Jr., Thomas D. Mathews, and Fonda E. Lindfors-Kearns

1991    Barrier Island Progradation and Holocene Sea-Level History in Southwest Florida. *Journal of Coastal Research* 7: 815–38.

Stojanowski, Christopher M., and Kent M. Johnson

2011   Brief Communication: Preliminary Radiocarbon Dates from Florida Crania in Hrdlička's Gulf States Catalog. *American Journal of Physical Anthropology* 145: 163–67.

Stuiver, Minze, and Henry A. Polach

1977   Discussion: Reporting of $^{14}$C Data. *Radiocarbon* 19: 355–63.

Tanner, William F.

1991   The "Gulf of Mexico" Late Holocene Sea Level Curve and River Delta History. *Gulf Coast Association of Geological Societies Transactions* 41: 583–89.

1992   Late Holocene Sea-Level Changes from Grain-Size Data: Evidence from the Gulf of Mexico. *The Holocene* 2: 249–54.

2000   Beach Ridge History, Sea Level Change, and the A.D. 536 Event. In *The Years without Summer: Tracing A.D. 536 and Its Aftermath,* edited by Joel D. Gunn, 89–97. BAR International Series 872. Archaeopress, Oxford.

Tykot, Robert H.

1998   Radiocarbon Chronology at the Narvaez/Anderson Site (8PI54). In *The Narvaez/Anderson Site (8PI54): A Safety Harbor Culture Shell Mound and Midden—A.D. 1000–1600,* compiled by Terrance L. Simpson, 54–58. Central Gulf Coast Archaeological Society, St. Petersburg.

Walker, Karen Jo

2013   The Pineland Site Complex: Environmental Contexts. In *The Archaeology of Pineland: A Coastal Southwest Florida Site Complex, A.D. 50–1710,* edited by William H. Marquardt and Karen J. Walker, 23–52. Institute of Archaeology and Paleoenvironmental Studies Monograph no. 4. Institute of Archaeology and Paleoenvironmental Studies, University of Florida, Gainesville.

Walker, Karen Jo, Frank W. Stapor, and William H. Marquardt

1994   Episodic Sea Levels and Human Occupation at Southwest Florida's Wightman Site. *Florida Anthropologist* 47: 161–79.

1995   Archaeological Evidence for a 1750–1450 B.P. Higher-than-Present Sea Level along Florida's Gulf Coast. In Holocene Cycles: Climate, Sea Levels, and Sedimentation. *Journal of Coastal Research,* Special Issue 17: 205–18.

Wang, Ting, Donna Surge, and Karen Jo Walker

2011   Isotopic Evidence for Climate Change During the Vandal Minimum from *Ariopsis felis* Otoliths and *Mercenaria campechiensis* Shells, Southwest Florida, USA. *The Holocene* 21: 1–11.

Wheeler, Ryan J.

2002   Harbor Key Temple Mound (8MA13): Vandal Pit Profile. Report on file, Florida Division of Historical Resources, Tallahassee.

White, Susan Lynn

1995   Technological and Formal Variability in Ceramics at Yat Kitischee. In Yat Kitischee: A Prehistoric Coastal Hamlet 100 B.C.–A.D. 1200, compiled by Robert J. Austin, 88–128. Report prepared for the Pinellas County Board of County Commissioners by Janus Research. On file, Florida Division of Historical Resources, Tallahassee.

Whitehurst, John C.

1988   Archaeological Investigations at Rattlesnake Midden (8HI981), Hillsborough County, Florida. MA thesis, Department of Anthropology, University of South Florida, Tampa.

Williams, J. Raymond

1979    Excavations at the Maximo Point Site, Pinellas County, Florida. Report prepared for the Florida Division of Archives, History, and Records Management. On file, Florida Division of Historical Resources, Tallahassee.

Willey, Gordon R.

1948    Culture Sequence in the Manatee Region of West Florida. *American Antiquity* 13: 209–18.

1949    *Archeology of the Florida Gulf Coast*. University Press of Florida, Gainesville.

Willis, Raymond F., and Robert E. Johnson

1980    Amax Pine Level Survey: An Archaeological and Historical Survey of Properties in Manatee and De Soto Counties, Florida. Report prepared for Environmental Science and Engineering, Inc. On file, Florida Division of Historical Resources, Tallahassee.

# 6

# Northwest Florida Woodland Mounds and Middens

## The Sacred and Not So Secular

MICHAEL RUSSO, CRAIG DENGEL, AND JEFFREY SHANKS

The northwest Florida panhandle coast has been called the heartland of the Swift Creek (AD 0–400) (figure 6.1) and Weeden Island cultures (AD 400–900) (Fairbanks 1982, 7; Sears 1973, 34), yet comparatively little data on either culture's pattern of intrasite settlement is available aside from that recovered by Moore (1902, 1918) from burial mounds. Moore identified most of these earthworks as small conical mounds from one to three meters high and 15 to 20 meters in diameter. As for their contents, he provided numerous but cursory descriptions of mound artifacts and inhumation orientations. But the spatial relations of mounds to other site types were less often mentioned largely because nonmound sites were rarely investigated.

In 1949, Willey attempted to synthesize Moore's mound descriptions with limited data from middens or shell middens. Based on pottery from mounds and middens, Willey defined the Swift Creek ceramic chronologies and other cultural traits. Middens were seen as containing 50 to 100 centimeters of black organic soils with shell, animal bone, and artifacts extending "30 to 100 meters in diameter." Representing the footprint of former Swift Creek villages, midden sites typically lay along marine (e.g., bay, marsh) shorelines; the village burial mound is located some 100 meters further inland. Willey concluded that pottery vessels of all shapes and surface designs were found in both mounds and midden contexts but that "many of the pottery vessels found with the dead are esoteric, complex, and non-utilitarian forms" (Willey 1949, 368–69). He speculated that multiple communities may have been linked to a single mound, that the unequal distribution of prestige pottery and exotic goods with certain burials indicated that some sort of social ranking and/or craft specialization may have existed among Swift

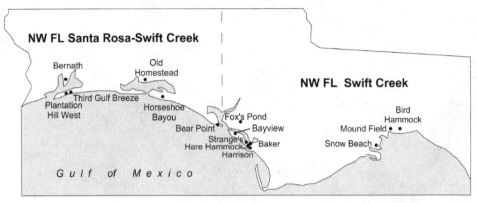

Figure 6.1. Location of select Swift Creek and Weeden Island ring middens in northwest coastal Florida.

Creek communities, and that the same individual(s) may have controlled the sacred and secular spheres of community life.

According to Willey, social inequality was not as apparent in the subsequent Weeden Island burial mounds, in which large-scale community caches of pottery were typically present rather than individualized mortuary offerings. Willey interpreted this to mean a decline in the prestige of Weeden Island priests and leaders. Although he does not suggest that craft specialists existed in Weeden Island communities, as he did for Swift Creek groups, he does note that Weeden Islanders made the most refined and unusual pottery in eastern North America, most of it used for "storage, drinking, eating or ceremonial purposes" rather than for cooking (Willey 1949, 406–7). Willey found the Weeden Island settlement and subsistence patterns to be virtually identical to those of the earlier Swift Creek groups. In some cases Weeden Island cultures continued to use the same Swift Creek burial mounds. Willey saw these shared burial locales and the Weeden Islanders' initial use of Swift Creek pottery motifs as evidence that the regional Swift Creek people were the direct ancestors of Weeden Island folks (Willey 1949, 580). Both cultures relied on shellfish, fish, terrestrial animals, and horticulture, although Weeden Island is presumed to have been more reliant on the latter.

A quarter of a century after Willey's publication, Sears (1973) took a new look at much of the same data (mostly Moore's mound studies) and devised a model to account for what he perceived as the differential distribution of Swift Creek and Weeden Island pottery and exotic artifacts among the region's mounds and middens. After Willey (1949) and Fewkes (1924), Sears (1973, 33–34, 39) formalized a dichotomy between mound and midden pottery: he referred to the vessels found in mounds as sacred and those found in villages as secular. He suggested that changes in the sacred/secular uses of pottery could be found among the region's Swift Creek and Weeden Island cultures. The earlier Swift Creek traditions used the same designs and utilitarian vessel forms in both secular and sacred spheres, although the better-made vessels and occasional trade vessels were exclusive to sacred mound contexts. In contrast to middens, mounds also contained vessels that had been ritually "killed" in the kiln, thus signifying their sacred function. In contrast to the Swift Creek pattern, Sears saw the sacred/secular dichotomy more strongly displayed in Weeden Island contexts, where vessel types in middens were generally restricted to limited utilitarian types such as simple bowls, collared bowls, and small jars. The more elaborated and compound forms that included effigy and pre-fired "killed" vessels were found exclusively in mortuary contexts.

Sears recognized that he was dealing with a meager database in formulating his sacred/secular dichotomy; few midden sites had been systematically excavated in northwest Florida. Thus, he cautioned that specific sacred/secular wares would likely differ among the widely dispersed Swift Creek and Weeden Island cultures. That is, we should not necessarily expect the same dichotomies to be found in the Big Bend area of Gulf Coast Florida as in, say, the Apalachicola Basin. Presumed utilitarian vessels in one region could become sacred vessels in another. The sacred/secular pottery dichotomy had to be worked out at each site (Sears 1973, 37–39). This prediction would be confirmed by later Weeden Island studies in Florida's interior (Milanich et al. 1984), but the proposed sacred/secular dichotomy in the panhandle has generally lacked comparative midden data. This is particularly true for one site type, the ring midden.

Observations of ring middens located near mounds were brought to the fore, first in three graduate theses on the Bird Hammock site (Allen 1954; Bense 1969; Penton 1970) and then in two papers presented at the 1974 annual meeting of the Society for American Archaeology (Brose 1979; Brose and Percy 1974; Percy and Brose 1974).[1] These papers greatly influenced our current operative model of Weeden Island/Swift Creek coastal settlement along Florida's Panhandle. Although only a few ring middens had been recognized or investigated in the region (Bense 1969; Penton 1970), Brose and Percy posited that ring midden sites represented the archeological footprints of Swift Creek and Weeden Island villages. Each village housed a small number of nuclear families who occupied the site on either a temporary or a permanent basis. In essence, Brose and Percy formalized a number of Willey's and Sears's observations on the functional aspects of both middens and mounds. Incorporating the sacred/secular dichotomy into what they called an explicitly processual model, Brose and Percy accounted for the presence of rare and unusual artifacts in the burial mounds as inland-derived exotica that, along with sacred pottery, was obtained specifically to be buried in mounds with coastal community members who had served in life as brokers with inland trading partners. In this model, exotic and other mortuary objects contained symbolic instead of or in addition to utilitarian value. The purpose of these inland-to-coastal "socio-symbiotic exchange systems" was to maintain and sanctify with traded objects relationships with inland groups from whom the coastal groups could seek subsistence support in times of environmental stress. Because the interment of exotica in the brokers' burials removed the valued sacra (sacred objects) from the exchange system, living individuals were incentivized to continue the system in order to maintain the flow of valued objects (Brose and Percy 1974, 10).

The Brose and Percy functional model was designed to account for all the available data of the time. It is thus resistant to change in the absence of new data from mounds or ring middens. Because most mounds have been destroyed by Moore and by subsequent development, ring and other middens have become the likely testing grounds for the sacred/secular processual model. Along Florida's northwest coast, recent investigations have identified numerous extant coastal ring middens that were heretofore unrecognized or underexamined. These sites offer potential insight into the practices that brought exotic pottery and other sacra into Woodland burial mounds. Below, we suggest that exotic burial objects and mortuary pottery made their way into the mound via ceremonies held at the ring midden site. However, to support this interpretation, we need to first discuss the presumption that ring middens in the region are only the epiphenomena of daily food consumption and other mundane activities.

## What Is a Ring Midden?

Willey (1949, 403) made the first, somewhat cursory attempt to fit features that would later be called ring middens into the regional settlement pattern. He thought they were either remnants of "old village fortifications" or were of "only ceremonial significance." Since then, archeologists have spent little time testing the possible multifunctionality of rings. Based on a small sample, Phelps (1969, 19) thought ring middens to be a rare site type he called "the infrequent circular midden embankment." In the absence of other description, a broader view of ring middens as functioning as something other than or in addition to refuse dumps cannot be inferred from his writing.[2] Percy and Brose, of course, saw them as villages associated with mounds, a model that was followed in subsequent syntheses (Bense 1994, 172; Milanich 1994, 145), although whether the ring middens were the actual village footprint or just the village refuse dumps is not always clear. A recurrent issue is whether the ring middens were occupied permanently or only seasonally (Bense 1969, 51; Bense 1994, 172; Bense 1998, 255; cf. Byrd 1994, 148, 157; Milanich 1994, 145; Nanfro 2004, 54; Penton 1970, 5; Phelps 1969, 19).

Aside from identifying the series and types of pottery, arguably the dominant processual goal over the last 50 years of ring midden studies has been to describe aspects of the environment that may have influenced the choice of settlement location. Among the few ring middens that have received detailed attention, research has focused on the periodicity of habitation using faunal and environmental analyses. At Bird Hammock, the shell and other faunal remains have been the topic of four master's theses and one PhD dissertation over the course of half a century. These works have all concluded that the Bird Hammock ring midden was a year-round Swift Creek/Weeden Island settlement whose inhabitants were dependent on the multiple ecozones of forests and estuaries for their survival (Allen 1954; Bense 1969; Byrd 1994; Nanfro 2004; Penton 1970).

At the Santa Rosa–Swift Creek Old Homestead site, faunal materials from pit features and the general levels of the ring midden elicited the same basic conclusion: that the ring midden consisted of subsistence refuse reflecting exploitation of multiple environments that allowed long-term annual occupations (Mikell and Pope 1996, 143). In contrast, Weeden Island ring middens, such as the Plantation Hill West (Byrd 1994; Mikell 1985) and Third Gulf Breeze (Doran 1985), were less faunally diverse and were interpreted as more strictly reliant on estuarine shell and fish species. This limited diversity suggested to at least one investigator that the Third Gulf Breeze site was only seasonally occupied (Byrd 1994, 79). Our own limited faunal analyses of samples from two Swift Creek ring middens (Baker's and Harrison) and three Weeden Island ring middens (Bayview, Strange's, and Hare Hammock) on Tyndall Air Force Base suggest a similar focus on estuarine shell and fish. Because the sample sizes were small, however, we could not draw definitive conclusions about the periodicity of settlement (Russo et al. 2006, 2009, 2011).

With few exceptions, inferences drawn from these faunal analyses have been axiomatic: all fauna in pits and midden deposits (both sheet and mounded) resulted from mundane subsistence activities, while considerations of other potential social practices involving shell and bone, including the use of shellfish remains as construction material or shellfish flesh as food in ceremonial feasting or ritual consumption, have largely been excluded from these analyses. Pits containing bone and shell are typically classified as storage or refuse pits for subsistence remains. When relatively large amounts of burned bone, burned shell, or burned soils are found in the pits, the features are interpreted as subsistence-related cooking pits or hearths (Bense 1969; Mikell and Pope 1996, 136; Nanfro 2004). Whether these pits are located within or below the ring midden or within the plaza, their classifications are similarly interpreted as quotidian in function (Bense 1994; Nanfro 2004). Although artifacts are typically present in both pit and ring middens, dark staining, fauna, and charcoal are typically the primary determiners of their function (e.g., Thomas et al. 1996, 48–70). Unless they are rare and exotic, artifacts are used only rarely in determinations of midden and feature function. In the wake of these perfunctory interpretations and what has been for the past half-century a focus on settlement as an environmentally adaptive strategy, shell ring middens have become de facto habitation sites in normative models.

We suggest that the assumption that food remains, regardless of their contexts, are quotidian in nature is potentially problematic in that it precludes from consideration other practices that might account for or be involved in their presence. Notable exceptions to this presumption do exist. At the Old Homestead site, for example, Thomas and Campbell (1996, 153, 158–59) compared ceramics found mostly in pits around the outside periphery of the plaza to ceramics found in the ring midden itself. They suggested that some activities in the plaza were likely ceremonial based on a higher frequency of Basin Bayou Incised ceramics, a ware they identified as Santa Rosa–Swift Creek's "finest" and probably sacred, having been recovered in a nearby mound (Willey 1949, 223–24). With the presence of sacred ceramics spatially related to fauna in the plaza pit features, they concluded that the plaza may have been the locus of "ritual feasting as well as other sacred activities." Identifying soot on many of the sherds and anticipating possible criticisms of interpreting sooted sherds as ceremonial, the authors cautioned that there was no inherent contradiction in using sacred vessels for cooking.

This idea that some pit features at ring-midden sites were ritual in nature was approached from a different perspective at the Bird Hammock ring midden. Trying to account for the low species diversity in the pit features compared to higher diversity found in the general ring midden deposits, Nanfro (2004, 53) noted that the pit features may have been the result of short-term ritual activities. While we do not believe that low species diversity alone is sufficient to identify ritual activity (low diversity could alternatively be related to a shorter period of use and to the fact that the pit was subject to fewer activities), the idea that fauna-filled pit features resulted from ritual feasting is a potentially testable hypothesis that includes low diversity as one possible expectation.

At the distinctive Bernath site where 17 human burials were discovered in the plaza, both refuse pits and cooking pits or hearths were found at the outer edge of the plaza and in the surrounding ring midden. Bense (1998, 263, 267) mentioned that some of the pits contained abundant shell and bone refuse of a "domestic" variety, while the ring midden generally lacked shell. Significantly, although the plaza pits contained what Bense referred to as domestic refuse, the pits were unusually large, over 2 meters in diameter and 1 meter deep. Another basin-shaped pit was 8 meters long—much larger than the typical pit features found at other ring midden sites (e.g., Thomas et al. 1996). The large sizes of the pits as well as their placement in a plaza containing ritualized burials suggested to Bense (1998, 263) a "nonutilitarian special function." Bense concluded that the ring midden was a habitation site of a leader where periodic ceremonies, including burials, were held.

Bernath was unusual, if not unique, not only for the discovery of burials in the plaza but also for the large pit and cooking features that marked consumption activities on a scale far greater than one would expect for a single family. These data alone suggest that ring midden sites may have served other than strictly utilitarian purposes. While no other Woodland ring is known to hold burials, many are physically close to and contemporaneous with burial mounds. Similar rituals and practices held for the dead at Bernath could have been held at other ring plazas associated with burial mounds. Yet with few exceptions, researchers have rarely asked what activities occurred in ring plazas next to burial mounds, why the rings were placed next to burial mounds, and how the rings differed in use from other types of midden sites.

Today, over twenty sites across the greater Florida Panhandle have been identified as either Swift Creek or Weeden Island ring middens (table 6.1). Many have multiple components but few have been closely investigated, and their primary periods of occupation are subject to further inquiry (Bense 1998; Russo et al. 2006, 2011; Stephenson et al. 2002, 319, 334; Thomas and Campbell 1991). Studies of the midden (as opposed to the plaza) components reveal that they generally consist of dark, organically stained soils intermixed with variable amounts of shell that may occur in pits or lenses. The predominant shell species seem to reflect shellfish abundance in the immediate environments; oyster is most often dominant along bays where freshwater inflow is substantial, and conchs and whelks are dominant in Gulf locales. However, our work at Tyndall Air Force Base and earlier studies indicate that ring middens are not "shell rings" in the Late Archaic sense in that dense amounts of shell do not necessarily demarcate the circumference of the ring midden. Shells are sparsely present or absent in some parts of a ring midden, and the resultant low relief often defies recognizable ring topography. In these cases, midden soil and/or artifact distribution may be the better markers of a midden's ring shape (Bense 1998, 267–68; Russo et al. 2009, 76, 91; Russo et al. 2011, 61, 97; figures 6.2 and 6.3).

Whether the ring middens are demarcated by topography, shell, ceramic distribution, or other materials, their shape may not be a clearly defined circle of midden with a central area containing little or no midden. Although these landscape features are called ring middens, they are rarely, if ever, closed, annular circles or rings. Typically they are irregular semicircles or discontinuous circles of variably dense midden deposits separated from each other by less dense midden that may lack shell entirely. The standard interpretation is that these discrete midden deposits represent individual incidentally deposited house middens (Milanich 2002, 363; Moore 1918, 564; Stephenson et al. 2002, 345–46). Areas with less midden, then, may reflect gaps/passageways between houses or household middens. This idea is supportable by our current mapping, which shows between three to nine localized dense shell deposits within the ring middens that may be linked to household activities (figures

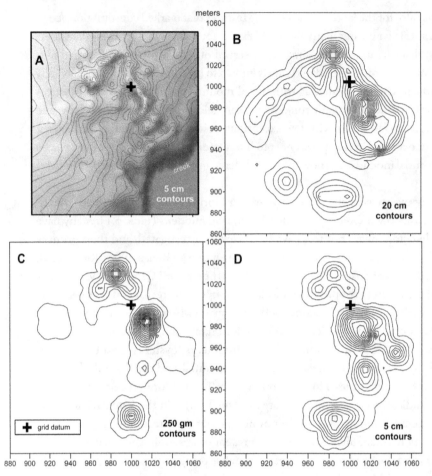

Figure 6.2. Strange's Ring Midden (8By1355) surface topography (A) and distributions of pottery (B), shell (C), and midden soils (D) based on 15-meter-grid shovel tests (Russo et al. 2011).

Table 6.1. Numbers of Weeden Island and Swift Creek mounds and rings along Florida's northwest coast containing rare and exotic materials and percentages of such materials

| Site Type | Effigy | Mica | Stone Celt | Lithic Point | Crystal Quartz | Hone & Sandstone | Ochre | Other |
|---|---|---|---|---|---|---|---|---|
| Mounds: N/% | 12/31 | 19/49 | 20/51 | 16/41 | 3/8 | 13/33 | 4/10 | 20/51 |
| Rings: N/% | 4/36 | 4/36 | 4/36 | 7/64 | 7/64 | 7/64 | 5/45 | 2/18 |

*Note*: The thirty-nine mounds reviewed were 8By1, 3, 5, 7, 8, 11–13, 15–22, 25–32; 8Gu1, 2; 8Fr1, 4, 5, 10, 11; 8Wa1, 4, 5, 8, 9, 10, 12; and SR29. The twelve ring middens were 8By29, 73, 137, 1347, 1355, 1359; 8SR8, 67, 986; 8Wa8, 9; and 8Wl58. In mounds the "other" category included stone and clay pipes, copper, galena, and worked shells. In rings the "other" category included a pearl and "mini-pots."

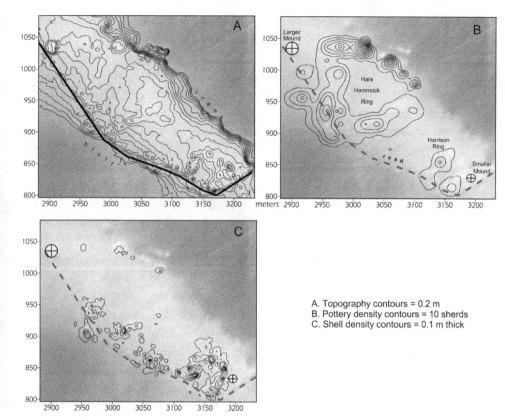

Figure 6.3. Hare Hammock Ring (8By1347), Harrison Ring Midden (8By1359), and the Larger and Smaller Mounds at Hare Hammock (8By30 and 31). Pottery based on 20-meter-grid shovel tests. Shell based on 1- to 5-meter grid probes.

6.2c and 6.3c; see also Russo et al. 2011, 97, figure 55). Yet although post molds have been found at rings, interpretations that they are associated with domiciliary structures are lacking (Bense 1998, 258; Thomas et al. 1996). This leaves open the possibility that the shell deposits may have arisen from activities other than those associated with individual house dumps. In the following section, we suggest that exotic and mortuary objects as well as public plazas at ring middens indicate possible uses of the sites other than those related strictly to quotidian shelter, consumption, and refuse disposal.[3]

## Ring Middens and Mounds in Northwest Coastal Florida

To assess what kinds of artifacts have been recovered from ring middens, we reviewed all ring middens on Tyndall Air Force Base and in other northwest Florida coastal areas that have been subject to modern excavation or large-scale systematic shovel testing. Our goal was to identify both materials that have traditionally been viewed as ritualistic or ceremonial (e.g., elite and special pottery and exotic minerals and stones) and with those that have been accepted as strictly quotidian. Our search found that these quotidian materials dominated site assemblages, but artifacts typically classified as ceremonial or otherwise special were widespread and sometimes relatively common. Archeologists, of course, have long recognized the presence of exotic, ritual, or elite artifacts in middens. As noted above, Sears (1973) recognized the presence of "sacred" artifacts in middens, particularly in Swift Creek contexts. But given his goal of establishing a dichotomy between sacred and secular, he was compelled to explain sacred-like midden artifacts as being of poorer quality and secular-like mound artifacts as being of higher quality. Then, having dealt with the troublesome fact that like objects were used in both sacred and secular contexts by the Swift Creek culture, Sears ultimately concluded that sacred/secular dichotomous spheres were apparent among all Woodland cultures (from Deptford to Weeden Island).

Our review indicates that the admixture of putative elite wares and mundane pottery actually occurs not only at Swift Creek ring middens but also at Weeden Island ring middens (see figure 6.4a and b).[4] Over a third of the ring sites we surveyed have yielded mica, polished greenstone and other foreign stone celts, and yellow and red ochre—all potentially non-quotidian artifacts—as well as fragments of figurines or effigy vessels, the latter of which, of course, have long been assumed to be the exclusive sacra of burial mounds. Mica, ochre, and effigy vessels have no apparent utilitarian purposes, and their presence implies some aspect of ritual at the ring sites. Celts, on the other hand, are valued utilitarian tools except when they are stylized and polished to such an extent that they lose efficiency as cutting implements. Several of the recorded celts, including one from Strange's Ring (8By1355), were of the stylized type (Russo et al. 2011; see also Bense and Watson 1977). Unfortunately, descriptions of most of these celts (particularly Moore's descriptions) are insufficient to assess whether they were used in functional or ceremonial ways.

The occurrence of effigy vessel fragments in ring site contexts suggests connections to ritual practices linking the ring sites, both plazas and middens, to their adjacent mounds, the presumed destined resting place for the pots.[5] We note, however, that effigy vessels are not all that common in the mounds themselves. Evidence of effigy vessels (including Swift Creek bas-relief and figurine vessels and Weeden Island whole pot and cutout effigies) was found in less than a third of the thirty-nine burial mounds in the region we surveyed (table 6.1). In comparison, effigy vessels (or more precisely, their fragments) occurred at about the same frequency in ring sites. When they are found in mounds, of course, effigy vessels are seen as definitive ritual objects, but when they are found in middens, their ritualistic aspects have been downplayed or ignored (e.g., Bense 1969, 28, 32; Bense and Watson 1979, 98, 127; Russo et al. 2006, 49–50).

That mica and polished stone celts are more commonly found in mounds (in roughly half of them) than in ring sites supports the theory that they were used in ritual. But their discovery in over a third of the rings suggests that these objects may have also been involved in rituals at rings (see also White 1992, 33, for an example of the occurrence of mica and clear quartz in nonring midden contexts). Ochre, mica, polished stone, and crystal quartz (which was found in 8 percent of the mounds and 64 percent of the rings) all exhibit rare visual aspects. These colorful, reflec-tive, glistening, and translucent materials were meant to be seen. Their presence in and near public ring plazas suggests that the plazas may have served as arenas for their conspicuous display in rituals, some of which may have been associated with mound burials, where these materials are also found.

In contradistinction to the sacred/secular dichotomy model, we found in our survey that most pottery in mounds is, in fact, of utilitarian types rather than specifi-cally mortuary wares. Although we have no accurate assessment of the numbers of sherds that came out of the burial mounds dug by Moore, in our sample, putative utilitarian pottery makes up 60 percent of Moore's pottery types as interpreted by Willey (1949), suggesting that burial mounds were actually places of interment for the most common plain and other daily-use cooking pots, many of which were used extensively before interment, rather than strictly places for formally sacred objects (see also Brose 1979; Wallis 2011, 190). This common placement of utilitarian pots in mounds echoes the observation that over 80 percent of 811 pots recovered from mounds in our study were simple collared bowls, a vessel type Sears (1973, 34) iden-tified as common, everyday ware.

Together, these data do not contradict the well-founded observations that burial mounds were places for interment of special ritual wares. But they do demonstrate that burial mounds primarily contain vessels that, in other contexts, would be con-sidered utilitarian. For example, at interior Weeden Island mounds, so-called elite pottery is considered to be ritualistically privileged for interment in burial mounds, although it is also found in ring middens (Milanich et al. 1984). This general pat-tern holds true along the northwest Florida coast, where elite wares may actually be more common in coastal ring midden contexts than in mounds (Russo et al. 2009).

## Summary

Based solely on shared material culture most obviously recognizable in ceramic design motifs and on Hopewellian interaction objects, Swift Creek and Weeden Island groups appear to have been deontic, ideologically pluralistic societies who shared various cosmological views through time and across space. Unfortunately,

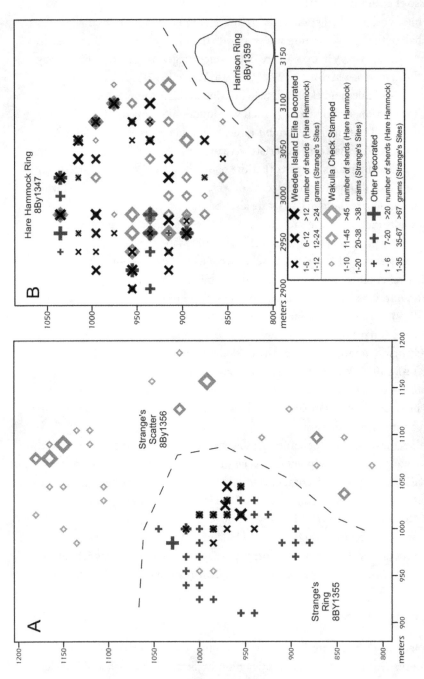

Figure 6.4. Weeden Island Series Decorated pottery distribution from systematic shovel test surveys at A) Strange's Ring Midden (8By1355) and Strange's Scatter (8By1356); and B) Hare Hammock Ring Midden (8By1347) and Harrison Ring (8By1359). Note the paucity of Weeden Island Series at 8By1359 and of Wakulla Check Stamped at 8By1355, which suggests temporally distinct deposits despite geographic proximity. *Sources:* A: Russo et al. 2011; B: Russo et al. 2009.

this geographically expansive assessment offers little insight into the "why" of local coastal settlement patterns wherein ring sites are placed adjacent to burial mounds, or vice versa, and ritual and utilitarian objects seemingly float freely between the long-supposed mutually exclusive cosmologic and domestic spheres—that is, the "sacred" and the "secular."

The Florida model (Brose 1979; Brose and Percy 1974; Percy and Brose 1974) posits that during coastal environmental stress the cultural relationships established between inland and coastal groups through trade in ideologically valued objects acted within the Hopewellian trade sphere to bring inland foods to the coastal communities. Unfortunately, to date, little or no archaeology has been undertaken that might test the accuracy of this hypothesis. Alternatively, Russo and colleagues (2011) have suggested that foods were shared among coastal communities in times of need. Along the coast, villages were situated among ecotones (e.g., bay estuaries, gulfside estuaries, freshwater rivers, beaches, high and low marshes, and a variety of terrestrial environments) that yielded both perennial (e.g., oyster) and season-ally abundant resources (e.g., scallops). In this model, subsistence needs were ful-filled from coastal resources and interactions among coastal groups. This hypothesis suggests that in times of seasonal and other food abundances, hosting groups held feasts, most likely at ring and other midden sites, thereby obligating neighboring kin groups to reciprocate in their times of abundance. These social obligations for sub-sistence reciprocation would have been shared among all coastal groups in times of need. Trade with inland partners certainly would have brought symbolically-valued objects to the coast and perhaps marriage partners as well. But relationships that mitigated subsistence stress may have been primarily coastal.

In either model, intrasite settlement patterns of coastal mound/ring complexes seem to have been at least partially based on both symbolic and subsistence needs. Their consistent placement near a variety of estuarine resources is surely related to economic maximization. But the proximity of mounds to ring sites and the inter-changeability of artifacts between mounds and rings suggest an ideological funda-ment. The Hopewell settlement in the Midwest consists of two distinct spheres, the "everyday" and the "high culture," or the dispersed, nearly invisible habitation sites and the grandly conspicuous earthwork sites. Whether archeologists assign these discrete emplacements to mutually exclusive kin groups or inclusive sodalities in charge of earthwork practices (Byers 2010, 283), the Hopewellian practice of dis-tancing monument from habitation site differs from the sacred/secular dichotomy proposed for northwest coastal Florida, where conspicuous mounds are located next to ring middens, the putative living areas of Swift Creek and Weeden Island groups. Of course, the sacred/secular dichotomy was not originally proposed to explain spatial relationships between mounds and middens; it was formulated to explain the apparent incongruence of pottery between the two site types. In fact, when the model was forwarded, coastal ring middens were largely unrecognized, or at least little studied (Sears 1973). Now that we have a better understanding of the spatiality and artifact contexts of ring middens, we can suggest that ritual materials ("the sacred") are found in both site types.

In our recent searches for five of Moore's long-lost Woodland burial mounds on Tyndall Air Force Base, heretofore unknown/uninvestigated ring middens were found to lie within 100 meters of each mound (Russo and Dengel 2010; Russo et al. 2009, 2011). This consistent proximity of mound and ring as well as Bense's (1998) identification of burials within plazas supports our proposition that the sacred/secular dichotomy among both Swift Creek and Weeden Island cultures was not strictly reified on the landscape. If rings were indeed habitation sites, mundane daily routines must have been periodically interrupted for burial and other rituals (e.g., Bense 1998). The open space of ring plazas facilitated verbal and visual communication and allowed for the manufacture, display, presentation, and symbolic negotiation of sacred objects destined for the mound. In these ceremonies, putative ritual objects were displayed and occasionally broken and their fragments lost within both ring midden and plaza contexts, while others were ritually buried in the plaza or discarded as ceremonial trash within the ring midden itself.[6]

Conversely, everyday tools such as pots, metates, and shells were used to prepare objects for display and ultimate burial in mounds and to prepare food to feed the ceremonial masses. In the process, these objects may have become sacralized, their use in ritual or sacred ceremonies excluding them from further mundane use. That is, they became ceremonial, as opposed to mundane, trash now subject to different rules of disposal (Walker 1995). The presence of shell and everyday pottery in burial mounds has most frequently been seen as offerings, for example, to feed the dead in preparation for the afterlife. Instead, it might have been refuse from ritual feasts whose discard could not occur in nonsacred contexts. In our ongoing work at the Swift Creek Harrison Ring, special ceremonial trash pit features that are isolated from the mundane refuse of the surrounding ring have been recovered in the plaza. These pits contain both exotic items (e.g., slate gorget, mica, ochre) and caches of ostensibly mundane objects (see endnote 6). Similar large pit features have been found in other ring plazas (Bense 1998). If exotic objects occur in these features, ritual function may be assigned. But typically in the absence of presumed ritual objects and in the presence of only seemingly mundane trash, these features are interpreted as storage pits that were infilled with anything handy after they were emptied.

Instead of an interpretation that sees only exclusively quotidian activities being practiced at ring sites, we suggest that daily routines among Swift Creek and Weeden Island groups were inseparable from their ideology. Rituals of varied scales likely occurred not just at times of burial but more frequently, even daily. The apparent interchangeability of object use between rings and mounds likely reflects the importance of the cosmological sphere in daily life. As archeologists, we need to consider both the mundane and the ritual at ring midden sites. That being said, there is little doubt that the burial mounds played an important—if not the most important—role in the spiritual lives of ring builders. But if ring middens and plazas were the habitation sites of the mound builders, the placement of rings and mounds in close proximity suggests that the cosmological was ever-present physically, visually, and spiritually in the communities' daily lives.

The incorporation of the cosmological sphere in daily life might also be observable in the orientation of mounds to rings. Some researchers (e.g., Snow 1998; Wallis 2011) have attempted to clarify cosmological specifics for Swift Creek and Weeden Island peoples. For Weeden Island groups, it has been hypothesized that celestial orientation influenced pottery designs and landscape orientations (Attison 2009; Milanich et al. 1984). Some archeologists have suggested an increase in agricultural production by Weeden Island groups (e.g., Brose and Percy 1974), a commonly cited impetus for the incorporation of sun cycles into rituals and landscape orientations. And certainly the oft-observed pattern of pottery caches on the east side of Weeden Island mounds suggests routine rituals related to solar orientations. Our own preliminary review of mound/ring orientations reveals a pattern of placement of burial mounds northwest of Weeden Island rings. This orientation is aligned generally toward the setting sun at winter solstice as viewed from the center of the ring plaza. In contrast, this pattern is not observable in the Swift Creek ring/mound complexes, and no mounds are known to be associated with the Santa Rosa–Swift Creek ring middens farther west (figure 6.5). Whether these apparent spatial orientations are universal or are linked to cosmological or geographical considerations remains to be investigated.

We are only beginning to study ring middens and their relationships to burial mounds. Although most Swift Creek and Weeden Island mounds in northwest Florida have been destroyed, at least a dozen largely intact ring middens promise new insights. The operative model of ring middens as representing the remains of villages, or at least their faunal refuse, has a sound evidentiary basis. But alternative hypotheses are needed to explain materials, features, and orientations that have not been and cannot be resolved by faunal analyses alone. Under what social negotiations did living occur at ring midden sites? Were they occupied by seasonal migratory groups from interior Florida (Bense 1998; Brose and Percy 1974), permanently by strictly coastal denizens (Byrd 1994; Russo et al. 2009, 2011), or occasionally during ceremonies associated with burials and/or food consumption (Russo in press)? A number of archeologists have suggested that ring sites were residences of specialists, such as cemetery and mound keepers, shamans, or chiefs (Bense 1998; Doran and Piatek 1985). But regardless of the

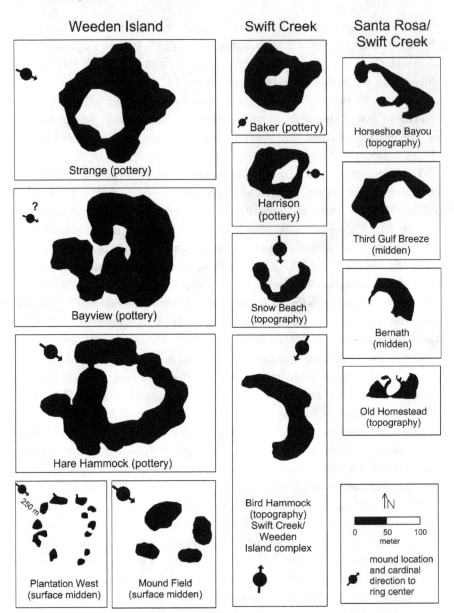

Figure 6.5. Cardinal orientations of Swift Creek and Weeden Island burial mounds and ring middens. Note that the location of Bayview and Plantation Hill West ring mounds are speculative (see Russo et al. 2011, 255–57; Doran and Piatek 1985, 90).

periodicity of occupancy or the specific quotidian practices at ring middens, the current data suggest that ring midden sites also served as places where rituals were performed and where, perhaps in the most significant rituals, living people negotiated the entrance of their dead into the sphere of the afterlife.

## Notes

1. The term "ring" and "ring midden" requires some discussion. Moore (1902, 1918) originally identified circular shell "enclosures" or ridges near a number of the mounds, noting mostly that the enclosures did not yield interesting pottery. Willey (1949) suggested that the enclosures were possibly the "remains of old village fortifications" or held some kind of "ceremonial significance" Willey (1949, 403). Sears identified no enclosing middens at his Tucker site excavations or in his paper on the sacred and secular (Sears 1963, 1973). None of the authors used the term ring to describe middens in the area. Bense (1969, 3, 19; cf. Penton 1970, 11) may have been the first to apply the term "ring" to Swift Creek and Weeden Island middens when she referred to Bird Hammock as a "midden ring" or "a ring of midden enclosing a level plaza." Later Percy and Brose (1974, 11) described similar middens as "∪-shaped or ring middens in use from the Early Swift Creek through Early Weeden Island." It is here, perhaps, that that the term ring and ring midden were first used interchangeably in reference to the Woodland features.

The term ring is also used as a shorthand for another archeological feature in the region, the Late Archaic period "shell ring," a construction variably different in form (taller), shape, and constituents (more shell than soil), if not in purpose, from the Woodland ring middens (Russo in press). In context, the use of "ring" to refer to either shell ring or ring midden is undoubtedly understandable. But when context is lacking, problems may arise (cf. the use of ring, ring midden, and shell ring in this chapter and in the White, Sassaman et al., and Saunders and Wrenn chapters in this volume). When readers encounter the term "ring" used to describe Woodland ring middens, they may need context to distinguish the features as either elements of a village (the common interpretation of ring middens) or as a monumental feasting site (a common interpretation of shell rings).

Additionally, using the term "ring" by itself may task the reader to determine if the writer is referring to the midden or the midden and the plaza together. That is, each ring midden—and each shell ring, for that matter—contains at least two recognized features, the midden and the plaza. When the writer states that the ring contains many pieces of pottery, it may be unclear whether he or she is referring to the midden, the plaza, or both.

With these factors in mind, we have attempted here, and elsewhere (Russo in press; Russo et al. 2006, 2009, 2011) to adhere to the term "ring midden" to keep separate the meaning-laden differences between Woodland ring middens and Archaic "shell rings" and to distinguish between midden and plaza at ring midden sites. The term "ring midden site" or "ring site" may be used when referring to both the plaza and the ring, and sometimes even the adjacent mound. "Ring" may be used alone if the context is clear that it means both the ring and the plaza. If we slip in our adherence, we hope that the context may provide the reader with our intended meaning.

2. Phelps (1969, 19) suggested another site type, the nondescript "midden dump," which was presumably more common and represented the dumping grounds of the nearby "temporary residences" that were often placed near burial mounds. This observation may have been one source of Brose and Percy's idea that each coastal Woodland village was associated with a burial mound. But it is not clear if the sites Phelps referred were rings. He warned readers that his data was limited.

3. Whether or not shell-bearing middens should be interpreted as purposeful or incidental mound construction has been debated in the context of Archaic shell rings (e.g., Marquardt 2010; Russo 2004). We suggest that whether Woodland ring middens are the phenomena or epiphenomena of domestic or ritual disposal, the placement and spacing of the refuse reflects proxemic and symbolic practices beyond that associated with routine, "incidental" disposal. In calling certain aspects of Weeden Island and Swift Creek ring middens possible incidental house midden discard, we report what others have interpreted, but we also note that these, like all interpretations, are susceptible to reappraisal subject to new data or theoretical perspectives. Routine discard into ring refuse deposits does not suggest that the rings were not intentionally made for purposes other than or in addition to discard. But the generally low relief of ring middens, which contrasts with that of many

Archaic shell rings (Russo 2004), suggests that attaining great height was not a likely goal of their construction.

4. Figure 6.4 compares Weeden Island elite decorated to utilitarian (other and Wakulla Check Stamped) decorated pottery at two rings and shows that both are found in the rings. Note that Wakulla Check Stamped may or may not be contemporaneous with the other Weeden Island series pottery in this region (Percy and Brose 1974; Milanich et al.1984; Willey 1949). At Strange's ring, Wakulla Check Stamped is relatively rare in the ring but abundant outside it. It is commonly intermixed with other wares at Hare Hammock, but it is relatively rare in Weeden Island elite contexts (20 out of 33 tests containing elite wares lacked Wakulla Check Stamped pottery). At both sites, this may indicate that later people who produced Wakulla Check Stamped wares had corporate memories of previous ancestral occupations and avoided reoccupation of those spots. Alternatively, if the check-stamped wares are contemporaneous with the elite, it suggests that elite utilitarian wares were differentially disposed of.

5. Some have rightfully questioned whether the mounds found next to middens in northwest Florida can be assumed to be contemporary (White 2010, 177). We certainly did not assume this in our analyses of the Tyndall Air Force Base mounds and ring middens. For the mound/ring complexes on Tyndall discussed here, we have radiocarbon dates on objects and human remains from two mounds and many more dates from ring middens. However, in light of the fact that destructive analyses of mound remains is effectively precluded in the future, the comparison of artifacts and geographic propinquity is destined to provide the best evidentiary base for making the case for the contemporaneous usage of rings and mounds (Russo et al. 2009; 2011). To this end, paddle matching of Swift Creek sherds found in mounds and ring middens has helped establish contemporaneity at the Baker Site and Hare Hammock (Russo et al. 2011), and developing reservoir effects for specific coastal waters has resulted in a refined capability to compare shell dates among mounds and middens (Shanks and Byrd 2012). Together these have helped demonstrate contemporaneity between the Tyndall Air Force Base mounds and the adjacent ring middens we have discussed in this chapter.

6. In reports in progress, crystal quartz, mica, Archaic-style stemmed lithic points, a slate gorget, a clay figurine head, and a cache of exhausted ground stone objects were found in plaza pits at the Harrison Ring in association with Swift Creek pottery and Swift Creek radiocarbon era dates. Only one 2 × 2 unit was excavated in the nearby Weeden Island period Hare Hammock ring plaza, but it yielded crystal quartz. Crystal quartz, mica, and ochre were also recovered from the surrounding ring midden along with "elite" or "prestige" pottery.

# References

Allen, Glenn

1954    Archaeological Investigations in the Northwest Coast of Florida. MA thesis, Florida State University, Tallahassee.

Attison, David

2009    Observations on Weeden Island Designs. Paper presented at the Weedon Island Conference, Tampa, FL.

Bense, Judith A.

1969    Excavations at the Bird Hammock Site (8WA30), Wakulla County, Florida. MS thesis, Florida State University, Tallahassee.

1994    *Archaeology of the Southeastern United States: Paleoindian to World War I*. Academic Press, New York.

1998    SantaRosa-Swift Creek in Northwestern Florida. In *A World Engraved: Archaeology of the Swift Creek Culture*, edited by Mark Williams and Daniel T. Elliott, 247–73. University of Alabama Press, Tuscaloosa.

Bense, Judith A., and Thomas C. Watson

1977    A Swift Creek-Weeden Island Village Complex in the St. Andrew Bay System of the Northwest Florida Gulf Coast: Analysis and Interpretation. Florida Master Site File, Survey 847, Tallahassee.

1979    A Swift Creek and Weeden Island "Ring Midden" in the St. Andrew Bay Drainage System on the Northwest Florida Gulf Coast. *Alabama Archaeology* 25(2): 85–137.

Brose, David S.

1979    An Interpretation of the Hopewellian Traits in Florida. In *Hopewellian Archaeology: The Chillicothe Conference,* edited by David S. Brose and N'omi Greber, 141–49. Kent State University Press, Kent, Ohio.

Brose, David S., and George Percy

1974    An Outline of Weeden Island Ceremonial Activity in Northwest Florida. Paper presented at the 39th annual meeting of the Society for American Archaeology, Washington, DC.

Byers, Martin

2010    The "Heartland" Woodland Settlement System: Cultural Traditions and Resolving Key Puzzles. In *Hopewell Settlement Patterns, Subsistence, and Symbolic Landscapes,* edited by A. Martin Byers and DeeAnne Wymer, 276–306. University Press of Florida, Gainesville.

Byrd, John Edward

1994    The Zooarchaeology of Four Gulf Coast Prehistoric Sites. PhD dissertation, University of Tennessee, Knoxville.

Doran, Glen H.

1985    Appendix II Faunal Analysis: Small Sample Analysis of Shellfish Remains from 8SR8, 8SR29, and 8SR67. In *Archaeological Investigations at Naval Live Oaks, Studies in Spatial Patterning and Chronology in the Gulf Coast of Florida,* by Glen H. Doran and Bruce J. Piatek, 183–87. National Park Service, Southeast Archaeological Center, Tallahassee.

Doran, Glen H., and Bruce J. Piatek

1985    *Archaeological Investigations at Naval Live Oaks, Studies in Spatial Patterning and Chronology in the Gulf Coast of Florida.* National Park Service, Southeast Archeological Center, Tallahassee.

Fairbanks, Charles H.

1982 [1949]    Introduction. In *Archeology of the Florida Gulf Coast,* by Gordon R. Willey, 1–15. Florida Book Store, Inc., Gainesville.

Fewkes, Jesse W.

1924    Preliminary Archeological Explorations at Weeden Island, Florida. *Smithsonian Miscellaneous Collections* 76(13): 1–26.

Marquardt, William H.

2010    Shell Mounds in the Southeast: Middens, Monuments, Temple Mounds, Rings or Works? *American Antiquity* 75(3): 551–70.

Mikell, Gregory A.

1985    Appendix II Faunal Analysis: Vertebrate Faunal Remains from 8SR29 and 8SR67. In *Archaeological Investigations at Naval Live Oaks, Studies in Spatial Patterning and Chronology in the Gulf Coast of Florida,* edited by Glenn H. Doran and Bruce J. Piatek, 163–82. National Park Service, Southeast Archeological Center, Tallahassee.

Mikell, Gregory A., and Jane Pope

1996    Faunal Analysis and Coprolite Discussion. In *Controlled Excavation at 8WL58, the Old Homestead Site: Completing the Compliance Process at Eglin Air Force Base, Okaloosa, Santa Rosa, and Walton Counties,* vols. 26–30, edited by Prentice M. Thomas Jr., Maria L. Schleidt Penalva,

L. Janice Campbell, and Mathilda Cox, 132–47. Report of Investigations no. 284. Prentice Thomas and Associates, Fort Walton Beach, Florida. On file, Florida Master Site File, Tallahassee.

Milanich, Jerald T.

1994    *Archaeology of Precolumbian Florida*. University Press of Florida, Gainesville.

2002    Weeden Island Cultures. In *The Woodland Southeast*, edited by David G. Anderson and Robert C. Mainfort Jr., 352–72. University of Alabama Press, Tuscaloosa.

Milanich, Jerald T., Ann S. Cordell, Vernon J. Knight Jr., Timothy A. Kohler, and Brenda J. Sigler-Lavelle

1984    *McKeithen Weeden Island: The Culture of Northern Florida, A.D. 200–900*. Academic Press, Orlando, FL.

Moore, Clarence B.

1902    Certain Aboriginal Remains of the Northwest Florida Coast, Part II. *Journal of the Academy of Natural Sciences of Philadelphia* 12: 127–358.

1918    The Northwestern Florida Coast Revisited. *Journal of the Academy of Natural Sciences of Philadelphia* 16: 513–81.

Nanfro, Claire Elizabeth

2004    An Analysis of Faunal Remains from the Bird Hammock Site (8Wa30). MS thesis, Florida State University, Tallahassee.

Penton, Daniel T.

1970    Excavations in the Early Swift Creek Component at Bird Hammock (8Wa30). MS thesis, Department of Anthropology, Florida State University, Tallahassee.

Percy, George, and David S. Brose

1974    Weeden Island Ecology, Subsistence and Village Life in Northwest Florida. Paper presented at the 39th annual meeting of the Society for American Archaeology, Washington, DC.

Phelps, David Sutton

1969    Swift Creek and Santa Rosa in Northwest Florida. *The Institute of Archeology and Anthropology Notebook* 1(6–9): 14–24.

Russo, Michael

2004    Measuring Shell Rings for Social Inequality. In *Signs of Power: The Rise of Cultural Complexity in the Southeast*, edited by Jon Gibson and Phillip Carr, 26–70. University of Alabama Press, Tuscaloosa.

In press    Ring Features of the Southeast U.S.: Architecture and Epiphenomena. In *The Cultural Dynamics of Shell Middens and Shell Mounds: A Worldwide Perspective*, edited by Mirjana Roksandic, Shiela Mendonc de Souza, Sabine Eggers, Meaghan Burchell, and Daniella Klokler. University of New Mexico Press, Albuquerque.

Russo, Michael, and Craig Dengel

2010    The History and Status of Sites 8By7, 8By8, and 8By9 on and near Tyndall Air Force Base. Southeast Archeological Center, National Park Service, Tallahassee. Submitted to Tyndall Air Force Base, Panama City, Florida.

Russo, Michael, Craig Dengel, Jeffrey Shanks, and Thadra Stanton

2011    Baker's and Strange's Mounds and Middens: Woodland Occupations on Tyndall Air Force Base. Southeast Archeological Center, National Park Service, Tallahassee. Submitted to Tyndall Air Force Base, Panama City, Florida.

Russo, Michael, Carla S. Hadden, and Craig Dengel

2009    Archaeological Investigations of Mounds and Ring Middens at Hare Hammock: Tyndall Air

Force Base. Southeast Archeological Center, National Park Service, Tallahassee. Submitted to Tyndall Air Force Base, Panama City, Florida.

Russo, Michael, Margo Schwadron, and Emily M. Yates

2006    Archeological Investigation of the Bayview Site (8By137): A Weeden Island Ring Midden. Southeast Archeological Center, National Park Service, Tallahassee. Submitted to Tyndall Air Force Base, Panama City, Florida.

Sears, William H.

1963    *The Tucker Site on Alligator Harbor, Franklin County, Florida.* Contributions of the Florida State Museum no. 9. University of Florida, Gainesville.

1973    The Sacred and Secular in Prehistoric Ceramics. In *Variation in Anthropology: Essays in Honor of John C. McGregor,* edited by Donald W. Lathrap and Jody Douglas, 31–42. Illinois Archaeological Survey, Urbana.

Shanks, Jeffrey, and Julia Byrd

2012    Shell Game: The Marine Reservoir Effect and the Chronology of a Woodland Mound and Ring Midden Complex on the Northwest Florida Coast. Paper presented at the 78th annual meeting of the Southeast Archaeological Conference, Baton Rouge, LA.

Snow, Frankie

1998    Swift Creek Design Investigations: The Hartford Case. In *A World Engraved: Archaeology of the Swift Creek Culture,* edited by Mark Williams and Daniel T. Elliott, 61–98. University of Alabama Press, Tuscaloosa.

Snow, Frankie, and Keith Stephenson

1998    Swift Creek Designs: A Tool for Monitoring Interaction. In *A World Engraved: Archaeology of the Swift Creek Culture,* edited by Mark Williams and Daniel T. Elliott, 99–111. University of Alabama Press, Tuscaloosa.

Stephenson, Keith, Judith A. Bense, and Frankie Snow

2002    Aspects of Deptford and Swift Creek of the South Atlantic and Gulf Coastal Plains. In *The Woodland Southeast,* edited by David G. Anderson and Robert C. Mainfort Jr., 318–51. University of Alabama Press, Tuscaloosa.

Thomas, Prentice M., and L. Janice Campbell

1991    The Elliott's Point Complex: New Data Regarding the Localized Poverty Point Expression on the Northwest Florida Coast, 2000 B.C.–500 B.C. *Geoscience and Man* 29: 103–19.

1996    Interpretations. In *Controlled Excavation at 8WL58, the Old Homestead Site: Completing the Compliance Process at Eglin Air Force Base, Okaloosa, Santa Rosa and Walton Counties,* vols. 26–30, edited by Prentice M. Thomas Jr., Maria L. Schleidt Penalva, L. Janice Campbell, and Mathilda Cox, 148–66. Report of Investigations no. 284. Prentice Thomas and Associates, Fort Walton Beach, Florida. On file, Florida Master Site File, Tallahassee.

Thomas, Prentice M., Jr., Maria L. Schleidt Penalva, L. Janice Campbell, and Mathilda Cox

1996    *Controlled Excavation at 8WL58, the Old Homestead Site: Completing the Compliance Process at Eglin Air Force Base, Okaloosa, Santa Rosa and Walton Counties,* vols. 26–30. Report of Investigations no. 284. Prentice Thomas and Associates, Fort Walton Beach, Florida. On file, Florida Master Site File, Tallahassee.

Walker, William H.

1995    Ceremonial Trash? In *Expanding Archaeology,* edited by James M. Skibo, William H. Walker, and Axel E. Nielsen, 67–79. University of Utah Press, Salt Lake City.

Wallis, Neill J.

2011    *The Swift Creek Gift: Vessel Exchange on the Atlantic Coast.* University of Alabama Press, Tuscaloosa.

White, Nancy Marie

1992    The Overgrown Road Site (8Gu38): A Swift Creek Camp in the Lower Apalachicola Valley. *Florida Anthropologist* 45(1): 18–38.

2010    Gotier Hammock Mound and Midden on St. Joseph's Bay, Northwest Florida. *Florida Anthropologist* 63(3–4): 149–82.

Willey, Gordon R.

1949    *Archeology of the Florida Gulf Coast*. Smithsonian Institution Press, Washington, D.C.

# 7

# North Gulf Coastal Archaeology
# of the Here and Now

KENNETH E. SASSAMAN, PAULETTE S. MCFADDEN, MICAH P. MONÉS,
ANDREA PALMIOTTO, AND ASA R. RANDALL

By some measures, over half of the population of the United States today lives on or near the coasts of the Pacific and Atlantic oceans and the Gulf of Mexico. In Florida, which boasts over 3,660 kilometers of tidal coastline, the proportion of coastal dwellers is much higher, over 75 percent of an estimated 18.8 million state residents in 2010 (Bureau of Economic and Business Research 2011). This is an increase in coastal population of nearly 200 percent in just 40 years. Indeed, Florida coastal populations and economies have witnessed accelerated growth over the past two centuries, and many expect that to continue into the future. Although a variety of stakeholders have alerted us to the vulnerabilities of unbridled coastal development (Hinrichsen 1998; Pilkey and Young 2009), those with the authority to change the course of Florida's history seem inclined to mortgage its future on continued, albeit now regulated, expansion (Schrope 2010).

The risks of demographic and economic expansion along Florida's coasts have come into sharper focus with greater understanding that coastal environments can sustain only so much human exploitation. Many such limits have been imposed or accentuated by the very interventions that made expansion possible, such as the alteration of lands and habitats, the extraction of ground water, the emplacement of infrastructure, the replenishment of beaches, and channelization. Others can be viewed as long-term, unforeseen consequences of intensified practices, such as commercial fishing, farming, consumption of fossil fuels, and industrial operations that pollute. In both cases, human perceptions of change hinder imagined alternatives, in the former case because of short-term future horizons and in the latter case because of truncated histories. Although modern Florida is defined by its unprecedented growth over the past two centuries, it represents but a fleeting moment in a history of human occupation that spans at least 130 centuries (ca.

13,000 years). Not only is Florida's recent past a small fraction of its total human past, it is destined to be a small fraction of its future, as the current rate of growth is not likely to be sustained for another 200 years.

Climate change is manifested on Florida's coasts by increased saltwater intrusion into freshwater aquifers, intensified coastal erosion, accelerated habitat destruction, and greater storm severity and frequency (Noss 2011; Pilkey and Young 2009). Projections of climate change for the next century render dubious any plan to expand the development of coastal lands that will be completely transformed by the end of this century. A one-meter increase in sea level by 2100 would flood 10 percent of Florida's inhabitable land (Weiss et al. 2011). Although a gradual, incremental rise in sea level could be accommodated by movement of coastal habitat landward where conditions allow, geological evidence suggests that sea levels in the past sometimes rose abruptly, overstepping surface geomorphology and drowning shorelines (Donoghue 2011). Moreover, emplacements of infrastructure and other modern alterations of coastal environments hinder adaptations to a changing shoreline, underscoring the need to seriously consider human withdrawal from the coastal zones that are most vulnerable. However, an imagined future of demographic retrenchment along the coast has little parallel (and hence no model for mitigative action) in Florida's recent past; it is, in fact, anathema to those whose only point of reference is unbridled expansion since the mid-nineteenth century.

The long view of Florida's past, however, reveals abundant prior experience with both drowned and emergent shorelines, human displacement and resettlement, and economic adjustments to changing coastal habitats. Thus, archaeology and history promise to lend some perspective on possible futures by considering current problems in the context of longer timeframes. This perhaps has always been the benefit of historical consciousness for humans in general, but in the modern era, the time before modernity has been unduly truncated by the temporality of progress, where the past bears little relevance moving forward (Harvey 1990). Archaeology and history that consider the challenges of human futures must strive to relocate and mobilize pasts that have been severed by the time-space compression of modernity.

An archaeology of the here and now is not an archaeology of modernity per se, but is rather an archaeology of the relationship between past human experiences and imagined futures. It starts not by asking what happened in the past but rather what might possibly happen in the future. Its point of reference is thus not a chronicle of extinct people with truncated histories but a series of alternative futures whose conditions and causes at any point in the past can be projected forward using observations of historical and archaeological records to infer both processes of long-term change and human interventions against change, all in the service of broadening future time horizons to imagine adaptations going forward.

Florida has a long history of coastal archaeology, much of it geared toward the investigations of environmental conditions that variously sustained and challenged occupation of the coast (Thompson and Worth 2011). The archaeological record of the last 4,000 years provides multiple examples of substantial human settlement in areas of favorable ecological conditions. Evidence of relatively large-scale intensive settlement is found on both the Atlantic and Gulf coasts, exemplified perhaps best by the Calusa of the Charlotte Harbor area (Marquardt 2004; Widmer 1988), a society whose level of sociopolitical complexity was underpinned by rich marine habitats and a capacity to modify environments for productive ends. The recent archaeology of the Calusa under the direction of Marquardt and Walker (2013) is one of the few examples of using the ancient past to create a bridge to solutions to modern challenges in Florida (Marquardt 1994), although coastal projects elsewhere in North America and beyond provide additional guidance about making such connections (e.g., Braje and Rick 2010; Rick and Erlandson 2008). Again, much of this work is geared toward the environmental conditions of coastal living. Less attention has been paid to the sociohistorical side of the equation, the realm of experience where perceptions of environmental change and imaginations of alternative futures are crafted, contested, and recrafted.

The Lower Suwannee Archaeological Survey was launched in 2009 to develop knowledge about long-term interactions between humans and their environment in a dynamic coastal setting for the purpose of informing contemporary and future issues (Sassaman et al. 2011). The project is still in its early stages and is expected to continue for decades to come, unfolding over a period when populations in some of the most vulnerable coastal areas will likely be relocated as sea levels overstep modern shorelines. The northern Gulf coast of Florida is one such area, where the low gradient of offshore terrain is highly vulnerable to changes in sea level that will expose abundant land with shoreline regression and flood equally vast areas with shoreline transgression. Known to modern Floridians as the "Nature Coast," the northern Gulf coast is largely undeveloped land, in part because of federal and state efforts to protect gulf coast habitat from development. Given the limited amount of previous archaeological research in the area, the Lower Suwannee Archaeological Survey is designed to compile basic information on the culture history of the area and thus help agencies such as the U.S. Fish and Wildlife Service with their legal obligations regarding historical preservation and at the same time ask questions that are relevant to Florida's future.

In keeping with an archaeology of the here and now, this chapter aims to illustrate alternative futures with histories of past experience, what we might call "futures past," to borrow from Koselleck (2004). We divide our examples into three categories. In the section on relocations, we use examples of site abandonment to consider the role that changes in sea level may have played in inducing resettlement. The establishment of new settlements we discuss in the emplacements section below are among the outcomes of transgressive seas, but here we emphasize deliberate human interventions against change, as in the terraforming of anthropogenic landscapes and the construction of elaborate mortuary facilities. We continue this theme of change in a section on resilience, in which histories of sustainability in cyclical regimes are threatened with structural change. In each of these sections we draw attention to the recent past of the study area to show how modern experiences of relocation, emplacement, and resilience resemble those of the ancient past. In particular, we highlight the town of Cedar Key in Levy County, a town whose history includes, among other fascinating events, its physical relocation after being destroyed by a hurricane in 1896 and, in the 1990s, its economic transformation as a leading producer of clams after a ban on gill-net fishing suspended "traditional" pursuits.

Background on the environment, culture history, and prior archaeological work in the study area is available elsewhere (Sassaman et al. 2011), and need not be repeated here. However, a few key features of this background bear mentioning. The 42-kilometer-long study area straddles the delta of the Suwannee River, the outlet of the only major gulf-draining river that has not been altered by dams or diversion canals (figure 7.1). The delta intercepts and overlies a complex surface geology of shallow limestone bedrock (Davis 1997, 165). Also overlying this karst topography are numerous relict paleodunes, some quite tall, that likely formed during the late Pleistocene, when sea levels were tens of meters lower than present and the shoreline tens of kilometers to the west. Shoreline erosion of these dunes contributes sand to an otherwise sediment-poor biome. Broad tidal marsh dominates the shoreline, and substantial oyster reefs parallel the coastline offshore. The long-term interplay of sedimentation, freshwater input, marsh formation, and oyster reef distribution is nicely illustrated by Wright et al. (2005) in their geological study of rising sea level in the Suwannee Delta during the Holocene.

Terrestrial archaeological evidence for human occupation of the Lower Suwannee region goes back to at least 4,000 years ago. Relative sea level has been rising in the region since the end of the Pleistocene, and shoreline settlements greater than circa 4,500 years in age are now inundated (Faught 2004). Prior work in the study area provides some insights about sites that were either destroyed long ago (e.g., Moore 1902, 1903, 1918; Stearns 1869; Wyman 1870) or have more recently been impacted by development or erosion (Borremans 1991a; Bullen and Dolen 1960; Dorian 1980; Jones 1992; Jones and Borremans 1991; Koski et al. 2003; Stojanowski and Doran 1998; Weinstein and Mayo 2006). Graduate student research at the University of Florida contributed intermittent but valuable field results in the late twentieth century (e.g., Borremans and Moseley 1990; Goldburt 1966; Kohler 1975).

The state inventory of recorded coastal sites in the study area includes around 111

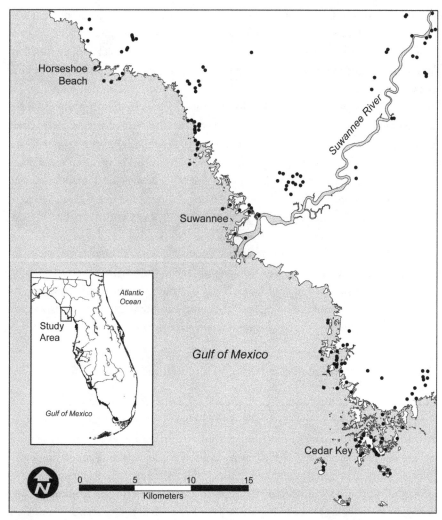

Figure 7.1. The Lower Suwannee Archaeological Survey study area on the northern Gulf coast of Florida, showing locations of sites on record in the Florida Master Site Files.

aboriginal sites, almost all of which have shell-bearing deposits (figure 7.1). The most intensive and sustained human settlement of what are now national wildlife refuges took place during the Deptford (ca. 500 BC–AD 250) and Weeden Island periods (ca. AD 200–900). Assemblages from sites of these periods often contain sherds of plain sand-tempered and Pasco limestone-tempered pottery. Swift Creek pottery is minor but pervasive. Its date is estimated at roughly AD 150–300, and thus it bridges the Deptford–Weeden Island continuum. Occasional fiber-tempered sherds attest to occupations during the Late Archaic Orange period (ca. 2500–1500 BC), and a consistent presence of spiculate-paste wares includes potentially early St. Johns pottery (ca. 1000 BC through possibly Weeden Island). Late St. Johns pottery (i.e., check-stamped wares, post–AD 750) occurs in only trace amounts. Finally, traces of Alachua (AD 700–contact) and Safety Harbor (AD 900–contact) pottery attest to late-period connections with populations up the Suwannee River and down the Gulf coast, respectively.

Mounds are recorded at 32 sites in the study area. Whether they are classified in the state site files as "shell" or "sand," mounds are distributed widely and include clusters of massive shell deposits (often with sand mounds) in the greater Cedar Key area (notably at Way Key) and at lesser locations north along the coast. Many of the sand mounds described by C. B. Moore and others consisted of mantles of sand overlying shell deposits, but mounds consisting entirely of sand are also known for the study area. Whether sand was emplaced over shell or deposited alone, the deceased were often interred in it. Burials also occur in what are described as "shell mounds," and these occur with relatively great frequency in shell deposits (middens?) that do not express much topographic relief. Burials are reported at about one-third of all sites in the study area. Thus, interment of the dead at sites in the study area was very common, and sometimes it was attended by the construction of mounds and the inclusion of elaborate material culture.

## Alternative Futures Past

Since 2009, the Lower Suwannee Archaeological Survey has conducted test excavations at eight sites in the study area and full-coverage reconnaissance surveys of two (dune) islands (McFadden and Palmiotto 2012; Monés et al. 2012; Sassaman et al. 2013; Sassaman et al. 2011). Testing has focused on exposing and dating stratigraphic sequences and on collecting bulk samples of midden matrix for analyses of vertebrate and invertebrate fauna. Specialized analyses involving ceramic petrography, geoarchaeology, and stable isotopes of oyster shell have also been launched. Although results to date are preliminary, we have begun to recognize patterns in the timing, siting, and structure of sites that enables us to infer a series of alternative futures for communities and individuals experiencing sea-level change. These patterns include examples of relocation, emplacement, and resilience.

### Relocation

Figure 7.2 shows stratigraphic profiles of seven of the eight sites we have tested in the project area (the eighth is a thin, single-component scallop midden on Way Key). The profiles are positioned in relative order, both horizontally (from north to south) and vertically (meters above mean sea level [amsl]). The basal components of these profiles range in elevation from 0.0 to 2.0 meters amsl, while elevations of their modern surfaces range from about 1.0 to 2.5 meters amsl. The deepest sequence among them is the 1.8-meter profile of the southern edge of Shell Mound, the shallowest the 0.5-meter profile of a test unit in the center of a shell ring on Deer Island. Most of the profiles contain distinct strata, some marked by unconformities of erosional events and/or depositional hiatuses. Strata include both autochthonous midden and masses of largely oyster shell with little to no inorganic matrix. Absolute dating of the beginning and endpoints of each stratigraphic unit will be needed to infer the duration of depositional activities, incidences of erosion, and depositional hiatuses. Although the 20 AMS assays obtained thus far offer some insight into patterned variation, they are but a modest start.

The earliest dated strata (ca. 4000 BP) exist at both low (< 0.3 meters amsl) and high (~ 1.7 meters amsl) elevations with assemblages indicative of substantial habitation (features, artifacts, diverse fauna, charcoal). Sea levels were still considerably lower than at present, and the shoreline was several kilometers west of its current position (Wright et al. 2005). That landforms elevated above and landward of the coastline were also locations of intensive habitation this early would suggest that coastal settlement during the Late Archaic period was broadly distributed across various landforms, including those located several kilometers inland from the coast. Despite variations in distance and elevation, all components of the Late Archaic period (through ca. 3300 BP) are dominated by oyster shell and marine fishes, a point to which we will return below.

Persistent, possibly intensified occupation of elevated landforms ensued over the Late Archaic period, presumably in concert with rising sea levels. The absence of low-elevation components dating to the last several centuries of this period may be simply due to sample bias, and we note that the profile at Cat Island suggests that post-4000 BP deposits were scoured by water. If so, this must have elapsed before ca. 1800 BP, the age of the late Deptford midden at a similar elevation on Little Bradford Island. The profiles of both Cat Island and Little Bradford provide some perspective on the cut-and-fill outcomes of storm surges at roughly modern sea levels. The upper 30–40 centimeters of each profile consists of finely bedded inorganic sands that rest unconformably on scoured archaeological midden. This was the outcome the so-called Storm of the Century, a 1993 cyclonic storm with a storm surge of over 2 meters.

After about 3300 BP, local populations relocated to sites other than those that have been investigated to date and we lose sight of them for the next 800 years. It is tempting to describe the change as the abandonment of the coast, but we simply do not know where local communities resettled. If they followed a regressing coastline, sites of this timeframe would be underwater today, as the sea level rose once again after about 2500 BP. This is the inference of settlement relocation along the South Atlantic coast, where Early Woodland denizens followed a retreating coastline during a time of global cooling (Brooks et al. 1989; DePratter and Howard 1981). Pro-

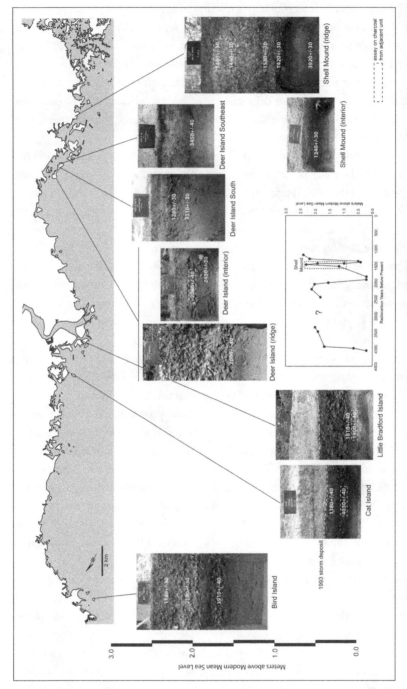

Figure 7.2. Stratigraphic profiles of seven sites tested in the study area, with locator map and inset graph showing the relationship between radiometric age of archaeostrata and elevations (meters) above modern mean sea level.

files of sites on elevated landforms in the study area lend some credence to the inference that sea level dropped after ca. 3300 BP. With the exception of Bird Island, Late Archaic strata with elevations at least 1.0 meter amsl are highly weathered, evidently due to excessive drainage and oxidation. In addition, all of the Late Archaic strata (including Bird Island) are overlain with a sandy stratum 10–20 centimeters thick. Because these overlying sands occur at elevations ranging from 0.5 to 2.0 meters amsl, they are likely to be pedogenic, not depositional. Pedogenesis resulting in the formation of a surface horizon of sand would require both adequate drainage and considerable time. The earliest reoccupation of any such locations was ca. 2500 BP, a hiatus of eight centuries. A similar period of time since the latest occupation of Deer Island (ca. 1300 BP) made possible the development of a surface horizon of sand not unlike that covering Late Archaic strata.

It is worth noting that one of the most distal islands of the northern gulf coast, North Key in the Cedar Key area, houses a midden that has basal elevations near the current sea level. Four C-13 corrected assays on marine shell from this midden range from ca. 3000 to 2400 BP (Borremans 1991b). Because we do not have precise provenience information on these samples and cannot be assured the assays are adequately corrected for the reservoir effect, we are reluctant to accept them uncritically. Nonetheless, the presumed age of this deposit falls in the time range that is "missing" from our inventory of sites. The distal position of North Key lends credence to the idea that communities during this interval relocated coastline settlement westward during a time of lower sea levels.

The resettlement of elevated landforms after about 2200 BP was accompanied by an intensive period of terraforming, when numerous rings, ridges, and mounds of shell were erected (see the section on emplacements below). The lowest of these are today only about 1.0 meter amsl, although they gained great height rather quickly, as in the accumulation of 7 meters of oyster shell at Shell Mound in just a century or two. It seems reasonable to suggest that a rapid rise in sea level (and possibly greater storm severity) encouraged settlement relocation to the highest elevations as well as public works projects to decrease the vulnerability of settlements to flooding. If that is the case, a reversal of sea level likely occurred over the next century or two, when low-elevation islands such as Little Bradford were again occupied. Settlement at sites near the modern sea level continued until at least 1350 BP. The most distal of the islands, Seahorse Key, was also settled during this interval and apparently continued to be occupied through about 1200 BP (Borremans 1991b), when most settlements were again relocated to elevated landforms. At over 16 meters amsl, Seahorse Key is the highest elevation in the study area and thus provided both refuge from high water during high sea-level stands and proximity to coastal biomes during low sea-level stands.

Relocations are not just events of the ancient past. On September 29, 1896, the town of Cedar Key was struck by a hurricane with winds estimated at 125 mph and a storm surge of over 3 meters. The town, which was located on the island of Atsena Otie, was destroyed, as were the stands of Eastern Red Cedar that were the basis of a thriving mill industry. For reasons that went beyond the storm damage itself, townspeople decided to relocate Cedar Key to a more protected inland island, Way Key. Long before then, Way Key had been the locus of intensive native settlement that started no later than 4,000 years ago and persisted intermittently through at least the fourteenth century. Many meters of shell midden, interspersed with sand mounds and other emplacements, had accumulated across much of Way Key, raising the elevation well beyond that of Atsena Otie and affording a secure foundation for a new, less vulnerable Cedar Key. The town's relocation in the late nineteenth century was merely the most recent of many such relocations in the past, and given the expectation that sea levels will rise in the future, it is unlikely to be the last.

## Emplacements

Every move away from a location that became vulnerable or inopportune because of changes in sea level was followed by an emplacement if people actually resettled in a new location, which apparently was often the case. Many such moves entailed returning to places of former settlement, in some cases perhaps with memories of previous lives, in others likely not. Whether or not they were stimulated by memories, emplacements at locations of former settlement often benefited from physical alterations that both elevated landforms above storm surge levels and rendered them less vulnerable to erosion (shell midden provides a resistant matrix against tidal erosion, for example). The relocation of the town of Cedar Key to Way Key would not have been such a good option had native predecessors never lived on the island and created such a firm foundation through landform alterations.

We regard the relocation of Cedar Key as a deliberate, planned event, for indeed it was. Arguably, the same could be said for the emplacement of shell and sand by coastal dwellers thousands of years ago. Emplacement in this sense is a discursive act, an instrument for moving forward. Just as Cedar Key mapped out its future with the emplacement of the town on Way Key, ancient people constructed village plans and associated facilities to materialize their own futures.

The many U-shaped shell ridges in the area surrounding Shell Mound bear witness to a flurry of terraforming at around 2000 BP (figure 7.3). Arcuate or semicircular ridges ranging in height from less than 1.0 to nearly 7.0 meters and from 20 to almost 200 meters long have been observed at many locations within a few kilometers of Shell Mound, itself the largest of the shellworks and seemingly at the center of a clustered distribution. Some "rings" are only barely circular in plan, as they consist of two parallel, slightly arcuate ridges. No matter what the shape or size, each configuration encloses a space that we infer to be habitation space. At the two rings we have tested thus far (Shell Mound and one at north end of Deer Island), a near-surface, thin-interior midden with pit features and only moderate amounts of shell contrasts with a thick column of mostly oyster shell in ridges. We suspect that ridges accreted episodically, although the shape of the accreting form may have been dependent on village layout from the start, so placement of even the initial loads of shell were not likely arbitrary. The size of ridges appears to be not just a function of time but also a function of the size of discrete depositional units (i.e., loads), and thus a function of human scale. The largest depositional units index large groups of people—not necessarily just residents—who were all engaged in mobilizing shell. In some cases, existing shell deposits may have been mined to fill in portions of accreting ridges, and we suspect that ridges sometimes went up rather fast. Four AMS assays from the southern edge of Shell Mound statistically cluster in the sixteenth and fifteenth centuries before the present, although we note that the core of this seven-meter-thick deposit has yet to be examined and Deptford pottery at the base suggests that shell began to accumulate closer to 2000 BP

Enclosures of shell offered practical value: with ridges closed to the northwest—the current direction of prevailing wind—ring interiors were sheltered from winds, which may have been detrimental under some conditions but were of obvious benefit during stormy weather, as we learned firsthand.

The practicality of shell ridges alone does not account for other emplacements associated with them, such as the sand mounds sited in the vicinity of Shell Mound. As we mentioned in the review of earlier work, sand mounds are generally mortuary facilities and they are most often associated with the Swift Creek and Weeden Island traditions of the region. The Hog Island mortuary mound, sited immediately to the west of Shell Mound across a narrow channel, contained scores of Swift Creek and Weeden Island vessels from both local and nonlocal sources (Harris-Parks 2012; Neill Wallis, personal communication 2013; Tallant n.d.), as well as galena, greenstone, and other exotic materials that were circulating across much of the region. It was thus a place of gathering not just for the living and the bodies of the deceased but also for diverse persons, as symbolized in objects from across the greater Southeast. The mound embodied a nuanced sense of history in indexing other places on the landscape, other objects, and other persons.

Many of the Weeden Island sand mounds observed at sites on Way Key were emplaced on older midden and were later encased in shell. In this respect, sand mounds transcended time and space by simultaneously referencing the past and enabling the future. All such historical or ritual acts exemplify the process by which places and landscapes develop significance beyond their practical utility (e.g., inhabitability, access to water, food, raw materials, information). They can be conceptualized as narratives about the past and about alternative futures. The same may be said for all types of "everyday" living, but in the elaborate facility that was the Hog Island

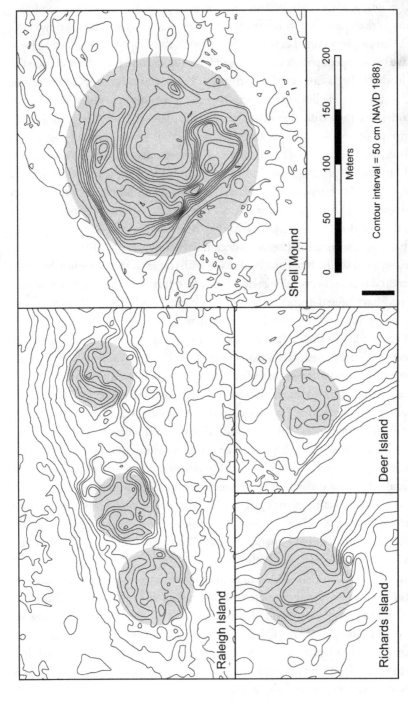

Figure 7.3. Examples of U-shaped and other arcuate shell ridges in the Shell Mound tract of the study area. LiDAR-generated maps courtesy of Asa R. Randall.

mortuary, for example, narratives were likely generalized to reach across cultural differences, including language. Referencing things with diverse origins, the narratives of material acts such as mounding and burials indexed other places and times and the people that populated them. It follows that practitioners of the Weeden Island religion drew from deeply historical and cosmopolitan frames of reference. They were thus perhaps challenged occasionally by conditions that threatened traditional beliefs and ways of life as sacred places such as mortuary mounds were impacted by rising seas. Did the very facilities, in this case ritual, that enabled the genesis and reproduction of networks of relocation become so fixed in place as to accentuate the vulnerability of people to changing water levels?

When Atsena Otie was abandoned in 1896, the only thing of consequence left behind was the town cemetery. Ever since, the persons interred at Atsena Otie have been a material link to a pivotal event, a reminder of a time when townspeople were wrested from their homes and relocated to a less vulnerable spot. Before water rises in the future and Atsena Otie is drowned, will these historical persons be disinterred and reburied, thus reentering the places of the living? Perhaps, but only if their descendants decide to take this action. In Weeden Island times, individuals were disinterred and reinterred occasionally, although they were not often relocated from places of initial interment except, perhaps, when destruction was an imminent threat. The Weeden Island Fowler Landing mound (Moore 1903, 364–70), located 16 kilometers up the Suwannee River, included 47 "bundle" burials, potentially individuals disinterred from coastal mortuaries and reinterred in locations far outside the vulnerabilities of coastal settings. The coastal mortuary at Hog Island contained an abundance of small bone elements such as toe and finger bones, in one case collected in a pottery vessel as if gathered together from a single event of disinterment (Tallant n.d.).

Other notable emplacements of historic Cedar Key include the infrastructure for transportation, commerce, and industry. Cedar Key became the western terminus of the Florida Railroad in 1860, which connected it to the Atlantic coast. Most of the island of Way Key was acquired by the railroad's president, David Levy Yulee, to house the terminal facilities. Way Key was platted as a town the following year, presaging the relocation of Cedar Key 35 years later, but not before the Civil War disrupted an era of otherwise steady growth. Indeed, the local economy boomed in the immediate postwar years, as new cedar mills were constructed on both Atsena Otie and Way Key, the latter so successful that its population exceeded that of the original town. When Henry Platt purchased the Florida Railroad in 1880, the future growth of Cedar Key seemed assured, but a dispute over selling the terminus at Way Key caused Platt to reroute the line to Tampa, which was completed six years later. Cedar Key's economic growth was curtailed, and by the time the 1896 hurricane struck, it was necessary to abandon not only Atsena Otie but also an entire way of life that was predicated on the town's connections via the railroad. Emplacements of infrastructure that had once made growth and prosperity possible through connectedness had the potential to become a drag on resilience.

## Resilience

Resilience is defined by ecologists as the ability of a complex system to withstand a disturbance and return to a state of equilibrium without undergoing structural change (Holling 1973). When it comes to the resilience of human societies, one could question the notion of equilibrium or steady-states and whether "systems" even exist outside the bounds of analytical perception. For our purposes here, the concept of resilience is useful for its nonlinear qualities, for providing an alternative to the notions of progress and growth on which the logic of capitalism is based. The history of Cedar Key, like the histories that elapsed before, is, if anything, nonlinear. More people lived in Cedar Key in the 1850s and the first century AD than live there today or at times in between. There was much greater wealth and industry right after the Civil War and in AD 500 than today or at times in between. And there were times when the oysters and other marine resources were so abundant and rich as to imagine infinite expansion of economy and population, but that proved not to be the case in the early 1900s and perhaps too as early as 3,300 years ago.

Just as the seas have never been always rising or always falling but simply changing, the histories of people on the northern Gulf coast have followed divergent, nonlinear paths. A constant state of change may have, in fact, precluded the development of more fixed and formalized relationships to the land, its resources, and to other people, leading not to the development of agricultural chiefdoms 1,000 years ago or to an urban center like Tampa in the late nineteenth century but instead a bastion of resilience. The sorts of structural changes known to throw complex ecosystems out of their adaptive cycles have no strong parallel in the cultural history of the study area, with the possible exception of cultural dispositions that arrived from without, as in the arrival of Weeden Island religion or the interventions of federal government since the Civil War (see below).

Resilience is certainly an apt description of life on the northern Gulf coast over the past 4,000 years, as it is today. We have already outlined several examples of relocation and emplacement that were at once responsive to change and proscriptive of futures. Here in closing we highlight briefly a few of the observations we have made about the subsistence economies of pre-Columbian communities to illustrate different forms of resilience involving natural resources.

Bird Island, located at the northern end of the study area, has a distinct stratigraphic sequence of early (ca. 4000 BP), middle (ca. 2200 BP), and late (ca. 1150 BP) components, the oldest separated from the other two by a thin stratum of sand, as noted earlier (McFadden and Palmiotto 2012). We do not have specific knowledge of the environmental conditions at each of these times, but apparently sea level was lower at the beginning of the sequence, when the shoreline was 4–5 kilometers west of its current position (Wright et al. 2005). Despite the distance from shore, Late Archaic residents of 4,000 years ago collected oysters and other marine shellfish as well as marine fish and turtles and transported them back to Bird Island. Freshwater and terrestrial resources apparently were not routinely collected, despite the fact that they were closer to the site. Without a point of comparison that predates 4,000 years ago, we can only imagine what prior experience was like, but we feel secure in suggesting that Late Archaic inhabitants of Bird Island came from a long lineage of coastal dwellers.

As sea levels rose and salt marsh began to form around Bird Island in the more or less modern configuration, the food choices of Deptford and Weeden Island residents did not vary appreciably from those of their Late Archaic predecessors. It would appear that the marine biomes that Late Archaic people traveled to had now arrived on the scene, enabling residents of Bird Island to confine most of their food gathering to the immediate area, if needed or desired. Of course, we do not know where particular oyster harvests were made, because later residents could have traveled just as far as their predecessors to collect food. However, we do know that whatever changes in environment took place from 4,000 to 2,200 to 1,150 years ago, they are not registered strongly in the archaeological record of food remains. Mobility clearly factors in as an instrument of resilience in at least the early period, while social networks of sharing that were embedded in community ritual was another likely measure of resilience in Weeden Island times.

Changes in food selection elsewhere in the study area provide a glimpse of changing sea levels and to human adjustments to "tradition" to facilitate persistence in place, yet another measure of resilience. The best example to date comes from Cat Island in the Suwannee Delta, where a 4,000-year-old midden dominated by oyster contrasts with a 1,400-year old midden dominated by Carolina marsh clam (*Polymesoda caroliniana*). The former contains no more than 5 percent clam by weight, whereas the latter consists of roughly 60 percent clam by weight (Sassaman et al. 2011).

Carolina marsh clam is adapted to low-salinity conditions made possible by a constant input of freshwater. Increased habitat for this species proximate to Cat Island could have been precipitated by either increased freshwater flow from the Suwannee River or the regression of the sea that shifted the freshwater plume seaward, or both. Sediment load is critical too for productive clam habitat, so spikes in production likely tracked marsh aggradation. The earliest use of marsh clam observed thus far is ca. 1800 BP, on nearby Little Bradford Island. This timing closely follows the period of intense oyster harvesting ca. 2000 BP, the time of the onset of terraforming. Perhaps the intensified use of marsh clam was not only an opportunistic use of an emergent new resource but was also encouraged by a downturn in the availability of oyster, exacerbated of course by the same changes in salinity that promoted marsh clams. Without metric data on changes in oyster size through time we must reserve any speculation about resource decline. However, oysters deposited during the Late Archaic period are substantially larger than those deposited later.

In the commercial era of modern Cedar Key we find again a shift from oyster to clam, in this case hard clam (*Mercenaria mercenaria*). In the early 1990s, following the release of contaminants from septic systems in the town of Suwannee, the federal government closed Suwannee Sound to oyster harvesting. A statewide ban on gill nets in 1995 dealt a second blow to a local economy based almost entirely on the sea. However, with government assistance and local resolve, fishermen in Cedar Key retooled to establish off-shore clam farms beginning in 1993. In a few short years, hard clam aquaculture was garnering annual sales of over $10 million, and the industry still thrives today. This remarkably nimble shift to commercial clamming qualifies as a measure of resilience inasmuch as it continues to be responsive to conditions that threaten its sustainability. Because the clamming industry depends so heavily on water quality, fishermen have teamed up with government agencies to monitor coastal waters (Colson and Strummer 2000), an effort that extends far beyond the coast to the entire Suwannee River valley, whose headwaters are in south-central Georgia. This effort emphasizes pollutants from modern technologies and land use. A deep time perspective alerts us to the need to anticipate changes in salinity in the coming decades as sea levels rise and thus of an ongoing need to plan for resilience.

## Conclusion

When we look past the historical particulars of technology, economy, and government, the recent and ancient pasts of the northern Gulf coast have much in common. That is not to say that life on the coast has never changed, for indeed change has been constant. The archaeological record of the study area consists of sequences of repeated emplacements and relocations, frequent realignments of people to coastal land and its resources. Yet we have no reason to suspect that the region was ever abandoned entirely over the past 4,000 years, despite dramatic storms, rising and falling seas, and changes in the availability of keystone resources. Instead, communities as far back as 4000 BP and as recently as the turn of the last century adjusted to emergent new circumstances and carried on. An enduring resilience appears to have been enabled, at least in part, by historical connections to places and persons of the past, both physically in the alteration of landscapes to enhance inhabitability and culturally in the changing meaning and value of ancestral places. If nothing else, the recent and ancient pasts of the northern Gulf coast have in common a series of places on the landscape—even entire landscapes themselves—that encode both records of futures past and guideposts for futures to come.

Looking forward, the research questions for an archaeology of the here and now must be relevant to the modern communities of Cedar Key, Suwannee, and Horseshoe Beach and to the U.S. Fish and Wildlife Service, which has jurisdiction over most of the study area. Many questions will be directed to the physical and natural sciences, whose data on environmental processes are needed for long-range planning. Archaeology adds to that repertoire of information by extending inquiry into human-environment relationships far beyond the reach of historic and contemporary records. However, in its understanding of the relationships among place, community, and history, archaeology brings a humanistic element that puts environmental data into perspective. The challenge moving forward is to broaden future time horizons with deep time perspectives so that decisions made for short-term gain do not lead to long-term, unforeseen consequences that would undermine a resilience that has served northern Gulf coast communities for over 4,000 years.

## References

Borremans, Nina T.

1991a  The Aboriginal Cemetery at Cedar Key (8LV4): Management Report. Institute of Archaeology and Paleoenvironmental Studies, University of Florida, Gainesville.

1991b  Unpublished notes and records on archaeological testing at Seahorse Key and North Key. On file, Florida Museum of Natural History, University of Florida, Gainesville.

Borremans, Nina Thanz, and Michael E. Moseley

1990  A Prehistoric Site Survey of the Cedar Keys Region of Coastal Levy County, Florida. Department of Anthropology, University Press of Florida, Gainesville.

Braje, Todd J., and Torben C. Rick (editors)

2010  Human Impacts on Seals, Sea Lions, and Sea Otters: Integrating Archaeology and Ecology in the Northeast Pacific. University of California Press, Berkeley.

Brooks, Mark J., Peter A. Stone, Donald J. Colquhoun, and Jan G. Brown

1989  Sea Level Change, Estuarine Development, and Temporal Variability in Woodland Period Subsistence-Settlement Patterning on the Lower Coastal Plain of South Carolina. In Studies in South Carolina Archaeology: Essays in Honor of Robert L. Stephenson, edited by A. C. Goodyear and G. T. Hanson, 91–100. South Carolina Institute of Archaeology and Anthropology, University of South Carolina, Columbia.

Bullen, Ripley P., and E. M. Dolan

1960  Shell Mound, Levy County, Florida. Florida Anthropologist 13: 17–23.

Bureau of Economic and Business Research

2011  Florida Statistical Abstract. Forty-fifth edition. Bureau of Economic and Business Research, University Press of Florida, Gainesville.

Colson, Suzanne, and Leslie N. Strummer

2000  One Shining Moment Known as Camelot: The Cedar Key Story. Journal of Shellfish Research 19: 477–80.

Davis, Richard A., Jr.

1997    Geology of the Florida Coast. In *The Geology of Florida*, edited by A. F. Randazzo and D. S. Jones, 155–68. University Press of Florida, Gainesville.

DePratter, Chester B., and James D. Howard

1981    Evidence for a Sea Level Lowstand between 4500 and 2400 Years B.P. on the Southeast Coast of the United States. *Journal of Sedimentary Petrology* 51: 1287–96.

Donoghue, Joseph F.

2011    Sea Level History of the Northern Gulf of Mexico Coast and Sea Level Rise Scenarios for the Near Future. *Climatic Change* 107: 17–34.

Dorian, Alan W.

1980    *Literature Search and Partial Cultural Resource Inventory of the Chassahowitzka, Cedar Keys, and Lower Suwannee National Wildlife Refuges.* Archaeological Research Reports no. 10. Southeast Archaeology Conservation Center, Florida State University Press, Tallahassee.

Faught, Michael K.

2004    The Underwater Archaeology of Paleolandscapes, Apalachee Bay, Florida. *American Antiquity* 69: 275–89.

Goldburt, J. S.

1966    The Archaeology of Shired Island. MA thesis, Department of Anthropology, University of Florida, Gainesville.

Harris-Parks, Erin

2012    A Petrographic Analysis of Weeden Island Pottery to Determine Provenance of Local and Nonlocal Wares. BA Honors thesis, Department of Anthropology, University of Florida, Gainesville.

Harvey, David

1990    *The Condition of Postmodernity: An Enquiry into the Origins of Culture Change.* Wiley Blackwell, Oxford.

Hine, Albert C., Daniel F. Belknap, Joan G. Hutton, Eric B. Osking, and Mark W. Evans

1988    Recent Geological History and Modern Sedimentary Processes Along an Incipient, Low-Energy, Epicontinental-Sea Coastline: Northwest Florida. *Journal of Sedimentary Petrology* 58(4): 567–79.

Hinrichsen, Don

1998    *Coastal Waters of the World: Trends, Threats, Strategies.* Island Press, Washington, DC.

Holling, C. S.

1973    Resilience and Stability of Ecological Systems. *Annual Review of Ecology and Systematics* 4: 1–23.

Jones, B. Calvin

1992    *Archaeological Evaluation of Lions Club Lot in Cedar Key, Florida: Salvage of Historic Burials and Preservation of Weeden Island (Pasco) Burial Area.* Florida Archaeological Reports 9. Bureau of Archaeological Research, Division of Historical Resources, Florida Department of State, Tallahassee.

Jones, Paul L., and Nina T. Borremans

1991    *An Archaeological Survey of the Gulf Hammock, Florida.* Institute of Archaeology and Paleoenvironmental Studies, University of Florida, Gainesville.

Kohler, Timothy A.

1975    The Garden Patch Site: A Minor Weeden Island Ceremonial Center on the Northern Peninsular Florida Gulf Coast. MA thesis, Department of Anthropology, University of Florida, Gainesville.

Koski, Steve, Jennifer Langdale, Jecyn Bremer, Lisa O'Steen, and Pamela Vojnovski

2003    *A Cultural Resource Assessment Survey of Four Parcels and Site Evaluation Study of 8DI29, 8DI150, and 8DI165 for the Suwannee River Dredging Project, Dixie County, Florida.* Technical Report 1070, New South Associates, Inc., Stone Mountain, Georgia.

Koselleck, Reinhart

2004    *Futures Past: On the Semantics of Historical Time.* Columbia University Press, New York.

Marquardt, William H.

1994    The Role of Archaeology in Raising Environmental Consciousness: An Example from Southwest Florida. In *Historical Ecology: Cultural Knowledge and Changing Landscapes,* edited by Carole L. Crumley, 203–21. School of American Research, Santa Fe, NM.

2004    Calusa. In *Handbook of North American Indians:* 14. *Southeast,* edited by R. D. Fogelson, 204–12. Smithsonian Institution Press, Washington, DC.

2010    Mounds, Middens, and Rapid Climate Change during the Archaic-Woodland Transition in the Southeastern United States. In *Trend, Tradition, and Turmoil: What Happened to the Southeastern Archaic?* edited by D. H. Thomas and M. C. Sanger, 253–71. Anthropological Papers of the American Museum of Natural History, vol. 93. American Museum of Natural History, New York.

Marquardt, William H., and Karen J. Walker (editors)

2013    *The Archaeology of Pineland: A Coastal Southwest Florida Village Complex, A.D. 50–1700.* Institute of Archaeology and Paleoenvironmental Studies, University of Florida, Gainesville.

McFadden, Paulette S., and Andrea Palmiotto

2012    *Archaeological Investigations at Bird Island (8DI52), Dixie County, Florida.* Technical Report 14. Laboratory of Southeastern Archaeology, Department of Anthropology, University of Florida, Gainesville.

Monés, Micah P., Neill J. Wallis, and Kenneth E. Sassaman

2012 *Archaeological Investigations at Deer Island, Levy County, Florida.* Technical Report 15. Laboratory of Southeastern Archaeology, Department of Anthropology, University of Florida, Gainesville.

Moore, Clarence B.

1902    Certain Aboriginal Remains of the Northwest Florida Coast, Part II. *Journal of the Academy of Natural Sciences of Philadelphia* 12: 128–358.

1903    Certain Aboriginal Mounds of the Florida Central West Coast. *Journal of the Academy of Natural Sciences of Philadelphia* 12: 361–438.

1918    The Northwest Florida Coast Revisited. *Journal of the Academy of Natural Sciences of Philadelphia* 16: 514–80.

Noss, Reed F.

2011    Between the Devil and the Deep Blue Sea: Florida's Unenviable Position with Respect to Sea Level Rise. *Climatic Change* 107: 1–16.

Pilkey, Orrin H., and Rob Young

2009    *The Rising Sea.* Island Press, Washington, DC.

Rick, Torben C., and Jon M. Erlandson (editors)

2008    *Human Impacts on Ancient Marine Ecosystems: A Global Perspective.* University of California Press, Berkeley.

Sassaman, Kenneth E., Paulette S. McFadden, and Micah P. Monés

2011    Lower Suwannee Archaeological Survey 2009–2010: Investigations at Cat Island (8DI29), Little Bradford Island (8DI32), and Richards Island (8LV137). Technical Report 10. Laboratory of Southeastern Archaeology, Department of Anthropology, University of Florida, Gainesville.

Sassaman, Kenneth E., Andrea Palmiotto, Ginessa J. Mahar, Micah P. Monés, and Paulette S. McFadden

2013    Archaeological Investigations at Shell Mound (8LV42), Levy County, Florida: 2012 Testing. Technical Report 16. Laboratory of Southeastern Archaeology, Department of Anthropology, University of Florida, Gainesville.

Schrope, Mark

2010    Unarrested Development. *Nature Reports Climate Change*, April 6, 2010. http://www.nature.com/climate/2010/1004/full/climate.2010.27.html, accessed May 2, 2012.

Stearns, R. E. C.

1869    Rambles in Florida. *The American Naturalist* 3: 349–56.

Stojanowski, Christopher M., and Glen H. Doran

1998    Osteology of the Late Archaic Bird Island Population. *Florida Anthropologist* 51: 139–45.

Tallant, Montague

n.d.    Unpublished Field Journal and Photographs on Excavations at Shell Mound and Sites in Vicinity, Levy County, Florida. On file, South Florida Museum, Bradenton, Florida.

Thompson, Victor D., and John Worth

2011    Dwellers by the Sea: Native American Coastal Adaptations Along the Southern Coasts of Eastern North America. *Journal of Archaeological Research* 19: 51–101.

Walker, Karen J., Frank W. Stapor, and William H. Marquardt

1995    Archaeological Evidence for a 1750–1450 BP Higher-Than-Present Sea Level Along Florida's Gulf Coast. In Holocene Cycles: Climate, Sea Levels, and Sedimentation, *Journal of Coastal Research*, Special Issue 17: 205–18.

Weinstein, Richard A., and Karen L. Mayo

2006    Historic Assessment and Cultural Resource Survey for the Suwannee River O&M Project's Upland Disposal Site, Dixie County, Florida. Coastal Environments Inc., Baton Rouge, LA.

Weiss, J. L., J. T. Overpeck, and B. Strauss

2011    Implications of Recent Sea Level Rise Science for Low-Elevation Areas in Coastal Cities of the Conterminus U.S.A. *Climatic Change* 105: 635–45.

Widmer, Randolph J.

1988    *The Evolution of the Calusa: A Nonagricultural Chiefdom of the Southwest Florida Coast*. University of Alabama Press, Tuscaloosa.

Willey, Gordon R.

1949    *Archaeology of the Florida Gulf Coast*. Smithsonian Miscellaneous Collections 113. Smithsonian Institution Press, Washington, DC.

Wright, Eric E., Albert C. Hine, Steven L. Goodbred Jr., and Stanley D. Locker

2005    The Effect of Sea-Level and Climate Change on the Development of a Mixed Siliciclastic-Carbonate, Deltaic Coastline: Suwannee River, Florida, U.S.A. *Journal of Sedimentary Research* 75: 621–35.

Wyman, Jeffries

1870    Explorations in Florida. In *Third Annual Report of the Trustees of the Peabody Museum of Archaeology and Ethnology*, 8–9. Harvard University, Cambridge, Massachusetts.

# 8

# The Modification and Manipulation
# of Landscape at Fort Center

VICTOR D. THOMPSON AND THOMAS J. PLUCKHAHN

The archaeology of Fort Center has been the subject of debate both within the region and further afield, especially regarding the antiquity of maize agriculture in southern Florida (Crawford et al. 1997; Fritz 1990; Hall 1976; Johnson 1990, 1991; Keegan 1987; Kelly et al. 2006; Lusteck 2006; Marquardt 1986; Milanich 1994, 2004; Steponaitis 1986; Wagner 2003; Windmer 2002; Yarnell and Black 1985). The Fort Center site contains over 24 earthworks, spans 1.5 kilometers east-west and 1 kilometer north-south, and is located at the junction of a river meander belt system, grass savannah, and oak hammock along Fisheating Creek (figure 8.1) (Thompson and Pluckhahn 2012; Sears 1982). While Fort Center is the most well-known and intensively researched site in the Belle Glade area, it is one of many large earthwork complexes that surround Lake Okeechobee. However, because people in the basin occupied Fort Center beginning around 800 B.C. up until the historic period, it is an ideal place for examining major shifts in cultural traditions.

Because of the size and complexity of its earthworks, Sears (1982; Sears and Sears 1976) suggested early on that maize agriculture was necessary for such constructions. This interpretation was based on his recovery of maize pollen from several contexts at the site. Since the late 1970s, Sears's (1982) view of Fort Center as an early agricultural village has influenced archaeological interpretations of site population estimates, the nature of social and political complexity in southern Florida, and the function of earthworks in the Lake Okeechobee region. This focus on maize agriculture has obscured many of the other potential insights regarding this fascinating region of Florida's Native American landscape.

In this chapter, we summarize new evidence from Fort Center that suggests that intensive maize agriculture was never a part of the site's economy and was likely absent from most of southern Florida. In light of this point, we then discuss the

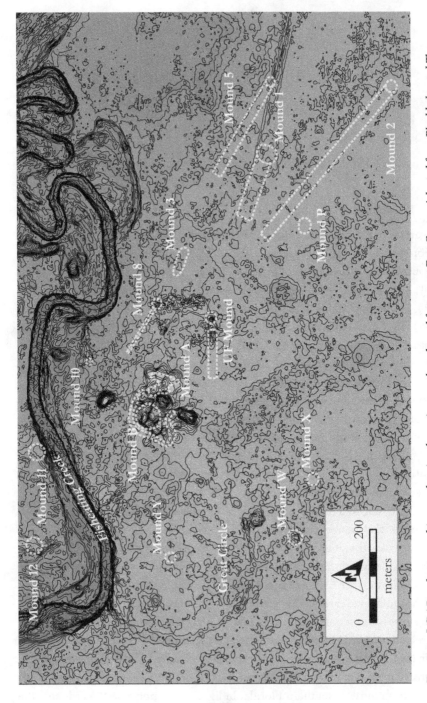

Figure 8.1. LiDAR and topographic map showing the various earthworks and features at Fort Center. Adapted from Pluckhahn and Thompson 2012.

nature of landscape modification and manipulation by the inhabitants of Fort Center from 800 BC up to the Spanish contact period. We also explore the obvious and not-so-obvious transformations of the Fort Center landscape. Following our summary of recent research, we then discuss what this means for the archaeology of Lake Okeechobee and southern Florida. The picture that is emerging is that the inhabitants at Fort Center were present in larger populations than was previously thought, at least at certain times, were able to mobilize labor for the construction of large-scale architecture, and manipulated the landscape using fire. All of these characteristics were facilitated by an economy and an ideology rooted in the wetland landscapes of the basin. This view not only has implications for research in southern Florida, but it also shapes our understanding of the variety of scales at which fisher-hunter-gatherer communities actively altered their environments (see Randall et al. this volume; Sassaman et al. this volume; Schober this volume).

## Note on Chronology

For our summary, we follow a generalized Belle Glade chronology for the site (Marquardt 2001, figure 12.3; see also Griffin 1988; Sears 1982). Although we recognize that there is room for refinement of these periods, this chronological framework provides a departure point for discussing the changing relationship between the inhabitants of Fort Center and the broader landscape.

## Maize at Fort Center?

Before moving on to our synthesis, we offer a brief critique of the evidence for maize (Sears 1982; Sears and Sears 1976) and a summary of our current paleoethnobotanical work at the site. There are a number of reasons to question the interpretation that the inhabitants of Fort Center were maize agriculturalists. These include the nature of the soils, the methods used to collect the original samples, identification of pollen remains, and the context of the original samples. In addition, we question the theory driving the interpretation, which may suggest that finding maize or some sort of agriculture was a foregone conclusion of the work from its inception. Sears notes in his National Science Foundation grant for the work at the site that:

> Some sort of agriculture is posited. The larger sites appear representative of societies which were too large and too complex to have been supported by hunting and gathering. Maize is a possibility, and the linear earthworks may have provided plots like the Mexican Chinampas. (Sears 1964, 3)

We do not wish to make much of this last point, but we do note that such a viewpoint could have possibly been a factor in creating confirmation bias in the research.

Johnson (1990, 1991) was the first to challenge Sears's interpretations for Fort Center. His analysis of the soils indicate that they were highly acidic, that the ditches were not periodically cleaned, and that the ditches were not uniformly dug into the spodic horizon, a practice that facilitates the draining of the fields for the growing of maize (cf. Sears 1982, 186). Thus, it appears that the environment around Fort Center, as Johnson argues, was poorly suited for maize agriculture.

In our 2010 excavations at the site, we recovered carbonized maize remains (Thompson et al. 2013). However, radiocarbon dating of these remains places them exclusively in the later historic period occupation of the site. Thus, we hypothesize that either the Seminole who occupied the area during the nineteenth century or later historic period peoples cultivated maize at the site (Thompson et al. 2013). No macrobotanical maize remains were recovered from secure prehistoric contexts from the new excavations (Morris 2012; Thompson et al. 2013).

Our recovery of carbonized maize macrobotanical remains leads us to our next critique of Sears's hypothesis. One of the carbonized maize specimens was recovered from some of the deepest levels in one of our test units at Fort Center, which contained primarily prehistoric artifacts (Thompson et al. 2013). If macrobotanical remains can penetrate this deep, most likely due to bioturbation, then pollen, which is more readily subject to such forces, certainly can do so. Little documentation accompanies the sampled contexts for Sears's Fort Center pollen remains. So any evaluation of context and its potential for contamination is difficult at best. In addition, it is uncertain whether (and unlikely that) Sears and colleagues followed modern standard procedures (e.g., cleaning of the trowel with distilled water) for the recovery of pollen samples, and if they did not, that introduces another potential source of contamination. We say this not to criticize Sears; indeed, he is to be commended for his forward thinking and use of new techniques, such as the collection of samples for microbotanical analysis at a time before concerns with such analyses had become widely incorporated into archaeological fieldwork. However, the lack of documentation about how Sears's pollen samples were collected makes it difficult to place confidence in his conclusions about maize agriculture.

Of all the contexts at Fort Center in which Sears identified maize, the pollen recovered from the paleofeces would seem to be the most secure, but there are several issues with these samples as well. First, none have been radiocarbon dated, although the fact that wood from the supposed pond platform was found over the top of these specimens would suggest that they are indeed prehistoric (Hogan 1978, 4). In addition none of the paleofeces have been definitively identified as human; identification was based on only size and texture (ibid., 13). Several tests could be conducted to evaluate if indeed these came from humans. Even if such tests were conducted, there is no documentation of them. Still, the recovery of pollen that is potentially maize is intriguing, and while a number of pollen grains in these samples (n = 3) are very large (n > 80 μm), they represent a minority. In addition, Sears (1982) identified potential maize pollen in only three out of the 50 paleofeces examined. In another study by Hogan (1978, 22) an additional 40 samples (although the abstract says 21) were examined and none were determined to contain maize pollen. Therefore, out of 90 pollen samples, a little over 3 percent contained potential maize pollen. Hogan (1978) offers the idea that these individuals were consuming a "ceremonial starvation stew" to account for the apparent lack of maize pollen in her samples. This, of course, is counter to Milanich's (1994, 290) suggestion that if maize was present at Fort Center, it likely played a role in ritual rather than in the subsistence economy.

In addition to possible contamination, there is the confounding issue of possible misidentification in the original studies. Sears and Sears (1976) attempted to rule out *Tripsacum* pollen, which can be misidentified as maize due to its large size. However, Austin (2006, 1222) suggests that the pollen may have been misidentified. Several other species that can be confused for maize are found in the region today or were found in the past, including wild cane (*Gynerium sagittatum*), sugarcane grass (*Saccharum giganteum*), and giant cane (*Arundinaria*) (Cummings and Yost 2011, 3; see also Thompson et al. 2013).

Sears's primary criterion for identifying the pollen as maize was the presence of Poaceae pollen greater than 50 μm. In our new microbotanical analysis, this was deemed too small; PaleoInstitute used a threshold of 65 μm (Thompson et al. 2013; Cummings and Yost 2011). This range is more consistent with the value used for Mexican cultivars, which can have lengths as small as 58 μm, but most of the mean values meet or exceed 70 μm (Holst et al. 2007). In our analysis of 12 samples from column excavations from the Fort Center research conducted in 2010, we recovered only one grain of pollen that was positively identified as maize, and it was from deposits dating to the later historic period occupation (Thompson et al. 2013). Although we found a large number of large Poaceae pollen, these most likely represent *Arundinaria* and not maize (Cummings and Yost 2011; Thompson et al. 2013). However, we did identify one wavy-topped rondal phytolith, a type that is considered to be diagnostic of maize cob material, which may indicate that maize cob material was present at Fort Center during the Belle Glade II period (ca. AD 200 to 900–1000) (Thompson et al. 2013). While this is intriguing, we remain cautious and suggest that this should be considered tentative given the uniqueness of the find, the absence of corroborating pollen remains, and the possible displacement of such remains in the soil profile (Thompson et al. 2013).

We remain highly skeptical that maize was present at Fort Center. Our interpretation of the wavy-topped rondal phytolith, if it does not represent contamination effects, is that it might be a nonlocal item—possibly part of ritualized trade or ceremonies, as Milanich (1994) and Hall (1976) suggest. Future work should explore this possibility through bioarchaeological analysis. We note that the few studies that have been conducted on Fort Center skeletal remains do not indicate heavy use of maize in terms of associated pathologies (e.g., dental carries) and are consistent with more of a fisher-hunter-gatherer way of life (see Miller-Shaivitz and Iscan 1991).

## Time and Fort Center's Earthworks

In this section, we consider the alteration of the landscape at this site and the timing of such alterations. Our main goal is to document the large-scale labor projects that occurred at Fort Center in order to place them in a context of a fisher-hunter-gatherer economy.

### Belle Glade I (800 BC to AD 200)

Construction of the largest of all the Fort Center earthworks, the Great Circle, began during the period of Fort Center's initial occupation (figure 8.2). Sears (1982) speculated that this feature was a type of irrigation technology, but our ongoing research has cast serious doubt on this assertion (Thompson et al. 2013; see also Johnson 1990, 1991). This earthwork encompasses ca. 93,836 sq. meters; its diameter is over 365 meters and its perimeter is circa 1130 meters (Thompson and Pluckhahn 2012). Our new excavations, coupled with work by Sears (1982), provide us with a conservative estimate that this feature was excavated to an average depth of 1.6 meters below the surrounding surface. The volume of soil moved is roughly calculated to be 13,607 cubic meters. As explained below, this translates to about 5,443 person-days for the construction of the Great Circle alone, using labor estimates provided in Erickson (2010) for the construction of ringed ditches in the Bolivian Amazon. This represents a considerable investment of labor and perhaps represents one of the largest earthen constructions associated with semi-fiber tempered pottery in Florida.

While the Great Circle is the best preserved of all the semi-circular earthworks, there were at least four additional ditch and berm constructions associated with this earthwork, which we refer to collectively as the Great Circle complex. Two of these earthworks are semicircular ditch-and-berm construction just on the interior of the Great Circle. In addition, another semicircular earthwork is located on the exterior of the Great Circle making the two form concentric semi-circles. Finally, Sears (1982) excavated a small mound (Mound Y) in the center of the Great Circle complex. Although we have no direct radiocarbon dates from these other earthworks, we hypothesize, following Sears, that at least some of these earthworks were either constructed prior to the construction of the Great Circle or shortly thereafter (Sears 1982; Thompson and Pluckhahn 2012, 56–57).

In our new microbotanical analysis of samples from Fort Center we note the

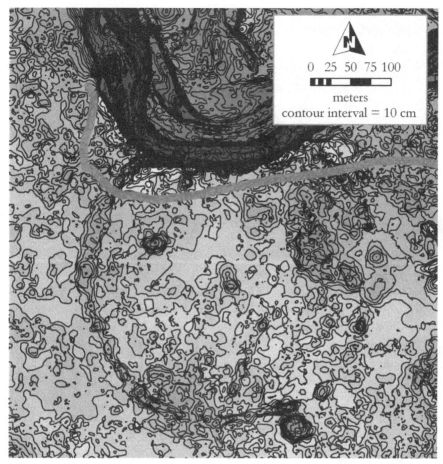

Figure 8.2. LiDAR and topographic map showing the Great Circle Complex. Adapted from Thompson and Pluckhahn 2012.

presence of many species adapted to some degree of forest opening (Thompson et al. 2013). This may be a by-product of the manipulation of the landscape through burning. The microbotanical analysis also revealed large amounts of microscopic carbonized remains from deposits dating to this period (figure 8.3). We interpret this to represent fires used in conjunction with cutting of vegetation for large-scale land clearance for the construction of the Great Circle and the other earthworks in the area. The practice of clearing land for earthworks is found elsewhere in the Americas. For example, researchers believe that in many cases, the construction of ring and circular earthworks in the Amazon also involved extensive clearing of the forest (Erickson 2010, 620). In addition to the time it took to actually excavate the Great Circle, inhabitants also likely cleared the forest with using both fire and cutting tools (e.g., stone axes). The land the Great Circle occupies plus a 100-meter buffer area would have encompassed an area of around 16.97 hectares. Carneiro (cited in Erickson 2010, 629) estimates that it takes approximately 377 person-days to clear one hectare of forest. Thus, around 6,398 person-days of labor in addition to the labor investment for excavation were required to complete the Great Circle.

In addition, our microbotanical analysis indicated the presence of wetland taxa in the paleoethnobotanical remains (Cummings and Yost 2011; Thompson et al. 2013). This is also consistent with what we know about the nature of the hydrological environment of the Fort Center landscape. The site is situated on an ecotone that encompasses three environmental zones, which include a meander belt, an oak hammock, and a grass savannah (Sears 1982). Because the Great Circle abuts Fisheating Creek, during the rainy season the ditch portion is often flooded to the point that airboats can be driven into a portion of the ditch (Fisheating Creek Wildlife Management, personal communication 2010). It is likely that the pre-drainage landscape of the Okeechobee area was much wetter than it is today (McVoy et al. 2011) and that the Great Circle was completely filled by seasonal flooding. A small water retention feature or "pond" is located along the southeastern edge of the Great Circle on the site opposite that of Fisheating Creek. Our coring of this feature indicates that it is still seasonally wet (see figure 8.1).

In addition to the mounds and earthworks associated with the Great Circle complex, a number of other mounds and structures were either built or occupied during this timeframe. These structures include the earliest deposits of Midden A and Midden B, which we now believe to be one roughly continuous midden along the creek bank (Thompson and Pluckhahn 2012). The occupants constructed several other mounds during this period, including Mounds 3, 12, 13, 11, and 14 (Sears 1982, 185). At least one of these structures, Mound 12, was constructed during the time when semi-fiber tempered pottery was in use at the site (Sears 1982, 139). Our radiocarbon dates suggest that Mound B was constructed sometime around 800 to 540 BC (Thompson and Pluckhahn 2012, table 1). Based on the evidence for early use and construction of many of the mounds at Fort Center, it may be useful at to separate a semi-fiber tempered period from Belle Glade I after the reanalysis of the previously excavated material at Fort Center is complete.

## Belle Glade II (ca. AD 200 to 900–1000)

During Belle Glade II, the occupants considerably expanded their activities at the site. It is during this time that new earthworks and features appeared on the landscape. Perhaps the most famous of the structures constructed during this time frame are those associated with the mound-pond complex. Situated east of the Great Circle complex, this architectural grouping is comprised of an earthen berm that incorporates and encircles a portion of two platform mounds (Mound A and B) and an artificially constructed pond (see figure 8.1). The fame of this section of the site

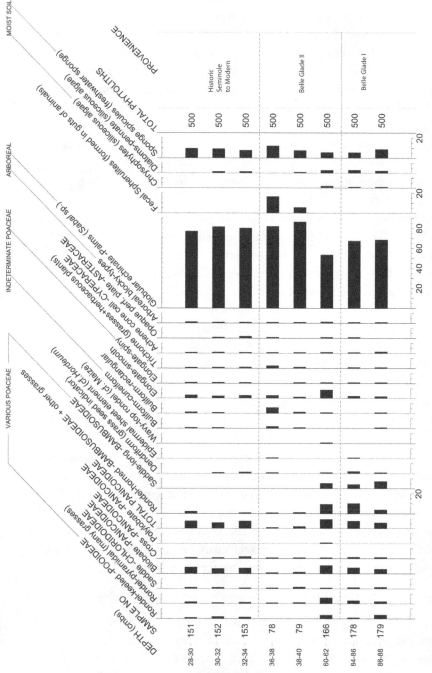

Figure 8.3. Adjusted pollen diagram for Fort Center. Adapted from Cummings and Yost 2011, Figure 2; and Thompson et al. 2013.

is mostly attributable to the extraordinary preservation of the wooden effigies that Sears recovered in his excavations of the mortuary pond.

Along with human remains, which represent a minimum of 150 individuals, Sears also recovered more than 100 (n = 100 to 150, depending on how they are counted) fragments of carved and unmodified preserved wood remains from the pond. Among these carvings were numerous effigies, mostly of animals that were local to the region, including many that represent distinct bird species (e.g., raptors) and large mammals (e.g., Florida panther) (Sears 1982, chapter 4). Sears (1982) speculated that these carvings were part of a large mortuary platform or some similar structure that sat over the pond (cf. Wheeler 1996, 95–97). Some of the wood recovered shows evidence of burning, which led Sears (1982, 165–67) to conclude that this was the ultimate cause of its collapse into the pond.

Sears's assessment that the mound-pond complex activities dated to the Middle Woodland period is correct. The ceramic sequence and radiocarbon dates Sears (1982) and Thompson and Pluckhahn (2012, table 1) ran support this idea. However, the mound-pond complex was occupied for some time after this period. And, as we note above, there is evidence to suggest that the site occupants constructed at least the beginning of one of the mounds (Mound B) early in the Belle Glade I period.

In addition to the occupation at mound-pond complex, the Great Circle area was still occupied during this time. Although features there were previously identified as two discrete occupation areas (Midden A and Midden B), we now think that this is a continuous midden that fronts the creek bank and extends for 400 meters (Thompson and Pluckhahn 2012, 56). In addition, there is evidence that the occupants of Fort Center either constructed or occupied two other mounds, Mounds 1 and 3, during this period.

Building these mounds and the artificial pond required coordinated suprahousehold labor efforts. However, accurate estimations of labor are difficult. Microbotanical analyses of deposits dating to this period continue to indicate open forest environments, which would have been indicative of heavy occupation at the site (Cummings and Yost 2011). In addition, there is evidence of even higher counts of microscopic charcoal for this period, which may suggest continued modification of the landscape using fire and/or a growing population at the site.

## Belle Glade III (AD 1000 to 1513)

It appears that during the Belle Glade III period, the occupants of Fort Center elaborated and used many of the circular-linear earthworks located along the eastern area of the site, which include Mounds 1, 2, 3, and 5 and their attached earthworks (see figure 8.1). The area that fronts Fisheasting Creek adjacent to the Great Circle (Midden A and B) also continued to be used during this period. Most interestingly, dates from Mound B and the pond also suggest that it continued to be occupied or altered during this period (Thompson and Pluckhahn 2012, 59). In addition to these mounds, several of the other linear earthworks terminating in mounds may have also been constructed near the end of this time frame and then continued be used during the Belle Glade IV period. These include both the UF Mound and Mound 8. This assessment is based on associated artifacts and the chronology Johnson (1996) developed for earthworks.

## Belle Glade IV (AD 1513 to 1763)

The mounds and linear earthworks (UF Mound and Mound 8) constructed at the end of the Belle Glade III period likely continued to be occupied during the Belle Glade IV period, as indicated by the recovery of artifacts of Spanish origin or trade items. In addition, Sears (1982, 200–201) documented a number of these artifacts as being from Mound B, indicating its continued use during the historic period. Mound A may have also been used during this time frame based on a single radiocarbon date that spans periods III and IV (see Thompson and Pluckhahn 2012, table 1).

The artifacts from the historic Spanish period that were recovered from Fort Center were likely traded in from the coast. During this time frame, the Calusa paramount polity controlled much of the distribution of such items. The capital of the polity was likely the site of Mound Key (Goggin and Sturtevant 1964; Marquardt 1988), which is directly down the Caloosahatchee River from Fort Center. It is likely that Fort Center was one of the principal towns on Lake Okeechobee, if not the principal town (Sears 1982). At the end of this time frame, much of southern Florida was abandoned due to a number of factors, which included slave raids, disease, and displacement by other groups (Marquardt 2001, 170–71; Worth 2003). By 1763, these processes had altered much of the Calusa landscape and no recognizable communities were left. By this point, the remnants of the Calusa people and many other groups from southern Florida had either migrated to Cuba or were absorbed by other ethnic groups that were occupying south Florida at the time (see Hann 1991; Marquardt 2001; Thompson and Worth 2011; Worth 2006).

For this period and Belle Glade III, the microbotanical analysis indicates some of the same patterns we note above. There is some uncertainty about the exact timing of environmental changes during these periods because of indications of bioturbation and the mixing of deposits in cases where we have samples dating to this time frame (i.e., the historic maize fragment from Unit 4; see Thompson et al. 2013). Nevertheless, we do note that during the later historic period occupation (after the turn of the nineteenth century), microscopic charcoal drops off dramatically, indicating abandonment of burning and control of the landscape using fire and/or depopulation of the site. In addition, there is a drop-off in species related to the cane family, which may be the result of the decrease in use of fire (which canebrakes depend on) and the increase in livestock grazing during the later historic period (Cummings and Yost 2011, 6).

## Summary Points

This brief overview of the earthworks at Fort Center reveals several important trends, all of which seem to accompany changes in the use of the landscape, specifically the use of fire, as evidenced by our microbotanical analysis. First, the largest of all the earth-moving projects occurred during the site's early occupation. The Great Circle required the largest labor investment compared to the labor required to construct the other earthworks at the site. That this structure was constructed during the earliest occupation suggests that Fort Center was an important point on the landscape from the time of its initial occupation. Furthermore, people in the basin were capable of mobilizing and coordinating massive labor projects prior to the development of any kind of complex polity (e.g., chiefdom).

Second, there appear to have been major earth-moving projects during all the recognized periods at Fort Center. Thompson and Pluckhahn (2012) point out that this indicates a continual reorganization of space and architecture at the site. In addition, the site's occupants were able to mobilize labor for earthwork construction under a wide variety of social, political, and environmental circumstances.

Finally, it appears that once earthworks were constructed, many were occupied or used for extended periods of time. This indicates that use and placement of new constructions were organized around an existing built environment. While the function and role of each earthwork likely changed over time, older constructions were integrated into any changes in the social and political order (Thompson and Pluckhahn 2012).

## Population, Monument Construction, and Landscape Alteration

Our discussion of the construction and use of the Fort Center earthworks both agrees with and departs from some of Sears's (1982) original interpretations of the site. Our work at Fort Center has corroborated Sears's ideas about the timing of the construction of many of the earthworks, although our new dates from the site indicate that occupations persisted for many of these structures far longer than the dates Sears proposed. The combination of these observations and our work challenging the hypothesis that the basis of the subsistence economy at Fort Center was agricultural (Thompson et al. 2013) has implications for estimates of the size of the population at the site, theories about why the earthworks were constructed, and analysis of the nature and degree of landscape modification in the area.

One of the most interesting aspects of our reevaluation of Fort Center relates to the site's resident population. While Sears never gives exact population estimates, statements throughout his monograph indicate that he does not believe that Fort Center had a substantial population. For example, he states that during the early historic (Belle Glade IV) period, "the same number of families—one or two at a time—lived on the site (1982, 200)." He also states that "at that time [the Belle Glade II period] there were a few other people on the site" (ibid., 174). By this, he means a few more people than the several families that he believed lived in the mound-pond complex at this time (ibid., 175).

Sears is correct to be cautious in assigning any sort of number to any one period for Fort Center. Indeed, while our work clarifies which mounds were occupied during each time frame, much more research needs to be done to refine some of the statements we have made in this chapter. That said, we suggest, based on the available data, that Fort Center's resident populations may have been larger than most estimates for the average site around the lake. At the very least, during some periods, the site experienced an influx of population from the surrounding landscape to engage in corporative labor projects (e.g., earthwork construction).

A few historic sources note that in the Belle Glade IV period the Lake Okeechobee district was part of the historic Calusa polity. Fontaneda, who was shipwrecked and lived at the Calusa capital of Mound Key, notes that the interior villages of the Lake Okeechobee region were much smaller than those along the coast and that most villages had between 20 and 40 inhabitants (Hann 1991, 159; Worth 2006). We suggest that this figure is meant to characterize the typical towns around the lake and that the major centers likely had larger populations. Based on the size of the site and the large amount of historic gold, silver, and other metal artifacts Sears documents for the site, we argue that Fort Center was one such town. Unfortunately, we can only speculate at this point about how large the actual population was at Fort Center.

Regardless of how large the population was at Fort Center, the inhabitants managed to significantly alter the landscape in a number of ways. Perhaps the most obvious of these alterations are the mounds themselves. This leads us to one of the central questions about Fort Center's built environment. Why were the mounds constructed? Sears (1982) thought that they were constructed to make drained field agriculture possible, specifically maize agriculture. Additionally, he believed that mounds served as the bases for houses (Sears 1982, 142–43), and Widmer (2002, 383) argues that mounds functioned to elevate houses above flood waters. He concurs with Sears that the linear mounds were used for growing maize when the drained field system failed due to rising sea levels (Widmer 2002, 383). Similarly, Hale (1984) suggests that the earthworks help redirect water away from the settlement. While these are intriguing hypotheses, a number of other sites in the basin that would have been subject to the same sorts of flooding events as at Fort Center do not have mounds. In fact, much of the habitation midden debris is adjacent to Fisheating Creek, thus calling this interpretation into question if other inhabitants at Fort Center resided in this area of the site. Further, the linear mounds and causeways at the site do not seem to function as raised areas for houses. And, as we have already established, the data do not support the maize agriculture hypothesis (Thompson et al. 2013). Finally, other large mound sites, such as the Ortona complex, are not located in savannahs, but in sandy scrub soils located on higher elevations (Carr et al. 1995, 258).

In contrast to these functional interpretations, several authors have emphasized the ceremonial and/or symbolic nature of the Lake Okeechobee earthworks (Carr et al. 1995; Goggin and Sturtevant 1964; Hall 1976). This interpretation, of course, does not preclude some of the more practical reasons for mound construction in the region, as many note the possibility that such architecture served multiple purposes (Carr et al. 1995). This view is much more in line with our own thinking about the mounds at Fort Center.

Like Carr et al. (1995), we view the purpose of the earthworks at Fort Center as not only multifunctional but also as malleable and fluctuating over time. That is, the function and meaning of mounds was not static and was constantly redefined or performed throughout the life history of a given mound. Thus, we note that at Fort Center, some mounds served as supports for domestic structures, which is not out of line with Sears's (1982) and Widmer's (2002) thoughts regarding some of the earthworks. However, we fundamentally disagree that linear earthworks and causeways were built to support maize agriculture or were designed *primarily* for the redirection of water (cf. Hale 1984; Sears 1982; Widmer 2002). Instead, we view these features as yet another way that some individuals (in addition to living on top of platform mounds) offset themselves from the rest of the population. The emergence of the circular linear earthworks during the Belle Glade III period could be a by-product of the development of complex polities in southern Florida at that time (Marquardt 1986, 1988; Thompson and Worth 2011; Widmer 2002). However, the use of mounds and earthen embankments may have had a long history at Fort Center, as we argue, following Sears (1982), that the semicircular embankment and mounds A and B were ceremonial specialists both lived and performed rituals during Belle Glade II times (Thompson and Pluckhahn 2012). However, we have no reason to believe that at this time the distinction between these individuals and others of the population was predicated on anything more than performed societal roles (e.g., shamans, ritual specialists).

Other earthworks, such the Great Circle, were used to control water. Although we cannot be sure exactly why such structures were created, several factors point to a ceremonial or ritual function. First, there is a mound in the center of the Great Circle. This pattern is not unlike the pattern found at other circular earthwork/mound pairings in the basin (Thompson and Pluckhahn 2012). This pattern is not restricted to

Florida, as circular earthworks surrounding central mounds, often containing burials, are present in other parts of the Americas, including Adena earthworks in the
American Midwest and mounds in highland Brazil (Clay 1987; Iriarte et al. 2008).
As Hall (1976) notes, the use of water as a barrier to spirits and as a symbol of the un-
derworld could have factored into such constructions. Furthermore, at Fort Center,
such constructions also appear to reference the local environment, as they are very
similar to oxbow lakes in the meander belt in the area (Thompson and Pluckhahn
2012). Thus, while such constructions may have had ceremonial and symbolic meaning, they most likely also provided fish during floods, as did the natural oxbow lakes
in the region (see Carr 2012). Thus, we view the earthworks as neither solely functional nor solely symbolic features. The practice of separating archaeological features
into such categories is rooted in a western ontology (Moore and Thompson 2012),
one that most likely would have not been part of the ideology of Fort Center.

In contrast to the more obvious alteration of mound building, the inhabitants
of Fort Center altered the landscape through less discernible ways. Increasingly,
archaeologists are aware of the fact that fisher-hunter-gatherers actively manipulate
landscapes for a variety of reasons (Thompson 2013). One of the best indications
of this at Fort Center is the high frequency of microscopic charcoal recovered from
deposits dating to the precontact periods for Fort Center. As we discussed earlier in
this chapter, we believe this pattern to be related to large-scale land clearance directly
linked to the construction of earthworks. This, of course, would have been done for
both practical reasons (e.g., cleared areas to construct the mounds) and aesthetic
reasons (e.g., lines of sight). Such activities would have added to the amount of planning and labor involved in the construction, manipulation, and maintenance of the
landscape.

## Considering Fort Center and Southern Florida

The lingering hypothesis of maize agriculture at Fort Center has heavily influenced
how researchers have interpreted the archaeology of the Lake Okeechobee basin.
We now have good reason to reject this hypothesis at Fort Center. Furthermore,
more recent macro- and microbotanical analyses have found no additional evidence
of cultigens, although a number of local plants likely contributed to the overall
economy of Fort Center (Hogan 1978; Morris 2012; Sears and Sears 1976; Thompson et al. 2013). Because of these reasons, Fort Center and likely most of southern
Florida should be seen as a landscape that was modified only by fisher-hunter-gatherer communities. These groups modified their environment, from the coasts to the
interior wetlands, by constructing mounds and canals and accumulating shell on a
monumental scale (see Carr 1985; Luer 1989a, 1989b; Marquardt 1988; Marquardt
and Walker 2012; Wheeler and Carr this volume). Researchers have long recog-

nized that these southern Florida sites were the product of fisher-hunter-gatherers, as were other areas of Florida, but only a few have discussed them in terms of issues related to complex hunter-gatherers (Pluckhahn et al. 2010; Marquardt 1986, 1988; Randall et al. this volume; Randall and Sassaman 2010; Russo 2004; Sassaman and Randall 2012; Sassaman 2010; Saunders and Russo 2011; Schwadron 2010; Thompson and Pluckhahn 2010).

Milanich (1994, 291) once stated that "the question of Okeechobee-region maize agriculture is one of most intriguing in Florida archaeology." We still believe that the Okeechobee Basin is one of the most fascinating areas of Florida archaeology, but the focus of research has changed from questions about whether maize agriculture was grown there to questions about the broader social history of the people of this region. Given the new information that we have regarding Fort Center, we must now consider it within the context of a fisher-hunter-gatherer economy and view it using the theoretical constructs associated with this literature. The manipulation of the landscape through earthen mounds and other activities that we document in this chapter are on a scale that is usually associated with only a few hunter-gatherer sites in the world (e.g., Poverty Point). Because Fort Center is not an isolated mound complex, but is part of a suite of sites in the basin and along the coast that also engaged in earthwork construction and landscape modification on a similar scale (Thompson and Worth 2011), we conclude that the southern Florida region in general represents one of the most extensively constructed built environments by hunter-gatherers in world prehistory (Thompson et al. 2013). If this view is correct, it forces us to consider the spectrum of social, historical, ritual, and political relationships that were possible in such economies. The focus of future research in this area should be not how such economies supported these populations, but rather how the environment and the social, political, and ritual histories of these peoples were intertwined and were part of a complex whole that structured the lives of the people of southern Florida for several millennia.

## Acknowledgments

We thank Asa Randall and Neill Wallis for their invitation to participate in their symposium "Precolumbian Archaeology in Florida: New Approaches to the Appendicular Southeast," organized for the 68th annual meeting of the Southeastern Archaeological Conference and in this volume. Our research was supported by funds from a National Geographic Society (Grant # 8772-10), The Ohio State University, and the University of South Florida. We thank Amanda Roberts Thompson, Hannah Morris, S. Margaret Spivey, and the Ohio State University 2010 archaeological field school students for their help. Our research would not have been possible without the support the Fisheating Creek Wildlife Management Area and staff at the Florida Bureau of Archaeological Research, particularly Beth Morford, Ryan

Wheeler, and Louis Tesar. We also thank William Marquardt, Karen Walker, Jerald Milanich, Ann Cordell, Mellissa Ayvaz, Elise LeCompte, Donna Ruhl, and Ellen Burlingame Turck for their assistance. Christopher B. Rodning, Asa Randall, Neill Wallis, and one anonymous reviewer provided helpful comments and edits that improved the quality of this chapter.

# References

Austin, Daniel F.

2006    *Florida Ethnobotany*. CRC Press, Boca Raton.

Carr, Robert

1985    Prehistoric Circular Earthworks in South Florida. *Florida Anthropologist* 38: 288–301.

2012    *Digging Miami*. University Press of Florida, Gainesville.

Carr, Robert, David Dickel, and Marilyn Masson

1995    Archaeological Investigation at the Ortona Earthworks and Mounds. *Florida Anthropologist* 48: 227–63.

Crawford, Gary W., David G. Smith, and Vandy E. Bowyer

1997    Dating the Entry of Corn (*Zea mays*) into the Lower Great Lakes Region. *American Antiquity* 62: 112–19.

Clay, Berley R.

1987    Circles and Ovals: Two Types of Adena Space. *Southeastern Archaeology* 6: 46–56.

Cummings, Linda S., and Chad Yost

2011    Pollen and Phytolith Analysis of Circular Earthwork Samples from the Fort Center Site, 8GL13, Glades County, Florida. Report submitted to the Department of Anthropology, The Ohio State University, Columbus, Ohio.

Erickson, Clark L.

2010    The Transformation of the Environment into Landscape: The Historical Ecology of Monumental Earthwork Construction in the Bolivian Amazon. *Diversity* 2: 618–52.

Fritz, Galye

1990    Multiple Pathways to Farming in Precontact Eastern North America. *Journal of World Prehistory* 4: 387–435.

Goggin, John M., and William T. Sturtevant

1964    The Calusa: A Stratified Non-Agricultural Society (with Notes on Sibling Marriage). In *Explorations in Cultural Anthropology: Essays in Honor of George Peter Murdock*, edited by Ward H. Goodenough, 179–219. McGraw-Hill, New York.

Griffin, John

1988    *The Archaeology of Everglades National Park: A Synthesis*. National Park Service, Southeastern Archaeological Center, Tallahassee.

Hale, Stephen

1984    Prehistoric Environmental Exploitation Around Lake Okeechobee. *Southeastern Archaeology* 3: 173–87.

Hall, Robert T.

1976    Water Barriers, Corn, and Sacred Enclosures in the Eastern Woodlands. *American Antiquity* 41: 360–64.

Hann, John H.

1991    *Missions to the Calusa*. University Press of Florida, Gainesville.

Hogan, Jacqueline

1978    Palynology of Ft. Center: Environmental Interpretations and Cultural Implications for a Central Florida Hopewellian Ceremonial Center. MA thesis, Department of Anthropology, Florida Atlantic University, Boca Raton.

Holst, Irene, J. Enrique Moreno, and Dolores R. Piperno

2007    Identification of Teosinte, Maize, and *Tripsacum* in Mesoamerica by Using Pollen, Starch Grains, and Phytoliths. *Proceedings of the National Academy of Sciences* 104: 17608–13.

Iriarte, Jose, J. Christopher Gillam, and Oscar Marozzi

2008    Monumental Burials and Memorial Feasting: An Example from the Southern Brazilian Highlands. *Antiquity* 82:947–961.

Johnson, William G.

1990    The Role of Maize in South Florida Aboriginal Societies: An Overview. *Florida Anthropologist* 43: 209–14.

1991    Remote Sensing and Soil Science Applications to Understanding Belle Glade Cultural Adaptations in the Okeechobee Basin. PhD dissertation, Department of Anthropology, University of Florida, Gainesville.

1996    A Belle Glade Earthwork Typology and Chronology. *Florida Anthropologist* 49: 249–60.

Keegan, William F.

1987    Diffusion of Maize from South America: the Antillean Connection Reconstructed. In *Emergent Horticultural Economies of the Eastern Woodlands,* edited by William F. Keegan, 329–44. Center for Archaeological Investigations Occasional Papers no. 7. Center for Archaeological Investigations, Southern Illinois University, Carbondale.

Kelly, Jennifer A., Robert H. Tykot, and Jerald T. Milanich

2006    Evidence for Early Use of Maize in Peninsular Florida. In *Histories of Maize: Multidisciplinary Approaches to the Prehistory, Linguistics, Biogeography, Domestication, and Evolution of Maize,* edited by John E. Staller, Robert H. Tykot, and Bruce F. Benz, 249–62. Elsevier Academic Press, Amsterdam.

Luer, George M.

1989a    Calusa Canals in Southwestern Florida: Routes of Tribute and Exchange. *Florida Anthropologist* 42: 89–130.

1989b    Further Research on the Pine Island Canal and Associated Sites, Lee County, Florida. *Florida Anthropologist* 42: 241–47.

Lusteck, Robert

2006    The Migrations of Maize into the Southeastern United States. In *Histories of Maize: Multidisciplinary Approaches to the Prehistory, Linguistics, Biogeography, Domestication, and Evolution of Maize,* edited by John. E. Staller, Robert H. Tykot, and Bruce F. Benz, 521–28. Elsevier Academic Press, Boston.

Marquardt, Willam

1986    The Development of Cultural Complexity in Southwest Florida: Elements of a Critique. *Southeastern Archaeology* 5: 63–70.

1988    Politics and Production Among the Calusa of South Florida. In *Hunters and Gatherers: History, Evolution, and Social Change,* vol. 1, edited by Tim Ingold, David Riches, and James Woodburn, 161–88. Berg, Oxford.

2001    The Emergence and Demise of the Calusa. In *Societies in Eclipse: Archaeology of the Eastern Woodlands Indians, A.D. 1400–1700,* edited by David Brose, Wesley Cowan, and Robert Mainfort Jr., 157–71. Smithsonian Institution Press, Washington, DC.

Marquardt, William H., and Karen J. Walker
2012    Southwest Florida During the Mississippi Period. In *Late Prehistoric Florida: Archaeology at the Edge of the Mississippian World*, edited by Keith Ashley and Nancy White, 29–61. University Press of Florida, Gainesville.

McVoy, Christopher W. Winifred Park Said, Jayanthya Obeysekera, Joel A. Vanarman, and Thomas W. Dreschel
2011    *Landscapes and Hydrology of the Predrainage Everglades*. University Press of Florida, Gainesville.

Milanich, Jerald T.
1994    *Archaeology of Precolumbian Florida*. University Press of Florida, Gainesville.
2004    Prehistory of Florida after 500 B.C. In *Handbook of North American Indians: Southeast*, edited by Raymond D. Fogelson, 191–203. Smithsonian Institution Press, Washington, DC.

Miller-Shaivitz Patricia, and Mehmet Yasar Iscan
1991    The Prehistoric People of Fort Center: Physical and Health Characteristics. In *What Mean These Bones: Studies in Southeastern Bioarchaeology*, edited by Mary L. Powell, Patricia Bridges, and Ann W. Mires, 131–47. University of Alabama Press, Tuscaloosa.

Moore, Christopher R., and Victor D. Thompson
2012    Animism and Green River Persistent Places: A Dwelling Perspective on the Shell Mound Archaic. *Journal of Social Archaeology* 12: 264–84.

Morris, Hannah
2012    Plant Use at Fort Center (8GL13), Florida. MA thesis, Department of Anthropology. The Ohio State University, Columbus.

Pluckhahn, Thomas J., and Victor D. Thompson
2012    Integrating LiDAR Data and Conventional Mapping of the Fort Center Site in Southcentral Florida: A Comparative Approach. *Journal of Field Archaeology* 37(4): 289–301.

Pluckhahn, Thomas, J., Victor D. Thompson, and Brent Weisman
2010    Toward a New View of History and Process at Crystal River (8CR1). *Southeastern Archaeology* 29: 164–81.

Randall, Asa R.
2011    Remapping Archaic Social Histories Along the St. Johns River in Florida. In *Hunter-Gatherer Archaeology as Historical Process*, edited by Kenneth E. Sassaman and Donald Holly Jr., 120–42. University of Arizona Press, Tucson.

Russo, Michael
2004    Measuring Shell Rings for Social Inequality. In *Signs of Power: The Rise of Cultural Complexity in the Southeast*, edited by John Gibson and Philip Carr, 26–70. University of Alabama Press, Tuscaloosa.

Sassaman, Kenneth E.
2010    *The Eastern Archaic, Historicized*. Altamira Press, New York.

Sassaman, Kenneth E., and Asa R. Randall
2012    Shell Mounds of the Middle St. Johns Basin, Northeast Florida. In *Early New World Monumentality*, edited by Richard Burger and Robert Rosenswig, 53–77. University Press of Florida, Gainesville.

Saunders, Rebecca, and Michael Russo
2011    Coastal Shell Middens in Florida: A View from the Archaic. *Quaternary International* 239: 38–50.

Sears, William H.
1964    *Prehistory of the Lake Okeechobee Basin*. National Science Foundation Grant Submission. Manuscript on file at the Florida Museum of Natural History, Gainesville.

1977    Seaborne Contacts between Early Cultures in Lower Southeastern United States and Middle through South America. In *The Sea in the Pre-Columbian World*, edited by Elizabeth Benson, 1–15. Dumbarton Oaks, Washington DC.

1982    *Fort Center: An Archaeological Site in the Lake Okeechobee Basin*. University Press of Florida, Gainesville.

Sears, Elsie, and William H. Sears

1976    Preliminary Report on Prehistoric Corn Pollen from Fort Center, Florida. *Southeastern Archaeological Conference Bulletin*, 19: 53–56.

Steponaitis, Vincas P.

1986    Prehistoric Archaeology in the Southeastern United States, 1970–1985. *Annual Review of Anthropology* 15: 363–404.

Schwadron, Margo

2010    Prehistoric Landscapes of Complexity: Archaic and Woodland Period Shell Works, Shell Rings, and Tree Islands of the Everglades, South Florida. In *Trend, Tradition, and Turmoil: What Happened to the Southeastern Archaic?* edited by David H Thomas and Matthew Sanger, 113–47. American Museum of Natural History, New York.

Thompson, Victor D., Kristen Gremillion, and Thomas J. Pluckhahn

2013    Challenging the Evidence for Prehistoric Wetland Maize Agriculture at Fort Center, Florida. *American Antiquity* 78: 181–93.

Thompson, Victor D., and Thomas J. Pluckhahn

2010    History, Complex Hunter-Gatherers, and the Mounds and Monuments of Crystal River, Florida, USA: A Geophysical Perspective. *Journal of Island and Coastal Archaeology* 5: 33–51.

2012    Monumentalization and Ritual Landscapes at Fort Center in the Lake Okeechobee Basin of South Florida. *Journal of Anthropological Archaeology* 31: 49–65.

Thompson, Victor D., and John E. Worth

2011    Dwellers by the Sea: Native American Adaptations along the Southern Coasts of Eastern North America. *Journal of Archaeological Research* 19: 51–101.

Wagner, Gail E.

2003    Eastern Woodlands Anthropogenic Ecology. In *People and Plants in Ancient Eastern North America*, edited by Paul Minnis, 126–71. Smithsonian Institution Press, Washington, DC.

Wheeler, Ryan

1996 Ancient Art of the Florida Peninsula: 500 B.C. to A.D. 1763. PhD dissertation, Department of Anthropology, University of Florida, Gainesville.

Widmer, Randolph J.

2002    The Woodland Archaeology South Florida. In *The Woodland Southeast*, edited by Robert C. Mainfort Jr., and David G. Anderson, 373–97. University of Alabama Press, Tuscaloosa.

Worth, John E.

2003    The Evacuation of South Florida, 1704–1760. Paper Presented at the Southeastern Archaeological Conference, Charlotte, North Carolina.

2006    The Social Geography of South Florida during the Spanish Colonial Era. Paper Presented at the Society for American Archaeology Meeting, San Juan, Puerto Rico.

Yarnell, Richard A. and M. Jean Black

1985    Temporal Trends Indicated by a Survey of Archaic and Woodland Plant Food Remains from Southeastern North America. *Southeastern Archaeology* 4: 93–106.

# 9

## Crafting Orange Pottery in Early Florida

### Production and Distribution

REBECCA SAUNDERS AND MARGARET K. WRENN

Why pottery was adopted around the world in general—and specifically in the time and place it was in the southeastern United States—has been a topic of considerable concern for archaeologists. In this chapter, we discuss the origin and trajectory of Orange pottery in northeast Florida, one of the earliest potteries in the United States, by comparing the assemblages at two Late Archaic period shell rings on the northeast Florida coast, Rollins Shell Ring (8DU7510) and Guana Shell Ring (8SJ2554).[1] The sites are just 25 miles (40 kilometers) apart, and they occupy similar environments: extensive estuaries west of the rings and beach resources nearby to the east (figure 9.1). However, the two sites are in distinct river drainages. Rollins is north of the St. Johns River in the Nassau River drainage and Guana is south of the St. Johns in the Guana River drainage. Hypothetically, the distinct drainage areas may have defined the geographic boundaries for the communities that built the rings, which we interpret as venues for feasting and other ceremonial activities (Saunders 2002, 2004a, 2004b). Rings were built "through feasting" (sensu Dietler and Hayden 2001, 9) by both local folk and, presumably, extralocal guests. The huge quantities of shell, which were sculpted into specific shapes, and the elaborately incised Orange pottery that was discarded in the rings (as ceremonial trash; Walker 1995; see also Wallis this volume; Wheeler and Carr this volume) were the result of "considerable labor to craft both places and objects for communal ritual" (Spielmann 2008, 38).

Stimulated by Spielmann's (2002, 2008) discussions of specialized craft production of ritual objects in small-scale societies, we asked whether specialists might have been involved in the production of Orange pottery for use in Archaic shell rings. This article contains the preliminary results of our search.

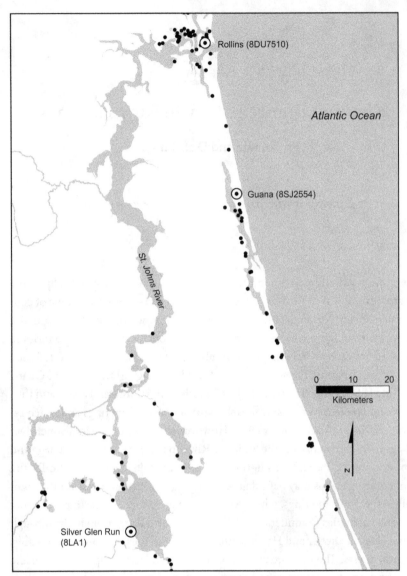

Figure 9.1. Location of the Rollins Shell Ring, the Guana Shell Ring, and other Late Archaic shell-bearing sites. Map by Asa Randall.

## Chronology

Orange pottery is one of three early wares that appeared in the Southeast at the beginning of the Late Archaic period. Two of these early wares, Stallings and Orange, are fiber tempered, but the two wares can easily be distinguished from each other because of different styles of surface decoration. Orange pottery is found throughout central Florida and along the Atlantic coast at least as far north as southern

Georgia and as far south as the Everglades, but the heartland of the ware appears to be in the St. Johns River Valley and the adjacent Atlantic coast (Milanich 1994). On the northern and western peripheries of the Orange Tradition, additional fiber-tempered types, St. Simons and Norwood, respectively, have been defined, but whether or not these are distinct enough from Orange to merit a separate type name remains debatable (Campbell 2004; Saunders and Hays 2004; White 2003 this volume). Stallings occurs north of the Altamaha River on the Georgia coast up to the Savannah River Valley (Sassaman 2004, figure 2.1), where it overlaps with Thoms Creek, the third early ware. Thoms Creek contains abundant sand inclusions and sometimes fiber. The designs on Thoms Creek ware are similar, if not identical, to those on Stallings ware.

The earliest dates for Archaic pottery are the radiocarbon results from Stoltman's (1966, 1974) excavations at Rabbit Mount, on the middle Savannah River. The oft-cited 4500 BP, uncorrected, uncalibrated dates (with large error ranges) calibrate to somewhere around 5000 BP for what was interpreted as an initial, plain, Stallings pottery horizon, which was thought to precede decorated pottery. Currently, the earliest date for Orange pottery comes from Sassaman's excavations at the Mouth of Silver Glen Run site (8LA1), at ca. 4500 cal BP (Sassaman 2003, table 1).[2] Sassaman (2004, 23) posited an initial Orange Plain horizon along "the south-central coast of present-day Georgia and northeast Florida" at around 5200–5000 BP, with subsequent regional variations emerging with distance. He attributed the variations to "different levels of social organization and sociopolitical differentiation among regional populations" (ibid., 39).

## The Function of Early Pottery

In terms of the function of early pottery, Sassaman (ibid., 24) suggested that the first Orange and Stallings wares were plain, flat-bottomed basins used for processing nut oils, meat and bone grease, and gastropods, all of which could be improved using indirect heat cooking (stone boiling using soapstone slabs). Sassaman's scenario is consistent with the "culinary hypothesis," one of the two major sets of models for the development of pottery (Garraty 2011; see also Rice 1999). In the culinary hypotheses, the invention or adoption of pottery increased the subsistence base, one way or another. The other set of hypotheses uses social models—variants of the premise that the earliest pottery fulfilled a social rather than an economic need. One of the principal proponents of the latter theory is Brian Hayden, who proposed that pottery, like all other products made of new materials, arose as a "prestige technology." Thus early pottery vessels were elaborate containers for the ceremonial presentation of food (Hayden 1995, 260). More mundane-looking early vessels were used to store and process prestige foods used in ritual contexts, especially feasting. Hayden predicted that the initial appearance and spread of pottery technology should occur among societies that engaged in reciprocal or competitive feasting. If this were true, Hayden maintained, we should expect "a rapid evolution towards labor-intensive, specialized production of highly decorated forms . . . with great emphasis on control of the medium and craft expertise" (ibid., 261). While one known ring is preceramic (Oxeye Island, 8DU7479), it may be no accident that shell rings and pottery appear together in the Late Archaic. Indeed, the culinary and the social models for the origin of pottery converge in the context of ritual feasting because of the need to process large amounts of food for participating bands.

However, Hayden's scenario is at odds with the traditional Orange period culture history. Based on stratigraphic excavations from numerous sites in Florida, Bullen (1972) transcribed a standard unilineal development for the ware (fully discussed in Milanich 1994; Sassaman 2003). In uncorrected radiocarbon years before present, plain fiber-tempered pottery appeared around 4000–3650 BP, followed by the appearance of rectilinear and (rarely) curvilinear incising (3650–3450 BP). In Bullen's analysis, the elaborate rectilinear incising of Orange III—the "apogee" of fiber-tempered development—was present between 3450 and 3250 BP, after which "designs are much reduced in variety and complexity" (Bullen 1972, 15). In this last period, which Bullen called a "transitional period" (although this periodization is no longer considered to be valid), sand and sponge spicules were added to the fiber-tempered pottery paste, and St. Johns pottery and Orange are found in the same contexts. According to Bullen, by 3000 BP, St. Johns spicule-paste wares had completely replaced Orange ware in northeast Florida. Elsewhere, quartz tempering became the norm.

Since most of Bullen's dates were on shell, 400 years can be added for isotopic fractionation, bringing Bullen's dates reasonably close to the current culture history for northeast Florida. However, Bullen's gradualist model, in which elaborate pottery decoration develops slowly from a plain base and the "apogee" of design elaboration occurs more than 500 years after its invention is at odds with the prestige model. Indeed, both Sassaman (2003) and Saunders (2004a) have shown that the incidence of incising in Orange assemblages is as much a function of site type as it is of time. Shell rings, such as the Rollins and Guana shell rings in Florida and the Fig Island site (38CH42) in South Carolina (Saunders 2002) have considerably more decorated pottery (over 40 percent of the assemblage) than contemporaneous sheet midden or non-shell sites (where assemblages include less than 10 percent decorated pottery) (Saunders 2004a). In addition, in the St. Johns River Valley, Randall and colleagues (this volume) found that a distinctive thick, incised Orange ware (used for food preparation in sacred contexts?) was found only in a few early shell mounds where feasting occurred. The preponderance of elaborately incised Orange ware in shell rings as opposed to shell middens and Randall's incised ware

are both consistent with the prestige hypothesis. At shell ring sites, we may be witnessing a "rapid evolution towards labor-intensive, specialized production of highly decorated forms" (Hayden 1995, 261). Other attributes of the Rollins pottery assemblage may indicate that pottery at shell rings was a prestige ware, including the technical excellence of design execution—the regularity of the width and depth of the incised designs; the skill required to incise the precise lines on the curved surface of the vessels; the preponderance of hard tooling and burnishing (which is present on 90 percent of vessel interiors and exteriors at Rollins); vessel forms—which at Rollins consist predominantly of wide, shallow, serving bowls, many (35 percent) with broad openings (> 51 centimeters); and the decorated rims or brims on the vessels (Saunders 2004a). Sooting is exceedingly rare at both Rollins and Guana, indicating that serving was the major function of vessels, not direct-heat cooking. There is no evidence (e.g., baked clay objects or soapstone slabs) for any kind of indirect-heat cooking. With deference to a multilineal approach to pottery evolution (that is, the idea that pottery may have emerged or have been adopted for different reasons in different areas), we note that although this lack of sooting appears to be consistent at coastal Orange sites, Sassaman (2003) found that at Orange sites along the St. Johns River, incised vessels were often heavily sooted while plain vessels were not. Clearly there is something quite different going on in terms of vessel use in the two regions. This is not too surprising given the different foodstuffs, the different processing needs of those foods, and the different construction and use of ceremonial/habitation sites on the St. Johns River compared to the Atlantic coast (Saunders and Russo 2011).

If decorated Orange ware was used predominantly in ceremonial contexts on the Atlantic coast, who made it? Late Archaic societies are generally considered to be band- or tribal-level societies and are envisioned as egalitarian or transegalitarian—not as hierarchical societies likely to have any degree of craft specialization.[3] (Spielmann [2002] explicitly rejects the idea that craft specialization is present only in ranked societies.) Most of us assume that women produced Orange pottery at the household level (e.g., Sassaman and Rudolphi 2001), strictly for use. But it is worth entertaining the notion that Orange as a prestige ware was the provenance of specialists. Hayden (1995, 260–61) remarked that at its inception, the potter's craft would require a great deal of specialized knowledge: about identifying and mixing the appropriate resources to produce the desired performance characteristics of a vessel; about which construction techniques to use; about the technical skill necessary to incise even the rather simple designs in the consistent manner in which they are executed; and about firing. Indeed, considering the transformative nature of firing pottery and the iconography involved in surface decorations (David et al. 1988), ritual specialists may have been necessary to create early pottery, in the same way that iron workers in parts of Africa were ritual specialists.

Spielmann (2002) researched feasting, craft specialization, and what she termed the "ritual mode of production" in small-scale societies—essentially how people intensify their economic activities in response to the sustained demand engendered by individual and communal ceremonial obligations. Somewhat like Hayden, Spielmann proposed that the primary motivation for subsistence intensification and craft specialization in small-scale societies was not about meeting the demand for basic subsistence but was rather about meeting the demand for "socially valued goods" used in ritual. While Hayden generally credits individual aggrandizers for stimulating production, Spielmann emphasizes the community. Spielmann (2002, 196–97) observed:

> This persistent emphasis on the scale of economic production necessary for ritual performance is critical to understanding economic intensification in general and craft specialization in particular in small-scale societies. Ritual does not simply regulate work; it demands work. Moreover, this work has an aesthetic quality to it beyond production for ordinary, everyday consumption, which may require a certain level of skill and affects the organization of craft production. In the ritual mode of production, the goal is not profits, but, rather, acceptable, often superlative performance and participation. Thus, feasting and craft production in small scale societies are supported not by elites but by numerous individuals as they fulfill ritual obligations and create and sustain social relations.

Indeed, Sassaman (2004, 39) postulated that such ritual demand resulted in what Hayden would perceive as the inevitable change from prestige to practical technology: "demand for serving vessels for feasting at centers of social interaction (competitive or otherwise) may have led to increased demand for vessels in general."

## Comparing the Pottery at Rollins and Guana Shell Rings

Did intensification or specialization appear at Rollins or Guana? In this section, we review some site characteristics and use Rollins, which has more extensive excavations than Guana, to estimate the amount of pottery produced for use at rings.

While not all Archaic shell rings were used as ritual enclosures reserved for special ceremonies, the evidence suggests that Rollins and Guana were used in this way (Saunders 2004b, 2010). These ring sites share many characteristics. As noted above, both are located in similar environments, and they are the same basic shape. However, the ring at Rollins is much larger than the ring at Guana (figure 9.2). By volume, Rollins contains some 9,252 cubic meters of shell, while Guana contains less than half that amount, 3,887 cubic meters (Russo 2006). Rollins is higher (up to 4.4 meters high along the western side) and it is elaborated with a series of "ring-

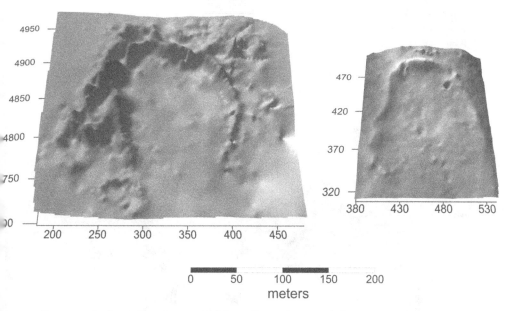

Figure 9.2. Surfer 11 3D surface maps of the Rollins and Guana shell rings, to scale. The highest point of Rollins is 4.4 meters; the highest point of Guana is 3.7 meters. North is up.

lets" that are particularly pronounced on the western and northern edges of the main ring. Only two of these ringlets are dated; one (F) is significantly older than the base of the main ring, while the other (D) is contemporaneous with the base (Saunders 2010). The main rings at Rollins and Guana appear to be contemporaneous; their calibrated dates cluster between cal 3600 and 3500 BP. Both rings have highly decorated Orange pottery assemblages.

In a series of short field seasons from 1998–2000, 20 1- × 2-meter units were excavated at Rollins (Saunders 2003, 2010) (figure 9.3). The units include three in the main ring plaza, three in ringlet plazas, one in the eastern arm, and eight contiguous units in a trench configuration through the western arm of the main ring (Trench 1). In addition, two units of 1 meter by 2 meters were located in the arms of two ringlets (D and F), and another was placed in an area south of the ring where shovel testing revealed a concentration of Orange pottery (Unit 12). Other units were located on the eastern arm of the ring and at the mouth of ringlet E. By volume, the excavations are a miniscule portion of the site, just over 43.8 cubic meters, or 0.47 percent of the shell volume at the site.[4] Nevertheless, one-hundred and sixty-six [5] distinct vessels have been recovered from the Rollins shell ring. Of that total, 139 distinct vessels were from Trench 1, which was purposefully placed in a swale rather than on one of the higher elevations of the western arm of the ring. The bulk of the vessels were from the six meters of shell deposits in the middle of the trench. While a final number is bound to be flawed, the number of pots in the main ring can be

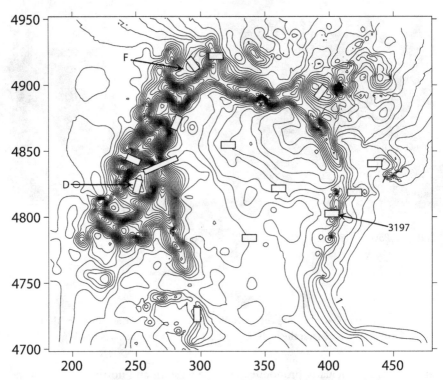

Figure 9.3. Surfer 11 contour map of the Rollins Shell Ring showing units of 1 by 2 meters, one of Russo's 1993 units of 2 by 2 meters, and the trench measuring 1 meter by 16 meters. Contour interval 10 centimeters. Units are not to scale. The ringlets D and E and unit 3197 mentioned in text are labeled. North is up.

extrapolated by determining the number of similar trenches that could be excavated on the ring. This was done by the simple expedient of treating the ring as a bracket, conservatively measured at 150 meters long on the west side, 150 meters wide along the northern portion of the ring, and 100 meters long on the east side. The resulting estimate of the minimum number of vessels (MNV) is 55,600.

A number of objections could be made concerning this result. First, of course, we have assumed that the frequency of pottery in Trench 1 is representative of the deposits in the rest of the ring. Also, there would be some overlap of trenches at the northeast and northwest corners, which possibly inflated the result—although again, the majority of the pottery is from the center of the trench, reducing this problem. In addition, as noted, Trench 1 was located in a 1-meter-high swale; higher areas on the west and north side of the ring could be expected to have more vessels. Furthermore, the estimate leaves out the ringlets altogether. Each of these factors should result in an underestimate. In addition, our procedures for establishing the MNV was strict and most likely also resulted in an underestimate (Wrenn 2012). If objections persist, note that, even when our figure is halved, the result is a lot of pots (but see below).

An appreciation of the intensity of pottery production for use at Rollins is enhanced by the recognition that the bulk of the site appears to have been constructed rapidly. Radiocarbon dates from the top and bottom of the shell deposits in Trench 1, from Unit 3197[6] on the opposite arm of the ring, and from a 2×2meter unit excavated by Russo in 1992 (Russo et al. 1993) are quite close. Ringlet D, one of the most massive of the ringlets at the Rollins site, is also contemporaneous with the main ring (table 9.1).

Given the intensity of pottery production, is it possible that some form of craft specialization was responsible for the surplus of technically and aesthetically superlative pots produced for use in Orange shell rings? Though some might balk at the suggestion of craft specialization in egalitarian fisher-gatherer-hunter societies, Spielmann (2002), drawing on ethnographic evidence from around the world, argued that craft specialization arose to produce surpluses of "socially valued goods" used in ritual, not in response to demands from elites. She noted that such goods can be identified by a number of attributes; for pottery she included an increase in burnishing, elaborate surface decoration, and large vessel size, all of which are attributes of the Rollins assemblage.[7] Spielmann also observed that the expectations of the community regarding the appropriate form of goods used in ritual promote standardization,[8] which increases the likelihood of specialization (Spielmann 2002, 201). Design homogeneity is further increased through trade in these vessels. For instance, despite the fact that Rio Grande potters in disparate villages produced the same Gila wares, vessels from a cluster of villages that specialized in their produc-

Table 9.1. Radiocarbon dates from the Guana shell ring

| Lab # | Provenience | Material | Corrected, B.P. | $\delta^{13}C$ | 2 /1 cal (intercept) 1/2caldelta R -5 ± 20 |
|---|---|---|---|---|---|
| WK-7438 | Trench 1, TU 1, Feature 1, top deposit, 33 cm bs | Oyster | 3600 ± 60 | -2.4‰ | 3660/3580–3420/3360 |
| Beta-119816 | Trench 1, TU 2, Feature 1, bottom deposit, 90–100 cm bs | Oyster | 3670 ± 70 | -2.5‰ | 3795/3680–3480/3400 |
| Beta-119817 | TU 3197 (east side of ring) base of shell | Oyster | 3710 ± 70 | -0.3‰ | 3830/3740–3540/3450 |
| Beta-50155 | 4850N/250E, 60–65 cm bs (Russo 1993) | Oyster | 3760 ± 60 | estimated | 3880/3800–3620/3530 |
| GX-30739 | TU 11 (Ringlet D) base of shell | Oyster | 3630 ± 70 | -3.6 | 3720/3630–3440/3360 |

tion were traded over 100 kilometers (Spielmann 2002, 199). In this respect, it is important to note that the similarity of Orange decoration across space was noted in the earliest research into Orange wares (Bullen 1972; Griffin and Smith 1954; see also Saunders 2004a). To the extent that designs manifested the cosmos and other religious iconography, the decoration of pottery might also have required special ritual knowledge that would also lead to specialization.

In her ethnographic research into the intensification of production, Spielmann (2002) noted that in many small-scale societies (of several hundred to several thousand people), different communities specialize in the production of ritual items. Communities that she studied in Melanesia could produce surpluses (from 12,000–35,000 vessels!) with only a modest level of intensification. Interestingly, the organization of production is different in societies with residential aggregation, in which the aforementioned community specialization occurs, and in societies that aggregate in ritual precincts distinct from communities, (as modeled for the Rollins and Guana sites). In the latter instance (one of Spielmann's cases is Hopewell enclosures), socially valued goods appear to be made by "multiple craftspeople" within the precinct itself instead of through community specialization (Spielmann 2002, 202).

To date, the only possible evidence for craft production at shell rings comes from the Fig Island Ring Complex (38CH42), where a test pit in one ringlet attached to the enormous Ring 1 produced a tremendous amount of pottery, shell tools, and other artifacts compared to the number of artifacts in all other excavation units. Unfortunately, however, it is not clear whether these artifacts were deposited in the ringlet wall as a result of production or whether they were discarded after use (or both). Certainly there was no evidence of pottery firing in the 1 × 2 meter unit that was excavated in that ringlet (Saunders 2002).

Despite the lack of direct evidence for pottery production at rings, it might be possible to determine whether there was some aggregation of pottery specialists, whether at the rings or in a nearby village context, that produced decorated Orange wares for use at the rings by comparing the technological and stylistic attributes of pottery at different rings. Those that study how designs are produced and distributed have long noted that the designs of closely interacting communities of potters are more similar to each other than to designs produced by potters with whom there is little interaction (e.g., Friedrich 1970 for a seminal example; Sassaman and Rudolphi 2001 for an assessment of variation in technological and stylistic attributes of Stallings wares). Especially if a standardized iconography is involved, assemblages produced by the "aggregated" potters might appear as what Redman (1977) and others (Crown 2007) have called the "analytical individual" and what Muller (1977) has termed a "microstyle" (Plog 1977). These terms were introduced in order to emphasize that it is extremely difficult to distinguish the works of an individual from a small group of artisans who work closely together. Muller (1977) and Redman (1977) remarked that distinguishing between the two is not as important as recognizing the high intensity of social interactions.

## Pottery Analysis

In order to determine whether an analytical individual might have produced pottery for use at ring sites across social boundaries (i.e., in two discrete drainages), we compared a number of technical and stylistic attributes of the pottery assemblages from Rollins and Guana. At the outset, however, we must note that there is a big difference in sample size between the two sites. The Rollins excavations were described above. At Guana, initially, 13 shovel tests were placed in the ring deposits, 15 were located in the center of the ring and in the immediate exterior of the ring (many of these were sterile), and one 1 × 2 meter unit was excavated in the apex of the ring (Russo et al. 2002). Subsequently, Saunders and Rolland (2005) placed a block excavation of 2 × 8 meters in the ring plaza (where a high concentration of bone was found during shovel testing) (figure 9.4). It is difficult to directly compare relative frequency of pottery at the two sites by, for instance, standardizing based on the relative amount of soil excavated, because the Guana shovel tests were all dug to one meter below the surface whereas the Rollins units were simply excavated to sterile soil. In the event, then, the assemblage of decorated sherds from Rollins totaled 646 sherds (MNV 166); at Guana, the number was 285 decorated sherds (MNV 61) (a ratio of 2.3:1 based on sherds and 2.7:1 based on MNV). The relative frequency of decorated to plain pottery at Guana is higher than at Rollins—51.3 percent sherds in the Guana main ring deposits were decorated (by sherd count; Russo et al. 2003, table 15) compared to 45 percent at Rollins (Saunders 2004a).

Our initial comparison of the design assemblages at Rollins and Guana was set up to extend the discussion of Orange technological characteristics and stylistic homogeneity at four sites in east-central and northeast Florida (Saunders 2004a) to include the Guana assemblage. Thus, a large number of attributes was recorded, including paste inclusions, interior and exterior burnishing, vessel form, vessel diameter, sherd thickness, land and groove width, groove depth, rim width, rim shape, and surface decoration. Wrenn (2012) reanalyzed both the Rollins and the Guana assemblage; she drew and scanned the design on each sherd, crossmending sherds/designs where possible. Ultimately, 131 discrete designs were identified in the two pottery assemblages. Once all the designs were recorded, they were placed in one of nine "motif groups": multiple-direction oblique lines, single-direction oblique lines, chevrons, horizontal or vertical lines (many sherds were difficult to orient, so these could not reliably be distinguished), crosses, nested motifs, crosshatching, alternat-

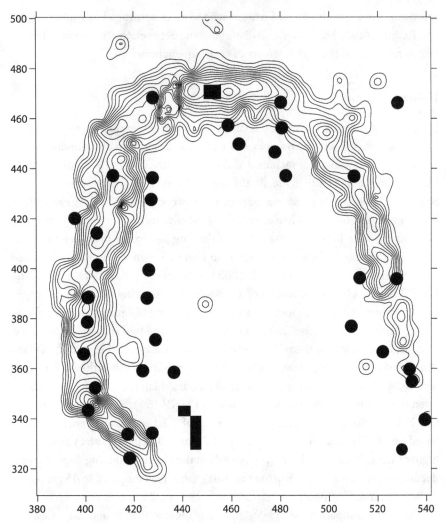

Figure 9.4. Surfer 11 contour map of the Guana Shell Ring showing locations of shovel tests of a unit of 1 by 2 meters at the apex of the ring and an excavation of a block 2 meters by 8 meters in the interior of the plaza. Contour interval 10 centimeters. Units are not to scale. North is up.

ing lines, and other. Representatives of each motif group were present at both sites,[9] reinforcing the notion of a good deal of stylistic homogeneity within the Orange tradition.

This stylistic homogeneity is one of the reasons we were prompted to look for some kind of craft specialization in the decorated wares at ring sites. Our investigations into this question are preliminary, and other avenues remain that could be used to study this question. However, for our first foray, we compared the characteristics of the most complex designs/motifs identified in each assemblage. Presumably these were the most likely to have been produced by specialists who had undergone long apprenticeships (Crown 2007; DeBoer 1990).

We selected 18 sherds from Rollins and 13 from Guana (figure 9.5) with complex designs requiring both a high level of motor control and precise placement of design elements—the marks of expert craftsmanship. At the outset, we can state with confidence that although the sherds from both samples shared design elements and design structure, no sherds with the same complex design were present at both sites. However, some attributes in the "complex" groups at the two sites were all but identical mean sherd thickness (10.3 millimeters at both), incision width (.95 and .97 at Rollins and Guana, respectively), incision depth (.56 and .59), and land width (1.97 and 1.96) (Wrenn 2012). However, these attributes were fairly similar in both simple and complex designs at both sites. The uniformity of these attributes may represent the "standardization" necessary in the production of socially valued goods (a standard stylus?), regardless of who drew the designs.

This result led us to scrutinize more technical aspects of design execution that reflect the habitus of individual motor control (Muller 1977; Plog 1977) in design

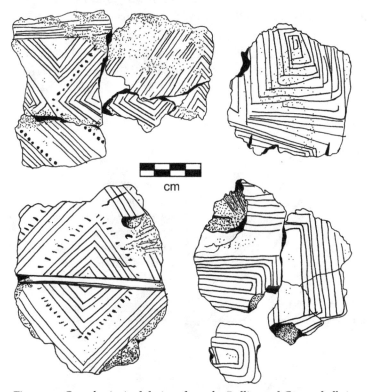

Figure 9.5. Complex incised designs from the Rollins and Guana shell rings. Top: Rollins Catalogue #144.16 (*left*); Rollins #91.9 (*right*). Bottom: Guana #106.21 (*left*); Guana #293.01 (*right*). Sherd drawings by Margaret Wrenn.

execution. These included the execution of incised lines and crosshatch formation (looking at the use of punctation and ticking would also be worthwhile, but the sample size from Guana [n = 2] was too low to be useful). There appeared to be three different styles of groove execution (incision) in the 31 sherds examined (figure 9.6). One style was noticeably straight and unwavering. The second was more inconsistent; linearity appeared to be the intent, but deviations—wobbly lines— were common (figure 9.7). The third type of incising was bowed. Again, linearity may have been the intent, but the line often bowed outward, always in the same direction. Thus, the groove was not completely linear, but it was consistent, not wobbly. Perhaps not surprisingly, the unwavering line was the most common. At Rollins, 50 percent of the complex-design sherds had unwavering lines; at Guana, the figure was even higher, at 84 percent. The inconsistent, wobbly execution was visible on 33 percent of the complex-design sherds at Rollins but was absent at Guana. Both site assemblages had examples of the bowed groove; 11 percent at Rollins and 25 percent at Guana.

There were three crosshatched sherds in the complex design assemblage from each site. To increase the sample size, we included all crosshatching from each site, resulting in a total of 29 sherds from Rollins and 9 from Guana. All crosshatched sherds in the two site assemblages were created by the same basic process. At both sites, a series of parallel incisions was first made in one direction and then another series was made over the first in an opposing direction (not always strictly perpen-

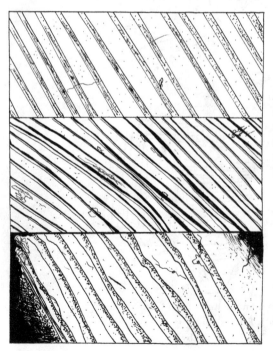

Figure 9.6. Differences in line execution in sherds found at the Rollins shell ring. *From the top*: straight-575.3, bowed-154.32, and wobbly-290.17. Drawing by Margaret Wrenn.

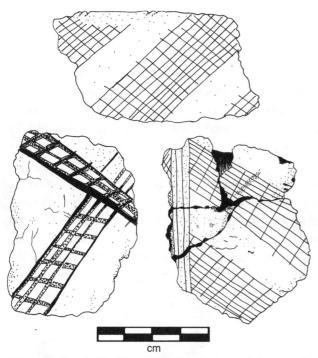

Figure 9.7. Crosshatched designs from the Rollins and Guana shell rings. See text for differences in execution of crosshatching in sherds found in the Rollins and Guana rings. *Top*: Guana Catalogue #91.02. *Bottom*: Rollins #123.14 (*left*); Rollins #676.01 (*right*). Sherd drawings by Margaret Wrenn.

dicular). However, motor movements involved in the creation of the crosshatching at the two sites were different. The Rollins crosshatching was formed by first incising a series of lines from the top left to the bottom right, while the second series was executed from the top right to the bottom left. At Guana, the order of incision was the opposite. First a series of lines was incised from the top right to the bottom left. These lines were superimposed by a group of lines drawn from the top left to the bottom right. There is a fundamental difference in the chaîne opératoire of crosshatching at the two sites.

We also examined aspects of the execution of angles in chevron, nested shape, and other (where applicable) designs in the complex design subsample. There were eight examples from Rollins and nine from Guana. First, we determined whether the angles were created using a single stroke or two strokes. When the angle was made using two strokes, we looked at how well the vertices of the angles lined up—whether they were straight or offset. At Rollins, 50 percent of the complex sherds with angled designs were made with a single stroke and 50 percent with a double stroke. At Guana, the majority (80 percent) was made with two strokes.

Taken together, these data, particularly the crosshatching data, suggest that different potting communities were responsible for the assemblages at Rollins and Guana.[10] Therefore, whatever surplus production might be involved must have been done at the intracommunity level, not between communities. This indicates either that festivities at the rings were conducted only at the intracommunity level or, if ceremonies involved communities from other drainages, that it was incumbent on the host community to provide serving wares. The latter conclusion would not be out of synch with ethnographic observations. However, Thompson et al. (2008) did suggest that Thoms Creek pottery may have been brought to the Sapelo Island rings for ceremonial purposes.

Although our preliminary conclusions are based on a small subsample of the respective design assemblages, we believe that the subsample of vessels with complex designs are the most likely to have been produced by craft specialists. The next step in the analysis is to prepare a more rigorous database of all designs and subject the database to cluster analysis, as described by Redman (1977) and Carr (1995). We could also look more closely within the design assemblages of both sites to determine how many potters (analytical individuals) are present at each site.

## Conclusions

While Hayden (1995) emphasized the role of competition and political aspirations among aggrandizers and Spielmann (2002) stressed the demands of the community in ritual performances, both researchers argued that pottery production emerged and intensified for social rather than utilitarian reasons. Under either model, early pottery was elaborated and produced by specialists. In this chapter, we looked for evidence that some Orange pottery was produced by the same craft specialists for ritual performances in two Late Archaic shell ring sites in northeast Florida. Specifically, we looked for distinctive traces of motor habits created by "analytical individuals." In this preliminary investigation, we found no evidence that pots with complex, well-executed designs from the Rollins and Guana shell rings were produced by the same individual. However, while our early investigations do not indicate that complex designs were created by potters for ritual use across drainages, we believe that our databases need to be increased and additional attributes need to be compared before we abandon our search for potting specialists in the Late Archaic. In addition, further analyses will be directed toward looking for specialized pottery production for ritual use within drainages and at individual rings or ring complexes.

As data increases, the complexity of Archaic societies continues to surprise us. After all, not that long ago, there were no Archaic mounds. Now we recognize not only mounds, but all manner of mound complexes, enclosures, shell rings, and other monuments. We wouldn't be at all surprised to find some heretofore unrecognized specialization in pottery production associated with Archaic shell rings.

## Acknowledgments

Many thanks to Asa and Neill for including us in the 2011 Southeastern Archaeological Conference symposium and in this volume. Special thanks to Asa for help with the maps and to Chris Rodning for spelling corrections.

## Notes

1. Note that, as Russo et al. (this volume) discuss, these coastal Archaic shell rings are distinct in both size and function from later Woodland period habitation rings.

2. The two 4800 cal BP dates in Sassaman, 2003, table 1, have relative areas of 7 percent and 14 percent, while the 4500 cal BP dates have 100 percent and 72 percent. In our estimation, the latter dates have more credence.

3. Specialization in production of pottery in Florida has been discussed by Milanich et al. (1997) for elite wares in the Weeden Island I period and by Luer (this volume) for utilitarian wares in the Safety Harbor period.

4. This is an admittedly sloppy measure, since the "volume" of the site as a whole is not known, and without extensive testing to determine the depth of deposits in all of the non-shell areas, no firm figure could be derived. However, the point that only a tiny portion of the site has been tested is valid. Unit 12 is not included in the volume estimate.

5. The single vessel from Unit 12, south of the ring, is not included in this vessel tally; a 1.8-meter-deep shell-filled feature in Unit 12 is dated to an earlier period than the most of the ring deposits.

6. The units excavated in 1998 were designated by the mapping coordinate number assigned by the digital transit for the southeast corner of each unit.

7. The association of these attributes with ceremonial vessels is, of course, not new.

8. Sassaman and Rudolphi (2001) also found design homogeneity in Stallings wares among three sites in the middle Savannah River. Interestingly, while the designs were similar, the technical attributes were not.

9. In surprisingly similar quantities, which we cannot yet address.

10. As noted, we are continuing to look at other aspects of the assemblages, especially firing practices. These too probably indicate separate potting communities.

## References

Bullen, Ripley P.
1972    The Orange Period in Peninsular Florida. In *Fiber-Tempered Pottery in the Southeastern United States and Northern Columbia: Its Origins, Context, and Significance*, edited by Ripley P. Bullen and James B. Stoltman, 9–33. Florida Anthropological Society Publications no. 6. Florida Anthropological Society, Gainesville.

Campbell, L. Janice, Prentice M. Thomas Jr., and James H. Mathews
2004    Fiber-Tempered Pottery and Cultural Interaction on the Northwest Florida Gulf Coast. In *Early Pottery: Technology, Function, Style, and Interaction in the Lower Southeast*, edited by Rebecca Saunders and Christopher T. Hays, 129–49. University of Alabama Press, Tuscaloosa.

Carr, Christopher
1995    A Unified Middle-Range Theory of Artifact Design. In *Style, Society and Person: Archaeological and Ethnological Perspectives*, edited by Christopher Carr, Jill E. Neitzel, 171–258. Plenum Press, New York.

Crown, Patricia L.

2007    Life Histories of Potters and Pots: Situating the Individual in Archaeology. *American Antiquity* 72: 677–90.

David, Nicholas, Judy Sterner, and Kodzo Gavua

1988    Why Pots Are Decorated. *Current Anthropology* 29(3): 365–79.

DeBoer, Warren R.

1990    Interaction, Imitation, and Communication as Expressed in Style: The Ucayali Experience. In *The Uses of Style in Archaeology*, edited by Margaret Conkey and Christine Hasdorf, 82–104. Cambridge University Press, Cambridge.

Dietler, Michael, and Brian Hayden.

2001    Digesting the Feast: Good to Eat, Good to Drink, Good to Think: An Introduction. In *Feasts: Archeological and Ethnographic Perspectives on Food, Politics, and Power*, edited by Michael Dietler and Brian Hayden, 1–20. Smithsonian Institution Press, Washington, DC.

Friedrich, Margaret Hardin

1970    Design Structure and Social Interaction: Archeological Implications of an Ethnographic Study. *American Antiquity* 35: 332–43.

Garraty, Christopher P.

2011    The Origins of Pottery as a Practical Domestic Technology: Evidence from the Middle Queen Creek Area, Arizona. *Journal of Anthropological Archaeology* 30: 220–34.

Griffin, John W., and Hale G. Smith

1954    The Cotten Site: An Archaeological Site of Early Ceramic Times in Volusia County, Florida. *Florida State University Studies* 16: 27–60.

Hayden, Brian

1995    The Emergence of Prestige Technologies and Pottery. In *The Emergence of Pottery: Technology and Innovation in Ancient Societies*, edited by William K. Barnett and John W. Hoopes, 257–66. Smithsonian Institution Press, Washington, DC.

Milanich, Jerald T.

1994    *Archaeology of Precolumbian Florida*. University Press of Florida, Gainesville.

Milanich, Jerald T., Ann S. Cordell, Vernon J. Knight Jr., Timothy A. Kohler, and Brenda J. Sigler-Lavelle

1997    *Archaeology of Northern Florida, A.D. 200–900: The McKeithen Weeden Island Culture*. University Press of Florida, Gainesville.

Muller, Jon

1977    Individual Variation in Art Styles. In *The Individual in Prehistory: Studies of Variability in Style in Prehistoric Technologies*, edited by James N. Hill and Joel Gunn, 23–40. Academic Press, New York.

Plog, Fred

1977    Archaeology and the Individual. In *The Individual in Prehistory: Studies of Variability in Style in Prehistoric Technologies*, edited by James N. Hill and Joel Gunn, 13–22. Academic Press, New York.

Redman, Charles L.

1977    The "Analytical Individual" and Prehistoric Style Variability. In *The Individual in Prehistory: Studies of Variability in Style in Prehistoric Technologies*, edited by James N. Hill and Joel Gunn, 41–54. Academic Press, New York.

Rice, Prudence M.

1999    On the Origins of Pottery. *Journal of Archaeological Method and Theory* 6: 1–54.

Russo, Michael

2006    *Archaic Shell Rings of the Southeast: U.S. National Historic Landmark Historical Context Study.* National Park Service, Washington, DC.

Russo, Michael, Ann S. Cordell, and Donna L. Ruhl

2003    The Timucuan Ecological and Historic Preserve: Phase III Final Report. SEAC Accession No. 899, Florida Museum of Natural History. Report Submitted to the Southeast Archaeological Center, National Park Service, Tallahassee, Florida.

Russo, Michael, A. S. Cordell, and D. L. Ruhl

1993    The Timucuan Ecological and Historic Preserve, Phase III Final Report. Southeast Archaeological Center, National Park Service, Tallahassee.

Russo, Michael, Gregory Heide, and Vicki Rolland

2002    The Guana Shell Ring. Report submitted to the Florida Department of State, Division of Historical Resources, Tallahassee.

Sassaman, Kenneth E.

2003    New AMS Dates on Orange Fiber-Tempered Pottery from the Middle St. Johns Valley and their Implications for Culture History in Northeast Florida. *Florida Anthropologist* 56: 5–14.

2004    Common Origins and Divergent Histories in the Early Pottery Traditions of the American Southeast. In *Early Pottery: Technology, Function, Style, and Interaction in the Lower Southeast,* edited by Rebecca Saunders and Christopher T. Hays, 23–39. University of Alabama Press, Tuscaloosa.

Sassaman, Kenneth E., and Wictoria Rudolphi

2001    Communities of Practice in the Early Pottery Traditions of the American Southeast. *Journal of Anthropological Research* 57: 407–25.

Saunders, Rebecca

2002    The Fig Island Ring Complex (38CH42): Coastal Adaptation and the Question of Ring Function in the Late Archaic (with William Green, Greg Heide, David S. Leigh, Mike Russo, and William Stanyard), edited by Rebecca Saunders and Mike Russo. Report submitted to the South Carolina Department of Archives and History under NPS grant #45-01-16441.

2003    Feast or Quotidian Fare?: Rollins Shell Ring and the Question of Ring Function. Report submitted to the Florida Department of Archives and History.

2004a   Spatial Variation in Orange Culture Pottery: Interaction and Function. In *Early Pottery: Technology, Function, Style, and Interaction in the Lower Southeast,* edited by Rebecca Saunders and Christopher T. Hays, 40–62. University of Alabama Press, Tuscaloosa.

2004b   Stratigraphy at the Rollins Shell Ring Site: Implications for Ring Function. *Florida Anthropologist* 57: 249–70.

2010    Rollins Redux: Rings, Ringlets, and Really Big Pits. Report submitted to the Florida Department of Archives and History, Tallahassee.

Saunders, Rebecca, and Christopher T. Hays

2004    Introduction: Themes in Early Pottery Research. In *Early Pottery: Technology, Function, Style, and Interaction in the Lower Southeast,* edited by Rebecca Saunders and Christopher T. Hays, 1–22. University of Alabama Press, Tuscaloosa.

Saunders, Rebecca, and Vicki Rolland

2005    Exploring the Interior of the Guana River Shell Ring (8SJ2554). Report submitted to the Florida Department of State, Division of Historical Resources, Tallahassee.

Saunders, Rebecca, and Michael Russo

2011    Coastal Shell Middens in Florida: A View from the Archaic Period. *Quaternary International* 239: 38–50.

Saunders, Rebecca, and Mike Russo (editors)

2002    The Fig Island Ring Complex (38CH42): Coastal Adaptation and the Question of Ring Function in the Late Archaic. Report submitted to the South Carolina Department of Archives and History, Columbia.

Spielmann, Katherine A.

2002    Feasting, Craft Production, and the Ritual Mode of Production in Small-Scale Societies. *American Anthropologist* 104: 195–207.

2008    Crafting the Sacred: Ritual Spaces and Sacred Places in Small-Scale Societies. Dimensions of Ritual Economy. *Research in Economic Anthropology* 27: 37–72.

Stoltman, James B.

1966    New Radiocarbon Dates for Southeastern Fiber-Tempered Pottery. *American Antiquity* 31: 872–74.

1974    *Groton Plantation: An Archaeological Study of a South Carolina Locality.* Monographs of the Peabody Museum no. 1. Harvard University Press, Cambridge, MA.

Thompson, Victor D., Wesley D. Stoner, Harold D. Rowe

2008    Early Hunter-Gatherer Pottery along the Atlantic Coast of the Southeastern United States: A Ceramic Compositional Study. *Journal of Island and Coastal Archaeology* 3: 191–213.

Walker, William H.

1995    Ceremonial Trash? In *Expanding Archaeology*, edited by James M. Skibo, William H. Walker, and Axel E. Nielsen, 67–79. University of Utah Press, Salt Lake City.

White, Nancy M.

2003    Late Archaic in the Apalachicola-Lower Chattahoochee Valley, Northwest Florida, Southwest Georgia, and Southeast Alabama. *Florida Anthropologist* 56: 69–90.

Wrenn, Margaret K.

2012    Designing Pots: Determining Orange Incised Design Variation and Distribution at the Rollins Shell Ring and the Guana Shell Ring in Florida. MA thesis, Department of Geography and Anthropology, Louisiana State University, Baton Rouge.

# 10

# It's Ceremonial, Right?

## Exploring Ritual in Ancient Southern Florida through the Miami Circle

RYAN J. WHEELER AND ROBERT S. CARR

Many popular accounts of the Miami Circle site proposed that the circle feature carved into the limestone at the mouth of the Miami River was the center of ritual activity. The remains of a shark, a sea turtle, and a bottlenose dolphin buried at the site were thought to represent ritual interments and one fanciful newspaper account speculated that the basin features comprising the site were animal effigies. This chapter considers the animal interments from the circle and elsewhere in southern Florida and explores what they may represent, including that they may be evidence of animal sacrifice. We also consider the animal interments in light of research on Native American beliefs about the nature of human and animal souls.

## The Miami Circle: A Case Study of Ritual in Southeastern Florida

News of the Miami Circle's discovery became widely known late in 1998 and set the stage for speculation by the press, archaeologists, and the public over the function and origin of this feature. The circle is 38 feet in diameter and consists of from 24 to 26 basins carved into the oolitic limestone at the mouth of the Miami River in downtown Miami, Florida (Carr and Ricisak 2000) (figure 10.1). Surrounding and overlying the circle are black earth midden deposits typical of the archaeological sites in the Miami area that contain artifacts such as shell tools, bone artifacts, local sand-tempered pottery sherds, ground stone tools, chipped chert artifacts, pumice, galena, and some sherds from other parts of the state. Taken in context, the material culture of the site is probably usual for the early formative Glades culture of the area, which seems to have participated in some fairly sophisticated local and regional exchange systems. The carved basin and hole features that make up the Miami Circle likely reflect local adaptations to building structures in areas where the limestone bedrock is at or near the surface. Subsequent excavations directly across the Miami River revealed another circular feature carved into the limestone that is associated with similar artifacts. Radiocarbon dates and material culture indicate that both circular features were made during the Glades I period (500 BC–AD 750) and surrounding environs were intensely occupied almost continuously up through European contact, when the residents of this large site group were known as the Tequesta.

Most of the wild claims about the circle have dissipated in the light of empirical research (for example, see Dixon et al. [2000] on the origin of basalt axes, as well as other scientific articles in three special issues of *The Florida Anthropologist*: December 2000, March–June 2004, and September–December 2006). The interments of a sea turtle carapace, a bottlenose dolphin skull, and a requiem shark, however, are unusual features and are theorized to be evidence of ritual activity (figure 10.2). The interment of animals or animal parts suggest sacrifice, the ritualized killing and offering of living beings as a gift to deities in exchange for favors or goodwill, a practice that some consider to be the basis for all ritual activity. In one definition, sacrifice consists of three elements: 1) killing a consecrated living being; 2) offering its life or life energy to a spirit or deity; and 3) receipt of a blessing or benefit through the col-

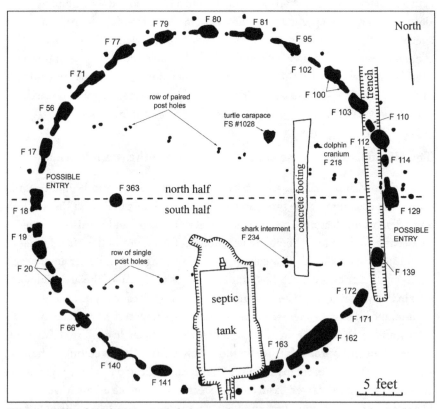

Figure 10.1. Sketch of the Miami Circle feature showing major components and animal interments. After Weisman et al. 2000.

lective consumption of the offering (see Bloch 1992; Humphrey and Laidlaw 2007, 270). In this chapter we will look critically at the Miami Circle animal interments in light of archaeological and ethnohistorical data from Florida and contemporary research on ritual and sacrifice. A central consideration is our ability to recognize sacrifice in the archaeological record.

a

Figure 10.2. Animal interments from the Miami Circle: a) requiem shark; b) reconstructed dolphin cranium and complete modern specimen; and c) loggerhead sea turtle carapace.

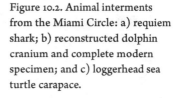

b

c

## The Miami Circle Animal Interments

The interments of a shark, a dolphin cranium, and a sea turtle carapace at the Miami Circle have already been described by Alison Elgart (2006; see also Wheeler 2008). All of the interments are local marine creatures; all date to approximately the same late time period, apparently well after the Miami Circle was built and used; and all were found in the eastern half of the circle. The turtle carapace and the bottlenose dolphin skull were quite near to one another. The shark seems to be the only interment of a complete animal. Each was interred in the black earth midden deposits overlying the Miami Circle feature. A summary of the three animal interment features is below.

### Shark Interment (Feature 234)

The shark interment (Feature 234) was encountered in excavation units 30 and 35, in the southeastern quadrant of the Miami Circle feature (Elgart 2006, 179, 181). The feature consists of a mass of teeth, representing the animal's head, oriented to the west, and articulated centra (vertebrae) extending to the east. Masses of dermal denticles (components of the shark's skin) were present as well. Measurements and preliminary identification indicate that it was a requiem shark (*Carcharhinus* sp.) 167 centimeters (5.5 feet) long. Bone collagen from the shark was radiocarbon dated at 670 ± 30 BP (Beta-134544, AD 1560–1680, 2-sigma calibrated age).[1]

### Turtle Carapace (FS #1028)

The loggerhead sea turtle (*Caretta caretta*) carapace (FS #1028) was recovered from Unit 64, in the northeastern portion of the Miami Circle (Elgart 2006, 181). The turtle carapace was not accompanied by any related skeletal elements and was found with its dorsal surface down. The proximal end of the carapace was oriented approximately to the east. It is the largest single object recovered from the Miami Circle excavations, other than the limestone cobbles found in some holes and basins. It is possible that the carapace represents a platter or similar artifact. Measurements of the carapace (it is 65 centimeters long) indicate that it is a subadult. Data from live measurements of nesting females in Broward County indicate that adult female carapace lengths range from 97 to 100 centimeters (Fletemeyer 1984, 32). Charcoal recovered in association with the carapace was radiocarbon dated at 420 ± 80 BP (Beta-167166, AD 1330–1650, 2-sigma calibrated age).

### Bottlenose Dolphin Cranium (Feature 218)

The fragmentary remains of a bottlenose dolphin (*Tursiops truncatus*) were found in units 32 and 33 (the northeast quadrant of the Miami Circle, just to the east of the sea turtle carapace described above) and were designated Feature 218 (Elgart 2006, 179). Reconstruction of the available bones indicates that most of the cranium is present, minus the teeth and the lower mandible. Radiocarbon dating of bone collagen from the dolphin skull produced an age of 690 ± 40 BP (Beta-161899, AD 1530–1680, 2-sigma calibrated age).

## Sacrifice among the Tequesta and Their Neighbors

Historic documents mention several instances of sacrifice among the native peoples of southern Florida. Notably, a short account by Escalante Fontaneda describes several forms of sacrifice among the sixteenth-century Calusa (Worth 1995). To paraphrase, the Calusa performed the following: 1) sacrifice of children upon the death of the cacique's son, so they could accompany the deceased in the afterlife; 2) sacrifice of servants upon the death of the tribal leader; 3) the annual sacrifice of a Christian captive in order to feed an idol that eats human eyes, including dances around the decapitated head; and 4) a fall sacrifice that involved performance by disguised shamans over a period of at least four months, with considerable dancing and attention to idols. In this last case it is not clear exactly what sacrifice is involved, although accounts of masked processions and the Calusa temple masks date from this same era (Hann 1991, 315–16; Childers 2003; Worth 1995, 344; Clark 1995). Escalante Fontaneda's list of sacrifices is suggestive of two distinct aspects of Calusa ritual: rites related to elite and chiefly power and rites of fertility and renewal. It is interesting to compare Calusa rituals with models of Mississippian religion by Lawrence Conrad (1989, 93) and Vernon Knight (1986), since the prevailing thought has been that there was little connection between the iconography and cosmology of the Mississippian Southeast and the local belief systems of people in southern Florida (Widmer 1989, 176–77, 179–80; Wheeler 1996).

The sacrificial practices Escalante Fonteneda described appear to have been widespread geographically and temporally in southern Florida, especially the sacrifice of captives (which was noted among the Uzita of Tampa Bay in the sixteenth century), sacrifice upon the death of a leader (which was found among the natives of the Florida Keys at this time as well), and the sacrifice of children. The account of the 1743 mission in southeastern Florida documents the Spanish intervention in the practice of sacrificing children. Interestingly, this sacrifice was intended to commemorate peace with a neighboring group (Childers 2003, 71). Another account involving child sacrifice comes from the short-lived mid-sixteenth-century Spanish mission to the Tequesta, where the niece of one the leading men became ill and died. Intervention by the Catholic priest led to the girl's burial in the Christian manner, but the Tequesta told the priests that if she had been interred in the traditional Tequesta way, the ritual would have included the sacrifice of four children (Hann 2003, 151–52). The account of 1743 Spanish mission among the remnants of several southern Florida groups indicates that the rituals of the sixteenth century seem to have persisted. Like their ancestors, these people had a temple with masks and the religious leader entered into an annual rite that involved fasting, dancing, and howling, some of which was aimed at controlling the weather (Childers 2003, 76–77). The description of this rite says that the religious leader "is exalted and dies and is resurrected sanctified." The association of sanctification and death seems to have existed among the Calusa of the sixteenth century as well; the observations of Jesuit cleric Father Juan Rogel indicate that fasting and running over a period of many days accompanied a number of rituals, including ceremonies dedicated to "idols" and burial of the dead. According to the account, the Calusa told the Spanish friar that their ancestors were able to see God during these rituals (Hann 1991, 242; 2003, 197–98). The account of the 1743 mission also mentions the sacrifice of food, tobacco, animal skulls, and other offerings to propitiate the spirits of the dead (Childers 2003, 77).

These accounts of sacrifice illustrate anthropologist Pierre Smith's structuralist dichotomies of periodic rites, such as life crises and calendrical holidays, which are balanced by occasional rites of affliction or enthronement. Smith also recognizes rites relating to the individual as opposed to collective rites (see Bell 1997, 174–76; Smith 1982, 108–9). In Smith's model, each periodic rite is assigned meaning and significance in the context of a complete sequence of rites. The rituals associated with life crises form a periodic system for the individual, while a sequence of annual or seasonal rites forms a periodic system for the collective. Smith's occasional rites are reactive and are tied to some type of disorder or imbalance, in contrast to the cycles of periodic ritual that can give rise to "an ordered series of eternal re-beginnings and repetitions" (Smith 1982, 109, 124–25). Rituals involving sacrifice seem to be important among the Tequesta and other southern Florida peoples, at least to outside observers. Sacrifice also seems to take a number of the forms in Smith's model, even including the occasional rites, such as the sacrifice of children to commemorate peace between neighboring groups. Many of these rituals of sacrifice, like the peace ritual, demonstrate the importance of ritual in civic and secular life, in contrast to the more traditional association of ritual and religion.

## Archaeological Examples of Sacrifice in Ancient Southern Florida

Elsewhere in Florida and the Southeast there is archaeological evidence for human sacrifice. For example, Lawrence Conrad (1989) discusses both ethnohistoric accounts of sacrifice among southeastern cultures such as the Natchez and Timucua and archaeological evidence for retainer burials at sites such as Cahokia. Despite written accounts of sacrifice in southern Florida, archaeological examples are difficult to discern. For example, excavations at sites from southern Palm Beach County through Broward and Miami-Dade counties and well to the west in Hendry County have discovered isolated human skulls—or in at least two cases, caches of human skulls—interred along with more conventional burials. There seems to be considerable variation in the treatment of these isolated skull interments. For example, at the Lauderhill Mound an isolated cranium was "embedded" in the rib cage of another burial, while at the Barnhill Mound, an isolated cranium was found in association with a postmold stain, leading to speculation that the skull had been mounted on a post (Bullen 1957, 33–34; Felmley 1991, 105–6) (figure 10.3). Excavations in the 1930s at the Surfside Mound located a cache of skulls near the mound center, while recent excavations at a site in Hendry County found at least 11 isolated skulls in a midden deposit, along with other, very scattered burials. A partial cranium buried with another individual at the Late Archaic Santa Maria site in Miami suggests some time depth for the interment of isolate skulls (Carr et al. 1984, 179). The isolated skulls and skull caches found in southern Florida may represent instances of sacrifice, but they also may represent interment of trophy skulls collected during battle or the crania of ancestors that were interred at various times with other decedents.

Keith Jacobi (2007) tackles the issue of human trophy taking in his consideration of archaeological data in the Tennessee River Basin, noting that many so-called isolate skulls and headless burials are the result of natural processes. Jacobi concludes that both antagonism and veneration of the dead are motivations behind trophy taking in the Southeast. Hally (2008, 260–61, 431–32, 447–48) describes burials that contain additional skeletal elements at the King site in northwestern Georgia, ranging from teeth to an entire bundle burial placed at the foot of another grave. He argues that these were war trophies.

Addressing the issue of Mississippian trophy taking and human skull collecting, James Brown and David Dye (2007) present a nuanced argument that the iconographic depiction of human skulls and heads that some have pointed to as evidence for warfare and sacrifice represent mythical hero personages and their activities (also see Hall 1989, 247, 256–57). Vernon Knight and Vincas Steponaitis (2011) look particularly at the Hemphill-style image on pottery, copper, stone, and shell artifacts at Moundville and suggest a connection with George Lankford's (2007) "Path of Souls" model, which unites a number of cosmological and astronomical themes. Knight and Steponaitis (2011, 213) mention that the skull and bone motifs could be interpreted in a variety of ways, as trophies taken in mythic combat or as allusions to Lankford's Path of Souls.

Although animal interments are rare, they have been reported from some sites in southern Florida. For example, federal relief excavations in the 1930s encountered "indeterminate animal" burials in the area surrounding the Surfside Mound in Miami-Dade County (Felmley 1991, 114–15). Excavators at the Margate-Blount site in Broward County found an area that they described as a "ceremonial precinct" adjacent to a cemetery and habitation site that contained a number of animal in-

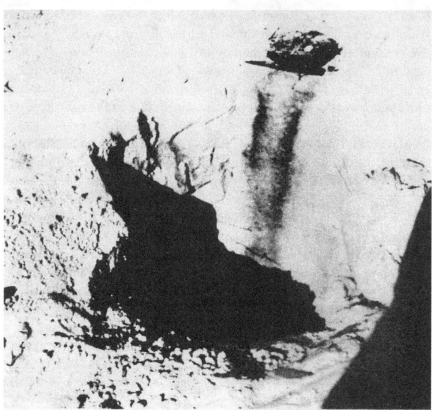

Figure 10.3. Human skull with post mold stain, Barnhill Mound, Palm Beach County. After Bullen 1957, figure 8.

terments, including an alligator, a coiled rattlesnake missing its head and tail, and turtles and raccoons (Felmley 1991, 102; Wheeler 1992, 94–95). Although human burials predominated at the Palmer Mound in Sarasota, several dog burials and one complete alligator were also interred there, along with what may be either two strands of sawfish (*Pristis* sp.) centra beads or portions of two sawfish (Bullen and Bullen 1976, 44–46, Plate 17) (figure 10.4). Other sites in Florida have partial interments of animals, usually the cranium. These include sea turtles, dolphins, and alligators (Carr and Steele 1993, 14; James Dunbar, personal communication November 2004; Elgart 2006, 184; Felmley 1991, 116–19; Johnson 1952, 36; Hermann Trappman, personal communication December 2003). Several patterns are suggested by the accounts of these rare interments of animals and animal parts, especially that many of the animals represented are aquatic creatures: alligators, sea turtles, bottlenose dolphins, and sharks. This is significant, especially in the context of Ian McNiven's (2003) research on seascapes and maritime ritual. He suggests that among Australian aboriginal fisherfolk, "most rituals attempted some form of spiritual control over the elements and marine animals" (338). Examples from Aus-

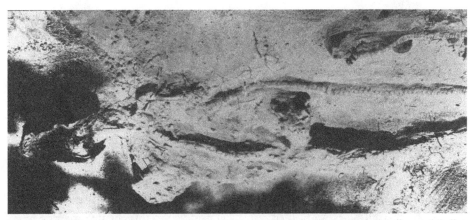

Figure 10.4. Alligator interment, Palmer Burial Mound, Sarasota County. After Bullen and Bullen 1976, plate 17.

tralia include one rare site with a collection of dugong bones and more common sites with geometric arrangements of stones, thought to be involved with hunting magic and the control of tides, respectively. Also, the diversity of animals that are interred, the variations in burial patterns, and the association of the animals that are buried is probably significant. Complete animal burials are very rare; while animal parts, especially skulls, are more common. In many cases there is a direct association with human burials or the animal burials occur near human mortuary areas. While the Miami Circle does not appear to be a human mortuary site, there is a burial area not too far distant to the south.

Accounts of animal burials in archaeological sites of the Southeast are rare, with the exception of dogs, though there are accounts of interment of animals and animal parts in the Caribbean and Mesoamerica. For example, three articulated crocodiles buried at the North Acropolis of Tikal in Guatemala could be considered dedicatory or commemorative offerings (Chase and Chase 1998, 324–26; also see Erica Hill's 2000 study of animal interments in the Southwest). Tanya Peres and Teresa Ingalls (2008) present one of the few studies of animal remains, both modified and unmodified, found in a Mississippian mortuary site. Their study is important and intriguing, since it hints that interment of animal remains may have been more widespread than was previously thought. Peres and Ingalls (2008, 9) found that along with shell ornaments and bone tools, some burials at the sixteenth-century David Davis Farm site in Tennessee also included unmodified animal bones and teeth. For example, 12 burials had unmodified beaver teeth.

As noted above, dog burials are the one animal interment routinely encountered in Florida and the Southeast. In fact, dog burials are well represented in the archaeological record in many parts of the world. While it is beyond the scope of this study to delve into the extensive literature on dogs and dog burials in Native America, it is worthwhile to consider some contemporary thinking about dog burials (e.g., Schwartz 1997). A recent popular article in *Archaeology* magazine concisely summarizes many of the human-dog interactions that have been documented archaeologically, including dogs as food, as companions, as deities, as tools, as sacrifices, and as guardians and guides for the dead (Lobell and Powell 2010). Jessica Zimmer's (2007) master's thesis on dogs in ancient Florida documents examples of dog bones found in refuse deposits, tools and ornaments made from dog bones and teeth, and dog interments. She concludes that the comparatively large number of dog bones found in midden deposits argues for the widespread use of dogs as food in prehistoric Florida, although she also found examples of single interments throughout the state, including cases from southern Florida. As with the interments of sharks, alligators, and other animals considered in this chapter, the dog interments in Florida do not seem to follow any clear patterns, though it is interesting that all of the complete animal interments are of animals that regularly appear to have been food items. Sharks, sea turtles, and alligators are well represented in midden deposits throughout peninsular Florida.

Darcy Morey's (2006) study of human-dog interactions is even more interesting. His discussion of dog burials worldwide considers the special relationship between dogs and humans, elaborating on many of the themes mentioned above. He tackles the difficult question of why dogs were buried, which certainly speaks to the question of these other animal interments. Morey (2006, 165–67) comes at this question in an intriguing way, arguing that elements of both companionship and spirituality are in play, ultimately suggesting that dogs may have been treated much like people in societies that practiced both dog and human sacrifice. Losey et al. (2011) consider the burials of a dog and a wolf in eastern Siberia and make the case that some individual animals were accorded human funerary treatment because they, like humans, were thought to possess souls. They make a complex argument based on the varied arctic and subarctic beliefs in animism, souls in general, and animal souls specifically that help explain some of the disparate treatment of animal remains, including those accorded burial. If the inhabitants of ancient southern Florida had similar beliefs, we may need to significantly alter our thinking about the role of animals in the belief system.

When we consider sacrifice—of both humans and animals—in southern Florida, the question is What happens to the remains of those sacrificed? Do they end up in the same spaces occupied by other burials or are they discarded or interred elsewhere? Individuals sacrificed to accompany the deceased elite may well end up in a burial mound or cemetery, but would captives sacrificed to a deity be afforded this treatment? Pawnee practices of human sacrifice that reenacted myths related to the Morning Star and other gods suggest that the victim's remains were not buried in traditional Caddoan ways but were instead scattered widely after the ritual killing

(Linton 1926). A bit closer to home, many of us living in southern Florida have encountered on beaches and roadsides the discarded paraphernalia from Santeria rituals, including the carcasses of sacrificed animals. Apparently, some southern Florida communities have even passed laws to prohibit this disposal of ritually sacrificed animals. However, we know little about sacrifice and trophy taking among the native people of southern Florida, so it is difficult to determine, for example, whether the human crania bowls known from sites in Palm Beach County are made from the skulls of murdered enemies or are the remains of venerated ancestors (Wheeler et al. 2002, 119–20). In much the same way, it is difficult to say what the isolated human heads found in some burial sites represent or if their burial treatment is similar to interments of animal heads.

## The Role of Sacrifice in Southern Florida

The Spanish accounts of sacrifice among the Calusa and their neighbors suggest that this activity had some significance in the broader belief systems of these people. The various types of sacrifice Escalante Fontaneda described in the sixteenth century are congruent with other information about the cosmology of the ancient inhabitants of southern Florida, namely that political leaders were prominent in the belief system and oftentimes found themselves in opposition to religious leaders. As John Hann (2003, 198–99) notes, the Calusa chiefly elite possessed esoteric religious knowledge that supported their claim to rule. Statements by the newly enthroned Calusa chief—namely that he was reluctant to forsake traditional religious practices for fear that he would lose support—indicate that the chief understood the complex relationship between religious belief and politics and that some of the attendant rites and rituals might specifically reinforce chiefly power at times of political unrest (Hann 2003, 199; Hann 1991, 224–25). Recall Pierre Smith's structuralist model of ritual, which distinguished between periodic and occasional rituals; the latter are associated with instances of imbalance or unrest in the broader sociopolitical system.

The shark, marine turtle carapace, and dolphin skull found at the Miami Circle give us the opportunity to consider the phenomenon of ritual sacrifice in southern Florida. The complete, articulated remains of a requiem shark is the most suggestive of sacrifice. The bottlenose dolphin skull and subadult sea turtle carapace may represent artifacts deposited at the site and may not be examples of ritual sacrifice. Erica Hill (2000), who studied animal interments in the southwestern United States, principally interments of birds such as raptors, turkeys, macaws, and parrots, suggests, based on the contexts of these interments, that they are "ceremonial trash." In other words, the birds were ritually dispatched and then buried after their feathers had been removed (Hill 2000, 388–89). The burial of the turtle carapace and the dolphin skull may be interments of such ceremonial trash or may represent the offering of "things" as opposed to sacrifices of animals.

That leaves the shark burial as a possible case of ritual sacrifice at the Miami Circle. Other examples of animal interments in southern Florida are very rare. Most notable are the burial of an alligator at the Palmer site near Sarasota and the burial of an alligator and other animals at the Margate-Blount site in northern Broward County (Bullen and Bullen 1976; Felmley 1991; Wheeler 1992). Evaluating each of these interments in terms of contemporary research on ritual and sacrifice leaves us with questions about what these interments really represent. For example, Russell (2012, 91) relates that some researchers confine discussions of animal sacrifice to domesticated beasts, leaving us to consider our examples as evidence of a hunting ritual. We can speculate that the rarity of these interments and their considerable variability means that they may be classed in Pierre Smith's definition of an occasional rite, one conducted only in times of great imbalance. It is also possible, considering what we know of Calusa beliefs about death and the nature of the human spirit, that such animal burials could be substitutes for human sacrifice, as in the case of the animal sacrifice involved in the Urad Mongol battle standard ritual (Humphrey and Laidlaw 2007, 263–64). It does appear that such sacrifices have a somewhat secular nature, perhaps tied to the instability of chiefly power that is evident during the European contact period in southern Florida, rather than to the masked dances and processions associated with the temple that call to mind first fruits rites. Also, while animal sacrifice and the interment of animals do not appear to have been widespread in the Mississippian Southeast, the iconography of Mississippian cultures often includes decapitated heads and figures dancing with human heads (see Hall 1989; Brown and Dye 2007). It is possible that blood sacrifice in southern Florida may have its origins in contacts with Mississippian groups and that after its adoption it may have been modified to include animal sacrifice on some occasions.

Spanish friars in the sixteenth century learned that the Calusa believed that upon an individual's death, some of their life energy migrated to the body of an animal and continued to move from animal to animal until it was almost dissipated. This may help explain the prominence of animal symbolism in the visual arts of the Calusa, the Tequesta, and their neighbors. It may also explain something about the nature of human and animal sacrifice in the context of a belief system that held that the world of animals and the world of humans were inexorably linked (Wheeler 1996) (figure 10.5). There has been a growing interest in the metaphysical connection between animals and humans in Native American belief systems. Building on Irving Hallowell's (1960) concept of "other-than-human persons," a number of authors have shown that Native American theologies often exhibit a considerable fluidity in notions of who or what is a person and may assign personhood to what western-

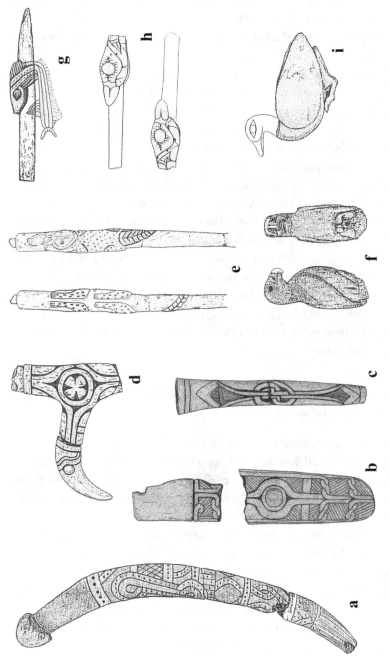

Figure 10.5. A sample of animal imagery from southern Florida: a) stylized rattlesnake, antler, Margate-Blount site (8BD41); b) pendant with eye and braid motif, bone (8DA140); c) plume holder with knot motif, bone (8DA5128); d) stylized vulture, antler, Margate-Blount; e) bas-relief carving of opossum, bone, Lyons-Lord site (8DA5128); f) hawk or peregrine falcon, antler, Florida Portland/Bamboo Mound (8DA94); g) freshwater eel, bone, Margate-Blount; h) deer head, bone, Onion Key (8MO49); and i) dabbler duck, antler, Margate-Blount. Drawings by Ryan Wheeler.

ers would think of as animals or inanimate objects (Hill 2011). In the Southeast, Dave Aftandilian (2011) has argued that Muscogee Creek and Cherokee peoples shared this conception of the soul. They viewed animals as spiritually powerful beings, participants in the creation of the world, and as relatives who live very much like humans. A recent review of the literature on Native American beliefs about the panther in the Southeast comes to a similar conclusion: panthers are frequently portrayed as clan progenitors and powerful beings, but they are also portrayed as persons living in villages and going about their daily lives (Wheeler 2011, 150). Could these animals, like the alligator or shark, which were regularly hunted and contributed significant protein to the native Florida diet, also have been considered "other than human persons?" If so, perhaps they could have served as an occasional stand-in during what would have normally been a human sacrifice. Ethnographers and archaeologists working in the arctic and subarctic have explored the metaphysical relationships between animals and humans. For example, Paul Nadasdy (2007) argues that among the Kluane in Alaska the social relationships between animals and humans transcend metaphor and go to the very core of native belief systems, governing decision making about hunting and wildlife management. Recall our consideration of canid burials and the argument Losey and his colleagues (2011) made that in Siberia some individual dogs and wolves were considered to have souls and were thus accorded human funerary treatment upon their deaths.

## Some Concluding Thoughts on Ritual and Sacrifice in Ancient Southern Florida

When the Miami Circle animal interments are considered in light of ethnohistoric documents, archaeological data, and contemporary thinking about ritual and sacrifice, they do not readily resolve the issue of ritual and sacrifice in ancient southern Florida. Despite that, we can suggest the following summary based on our consideration of these unusual features.

Ethnohistoric documents spanning the sixteenth through the early eighteenth centuries indicate that human sacrifice was employed on a variety of occasions, often in conjunction with what could be termed "occasional" rituals. These rituals may have had a secular purpose and origin that was related to the arrangement, balance, and imbalance of chiefly power in southern Florida. It is possible that human sacrifice was a fairly recent addition to the rituals of ancient southern Florida, perhaps borrowed from neighbors in other parts of the Southeast, and was appended to older rites that focused on the temple and mask complex. This may explain the scant archaeological evidence for human sacrifice in southern Florida and the willingness of native peoples to forego sacrifice when challenged by the Spanish.

Despite the historic accounts of sacrifice, archaeological evidence for human sacrifice is scant or dubious. The isolate human skull burials found at a number of southern Florida sites could be interpreted in a variety of ways: as the product of taphonomic processes, as trophy skulls, as secondary burials, or as some evidence of sacrifice. However, there is nothing to suggest which is the case or if they represent some other cultural practice. McNiven (2003, 338) points out that among fisher-folk in Australia, sites associated with turtle-hunting magic might feature skulls and carapaces of previously hunted turtles and the skulls of successful hunters who may provide skilled guidance and aid to living hunters.

The interment of animals or animal parts occurred very rarely in southern Florida. When it is encountered, the animals involved often are aquatic species such as sharks and alligators and frequently have some association with human mortuary sites. Interments of complete animals, like the shark at the Miami Circle, are exceedingly rare. It is possible that these interments represent ritual sacrifice, but it also is possible that they represent other cultural practices. For example, the turtle carapace and the dolphin skull may represent the discard of large artifacts like a platter or a skull from which teeth were extracted or they could represent "ceremonial trash," essentially the burial of things used in some rite or ritual.

If the animal interments represent ritual sacrifice, it is possible that the animals were stand-ins for human counterparts, either because of beliefs about the interconnectedness of human and animal souls or because human victims were unavailable. The concept of "other than human persons" seems to be widespread in Native America and may well have played a central role in ancient Florida and Southeastern cosmologies, especially among groups that focused on hunting and gathering.

While evidence of interments of animals such as the shark at the Miami Circle and the alligators at Margate-Blount and Palmer is found only rarely, burials of canids appear to have been more common. Burials of dogs and other canids may be helpful in understanding other animal interments. Moving beyond sentimental interpretations of dog burials, it may be that some dogs, and by extension, some other individual animals, were considered to have souls and thus were accorded funerary treatment like other humans. In either case, it may be productive to explore the idea of "other than human persons" in the cosmology of native Florida and the Southeast. As in the arctic and subarctic, where anthropologists and archaeologists have explored the metaphysical relationships between humans and animals, it may be that these relationships in ancient Florida and the Southeast were more complicated than was previously believed. This may be especially true in peninsular Florida, where relations with game animals and fish were very important.

In considering the question posed at the outset—Are the burials of a shark, a sea turtle carapace, and a dolphin skull at the Miami Circle sacrifices?—we do not have an answer. European documents tell us that human sacrifice in southern Florida among the Tequesta, the Calusa, and their neighbors were made for a variety of reasons, ranging from retainer burials to propitiatory offerings made to celebrate a peace accord. Animal sacrifice is not mentioned in the literature, though one eighteenth-century account does indicate that animal skulls were left as offerings along with food and other items at a cemetery. Archaeological evidence of both human and animal sacrifice is scant in southern Florida. Evaluating archaeological features using the anthropological literature on sacrifice is difficult, especially as there is some debate about what sacrifice is. For example, in contrast to the definition presented at the outset of this chapter, McClymond (2004) presents an alternative view of sacrificial ritual in which animal sacrifice may not be the defining event and in which sacrifice of other classes of objects (including inanimate objects) are just as prominent and important. The somewhat unusual case of human sacrifice in the Buddhist Urad Mongol battle standard ritual mentioned above points to the complexity and considerable variation in sacrifice of any kind. We find that the ontological concept of "other than human persons" may be helpful in understanding animal burials in southern Florida. There is considerable indication in the broader sacred literature of the Native American Southeast to suggest that this may have been a fundamental principle in the cosmologies of Southeastern tribes, including the Tequesta, the Calusa, and their neighbors. If this is the case, some animal species and some individual animals, including game animals, major predators, and canids, may have been considered to have souls, to be, essentially, people. For this reason, upon their deaths they were accorded burial like other humans. This principle may have included what we would consider to be inanimate objects as well. That this was part of the belief system in southern Florida, where fishing, hunting, gathering, and collecting formed the base of the economy, is, perhaps, not surprising. The hunters and gatherers of southern Florida likely had a long and close relationship with their prey, one that very well may have included social and kinship bonds and obligations. While some might argue that the animals in question must have been killed and interred by humans, and thus have constituted sacrifice, it is not clear that they are merely stand-ins for human sacrifice victims, perhaps substituted because of ontological beliefs about the nature of human and animal souls. Refocusing our approach and considering the significance of seascapes and maritime ritual will likely be productive and would be consistent with the ontological approach that adds some clarity to our interpretation of seemingly enigmatic features and sites. Further study of the metaphysical and ontological beliefs of the Southeastern tribes may further illuminate the rare and enigmatic case of animal interments.

## Acknowledgments

Many thanks to Neill Wallis and Asa Randall for inviting us to participate in the 2011 Southeastern Archaeological Conference symposium that formed the basis for this book. Thanks also to Chris Rodning and an anonymous reviewer who read this chapter and helped connect our thinking to the broader world of the Southeast.

## Notes

1. This date was made on bone collagen extracted from the cartilaginous centra of the shark and calibrated using a marine calibration curve rather than the INTCAL98 curve. See Widmer (2004) for more on radiocarbon dates from the Miami Circle.

## References

Aftandilian, Dave

2011    Toward a Native American Theology of Animals: Creek and Cherokee Perspectives. *Cross Currents* 61: 191–207.

Bell, Catherine

1997    *Ritual: Perspectives and Dimensions*. Oxford University Press, New York.

Bloch, Maurice

1992    *Prey into Hunter: The Politics of Religious Experience*. Cambridge University Press, Cambridge, UK.

Brown, James, and David H. Dye

2007    Severed Heads and Sacred Scalplocks: Mississippian Iconographic Trophies. In *The Taking and Displaying of Human Body Parts as Trophies by Amerindians*, edited by Richard J. Chacon and David H. Dye, 278–98. Springer, New York.

Bullen, Ripley P.

1957    The Barnhill Mound, Palm Beach County, Florida. *Florida Anthropologist* 10: 23–36.

Bullen, Ripley P., and Adelaide K. Bullen

1976    *The Palmer Site*. Florida Anthropological Society Publications no. 8. Florida Anthropological Society, Gainesville.

Carr, Robert S., M. Yasar Iscan, and Richard A. Johnson

1984    A Late Archaic Cemetery in South Florida. *Florida Anthropologist* 37: 172–88.

Carr, Robert S., and John Ricisak

2000    Preliminary Report on Salvage Archaeological Investigations of the Brickell Point Site (8DA12), Including the Miami Circle. *Florida Anthropologist* 53: 260–84.

Carr, Robert S., and Willard Steele

1993    An Archaeological Assessment of the Hutchinson Island Site (8MT37), Martin County, Florida. Technical Report No. 68. Archaeological & Historical Conservancy, Inc., Miami. On file, Florida Master Site File, Florida Division of Historical Resources, Tallahassee.

Chase, Diane Z., and Arlen F. Chase

1998    The Architectural Context of Caches, Burials, and Other Ritual Activities for the Classic Period Maya (as Reflected at Caracol, Belize). In *Function and Meaning in Classic Maya Architecture*, edited by Stephen D. Houston, 299–332. Dumbarton Oaks Research Library and Collections, Washington, DC.

Childers, R. Wayne

2003    Historical Notes and Documents: Life in Miami and the Keys: Two Reports and a Map from the Monaco-Alaña Mission, 1743. *Florida Historical Quarterly* 82: 59–82.

Clark, Merald

1995    Faces and Figureheads: The Masks of Prehistoric South Florida. MA thesis, Department of Anthropology, University of Florida, Gainesville.

Conrad, Lawrence A.

1989    The Southeastern Ceremonial Complex on the Northern Middle Mississippian Frontier: Late Prehistoric Politico-Religious Systems in the Central Illinois River Valley. In *The Southeastern Ceremonial Complex: Artifacts and Analysis*, edited by Patricia Galloway, 93–113. University of Nebraska Press, Lincoln.

Dixon, Jacqueline Eaby, Kyla Simons, Loretta Leist, Christopher Eck, John Ricisak, John Gifford, and Jeff Ryan

2000    Provenance of Stone Celts from the Miami Circle Archaeological Site. *Florida Anthropologist* 53: 328–41.

Elgart, Alison A.

2006    The Animal Interments at the Miami Circle at Brickell Point Site (8DA12). *Florida Anthropologist* 59: 179–89.

Felmley, Amy

1991    Prehistoric Mortuary Practices in the Everglades Cultural Area, Florida. MA thesis, Department of Anthropology, Florida Atlantic University, Boca Raton.

Fletemeyer, John R.

1984    Report, Sea Turtle Monitoring Project. Prepared by Nova University for Broward County Environmental Quality Control Board, Fort Lauderdale. On file, Broward County Sea Turtle Conservation Program, Nova Southeastern University Oceanographic Center, Dania Beach.

Hall, Robert L.

1989    The Cultural Background of Mississippian Symbolism. In *The Southeastern Ceremonial Complex: Artifacts and Analysis*, edited by Patricia Galloway, 239–78. University of Nebraska Press, Lincoln.

Hallowell, A. Irving

1960    Ojibwa Ontology, Behavior, and World View. In *Culture in History: Essays in Honor of Paul Radin*, edited by Stanley Diamond, 19–52. Columbia University Press, New York.

Hally, David J.

2008    *King: The Social Archaeology of a Late Mississippian Town in Northwestern Georgia*. University of Alabama Press, Tuscaloosa.

Hann, John H.

1991    *Missions to the Calusa*. University Press of Florida, Gainesville.

2003    *Indians of Central and South Florida, 1513–1763*. University Press of Florida, Gainesville.

Hill, Erica

2000    The Contextual Analysis of Animal Interments and Ritual Practice in Southwestern North America. *The Kiva* 65: 361–98.

2011    Animals as Agents: Hunting Ritual and Relational Ontologies in Prehistoric Alaska and Chukotka. *Cambridge Archaeological Journal* 21: 407–26.

Humphrey, Caroline, and James Laidlaw

2007    Sacrifice and Ritualization. In *The Archaeology of Ritual*, edited by Evangelos Kyriakidis, 255–76. Cotsen Institute of Archaeology, University of California, Los Angeles.

Jacobi, Keith P.

2007    Disabling the Dead: Human Trophy Taking in the Prehistoric Southeast. In *The Taking and Displaying of Human Body Parts as Trophies by Amerindians*, edited by Richard J. Chacon and David H. Dye, 299–338. Springer, New York.

Johnson, William R.

1952    Lepidochelys kempii and Caretta c. caretta from a South Florida Indian Mound. *Herpetologica* 8: 36.

Knight, Vernon J., Jr.

1986    The Institutional Organization of Mississippian Religion. *American Antiquity* 51: 675–87.

Knight, Vernon J., Jr., and Vincas P. Steponaitis

2011    A Redefinition of the Hemphill Style in Mississippian Art. In *Visualizing the Sacred: Cosmic Visions, Regionalism, and the Art of the Mississippian World*, edited by George E. Lankford, F. Kent Reilly III, and James F. Garber, 201–39. University of Texas Press, Austin.

Lankford, George E.

2007    The "Path of Souls": Some Death Imagery in the Southeastern Ceremonial Complex. In *Ancient Objects and Sacred Realms: Interpretations of Mississippian Iconography*, edited by F. Kent Reilly III and James F. Garber, 174–212. University of Texas Press, Austin.

Leonard, Andrew L. Allen, Anne M. Katzenberg, and Mikhail V. Sablin

2011    Canids as Persons: Early Neolithic Dog and Wolf Burials, Cis-Baikal, Siberia. *Journal of Anthropological Archaeology* 30: 174–89.

Linton, Ralph

1926    The Origin of the Skidi Pawnee Sacrifice to the Morning Star. *American Anthropologist*, new series 28: 456–66.

Lobell, Jarrett A., and Eric Powell

2010    More Than Man's Best Friend. *Archaeology* 63: 26–35.

Losey, Robert J., Vladimir Bazaliiskii, Sandra Garvie-Lok, Mietje Germonpré, Jennifer A. Leonard, Andrew L. Allen, Anne M. Katzenberg, and Mikhail V. Sablin

2011    Canids as Persons: Early Neolithic Dog and Wolf Burials, Cis-Baikal, Siberia. *Journal of Anthropological Archaeology* 30: 174–89.

McClymond, Kathryn

2004    The Nature and Elements of Sacrificial Ritual. *Method and Theory in the Study of Religion* 16: 337–66.

McNiven, Ian J.

2003    Saltwater People: Spiritscapes, Maritime Rituals and the Archaeology of Australian Indigenous Seascapes. *World Archaeology* 35: 329–49.

Morey, Darcy F.

2006    Burying Key Evidence: The Social Bond Between Dogs and People. *Journal of Archaeological Science* 33: 158–75.

Nadasdy, Paul

2007    The Gift in the Animal: The Ontology of Hunting and Human-Animal Sociality. *American Ethnologist* 34: 25–43.

Peres, Tanya M., and Teresa L. Ingalls

2008    Native and Exotic Animals from Mississippian Mortuary Contexts at the David Davis Farm Site (40HA301), Tennessee. Report submitted to Tennessee Council of Professional Archaeologists. Department of Sociology and Anthropology, Middle Tennessee State University, Murfreesboro.

Russell, Nerissa

2012    *Social Zooarchaeology: Humans and Animals in Prehistory*. Cambridge University Press, Cambridge.

Schwartz, Marion

1997    *A History of Dogs in the Early Americas*. Yale University Press, New Haven, CT.

Smith, Pierre

1982    Aspects of the Organization of Rites. In *Between Belief and Transgression: Structuralist Essays in Religion, History and Myth*, edited by Michel Izard and Pierre Smith, 103–28. University of Chicago Press, Chicago.

Weisman, Brent R., Herschel E. Shepard, and George Luer

2000    The Origin and Significance of the Brickell Point Site (8DA12), also Known as the Miami Circle. *Florida Anthropologist* 53: 342–46.

Wheeler, Ryan J.

1992    Time, Space and Aesthetics: Decorated Bone Artifacts from Florida. MA thesis, Department of Anthropology, University of Florida, Gainesville.

1996    Ancient Art of the Florida Peninsula: 500 B.C. to A.D. 1763. PhD dissertation, Department of Anthropology, University of Florida, Gainesville.

2004    Bone Artifacts from the Miami Circle at Brickell Point (8DA12). *Florida Anthropologist* 57: 133–58.

2008    National Historic Landmark nomination, Miami Circle at Brickell Point (8DA12), Miami, Miami-Dade County, Florida, National Historic Landmark System #01001534. Electronic document, http://www.nps.gov/nhl/designations/samples/fl/MiamiCircle.pdf, accessed October 2, 2011.

2011    On the Trail of the Panther in Ancient Florida. *Florida Anthropologist* 64: 139–62.

Wheeler, Ryan J., William Jerald Kennedy, and James P. Pepe

2002    The Archaeology of Coastal Palm Beach County. *Florida Anthropologist* 55: 119–56.

Widmer, Randolph J.

1989    The Relationship of Ceremonial Artifacts from South Florida with the Southeastern Ceremonial Complex. In *The Southeastern Ceremonial Complex: Artifacts and Analysis*, edited by Patricia Galloway, 166–80. University of Nebraska Press, Lincoln.

2004    Archaeological Investigations at the Brickell Point Site, 8DA12, Operation 3. *Florida Anthropologist* 57: 11–57.

Worth, John E.

1995    Fontaneda Revisited: Five Descriptions of Sixteenth-Century Florida. *Florida Historical Quarterly* 73: 339–52.

Zimmer, Jessica

2007    Native Americans' Treatment of Dogs in Prehistoric and Historic Florida. MS thesis, Department of Anthropology, Florida State University, Tallahassee.

# 11

## Woodland and Mississippian in Northwest Florida

### Part of the South but Different

NANCY MARIE WHITE

Like many other famous landforms with peninsulas (such as Italy), Florida has an "appendicular" portion extending into and surrounded by the sea and another connecting it to the edge of the continent; the archaeology of these two land features differs accordingly. My work is at the mainland edge, in the Apalachicola/Lower Chattahoochee Valley of northwest Florida. The prehistoric material record here demonstrates great continuity with mainstream southeastern archaeological traditions but also has far-flung connections and some unique aspects. New data from several sites in this valley and in the St. Joseph Bay region at the southwestern edge of the Apalachicola delta (figure 11.1) show great variability yet some geographic and temporal correspondences among distinctive Woodland and Mississippian manifestations.

There is now evidence for mound construction in Early Woodland (Deptford) times at both the top and bottom of the valley. Middle Woodland combines Swift Creek, *early* Weeden Island, and even sometimes Marksville-like ceramic traditions with unusual stone and other artifacts at both fancy burial mounds and humble campsites, contradicting the received notion of the "sacred-secular" dichotomy. The Late Woodland (*late* Weeden Island) adaptation abandons the emphasis upon exotics, perhaps to concentrate inland on developing maize agriculture. Late prehistoric Fort Walton sites include typical Mississippian large villages and platform mounds, but they also include distinctive ceramics and reuse of Woodland ritual/monumental sites. Interior riverine Fort Walton farming settlements contrast with coastal sites, where the collection of aquatic species persisted. Extra-regional exchange was continual, but there is no evidence for outright migration of societies during prehistoric times.

This chapter describes the record (summarized in table 11.1) of Native American settlement from Paleoindian through contact periods, and it challenges some archaeological orthodoxies for the northwest Florida region. Besides dismissing

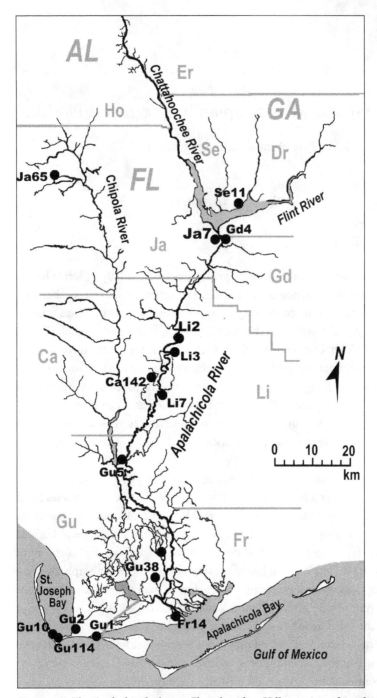

Figure 11.1. The Apalachicola–lower Chattahoochee Valley region of northwest Florida, showing locations of sites discussed in this chapter. (State numbers 8 and 9 are eliminated from the labels; state and county designations are in gray.)

Table 11.1. Later prehistoric cultural chronology in the Apalachicola–lower Chattahoochee Valley, northwest Florida

| Period | Ceramic series | Dates | Diagnostic ceramics |
|---|---|---|---|
| Early Woodland | Deptford | 500 BC–AD 200? | Deptford Linear Check-Stamped, Deptford Simple-Stamped, Deptford Fabric-Marked, tetrapods |
| Middle Woodland | Swift Creek–early Weeden Island | AD 200–700 | Swift Creek Complicated-Stamped, Weeden Island Incised, Punctate, Plain, and Zoned Red |
| Late Woodland | Late Weeden Island | AD 700–900? | Wakulla Check-Stamped, occasionally Carrabelle Punctate or Incised, Keith Incised |
| Mississippi | Fort Walton | AD 900–1650? | Fort Walton Incised, Lake Jackson, Marsh Island Incised |

the sacred-secular idea, I suggest that we reject names of "complexes" and "phases" based on single sites or other untested hypotheses; eliminate "Weeden Island" as a cultural entity and refine its meanings as two different ceramic complexes; identify how the distinctiveness of Middle Woodland culture carries on into Fort Walton times, perhaps for the maintenance of a specific identity; and show that while socio-economic interaction was widespread, clear evidence for real population movement appears only after the Old World invasion.

## Archaeological and Environmental Background

The Apalachicola/lower Chattahoochee valley is the lowest 135 river miles (217 kilometers) of the large river system that originates in the north Georgia mountains, the only Florida river with a component of melted snow, and the largest river in the state in terms of flow. The upper portion of the region is farmland today, with some low meander belts and backswamps. On the east side are unusual high bluffs with rare animal and plant species. The lower valley is mostly low wetlands that include estuaries and bays on the coast surrounded by barrier formations. This was a culturally consistent region throughout prehistory, and it extends another 25 river miles (40 kilometers) upstream (where the Chattahoochee River is the border between Alabama and Georgia), beyond which the archaeology becomes very different. However, I concentrate on the Florida portion for this chapter.

C. B. Moore (1901, 1902) explored here as early as 1900 (Brose and White 1999) and returned often (Moore 1903, 1907, 1918), seeking beautiful pottery in burial mounds. Even in his day, as he frequently noted, the sites he explored had been heavily looted. There is documentation for artifacts obtained earlier in the nineteenth century from Moore's sites, including materials other explorers donated to the Smithsonian (White 2010, 2012) and the British Museum.

Gordon Willey (1999 [1949]) was the first to synthesize the archaeology of this region (and others along Florida's Gulf coast), setting up temporal sequences that still work well, except for calendrical chronology, as he did not yet have radiocarbon dates (see Austin et al. this volume). However, in the many decades since, although we have better interpretive tools, good dates, and tons more data, we have suffered from the "operationalizing" of Willey's terms to permit easy reference for the purposes of both research and cultural resources management. Willey's overlapping ceramic series were transformed into real cultural entities, confusing the chronological picture and making comparisons across time and space difficult. Well over a thousand site records for the region are now pigeonholed into cultural names, such as simply "Weeden Island," that often are useless for interpretation. Hence the revision and synthesis in this chapter.

## Before Woodland

Larger, more accurate databases for the region are now assembled. They show that Paleoindian settlement was intensive not in the main valley but along the large western tributary, the Chipola River (e.g., Tyler 2008), probably because it was the main river channel during the Pleistocene. From Early Archaic onward, both riverine and upland settlement was widespread everywhere. Preceramic Late Archaic is hard to recognize, but by around 4,000 years ago there was fiber-tempered pottery that was made of clay mixed with Spanish moss and was plain-surfaced or (rarely) simple-stamped (White 2003a, 2003b). It was originally named St. Simons Plain or Orange ware (Bullen 1958; Willey 1999 [1949], 352), then was relabeled "Norwood" by Phelps (1965), for reasons apparently related to that fact that it has some sand with the fiber in the paste.

A lack of further comprehensive research did not prevent this name from catching on. Norwood became a "phase" name in northwest Florida (Phelps 1966), even though the pottery was not that distinctive and was not associated with anything else very specific to the region, contrary to what a phase is supposed to indicate. The sand in the paste (e.g., Bullen 1972, 19) was thought to indicate some transitional character leading into Early Woodland sand-tempered pottery. Of course this is far too simplistic, and the presence, absence, or amount of sand in the temper has now been assessed in great detail and has been determined to be unrelated to age, while the simple-stamped variant is known only at a few sites on the coast (White 2003b).

Both fiber-tempered plain and simple-stamped wares are variants of the earliest pottery seen widely across the Southeast. At coastal shell middens, they may be associated with clay "balls" or "objects," large numbers of chert microtools, and other items similar to Poverty Point material culture in Louisiana. While sites with these materials were placed in a taxon called "Elliott's Point Complex" simply because they were in Florida, they clearly demonstrate commonalities in coastal and wetland adaptation all along the Gulf coast and do not need a separate archaeological name (White 2003a; White and Estabrook 1994). Fiber-tempered pottery is still so sparse at sites where it occurs that it is difficult to distinguish the preceramic from the ceramic Late Archaic and to sort out the timing of the first appearance of ceramics in relation to Poverty Point associations. But the Late Archaic provides stronger evidence of well-established cultural interaction over very long distances, east-west along the coast and north-south up the river.

A popular archaeological topic and one focus of this volume is the earliest evidence of ritual, including construction of mounds for burials or other purposes. Raised occupation surfaces do not necessarily mean special activities beyond daily chores or keeping dry, but deliberate construction does mean a lot of labor. So far there is no evidence for Archaic mounds of any kind in this region (White 2004). No sand mounds are known, and freshwater shell middens are flat riverbank strata that incorporate shells and other refuse into dark midden soils. While mound building using shell midden soils is now hypothesized in many coastal areas, it does not appear in the Archaic in the Apalachicola delta. Some sites have been labeled "shell mounds" simply because the accumulated oyster and *Rangia* shells were mounded in flat, rounded, or multilobed formations, usually with multiple prehistoric cultural components (White 1994). So far there is no way to tell if this was done for some specific purpose or if it was just how everyday refuse accumulated. No shell ring sites are known. While many of these mounded-shell sites are curved, banana-shaped, or tighter, they reflect the curve of the stream banks along which people harvested the shellfish. Many of these shell middens have long records of habitation extending two to four millennia. One reason may be that they are easy to see, white amid the dense green of the forested wetlands, and easy to find and use again for a raised, dry camp. People surely knew these sites had been walked on by ancestors, but we do not know whether that made them sacred or just convenient.

## Early Woodland

By Early Woodland times, inhabitants of the Apalachicola–lower Chattahoochee region were indeed deliberately building mounds for burials and other less-understood reasons and were including shell as construction material in coastal areas. However, material culture that is indicative of elaborate rituals is not prominent.

Willey (1999 [1949], 353) originally recognized Early Woodland by the diagnostic Deptford- period ceramic types Linear Check-Stamped, Simple-Stamped, and Bold Check-Stamped. The first is the easiest to recognize; the lands of one direction in the checkerboard pattern are more prominent than those of the other direction. Deptford Simple-Stamped has mostly resisted efforts to subdivide it into two types based on orientation of the parallel-line stamping. Whether it is done with a single dowel or a paddle carved in straight lines, the stamping could result in simple lines or crisscrossed lines, and labeling the latter a separate type ("cross-stamped"; Phelps 1966) results in sherds from the same vessel having different type names!

What Willey (1999 [1949], 357) described as "bold" checks that were characteristic of Deptford overlap in size with checks on ceramics of many other time periods over 1,500 years that had similar tempers (sand, grit, grog) and often similar rim treatments too (Marrinan and White 2007). Without linearity of the checks or a basal sherd with a podal support or an associated chronometric date, it is impossible to distinguish Deptford "Bold" Check-Stamped. Willey's (1999 [1949], 387) Middle Woodland type Gulf Check-Stamped occasionally has scalloped or notched rims. His Late Woodland–Fort Walton Wakulla Check-Stamped (ibid., 437–39) has a huge number of different shapes, rim varieties, and check sizes. Even the protohistoric Leon Check-Stamped (ibid., 491), which is supposedly distinguished by larger checks, can have small checks too (Marrinan and White 2007, figure 4). Thus, for those few checked sherds that can clearly be assigned to Early Woodland, the type name Deptford Check-Stamped is sufficient.

However, the ubiquity in the Apalachicola–lower Chattahoochee region of sites with only check-stamped and plain sherds has resulted in enormous confusion. Like many others, I once classified them all as Late Woodland (White 1981). While this sounds like an easy mistake to fix, it is not, and many of our archaeological misconceptions stem from this kind of initial classification and naming process. As in any science, taxonomy becomes a shorthand for understanding the bigger picture. Once a type or phase name is bestowed, one can quickly build chronologies and interpretations, but these often become ever more derived scenarios. If the initial characterization is incorrect, everything that follows is questionable.

## Chattahoochee Landing

One example of this derived interpretation is found at the Chattahoochee Landing site (8GD4; see figure 11.1), a multi-mound complex just below the Flint-Chattahoochee confluence on the upper Apalachicola riverbank. Here the large amount of check-stamped pottery led to using the site name for an early "phase" in a hypothesized Fort Walton cultural sequence (Scarry 1990). However, much of this pottery was already known to be Deptford, based on the presence of several linear check-stamped sherds (Bullen 1958, 351–52; Marrinan and White 2007, 296; White 1982, 137–42). Comprehensive investigations at the site were undertaken in

2011 (White 2011a) confirming this Early Woodland component, apparently even for the earliest mounds.

Chattahoochee Landing was investigated by Moore (1903, 491–92), who noted seven mounds and declared that all were "domiciliary" because he found no burials or fancy pots. After compiling data on professional and private collections and local oral histories, I reconstructed the locations and contents of the mounds (White 2011a). Remnants of flat-topped Mounds 1 and 2 sit on the riverbank, and small Mound 4 sits back away from the river. Mound 2 (Brose and White 1999, figure 6) is a large platform (temple mound) that was probably once 10 to 11 meters high. It has Fort Walton pottery around it, including cob-marked sherds indicative of maize agriculture. A nearly three-meter profile of the exposed, eroding face of Mound 2 that was cleaned in 1975 showed many activity layers, multicolored strata, burned surfaces, and basket loading, but it did not produce diagnostic materials to establish the age(s) of the components.

When the eroding face of Smaller Mound 1 (which originally was the backslope of the mound away from the river) was cleaned in 2011, the process exposed seven strata extending nearly a meter deep. Stratum VII was a black midden layer with indeterminate check-stamped sherds that was as deep as the current surrounding ground surface. Though it was not excavated more than six centimeters below its top, the best estimate is that it is Deptford in age and represents either occupation before mound building or the earliest stage of mound building. Some 35 centimeters above it, a feature in Stratum IV was AMS radiocarbon dated to cal AD 540 to 620 (2-sigma; Beta-306923). The dated material was not charcoal, as was originally thought, but organic sediment that could have been in the soil earlier than the feature event, according to the experts at Beta Analytic. This date is within the later part of Middle Woodland. Since no evidence of a Middle Woodland component has been found at the site and the date may be slightly and erroneously early, Stratum IV is most probably Late Woodland.

An approximately 1.5-meter-deep profile exposed in 1975 of Mound 4 showed a flat black layer at the base, maybe the same probable Deptford midden. It produced a projectile point that could be classified as Florida Archaic Stemmed (Bullen 1975, 32) or Cotaco Creek (Cambron and Hulse 1986, 33), which can be either Archaic or Woodland. On top of this black midden were three sloped mound strata of strikingly different colors. The locally ubiquitous red clayey sand constituted the earliest mound layer, overlaid by a white stratum and then another reddish layer under the topsoil. These colors must have had significance, since the soils had to be obtained from different sources. Mound 4 has both (indeterminate) Woodland and Fort Walton components.

There is a good-sized Fort Walton occupation at Chattahoochee Landing. These later people probably disturbed earlier cultural deposits and added to the mounds.

They undoubtedly found this just as strategic a location, right below the river forks, as earlier peoples had. Across the river is the Curlee site (8JA7), a large Fort Walton village and cemetery (White 1982). As described below, Fort Walton people reoccupied many Woodland mound sites, probably for both utilitarian and ideological reasons. But none of the mounds at Chattahoochee Landing has produced any evidence for burials or ceremonialism. They may indeed have served as structure platforms, as Moore suggested. The labor required to construct them and whatever buildings they elevated may have made them special monuments. During the annual flood season in late winter, the riverbank is often underwater but Mound 2 becomes an island (figure 11.2), as it was documented to be even in March 1838 (de Castelnau 1948, 206). The fact that it was a high, dry space amid and above the annual floodwaters may have made this mound a symbol of individual or community power and persistence, while it also provided a spot for river travelers to rest securely, as it did when it supported a nineteenth-century inn.

Before leaving Chattahoochee Landing, I would like to make a comment on pottery typology. Proposing a new classification scheme for Fort Walton ceramics using the type-variety method, Scarry (1985, 231) named a variety of Wakulla Check-Stamped after the Chattahoochee Landing site, characterizing it as having rectangular small checks. The examples cited were two of four check-stamped sherds in a photo in Bullen's (1958, Plate 73a, b) original work on the site. But Bullen (ibid., 352) had noted that there was little variation among check-stamped sherds

Figure 11.2. Chattahoochee Landing Mound 2 (the temple mound) becomes an island during the late winter flood season, when the riverbank is underwater (photo taken by author from old US 90 bridge on March 1, 1980; view facing east-southeast). Perhaps platform mounds were also constructed to elevate structures above flood or wetland levels. Photograph by the author.

throughout the midden and that there was a Deptford component. If rectangularity of checks was the crucial attribute, it was never quantified, either in terms of check dimensions or in what proportion of the entire check-stamped assemblage was rectangular. A single vessel or large sherd often manifests both square and rectangular checks, probably due to the movement of wet clay after stamping and before firing or the irregularities of a hand-carved paddle. The point is that most check-stamped sherds should be labeled using only lowercase generic names if they have no distinguishing characteristics. Lumping is a better approach until robust datasets support splitting.

## Middle Woodland

Middle Woodland in the Apalachicola–lower Chattahoochee valley region, as elsewhere, is the time of the height of burial mound construction and mortuary ritual involving fancy ceramics and exotic materials brought from afar. But ceramics are the source of much misunderstanding in interpretation. Willey (1999 [1949]) unfortunately defined a Santa Rosa–Swift Creek and two Weeden Island cultural periods based on the presence of pottery types that used these two names, but in a confusing and overlapping fashion. The type names became the shorthand for chronology, reified as cultural entities.

In this region there is little Santa Rosa pottery (perhaps five to ten sherds in the whole valley), which is more common in the western panhandle. However, Swift Creek Complicated-Stamped and early Weeden Island (Willey's Weeden Island I) Incised, Punctated, modeled, cutout, and red-painted ceramic types both occur, usually *together* at both habitation and mound sites. The complicated-stamped pottery *may* be slightly earlier, according to two kinds of evidence. First, it is occasionally seen in possible association with some Deptford diagnostics (White 1994, 29–38), though it has not yet been dated in those contexts to establish that components are not mixed. Second, where it has been dated in strata unmixed with Weeden Island types it seems to be slightly earlier. At the Overgrown Road site, 8GU38 (White 1992), a small camp in the lower valley, a refuse pit with a complicated-stamped and a few plain sherds was dated to cal AD 407 ± 76 (1-sigma).[1] West of the region some 100 kilometers, on St. Andrew Bay, a shell midden near a mound with Swift Creek only has been dated to AD 290 and 380 (Russo 2009; Shanks 2009).

We continue working on the Otis Hare site, 8LI172, in the middle valley, a freshwater shell midden one meter thick, where Middle to Late Woodland deposits are buried under another meter of recent alluvium. Radiocarbon dates were obtained on charcoal from Unit 1, where the midden was dug in five-centimeter levels. The earliest, Level 14, had only Swift Creek pottery and produced two dates: 1530 ± 50 or cal AD 514 ± 62 (Beta-46705) from the level itself, and 1480 ± 70 BP(Beta 46703) or cal AD 547 ± 74 from a small pit feature extending below it (2-sigma; Cologne 2012). Levels above this feature had sherds of both Swift Creek and Weeden Island types.

Even if there is a century or more of difference between the time of first appearance of these two ceramic series, they nearly always occur together at the same sites. Of at least 30 mound sites known in the valley region, only one (Indian Pass, 8GU1) has early Weeden Island pottery but no Swift Creek, and only three (Bristol, 8LI3; Estiffanulga, 8LI7; Howard Creek, 8GU41) have Swift Creek but no early Weeden Island ceramics. There is also the issue of sample size and happenstance; the next investigator might find a sherd of the other ceramic series.

The diagnostic early Weeden Island types are Weeden Island Incised, Weeden Island Punctated, Weeden Island Plain (when it can be discerned from either cutout or modeled vessel shapes, unusual rim shapes, or red painted surfaces), and Weeden Island Zoned Red. These types disappear after the Middle Woodland, as did Swift Creek and other complicated-stamped ceramics. Willey put other less diagnostic and more long-lasting types into his Weeden Island catchall category. These include Carrabelle Punctate, Carrabelle Incised, and Keith Incised and a few others that are less common; they all hang on into Late Woodland and so are less diagnostic.

The Middle Woodland period in the region thus combines both Gulf and Appalachian traditions across the South as well as other influences. Recent work at the Gotier Hammock mound (8GU2) on St. Joseph Bay (White 2010) uncovered a jar of the type Basin Bayou Incised (Willey 1999 [1949], 374–76), which is a sand-tempered Florida version of Marksville Incised, a type known in the Lower Mississippi Valley (Phillips, Ford, and Griffin 2003 [1951]). Basin Bayou Incised is also found westward along the Gulf into Alabama (Dumas 2008; Price 2008, 156). Soot encrusted on a jar from Gotier Hammock has been dated to cal AD 610–80 (2-sigma), indicating the very latest Middle Woodland. Similar late dates have been associated with this type in Alabama. Given the blending of so many ceramic traditions and the relatively late dates, Middle Woodland is best called Middle Woodland—meaning mound burials and fancy stuff—until it is gone by about AD 650–700. This is better than ceramic-based names such as "Weeden Island," which can signify so many different things. If the term must be used, perhaps to describe ceramic types present at a site, it should specifically be *early* Weeden Island to avoid all the confusion.

## Sacred, Secular, Special, Fancy

Basin Bayou Incised has designs in loops and scrolls that are similar to both incised patterns on early Weeden Island pots and stamped designs on Swift Creek pots. These elements change only subtly through time and continue on late prehistoric

Fort Walton ceramics. The symbolism of such motifs, which occur throughout the South, remains unknown.

An important aspect of Middle Woodland archaeology in the Apalachicola–lower Chattahoochee Valley and other regions is that both burial mounds and domestic sites have imported and unusual materials—mica, copper, figurines, multicolored exotic cherts, and other stones—for show or status or ideological reasons. The dated feature noted above at 8GU38 contained a smoothed hemisphere of clear quartz among the sherds, chert, charred wood, and other camp refuse (White 1992). The freshwater shell midden at 8LI172 produced a mica cutout in the shape of an arrowhead that was similar to two from mounds in the middle valley (Bristol Mound and Aspalaga mounds; Moore 1903, 474–80, 482) but also to one from another domestic context at Sealy's Plantation (9SE11), some 65 kilometers upriver on a tributary of the lower Flint River in Georgia (Kelly 1960, 37–39; artifact viewed at the state collections, University of Georgia, Athens). Many more such examples could be given. Furthermore, burial mounds frequently included the plain, ugly pottery that Moore often complained about ("inferior ware") and others have noted (Brose 1979, 142; Tesar and Jones 2009, 22). At Gotier Hammock mound, plain and fancy pottery occurred together, and both have baked-on soot from some kind of cooking (White 2010). It is time to abandon the "sacred-secular" dichotomy (Sears 1973) that postulates that ornate things were used for mortuary ceremony and more mundane artifacts had everyday functions. The evidence has long contradicted this notion. Mound ritual may have transformed whatever artifacts were used into more honored objects, whether they were specially and elaborately crafted or not.

But why the obsession with exotics during the Middle Woodland? And how is variation from site to site, burial to burial explained? People everywhere balance individuality with group practice, in different proportions. Burial planners might have combined traditional pan-regional ritual elements with what was lately in style and with things that were specific to a family or individual, much like, say, modern wedding or party planners do. Funerals and burials are rites of passage (like weddings) that transform the parties involved and thus merit extra expense (consuming expensive goods). But a fascination for imported artifacts might also reflect a temperament that was open to novelty or a delight in the unusual, as opposed to a focus on the utilitarian and/or an isolationist philosophy.

As hypothesized elsewhere (White et al. 2012), the imported objects were probably obtained through extensive supply networks that sent local resources long distances into the interior South and Midwest in exchange for metals, exotic stones, and other fancy commodities. Gulf coast whelk and conch shells that appear in Ohio Hopewell, for instance, represent socioeconomic interaction systems that were in place probably from the Late Archaic onward. In addition to abundant large shells (especially in the region of salty St. Joseph Bay), other desirables from northwest Florida may have included indigenous yaupon holly leaves (for Black Drink) and maybe marine or estuarine smoked seafood or other nonpreserved goods. We cannot leave out the possibilities of exchange in more abstract things such as songs, dances, stories, poems, rituals, and other knowledge that tied together ceremonial practice throughout the eastern United States as early as the Early Woodland.

## Pierce Mounds

One site famous for exotics is Pierce (Moore 1902, 217–29), which is labeled 8FR14 and includes five mounds (A through E) but also encompasses at least five others (Singer Mound, 8FR16; Cemetery Mound, 8FR21; Mound Near Apalachicola, 8FR20; Cool Spring Mound, 8FR19; an unnamed temple mound) and a long shell midden ridge along the old riverbank at the mouth of the Apalachicola River. Continuing University of Southern Florida investigations (White 2007, 2012) show that the west side of a possible oval of mounds contains the Early and Middle Woodland components, seen both in the shell and nonshell midden and in Mounds A, B, and C. These mounds have strata of both sand and shell, probably gathered from the already discarded midden garbage to use to cover burials. Early Woodland Deptford ceramics came from Mounds C (linear check-stamped from looted deep levels) and A (a tetrapodal plain vessel obtained by Moore [1902, 227]; National Museum of the American Indian cat. no. 174531.000). The 99 burials in Mound A were oriented in several different ways, and grave goods included stone points and plummets, freshwater pearls, copper tubes, silver-covered copper disks, shell beads, shell drinking cups, and even a pendant of bison bone. The several Weeden Island Zoned Red vessels include one with an incised pattern in the shape of human hands, one with a flower-like incised design, and one in a U-shape with two flaring necks. A famous vessel shaped into a ribbed, spiraling tube is thought to be an effigy of a ram horn or a grub worm. Many of these artifacts represent extreme long-distance exchange in both materials and ideas.

The Fort Walton component at Pierce is on the east side, where the flat-topped temple mound made of shell constitutes another part of the oval of mounds and anchors a large late prehistoric village. Perhaps reverential memory (or invented memory) of the existing sacred monumental places that the earlier mounds represented inspired new uses of their own real or imagined past for the Fort Walton people who came back there. Or perhaps they never left and an intervening Late Woodland occupation is less visible at the site.

## Late Woodland: Late Weeden Island

A good reason Late Woodland is not always visible is that it is characterized by mostly check-stamped and plain pottery. Willey (1999 [1949], 396–407) hampered us in naming the Late Woodland ceramic series "Weeden Island II" because it is not like his Middle Woodland (early) Weeden Island I. Late Weeden Island, which has a reasonable beginning date of around AD 700, occasionally has other ceramic types such as Carrabelle and Keith, as noted, but complicated stamping and Weeden Island Incised and Punctate disappear. Late Woodland is a much better term, instead of using "Weeden Island" as a cultural entity that is by this time very different from Middle Woodland.

Mound building apparently died out or became rare during Late Woodland times. A few mounds are indeed noted as having mostly check-stamped and plain ceramics (e.g., Kelly 1960), and others might have originated during the Middle Woodland and had continued use during the Late Woodland, albeit with more mundane pottery. For example, at the Mound at Bristol (8LI3) noted above (Moore 1903, 474–80), most of the pottery was check-stamped, but there were also a Swift Creek Complicated-Stamped, a Weeden Island Incised, and three Weeden Island Plain pots. The probable Late Woodland mound stratum at Chattahoochee Landing is noted above.

Ceremony was probably not unimportant during the Late Woodland. But what happened to the fancy artifacts from Middle Woodland times? Did practices change and thus prohibit interment of valuables with the dead? Or were these items stored away and saved for generations or centuries? At the Yon (8LI2) and Corbin-Tucker (8CA142) sites in the middle valley there are Fort Walton burials with charcoal from wooden objects that have produced far earlier radiocarbon dates (Du Vernay 2011; Marrinan and White 2007, table 2; White 1996), perhaps because they were long-curated artifacts that were finally interred with persons who might have been the last of a lineage or were interred for some other reason to remove them from the realm of the living. Perhaps by this time ritual artifacts consisted more typically of perishable materials. Rather than think of late Weeden Island folks as boring, we could imagine them with colorfully painted bodies, clothes, walls, gourd vessels, bark images of spiritual beings, and other items. By Late Woodland times, some maize had appeared in the interior (Milanich 1973). Maybe more energy was spent learning how to intensify gardening into farming at this time instead of doing fancy craftwork.

## Mississippi Period: Fort Walton

Whatever happened during the Late Woodland, the transition into Fort Walton was smooth and internal, and many Woodland sites were reoccupied (or continued to be occupied more intensively or more visibly). Perhaps mounds had always been hallowed places and thus were attractive to Fort Walton societies of increasing complexity. I have not said much about sociopolitical organization here, but consolidation of power by emerging hereditary leaders may have involved claiming a heritage of obvious antiquity, visibility, and monumental character. Middle Woodland mounds were reused by Fort Walton peoples all over the region, from Waddell's Mill Pond (8JA65) on the upper Chipola (Tesar and Jones 2009) to Chipola Cutoff mound (8GU5) in the lower valley (White 2011b) to Richardson's Hammock (8GU10), a large-gastropod burial mound and shell midden on St. Joseph Bay (White et al. 2002).

Fort Walton was distinctive among a host of other Mississippian adaptations in the Southeast (Marrinan and White 2007; White et al. 2012). It included maize agriculture, temple mound centers, and ceramics in mostly typical Mississippian shapes. However, Fort Walton pottery was not shell-tempered like most other Mississippian wares, and it featured at least one unusual vessel shape, the six-pointed (rarely five-pointed) Fort Walton Incised open bowl. Curiously, there were very few chipped-stone tools as compared with contemporaneous archaeological manifestations elsewhere or with cultures before and after Fort Walton in this same region. These and other characteristics cannot be interpreted in any other way except as a deliberate assertion of regional identity, one originally rooted in Middle Woodland traditions that may have been attenuated or expressed differently but not forgotten during Late Woodland times.

Continuity with the Woodland period is seen in many areas. For example, Fort Walton ceramic tempers are similar to what they had always been—sand, grit, and grog—but with a heavier emphasis on grit. Also, design elements and vessel forms appear to be related, as seen in figure 11.3. Though separated in time by perhaps a half-millennium, the Weeden Island Incised and one Fort Walton Incised bowls have similar plain necks, while the other Fort Walton Incised neck has parallel incisions below a ticked rim. Vessel bodies are all plain below the decorative band, which consists of zoned punctations and incisions in curvilinear or rectilinear variants of waves or scrolls. Other formal similarities from Middle Woodland to Fort Walton appear in elbow-shaped pipes, bird and other animal effigies on rims, ticks along rim lips, zones of punctations set off by incisions, stylistic motifs such as loops and scrolls, and even some vessel shapes, from simple bowls to the shallow bowl or plate with a wide, nearly horizontal decorated rim. Equally important, Fort Walton ceremonial expression includes much of the same exotic character seen during the Middle Woodland: greenstone celts, copper disks, shell cups, other burial goods. Undoubtedly the long-distance exchange networks continued, probably intensified, so that Fort Walton peoples could obtain the exotic stone and metals and Mississippi- period cultures throughout the South could get the lightning whelk shells so important to their ceremonial activities. (Such hypotheses may become more clearly supported as trace element analyses begin to allow source documentation for the raw materials in these artifacts.)

Figure 11.3. Comparison of ceramics from Middle Woodland and Fort Walton periods. *Top left*: Weeden Island Punctate bowl from Porter's Bar (8FR1), Middle Woodland mound. Top right: Fort Walton Incised bowl from Pope Lake site (8JA391). *Bottom*: Fort Walton Incised bowl from east side of Pierce Mounds (8Fr14). *Sources: top left*, Adapted from Moore 1902, figure 180; *top right and bottom*, Drawings by M. B. Fitts for the USF Anthropology Department.

Plenty of maize remains have been recovered to document Fort Walton intensive agriculture (White et al. 2012) but they appear to be confined to the riverine interior. In the lower valley and coastal/estuarine areas the sites have so far produced no evidence for cultivation, just the same aquatic species seen in faunal assemblages from earlier Woodland and Archaic strata, confirming that Florida coasts have one of the longest records of hunter-gatherer-fisher adaptation.

The Fort Walton component at the Chattahoochee Landing site (8GD4), which is described above, includes a platform mound construction for some nonmortuary purpose. Pierce (8Fr14), at the other end of the valley, is another example of the Fort Walton reoccupation of a Woodland monumental center. C. B. Moore never mentioned Fort Walton materials there; he only described what he called a shell heap on the east side: the platform temple mound amid the Fort Walton village. A core sample that was taken just east of this mound in the shell midden produced charcoal a meter deep that was radiocarbon-dated to 780 ± 40 BP or cal 1220–1300 (2-sigma; White 2007, 2012). At the southeastern end of the oval of mounds are three low platform mounds (E, F, G) of sand. Testing in them produced almost nothing cultural, suggesting that they, too, might be structure platforms, as is hypothesized at Chattahoochee Landing. Daub fragments from the thick Fort Walton midden indicate some kind of structures.

## The End of Fort Walton

Fort Walton ceramics at Pierce were typical: Fort Walton Incised, Lake Jackson, Point Washington Incised, and some of the ubiquitous check-stamped pottery, which hangs on a few centuries past the Late Woodland. During very late Fort Walton times in this region, the appearance of some new and very different evidence suggests that the fate of the indigenous peoples was changing enormously. Though this book is about prehistoric Florida, it is important to review how prehistory ends.

The first type of evidence is early contact period Spanish material, which is found in very small quantities and at only four sites so far (White 2011b). It includes glass beads, an iron spike, and some unusual items of apparently aboriginal manufacture, such as clay mushroom-shaped objects and lobed rectangular shell buttons that are considered protohistoric in Alabama and elsewhere. No Spanish are recorded in this valley before the late 1600s, but the conflict and disease they brought must have been transported into the region earlier by indigenous peoples. One of the four sites, Corbin-Tucker (8CA142) in the middle valley, has a cemetery with both prehistoric and protohistoric burials. One of the latter was an adult female with an embossed copper disk on her forehead, a large greenstone celt under her chin, and a scattering of sherds, including some from a six-pointed Fort Walton Incised bowl. It is not hard to imagine the sacred ground inhabited by prehistoric ancestors remaining important for cemetery ritual during a time of upheaval and cultural loss.

A second kind of unusual evidence is Lamar pottery, which has sloppy complicated-stamped designs and distinctive rims with a wide fold and notches or an added, notched appliqué strip. In the Tallahassee region, Lamar is called Jefferson ware and is associated with natives at Spanish missions. But in the Apalachicola region, Lamar is now recognized as something new that represents unknown protohistoric Indians who settled in the region only briefly. At the Yon site (8LI2) in the middle valley, a Fort Walton temple mound and village that has been dated to AD 1200–1250 is overlaid by a Lamar component dating to around 1700 (Du Vernay 2011; White 1996; White et al. 2012). At the Lighthouse Bayou site (8GU114), a large-gastropod shell midden on St. Joseph Bay, individual shell piles with Lamar pottery have produced two similar dates (White 2005, 31–34). While associating ceramics with ethnicity is tricky, Lamar is very different from what came before it. Further, it is only present at a few sites in three areas: around the forks in the upper valley, around Yon in the middle valley, and on the barrier island–peninsula formations on the coast. It may represent inhabitants fleeing the destruction of the missions in 1704 or some other mobile groups who stayed briefly in an area that was becoming empty of the original natives and their Fort Walton material culture. Later peoples moving in, Creeks who later turned into Seminoles, made distinctive Chattahoochee Brushed pottery and lived at sites that are mostly historically recorded, though Lamar may represent some proto-Creek groups.

## Summary

Florida is not necessarily on the periphery of the South. In both Woodland and Mississippi- period times, northwest Florida was squarely in the middle of important developments in ritual, craftwork, socioeconomic interaction, and monument construction, even though it is located at the edge of the continent. A wealth of evidence exists for continual long-distance exchange and influence in both utilitarian and special commodities and in political and ceremonial practices. Nonetheless, by Middle Woodland times a distinctive material culture blended Swift Creek, early Weeden Island, and other contemporaneous traditions. This became the foundation for what can only be termed a specific regional identity that continued through late prehistory. Because important topics for this volume are population movement and long-distance interaction, it is important to note that although exchange of exotics had been going on for many millennia, the possibility of real migration in this valley, groups moving in from afar, is so far supported only by the evidence from protohistoric times, as the original native culture disappeared.

## Notes

1. All radiocarbon dates not calibrated by Beta Analytic were done using Cologne Radiocarbon Calibration & Paleoclimate Research Package's CalPal Online Interactive online radiocarbon calibration, at http://www.calpal.de, accessed 9 April 2012.

## References

Brose, David S.
1979    An Interpretation of Hopewellian Traits in Florida. In *Hopewell Archaeology: The Chillicothe Conference*, edited by David S. Brose and N'omi Greber, 141–49. Kent State University Press, Kent.
Brose, David S., and Nancy Marie White (editors)
1999    *The Northwest Florida Expeditions of Clarence Bloomfield Moore*. University of Alabama Press, Tuscaloosa.
Bullen, Ripley P.
1958    Six Sites Near the Chattahoochee River in the Jim Woodruff Reservoir Area, Florida. River Basin Surveys Papers no. 14. *Bureau of American Ethnology Bulletin* 169: 316–58. Smithsonian Institution, Washington, DC.
1972    The Orange Period of Peninsular Florida. In *Fiber-Tempered Pottery in the Southeastern United*

*States*, edited by Ripley P. Bullen and James Stoltman, 9–33. Florida Anthropological Society Publication No. 16. Florida Anthropological Society, Fort Lauderdale.

1975    *A Guide to the Identification of Florida Projectile Points.* Rev. ed. Kendall Books, Gainesville, FL.

Cambron, James W., and David C. Hulse

1986    *Handbook of Alabama Archaeology.* Part 1, *Point Types.* Rev. ed. Ed. David DeJarnette. Alabama Archaeological Society, Huntsville.

De Castelnau, Comte (Francis La Porte)

1948    Essay on Middle Florida, 1837–38 (Essai sur la Floride du Milieu). *Florida Historical Quarterly* 26: 199–255. Trans. Arthur R. Seymour. Foreword by Mark F. Boyd.

Dumas, Ashley A.

2008    New Data for the Middle Woodland Period on the Alabama Gulf Coast. Poster presentation at the 65th annual meeting of the Southeastern Archaeological Conference, Raleigh, NC.

Du Vernay, Jeffrey

2011    The Archaeology of Yon Mound and Village, Middle Apalachicola River Valley, Northwest Florida. PhD dissertation, Department of Anthropology, University of South Florida, Tampa.

Kelly, A. R.

1960    A Weeden Island Burial Mound in Decatur County, Georgia: the Lake Douglas Mound, 9DR21. Report No. 1. University of Georgia Laboratory of Archaeology, Athens.

Marrinan, Rochelle A., and Nancy Marie White

2007    Modeling Fort Walton Culture in Northwest Florida. *Southeastern Archaeology* 26: 292–318.

Milanich, Jerald T.

1973    Life in a 9th Century Indian Household, a Weeden Island Fall-Winter Site on the Upper Apalachicola River, Florida. *Florida Bureau of Historic Sites and Properties Bulletin* 4: 1–44.

Moore, Clarence Bloomfield

1901    Certain Aboriginal Remains of the Northwest Florida Coast. *Journal of the Academy of Natural Sciences of Philadelphia* 11: 421–97.

1902    Certain Aboriginal Remains of the Northwest Florida Coast, Part II. *Journal of the Academy of Natural Sciences of Philadelphia* 12: 127–358.

1903    Certain Aboriginal Mounds of the Apalachicola River. *Journal of the Academy of Natural Sciences* 12: 440–90.

1907    Mounds of the Lower Chattahoochee and Lower Flint Rivers. *Journal of the Academy of Natural Sciences of Philadelphia* 13: 426–56.

1918    The Northwestern Florida Coast Revisited. *Journal of the Academy of Natural Sciences of Philadelphia* 16: 514–80.

Phelps, David S.

1965    The Norwood Series of Fiber-Tempered Ceramics. *Southeastern Archaeological Conference Bulletin* 2: 65–69.

1966    Early and Late Components of the Tucker Site. *Florida Anthropologist* 19: 11–38.

Phillips, Philip, James A. Ford, and James B. Griffin

2003 [1951]        *Archaeological Survey in the Lower Mississippi Alluvial Valley, 1940–1947.* Papers of the Peabody Museum of American Archaeology and Ethnology 25. University of Alabama Press, Tuscaloosa.

Price, Sarah E.

2008    Phase III Archaeology at Plash Island, Archaeological Site 1BA134, in Baldwin County, Alabama. Center for Archaeological Studies, University of South Alabama, Mobile.

Russo, Michael

2009    Presentation on the archaeology at Tyndall Air Force Base at the symposium entitled Rethinking Weeden Island: A Pottery Potlatch, February 2009, Weedon Island Preserve Cultural and Natural History Center, St. Petersburg, FL.

Scarry, John F.

1985    A Proposed Revision of the Fort Walton Ceramic Typology: A Type-Variety System. *Florida Anthropologist* 38: 199–233.

1990    Mississippian Emergence in the Fort Walton Area: The Evolution of the Cayson and Lake Jackson Phases. In *The Mississippian Emergence*, edited by Bruce D. Smith, 227–50. Smithsonian Institution Press, Washington, DC.

Sears, William H.

1973    The Sacred and the Secular in Prehistoric Ceramics. In *Variation in Anthropology: Essays in Honor of John C. McGregor*, edited by Donald Lathrap and Jody Douglas, 31–42. Illinois Archaeological Survey, Urbana.

Shanks, Jeffrey H.

2009    Baker's Mound (8BY29)—a Swift Creek Sand Mound and Ring Midden. Paper presented at the annual meeting of the Southeastern Archaeological Conference, Mobile, AL.

Tesar, Louis D., and B. Calvin Jones

2009    The Waddells Mill Pond Site (8Ja65): 1973–74 Test Excavation Results. Florida Department of State, Bureau of Archaeological Research, Tallahassee.

Tyler, William D.

2008    The Paleoindian Chipola: A Site Distribution Analysis and Review of Collector Contributions in the Apalachicola River Valley, Northwest Florida. MA thesis, Department of Anthropology, University of South Florida, Tampa.

White, Nancy Marie

1981    *Archaeological Survey at Lake Seminole*. Cleveland Museum of Natural History Archaeological Research Report no. 29. Submitted to the U.S. Army Corps of Engineers, Mobile, AL.

1982    The Curlee Site (8JA7) and Fort Walton Development in the Upper Apalachicola-Lower Chattahoochee Valley, Florida, Georgia, Alabama. PhD dissertation, Department of Anthropology, Case Western Reserve University.

1992    The Overgrown Road Site (8GU38): A Swift Creek Camp in the Lower Apalachicola Valley. *Florida Anthropologist* 45: 18–38.

1994    *Archaeological Investigations at Six Sites in the Apalachicola River Valley, Northwest Florida*. NOAA Technical Memorandum NOS SRD 26. U.S. Dept. of Commerce, National Oceanic and Atmospheric Administration, National Ocean Service, Office of Ocean and Coastal Resource Management, Sanctuaries and Reserves Division, Washington, DC.

1996    Test Excavations at the Yon Mound and Village Site (8LI2), Middle Apalachicola Valley, Northwest Florida. Report to the Florida Division of Historical Resources, Tallahassee. Department of Anthropology, University of South Florida, Tampa.

2003a    Testing Partially Submerged Shell Middens in the Apalachicola Estuarine Wetlands, Franklin County, Florida. *Florida Anthropologist* 56: 15–45.

2003b    Late Archaic in the Apalachicola/Lower Chattahoochee Valley of Northwest Florida, Southwest Georgia, Southeast Alabama. *Florida Anthropologist* 56: 69–90.

2004    Late Archaic Fisher-Foragers in the Apalachicola-Lower Chattahoochee Valley, Northwest Florida-South Georgia/Alabama. In *Signs of Power: The Rise of Cultural Complexity in the Southeast*, edited by Phil Carr and John Gibson, 10–25. University of Alabama Press, Tuscaloosa.

2005    Archaeological Survey of the St. Joseph Bay State Buffer Preserve, Gulf County, Florida. Report to the Apalachicola National Estuarine Research Reserve, Eastpoint, Florida, and the Division of Historical Resources, Tallahassee. Department of Anthropology, University of Southern Florida.

2007    Pierce Mounds, an Ancient Capital in Northwest Florida. Paper presented at the 58th annual meeting of the Florida Anthropological Society, Avon Park, May.

2010    Gotier Hammock Mound and Midden on St. Joseph Bay, Northwest Florida. *Florida Anthropologist* 63: 149–82.

2011a   Archaeology at Chattahoochee Landing, Gadsden County, Northwest Florida. Report to the Florida Fish and Wildlife Conservation Commission and the Division of Historical Resources, Tallahassee. Department of Anthropology, University of Southern Florida.

2011b   Middle Woodland and Protohistoric Fort Walton at the Lost Chipola Cutoff Mound, Northwest Florida. *Florida Anthropologist* 64: 241–73.

2012    Pierce Mounds Complex, An Ancient Capital in Northwest Florida. Draft report submitted to landowner George Mahr, Apalachicola, Florida. Department of Anthropology, University of South Florida.

White, Nancy Marie, Jeffrey P. Du Vernay, and Amber J. Yuellig

2012    Fort Walton Culture in the Apalachicola Valley, Northwest Florida. In *Late Prehistoric Florida: Archaeology at the Edge of the Mississippian World*, edited by Keith Ashley and Nancy Marie White, 231–74. University Press of Florida, Gainesville.

White, Nancy Marie, and Richard W. Estabrook

1994    Sam's Cutoff Shell Mound and Late Archaic Elliott's Point in the Apalachicola Delta, Northwest Florida. *Florida Anthropologist* 47: 61–78.

White, Nancy Marie, Christopher Smith, Nelson Rodriguez, and Mary Beth Fitts

2002    St. Joseph Bay Shell Middens Test Excavations, Gulf County, Florida, 2000–2002. Report to the Department of State, Division of Historical Resources, Tallahassee. Department of Anthropology, University of Southern Florida.

Willey, Gordon R.

1999 [1949]    *Archeology of the Florida Gulf Coast.* Smithsonian Miscellaneous Collections no. 113. University Press of Florida, Gainesville, 1999.

# 12

# Ritualized Practices of the Suwannee Valley Culture in North Florida

NEILL J. WALLIS

The study of ritual in archaeology often has been closely tied to the excavation and interpretation of mortuary contexts. From its colonial beginnings until just over half a century ago, much archaeology in southeastern North America took mortuary ritual as its primary focus because of its inherent visibility in mounds across the landscape and their association with finely crafted artifacts. In Florida, as elsewhere, early antiquarians such as C. B. Moore (e.g., Mitchem 1999a, 1999b) pursued burial mounds instead of nonmounded sites in large part because they yielded "relics" that satisfied Anglo-American aesthetic sensibilities and curio cabinets. It has been the important task of archaeologists in the last half-century or so to document more completely the lives of people who participated in mortuary ritual by turning focus to the habitation areas, or villages.

Yet villages were places of much more than quotidian daily life, and the common division of "mound" and "village" in archaeological parlance at best does little justice to, and at worst disavows, the diverse and sometimes ritualized practices that evidently took place adjacent to mounds and other places where resident populations apparently lived (see, for example, Russo et al. this volume). Moreover, the often-repeated and -criticized "sacred" and "secular" categories that Sears (1973) applied to Woodland ceramic types parallel our shorthand site categories and perhaps further homogenize the complex realities of past ritualities (see White this volume). Obfuscating terminologies aside, a practice-centered approach is clearly warranted, one that investigates ritualization as a process instead of ritual as a typological distinction. According to this view, which is grounded in practice theory (Bourdieu 1977; Giddens 1984), myriad practices in a variety of locales, not just mounds, have the potential to become ritualized, and mortuary and religion are only two of many implicated categories (Bell 1997). From this perspective, questions move away from trait lists of traditions to investigations of the process by which commonplace practices such as manufacturing tools, constructing houses, cooking, traveling, or consuming food, to name a few, might become formalized performances with considerable symbolic import and might sometimes be transformed into ostentatious spectacles (e.g., Gosden 2005; Keane 2003, 2005; Pauketat and Alt 2005).

This chapter examines some of the evidence for ritual practices in late pre-Columbian contexts after around AD 700 in north Florida, the region surrounding the Middle Suwannee River (figure 12.1). In this region lies a site that is often upheld as one of the premier examples of Middle Woodland mortuary ritual, ceremonialism,

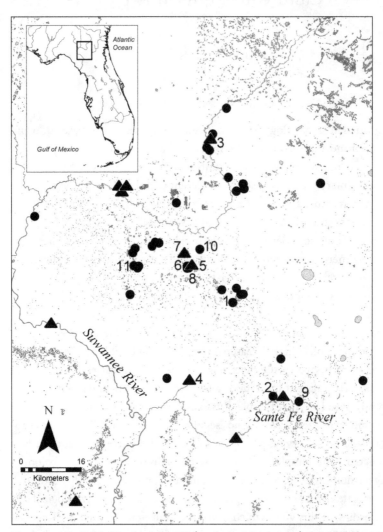

Figure 12.1. Probable Weeden Island II (marked with triangles) and Suwannee Valley culture (marked with circles, except for 2 and 8) sites in north Florida. 1) Alligator Lake; 2) Alligood; 3) Carter Mound I; 4) Fig Springs; 5) Indian Pond; 6) Johns Pond; 7) Leslie Mound; 8) McKeithen; 9) Palmore; 10) Parnell Mound; 11) Peacock Lake Mounds. *Sources*: Florida Master Site File data and descriptions in Sigler-Lavelle 1980a and Johnson 1986, 1987, and 1991.

and population aggregation in the Deep South, the McKeithen site (8CO17) (Milanich et al. 1984, 1997). The very large horseshoe-shaped village studded by three earthen mounds provides unparalleled evidence of an entire mortuary program, from charnel structures (on Mound A) to the residence and tomb of a religious specialist (in Mound B) to a mortuary mound with abundant bundle burials (Mound C). Moreover, the solitary burial in a platform mound of a ritual specialist who, according to stable isotope analysis, ate far more maize or maritime foods than anyone else in the large resident population, has led to frequent mention of incipient social complexity that did not reach its zenith until the following Mississippi period (Kelly et al. 2006; Turner et al. 2005). Curiously, attributes commonly associated with sociopolitical complexity at later Mississippian seats of power, such as planned mound complexes with plazas and domiciliary platform mounds, site-size hierarchies, intensive maize agriculture, and various prestige goods of mineral, metal, and stone (many with iconography, as seen at major mound centers of the Mississippian Southeast) are entirely lacking in Mississippi period north Florida. This appears especially troubling to some, because ethnohistoric accounts show that "the Suwannee Valley region was unquestionably characterized by chiefly social organization at the time of first European contact" (Worth 2012, 169).

From the vantage point of McKeithen, however, what is much more troubling is the perception, which easily could be garnered from existing work (or lack thereof), that with the decline of an ostentatious mortuary program that brought populations to an aggregated center, ritual seems to have been attenuated severely in north Florida. Indeed, McKeithen is often viewed as a major ceremonial center in the Middle Woodland Southeast, while the region became an apparent cultural backwater during the Late Woodland and Mississippi periods and is rarely mentioned in wider treatments of late pre-Columbian history. This characterization is primarily attributable to lack of investigation rather than to the absence of data and perhaps also to a scholarly obsession with Mississippianization, in which north Florida residents took little obvious part. However, there are long-standing continuities in ritualized practice in north Florida related to the importance of intercommunity gatherings at mound centers and the feasts that apparently took place there.

This chapter evaluates ritualization in late pre-Columbian north Florida through a focus on the shifting role of the "ceremonial center" (e.g. Anderson 1998; Stephenson et al. 2002). The analysis consists of two parts. First, it evaluates suggested temporal shifts in population aggregation and dispersal in relation to mound centers (e.g., Milanich 1996, 36–37) using extant data from the Florida Master Site File (FMSF) and unpublished reports. These data are difficult to match with a model of abrupt changes following the abandonment of McKeithen and instead could indicate considerable continuity in patterns of settlement and convergence at ceremonial centers. Second, the chapter considers evidence for ritualized mound-adjacent practices beyond the act of burial, especially feasting. Behind the more celebrated aspects of the McKeithen Weeden Island mortuary program, the ornate earthenware vessels and burial rites, was the associated preparation and consumption of animals (particularly deer) that have been labeled feasts (Knight 2001; Milanich et al. 1997, 102). While late period burial practices in the region seemed to have eschewed the fineries of previous Weeden Island mortuary paraphernalia, new evidence from the Parnell Mound (8CO326) indicates that by around AD 1200, feasting had become a ritualized spectacle on a truly grand scale that went far beyond its humble antecedents at McKeithen. These data indicate that ritual and population aggregation may not have been diminished at all but instead shifted to practices and events that had previously been less emphasized, and operated according to different temporalities.

## North Florida Chronology, Settlement Patterns, and Aggregation

Nearly three decades ago, Milanich and colleagues (1984) defined the McKeithen Weeden Island culture of north Florida based mainly on extensive excavations at the McKeithen site (8CO17). The Middle Woodland culture was characterized by nucleated villages with mounds, distinctive ceramic styles that included Weeden Island mortuary and prestige wares, a hunter-gatherer subsistence pattern, and some degree of status differentiation, presumably linked to the convergence of related groups, perhaps lineages, at mound centers. Concurrent with the McKeithen excavations, the survey efforts of Brenda Sigler-Lavelle (1980a, 1980b) identified what were presumed to be Late Woodland sites that postdated McKeithen scattered throughout portions of Columbia and Suwannee counties. Compared to earlier patterning, these sites were less dense, more dispersed, and more numerous. Milanich (1994, 1996) later surmised that this dispersed settlement pattern may have corresponded with the adoption of maize agriculture, similar to that suggested for the contemporaneous Wakulla Weeden Island culture of the Florida panhandle (see also White this volume). Ken Johnson (1986, 1987, 1991) subsequently identified clusters of even later sites, some of which were eventually identified as representing the Suwannee Valley archaeological culture (Weisman 1992; Worth 2012). Together, all of this work seemed to indicate that settlement patterns changed over time, from aggregation at ceremonial centers during Weeden Island I (ca. AD 200 to 750) to dispersal during Weeden Island II (ca. AD 750 to 1000; perhaps with the adoption of maize agriculture) and then back to aggregation that featured more chiefdom-like political structures that were presumably associated with the Suwannee Valley culture during the few centuries before European encounters (ca. AD 1000 to 1500; Milanich 1996, 36–37; Worth 2012).

This model of aggregation and dispersal is difficult to match with extant archaeological data. In fact, despite several vigorous research projects in the 1980s and 1990s (Milanich et al. 1984; Johnson 1991; Weisman 1992), the archaeological record of late pre-Columbian north Florida is among the least understood in the state. Owing to both a lack of consistent archaeological research in the region over the last century and oftentimes mixed or ephemeral late components, the eight or nine centuries following the abandonment of the well-known Middle Woodland McKeithen site, in particular, have remained somewhat unclear. Indeed, Weeden Island II has not been the focus of new research in north Florida since its initial description based on Sigler-Lavelle's (1980a, 1980b) work (Milanich et al. 1997, 201–8), and the Suwannee Valley archaeological culture was defined in a preliminary way only two decades ago (Weisman 1992) and was refined only months ago (Worth 2012). Nonetheless, a reappraisal of settlement patterns and population aggregation at ceremonial centers is possible with available data. These data show that there may be more continuity in settlement and aggregation centers than has previously been described.

## Chronology

In order to begin approaching these continuities, we must first unravel the idea of settlement change, which seems to correspond as much to expectations as it does to available archaeological data. Evaluating the existence of changing settlement patterns has been significantly frustrated by the absence of absolute dates and limited development of the late period chronology until very recently. John Worth (2012) has refined the Suwannee Valley pottery series based on work on pre-Columbian components at the Fig Springs site. Drawing on Worth's assessment, we should be able to parse the north Florida timeline into Weeden Island I (contemporaneous with McKeithen and perhaps ending around AD 750), Weeden Island II (ending around AD 1000 or a bit earlier), and Suwannee Valley (ending at around 1500). To summarize very briefly, Weeden Island I village assemblages are characterized by an overwhelming majority of sand-tempered plain sherds (83 percent at McKeithen Village) and minor occurrences of decorated types such as Weeden Island Punctated, Weeden Island Incised, Carrabelle Incised, Carrabelle Punctated, Keith Incised, Swift Creek Complicated Stamped, and Wakulla Check Stamped types. Weeden Island II assemblages contain a diminished percentage of plain wares (making up between 50 and 70 percent), an increase in Wakulla Check Stamped and Suwannee Valley series types, and a decrease in Weeden Island decorated types. Suwannee Valley assemblages contain notably few sand tempered plain sherds (less than 10 percent) and an abundance of Lochloosa Punctated, Fig Springs Roughened, and Prairie Cord-Marked, with minor occurrences of Alachua Cob-Marked (late) and various incised, impressed, and pinched surface treatments of the Suwannee Valley series that are reminiscent of the Weeden Island series. These latter types include Fig Springs Incised, Trestle Point Shell Impressed, and the unappealingly named Grassy Hole Pinched (Worth 2012). Only a single radiocarbon date is published for Weeden Island II, from a late context at McKeithen (Milanich et al. 1997, 56). Seven previously published radiocarbon dates are associated with the Suwannee Valley culture. Four come from charcoal at the Fig Springs site (8CO1) and together denote a 2-sigma range of cal AD 980 to 1660 (Worth 2012, 157). Three AMS assays from soot on Suwannee Valley series vessels from the Suwannee Sinks Site (8SU377) yielded 2-sigma ranges from cal AD 1010 to 1210 (Heller et al. 2012, 125). An eighth date for the Suwannee Valley culture is recorded in this chapter (see below), and more are forthcoming. Aside from occasional cobmarked sherds, evidence for maize in pre-Columbian contexts in north Florida is scant at best, and no maize has ever been directly dated (but see Worth 2012).

Settlement

An initial and naïve goal of this project was to systematically identify sites associated with archaeological cultures and time periods and analyze their spatial distribution. The improbability of this task became quickly apparent, with several specific complicating factors. First, and predictably, existing literature and FMSF data tend to use antiquated and more homogenous designations than those recently defined by Worth (2012; and in Weisman 1992). Most sites have been labeled Weeden Island, although few have been investigated (see White this volume for a similar situation). The taxonomic problem is therefore twofold: many sites were recorded using an underdeveloped pottery typology and chronology and the vast majority of sites are identified only through surface collections and surface surveys. Second, the surveys of Sigler-Lavelle (1980a, 1980b) and Kenneth Johnson (1986, 1987, 1991) are still the most comprehensive and detailed investigations of sites in the region, and their results, though they were working with inchoate chronologies, tend to indicate that multicomponent sites are the norm in north Florida. A perusal of collections at the Florida Museum of Natural History (FLMNH) from these surveys with an eye for recently defined Suwannee Valley series types confirms that multiple (and mixed) components are common. A thorough investigation of these collections using new typologies, a battery of radiocarbon assays, and new systematic excavations are all necessary to generate enough data to satisfactorily assess settlement patterns. Even with these limitations, however, some basic conclusions can be drawn.

Starting with the most obvious conclusion, there are no known sites in north Florida contemporaneous with McKeithen that are nearly as big or as dense or contain three mounds. At the time of the McKeithen work, a survey area comprised of Columbia County and portions of Suwannee and LaFayette counties contained only 27 sites that were deemed to be Weeden Island (11 of which had mounds), and 10 more were identified as probable Weeden Island sites (Milanich et al. 1997, 38–39). Today there are 66 sites in this survey area that are listed as "Weeden Island" in the FMSF. Only five have mounds and the rest are mostly small ceramic scatters. Only six sites are listed as having Weeden Island I components, and this does not include McKeithen, which raises serious concerns about the utility of these data. Today there is a grand total of 48 mounds listed for this area, and they are nearly all unassigned to a specific culture or time period. Even those that are designated as Weeden Island have seen little or no professional investigation and in fact may not be Weeden Island, as was discovered recently at the Parnell Mound (8CO326).

Because the term "Weeden Island" has been used often to describe nearly a millennium of occupation in north Florida, from around AD 200 to 1000 or even later, many sites might be better labeled "Weeden Island II," or Suwannee Valley culture. Based on available reports, there are very few sites in the region that could be confidently called Weeden Island I, and most are quite small, with "ceramic scatters" predominating. Besides McKeithen, there is only one other Weeden Island I site of any size recorded in the region, the Alligood site, which is defined as a modest-sized village without a mound located near the Santa Fe River about 40 kilometers southeast of McKeithen (Johnson 1991). Thus, during Weeden Island I, village aggregation is evident only at the McKeithen site and there is little to indicate that people congregated at even a remotely similar scale anywhere else in the region.

The majority of sites that Sigler-Lavelle documented postdated McKeithen and were called Weeden Island II by Milanich and colleagues (1984) to designate a time period that now also includes the Suwannee Valley culture. These late sites, which were not recorded in the FMSF, were deemed to be more abundant and less dense than Weeden Island I sites. In the FMSF, only nine sites in the region are listed as having Weeden Island II components, but this count may be limited by inconsistent terminology. Some of the sites investigated by Sigler-Lavelle, such as Carter Mound I, Leslie Mound, and Johns Pond, may also contain major Weeden Island II components, identified on the basis of large quantities of sand-tempered plain sherds and significant presence of Wakulla Check-Stamped pottery. However, most sites with significant percentages of plain pottery have collected assemblages too small to confidently assign a temporal range, a problem Milanich and colleagues have described (1997, 201–2). Thus, we simply cannot accurately assess the distribution of Weeden Island II sites. The sites that do seem to be Weeden Island II, such as Leslie Mound, are certainly less dense and smaller than McKeithen (as are all sites of any time period) and tend to contain a single burial mound and adjacent village, but we cannot say with any confidence that these sites are more numerous than the preceding period. The period between Weeden Island I and Suwannee Valley culture, around AD 750 (or earlier) to 1000, will thus remain unclear until more fieldwork is done.

Many of the sites, but not all, traditionally labeled Weeden Island II are actually

Suwannee Valley culture sites according to the revised chronology. Using survey data, Kenneth Johnson (1991) defined site clusters among late sites in north Florida, and it seems that this was one of Milanich's (1994, 349–53; 1996, 35–36) reasons for defining increasing aggregation of late settlements. However, most of Johnson's (1991) site clusters center on known Spanish missions, and the sites might very well date to the mission period. While mission-era assemblages presumably could be confidently differentiated from pre-Columbian Suwannee Valley assemblages, Johnson's limited survey data do not lend themselves to such discernment. What is more important, however, is that the only substantial pre-Columbian sites in Johnson's survey, which all seem to contain significant Suwannee Valley components based on his descriptions of assemblages, are solitary, not clustered. These include Palmore (AL189), South End (at Fig Springs, 8CO1), Indian Pond's (CO229) East Lower Slope, and Peacock Lake Mounds (SU174). Only Palmore and Peacock Lake contained burial mounds. Parnell (8CO326) can now be added to the list of large Suwannee Valley sites and may have a similar layout to Palmore, with a solitary burial mound, a seemingly horseshoe-shaped distribution of artifacts (i.e., the village), and nearby small contemporaneous sites (Johnson 1991, 277). Although large Suwannee Valley sites are not clustered, a prevalent pattern seems to be several small sites surrounding a mound. These may be small hamlets related to an agricultural subsistence regime, but it is difficult to judge whether the distribution is much different from Weeden Island I sites.

In summary, available data neither easily support nor refute a model of shifting settlement patterns because there are too many gaps in our knowledge to conduct an adequate diachronic analysis. It seems that there are indeed numerous small sites that are Suwannee Valley culture, and no site of any period compares to the size of McKeithen. Regardless of the details of settlement, however, it is worth noting the persistence of mounds as apparent population aggregators, whether people lived among the mounds, as proposed for McKeithen, or in nearby hamlets, as proposed for Suwannee Valley culture. Moreover, major mound centers tend to be located in similar locales fairly proximate to one another. In other words, mound sites cluster in a diachronic fashion. The densest and longest-lived place of aggregation may be the area that includes McKeithen, Leslie, Indian Pond, and Parnell. Besides Indian Pond, which is a major multicomponent site without a mound, each of these sites could be considered one of the major mound and village complexes at the time of their respective occupations. Each mound site is essentially comprised of a single component and is located less than five kilometers from the previous mound center, which means that they are all centrally located in the north Florida region. Instead of denoting entirely different scales of ceremonial gathering and population aggregation, these sites may have been inflected by different ritualized practices.

## The Parnell Mound (8CO326)

The Parnell Mound site (8CO326) offers significant opportunities to understand ritualized practices at mound centers during the Mississippi period in north Florida. In the summers of 2011 and 2012, the Florida Museum of Natural History produced a topographic map of the site, delineated the distribution of artifacts through systematic shovel testing and test excavations, and excavated a large pit feature 30 meters NNW of the mound summit (figure 12.2). The sand mound is situated on the edge of a terrace that overlooks Indian Mound Swamp, a formerly large pond that is now dry after intentional draining in the 1980s. The elevated terrace greatly enhances the apparent height of the mound when viewed from downslope (west or south). The mound is heavily deranged after illicit digging, some of it with heavy machinery, but its original dimensions are apparent: 27 meters across and between 2 and 3.5 meters high above the natural ground surface from various vantage points along the terrace. The mound has never been professionally excavated, though human remains were encountered by earthmoving activities and amateur excavations more than 50 years ago. An auger test in a treasure hunter's hole in the top of the mound recovered one Fig Springs Roughened (var. Ichetucknee) sherd at an elevation near the pre-mound ground surface, providing confirmation that the mound is likely to be associated with the Suwannee Valley culture and dates to the Mississippi period or later.

Artifacts are distributed across an area 200 meters wide around the mound but

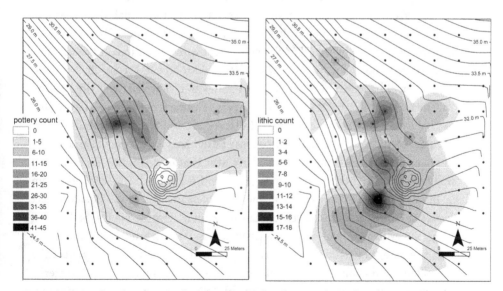

Figure 12.2. Artifact distributions based on interpolated counts from shovel tests, superimposed on 0.5-meter topographic contours of the Parnell Mound and surrounding environment. Elevations are meters above mean sea level.

are concentrated in several distinct clusters (figure 12.2). As interpolated from shovel tests, two of the densest clusters contain both potsherds and lithic artifacts (predominantly flakes) while the assemblages from a few other lower-density clusters are nearly mutually exclusive in terms of material culture. Artifacts are most concentrated between 50 and 80 centimeters below the ground surface within a biopedoturbated B Horizon. This vertical distribution is found throughout the site and at the nearby Buck site (8CO1201; see below) and likely reflects significant pedogenesis over the last eight centuries. While all but a few of thousands of sherds are of the Suwannee Valley series, or contemporaneous types, some patinated flakes and occasional Florida Archaic Stemmed hafted bifaces denote an earlier component represented by some of the lithic artifacts to the south of the mound.

High-density and discrete clusters of artifacts near the mound are not recorded for a habitation site in this region, particularly among late sites that are generally assumed to be low density compared to McKeithen (Milanich 1994, 349–51). Parnell can be distinguished through comparison with two presumed residential sites of vastly different scales, McKeithen and the Buck site (8CO1201). In Kohler's interpolation of artifact densities in the McKeithen village, artifacts were more or less continuously distributed across an area of nearly 500 meters between mounds. Using Kohler's artifact density ranges, only three small areas at Parnell, each between 20 meters and 40 meters wide, would match the number of artifacts per cubic meter (greater than 78) that characterizes the continuous distribution of McKeithen's northern ridge (Milanich et al. 1997, 54). Each of the Parnell artifact clusters more closely mirrors the spatial scale of the Buck site (8CO1201), a high-density area of lithic debitage and Suwannee Valley series sherds approximately 30 meters wide that was investigated by the FLMNH concurrent with excavations at Parnell. This site is located 500 meters to the NNW of Parnell Mound and seems likely to represent a small habitation (or hamlet) that seems to characterize this time period (Milanich 1994, 1996). Although the numbers of artifacts per volume of excavated material are comparable in select areas of all three of these sites and illustrate important differences in scale, the comparison may be dubious in the case of Parnell. This is because the Parnell clusters, particularly near Feature 1, contain exceptionally large sherds. These sherds tend to average two or three times the size of sherds from the Buck site, making comparison of counts problematic. Perhaps the small artifact clusters at Parnell are also far denser than any context recorded in the McKeithen village, but artifact weights are necessary to evaluate this assertion.

In any case, the artifact distribution at Parnell does not seem to reflect the typical habitation context of a hamlet or village. There is far too much material concentrated in a few small areas, and it tends to include notably large sherds that have been subjected to little postdepositional breakage. In other words, these distributions are the result of discrete events and rapid deposition; they are not the detritus of everyday living but are what might be expected in the event of a feast or other ritualized occasion.

## Feasting Rituals

Thorough investigation of a large feature at Parnell supports the notion that much of the mound-adjacent archaeology of the site is the result of special gathering events rather than refuse from everyday living. A shallow pit approximately 2.5 meters by 3 meters in diameter and more than half a meter deep is located 30 meters NNW of the mound summit (figure 12.3). A lens of dense charred wood, more than 10 centimeters thick in some places, defined the base of the feature and was covered by an organically stained stratum that was rife with faunal remains and artifacts. Surrounding the wide pit were areas of very high artifact density that extended about two meters beyond the pit margins. The feature presents clear evidence of burning and rapid deposition of fauna and artifacts and represents a roasting pit or earth oven that was subsequently filled with the remains of a very large meal.

Laboratory analysis is not yet complete, but results from just over half the feature indicate an exceptionally dense and surprisingly diverse faunal assemblage. More than 5,000 large fragments of deer bone representing at least 88 individuals were

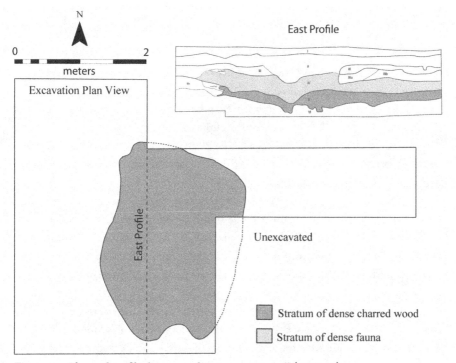

Figure 12.3. Plan and profile diagrams of Feature 1 at Parnell (8CO326).

located within this massive pit and the immediately surrounding deposit. Deer are represented by the full suite of cranial and axial elements, but the latter are most common. Among the axial parts, the meat-bearing long bones are most common, followed by pelves, scapulae, and some thoracic and lumbar vertebrae. Cutmarks are evident on some specimens, generally confined to the epiphyseal ends. Many of the long bones appear to have been buried whole and often in association with other bones of the same limb (femurs, fibulae, and tibiae; humerus, radii, and ulnae) and vertebrae were often articulated. These elements are likely to be the remains of shoulders and haunches that were roasted whole. The size of individual deer is fairly consistent; they represent primarily adults, although subadults and occasional fawns are present. One deer antler attached to the skull indicates a fall or winter kill.

Other mammals in the assemblage include opossums, rabbits, squirrels, unidentified rodents/small mammals, dogs, and black bears, each representing just one or two individuals. Other identified fauna include turkeys, turtles (cooters and gopher tortoises are most prevalent, followed by mud/musk, box, soft-shell, and snapper turtles), and fish (primarily mullet, but also jack, ladyfish, carcharhinid shark, freshwater catfish, and largemouth bass). About 25 percent of the total number of individual specimens shows evidence of burning but is confined mostly to small fragments of long bones or unidentified elements rather than the larger or more complete elements.

More than 4,500 pottery sherds were associated with this mass of bone, many of them very large sherds representing significant portions of vessels. These sherds differ from other areas of the site not only in their size but also in the size of the vessels of which they are portions. Based on orifice curvatures, many of these vessels were very large—the average opening was more than 30 centimeters (n = 62; SD = 9.5) and at least 15 vessels had openings larger than 40 centimeters. Lochloosa Punctated sherds made up nearly half the assemblage, followed by Fig Springs Roughened (ca. 20 percent), sand-tempered plain (ca. 20 percent), and Prairie Cord-Marked (ca. 5 percent), as well as occasional St. Johns Plain, St. Johns Check-Stamped and at least two Marsh Island Incised sherds (Hall 2013).

Abundant lithic artifacts were also located within the feature. These included over a dozen Pinellas points, most made of a poor-quality local phosphate chert, numerous lithic flakes that included several varieties of chert and silicified corals, sandstone abraders, and "nutting stones," the latter defined by numerous small cupules ground into flat slabs of sandstone. Also encountered were numerous large iron concretions that were notably larger and more abundant than other areas of the site, where they were found at the bottom of excavations above a culturally sterile clay horizon. Some of these iron concretions within and around the feature may have been sought for iron ore. Three small nodules of hematite were also encountered within the feature, along with two unmodified quartz crystal fragments.

AMS assays on charred wood from near the base of the feature yielded a 2-sigma calibrated range of AD 1160 to 1260(Beta-323913), firmly anchoring it to the Mississippi period.

Although laboratory analysis is still under way and quantitative data are not yet complete, Feature 1 at Parnell is clearly a remarkable record of ritualized practice, including feasting. What makes a meal a feast? The archaeological signatures of feasting are contextually variable, and archaeologists sometimes struggle to differentiate daily food consumption from more extraordinary contexts. Nonetheless, Nerissa Russell (2012, 377–92) has recently outlined a nearly comprehensive list of the archaeological characteristics of feasting that can serve as aids in its identification. Among these indicators are 1) spatial associations of fauna with places of ritual such as temples, mounds, or human burials, and highly visible areas like village plazas; 2) an unusually large quantity or high density of fauna deposited in a single event or over a short period of time; 3) association of fauna with feasting paraphernalia (e.g. large vessels); 4) foods in much different proportions than daily fare (e.g., a broad spectrum foragers creating a deposit with low species diversity and equitability); 5) limited portions of the body represented, especially meat brought in with articulated joints; 6) larger than usual portions of animals; 7) remains that are less processed than usual; 8) special cooking methods that add value through display (such as roasting); and 9) formal and rapid burial of remains that tend to preserve articulated elements (Kelly 2001; Stephanie Knight 2001; Russell 2012). While a single feasting context may rarely exhibit all of these characteristics together, Feature 1 at Parnell most assuredly does. The feature is proximate to and in full view of a large burial mound, contains materials such as quartz crystal and ochre that are more common in mortuary contexts, contains foot elements of bears and cranial elements from dogs that are not common food remains, is filled with portions of cooking vessels larger than those found elsewhere at the site, appears to contain a small proportion of other fauna that were likely parts of the diet (e.g., other mammals, birds, reptiles, and fish), contains articulated shoulders and haunches, and appears to have been deposited and covered over in a single event and not disturbed again (until our excavations).

Meat of large animals is particularly common feasting fare throughout much of the world, and deer is a likely candidate in the pre-Columbian Southeast. There is a long history of feasting with deer in the Southeast, and as Vernon Knight (2001) discusses, several recorded instances of faunal remains at Woodland platform mounds, including McKeithen, might be interpreted this way. These platform mounds also exhibit evidence of large posts and smaller scaffolding that was repeatedly emplaced and removed, which Vernon Knight (2001, 324) infers was associated with the conspicuous display of cuts of meat slated for feasting. At both the Walling site, in northern Alabama, and McKeithen, just seven kilometers SSW of

Parnell, high meat-bearing portions of deer dominated the faunal assemblages. At McKeithen, both haunches and shoulders were present, comprised of 10 femora, 20 tibia, 8 humeri, and 10 scapulae (Milanich et al. 1997, 102). These, and a few other elements, from two middens on Mound A at McKeithen made up a minimum of nine individuals. In comparison, the excavation of Feature 1 at Parnell uncovered several hundred deer long bones, scapulae, and vertebrae. The density of bone is truly staggering and conservatively represents a minimum of 88 individual deer.

The ceremonial importance of animals, particularly deer, among the ethnohistoric Timucua is well documented in Pareja's Confesionario (Spike 2006). There is more than an analogical correspondence here, as the Suwannee Valley archaeological culture is presumed to represent the direct ancestors of the Utina Timucua described in Spanish accounts (Worth 2012). Whether Feature 1 at Parnell represents something akin to a "First Fruits" ceremony that was so important among Timucuan groups is difficult to ascertain. There seem to have been many different rituals related to First Fruits at various scales that involved numerous kinds of food, but the first deer taken in the spring season was a particularly important event. Still unknown are how many deer or other prey were taken for these rituals. An annual renewal ceremony described and illustrated by Jacques LeMoyne, however, involved a single large stag prepared and mounted on a tree (Spike 2006, 17). Judging by the sheer quantity of meat consumed at Parnell during the event that ended in Feature 1, the scale of this feast may surpass any documented Timucua celebrations. Beyond the sheer size and density of the feature at Parnell, other indications of a ritual deposit are the inclusion of dog and bear elements, potentially pieces of animal guardians, and the ochre and quartz crystals that have potent properties in some Native American worldviews (Brown and Emery 2008; Vanpool and Newsome 2012; Zedeño 2009).

Regardless of its relationship to later rituals described in Spanish accounts, the feast and subsequent emplacement of associated materials near the mound at Parnell is likely to have been an event that initiated or consecrated the mound as an important place. Furthermore, and in contrast to the lack of conventional signs of sociopolitical complexity in north Florida normally associated with Mississippianization, feasts of this scale may have been linked to attempts to enhance hosts' prestige, wealth, and power. Indeed, feasts are often a form of gift (Mauss 1970 [1925]) and can be effective ways to convert economic to symbolic capital through the creation of networks of obligation. Michael Dietler (2001) describes three categories of feasts: empowering (competitive and leveling), patron-role (redistributive), and diacritical (elite reinforcing). While these categories are not mutually exclusive, Dietler's description of empowering feasts may best explain the event at Parnell. Empowering feasts include the classic ethnographic examples of the potlatch of the northwest coast and the *moka* of Papua New Guinea, in which the escalating competition of feasts tends to impoverish a host in the short term but obligates others in ways that pay long-term benefits. "Work-party" feasts are one such type of event in which food is ceremoniously supplied to marshal labor for large construction projects. It is tempting to imagine a large feast at Parnell among a gathering of many people from throughout the region in anticipation or celebration of the construction of the mound.

In any case, Feature 1 at Parnell and the high-density clusters of artifacts at the site are evidence of ceremonial occasions that brought together a large number of people from far and wide, enough to capture and consume numerous deer on a single occasion. These results contrast starkly with the results of excavations in late period burial mounds that give the impression of provincialism and little concern for ceremonial regalia. But instead of becoming more isolated and less practiced in ritual during the Mississippi period in north Florida, the contexts of some rituals shifted away from the mound and there was an escalation of ritualized performance surrounding the hunting, preparation, and consumption of deer and other animals.

## Conclusions

Ceremonial centers were important features of the north Florida landscape for nearly a millennium after the abandonment of the McKeithen site. The ephemeral nature of the villages adjacent to many Late Woodland or Mississippi period mounds and the clustered high-density areas recorded at Parnell each indicate that mounds were not surrounded by large residential populations. Rather, what seems likely is that habitation sites were located away from mounds and people converged at these places for important ritual occasions, such as burial ceremonies, mound construction, and feasts. Parnell has a lower density or smaller extent of archaeological deposits compared to McKeithen because the practices that took place there may have been restricted to periodic ceremonial events, not habitual and repeated actions of permanent residents. A similar convergence of participants from afar may have occurred at the McKeithen site, but there has been little investigation of small Weeden Island I sites from which people may have traveled.

Weeden Island II and Suwannee Valley culture burial mounds do not contain nonperishable accoutrements like those that are typical of Weeden Island I burials, particularly ornate pottery, nor do they contain the finery of Mississippian burials that has been found at places such as Lake Jackson (Jones 1982). However, contrasting with this relative austerity in mortuary tradition, Feature 1 at Parnell showcases the grand scale of the feasting event. Much work is left to be done to precisely characterize this feature, explore evidence of feasting in the preceding centuries, and better understand the history and process of ritualized food consumption in north Florida. Like the mortuary practices at McKeithen that incorporated objects made in distant locales (Pluckhahn and Cordell 2011), the geographic scale of social interaction facilitated by feasts may have extended beyond the north Florida region. The incorporation of quartz crystals, sharks teeth, and potentially nonlocal Marsh Island Incised and St. Johns Check-Stamped pottery in the feasting deposit at Parnell indexes interregional connections. Notably absent are any of the trademarks of Mississippian culture that are present at contemporaneous Fort Walton sites to the west and St. Johns II sites to the east (see Ashley this volume; White this volume). Given the scale of ceremonial events evident at Parnell, the absence of traditional Mississippian ritual objects is unlikely to be due to the leaders' inability to connect to exchange networks. Instead, it may represent alternative traditions that actively eschewed the hegemony of Mississippian politics that surrounded them.

## Acknowledgments

I am grateful to have been able to summarize partial results from ongoing analyses of the Parnell site Feature 1 assemblage: faunal analysis by Meggan Blessing and pottery analysis by Kristen Hall. Thanks to the FLMNH Environmental Archaeology and Ceramic Technology laboratories for support for this research.

## References

Anderson, David G.
1998    Swift Creek in Regional Perspective. In *A World Engraved: Archaeology of the Swift Creek Culture*, edited by Mark Williams and Daniel T. Elliot, 274–300. University of Alabama Press, Tuscaloosa.

Bell, Catherine M.
1997    *Ritual: Perspectives and Dimensions*. Oxford University Press, New York.

Bourdieu, Pierre
1977    *Outline of a Theory of Practice*. Cambridge University Press, Cambridge.

Brown, Linda A., and Kitty F. Emery
2008    Negotiations with the Animate Forest: Hunting Shrines in the Guatemalan Highlands. *Journal of Archaeological Method and Theory* 15: 300–337.

Dietler, Michael
2001    Theorizing the Feast: Rituals of Consumption, Commensal Politics, and Power in African Contexts. In *Feasts: Archaeological and Ethnographic Perspectives on Food, Politics, and Power*, edited by Michael Dietler and Bryan D. Hayden, 65–114. Smithsonian Institution Press, Washington, DC.

Giddens, Anthony
1984    *The Constitution of Society: Outline of the Theory of Structuration*. University of California Press, Berkeley.

Gosden, Chris
2005    What Do Objects Want? *Journal of Archaeological Method and Theory* 12: 193–211.

Hall, Kristen C. D.

2013    Reexamining Suwannee Valley Pottery: A Typological and Formal Analysis of Pottery in Feature 1 at Parnell Mound. BA thesis, University of Florida, Gainesville.

Heller, Nathanael, William P. Barse, R. Christopher Goodwin, Sean Coughlin, Brian Ostahowski, Sherman W. Horn III, Charlotte Donald Pevny, Raegan Buckley, and Haley Holt

2012    Phase III Archaeological Data Recovery at Site 8SU377, Suwannee County, Florida. Manuscript on file, Department of Historical Resources, Tallahassee.

Johnson, G. Michael, and Timothy A. Kohler

1987    Toward a Better Understanding of North Peninsular Gulf Coast Florida Prehistory: Archaeological Reconnaissance in Dixie County. *Florida Anthropologist* 40: 275–86.

Johnson, Kenneth W.

1986    Archaeological Survey of Contact and Mission Period Sites in Northern Peninsular Florida. Report on file, Florida Division of Historical Resources, Tallahassee.

1987    The Search for Aguacaleyquen and Cali. Report on file, Florida Division of Historical Resources, Tallahassee.

1991    The Utina and the Potano Peoples of Northern Florida: Changing Settlement Systems in the Spanish Colonial Period. PhD dissertation, University of Florida, Gainesville.

Jones, B. Calvin

1982    Southern Cult Manifestations at the Lake Jackson Site, Leon County, Florida: Salvage Excavation of Mound 3. *Midcontinental Journal of Archaeology* 7: 3–44.

Keane, Webb

2003    Semiotics and the Social Analysis of Material Things. *Language and Communication* 23: 409–25.

2005    Signs Are Not the Garb of Meaning: On the Social Analysis of Material Things. In *Materiality: Politics, History, and Culture*, edited by Daniel Miller, 182–205. Duke University Press, Durham, NC.

Kelly, Jennifer A., Robert H. Tykot, and Jerald T. Milanich

2006    The Importance of Maize in Florida Through the Contact Period. In *Histories of Maize: Multidisciplinary Approaches to the Prehistory, Linguistics, Biogeography, Domestication, and Evolution of Maize*, edited by John E. Staller, Robert H. Tykot, and Bruce F. Benz. Academic Press, Waltham.

Kelly, Lucretia S.

2001    A Case of Ritual Feasting at the Cahokia Site. In *Feasts: Archaeological and Ethnographic Perspectives on Food, Politics, and Power*, edited by Michael Dietler and Bryan D. Hayden, 334–67. Smithsonian Institution Press, Washington, DC.

Knight, Stephanie

2001    Beasts and Burial in the Interpretation of Ritual Space: A Case Study from Danbury. In *Holy Ground: Theoretical Issues Relating to the Landscape and Material Culture of Ritual Space Objects*, edited by A. T. Smith and A. Brookes, 49–59. British Archaeological Reports, International Series. Archaeopress, Oxford.

Knight, Vernon J., Jr.

2001    Feasting and the Emergence of Platform Mound Ceremonialism in Eastern North America. In *Feasts: Archaeological and Ethnographic Perspectives on Food, Politics, and Power*, edited by Michael Dietler and Bryan D. Hayden, 239–54. Smithsonian Institution Press, Washington, DC.

Mauss, Marcel

1970 [1925]   *The Gift: Forms and Functions of Exchange in Archaic Societies.* Translated by I. Cunnison. Cohen and West Ltd., London.

Milanich, Jerald T.

1994    *Archaeology of Precolumbian Florida.* University Press of Florida, Gainesville.

1996    *The Timucua.* Blackwell, Oxford.

1998    *Florida's Indians from Ancient Times to the Present.* University Press of Florida, Gainesville.

Milanich, Jerald T., Ann S. Cordell, Vernon J. Knight Jr., Timothy A. Kohler, and Brenda J. Sigler-Lavelle

1984    *McKeithen Weeden Island: The Culture of Northern Florida, A.D. 200–900.* Academic Press, Orlando.

1997    *Archaeology of Northern Florida, A.D. 200–900: The McKeithen Weeden Island Culture.* University Press of Florida, Gainesville.

Mitchem, Jeffrey M. (editor)

1999a   *The East Florida Expeditions of Clarence Bloomfield Moore.* Introduction by Jeffrey M. Mitchem. University of Alabama Press, Tuscaloosa.

1999b   *The West and Central Florida Expeditions of Clarence Bloomfield Moore.* Introduction by Jeffrey M. Mitchem. University of Alabama Press, Tuscaloosa.

Pauketat, Timothy R., and Susan M. Alt

2005    Agency in a Postmold? Physicality and the Archaeology of Culture-Making. *Journal of Archaeological Method and Theory* 12: 213–36.

Pluckhahn, Thomas J., and Ann S. Cordell

2011    Paste Characterization of Weeden Island Pottery from Kolomoki and Its Implications for Specialized Production. *Southeastern Archaeology* 30: 288–310.

Russell, Nerissa

2012    *Social Zooarchaeology: Humans and Animals in Prehistory.* Cambridge University Press, Cambridge.

Sears, William H.

1973    The Sacred and the Secular in Prehistoric Ceramics. In *Variations in Anthropology: Essays in Honor of John McGregor,* edited by Donald Lathrap and Jody Douglas, 31–42. Illinois Archaeological Survey, Urbana.

Sigler-Lavelle, Brenda J.

1980a   On the Non-Random Distribution of Weeden Island Period Sites in North Florida. *Southeastern Archaeology Conference Bulletin* 22: 22–29.

1980b   *The Political and Economic Implications of the Distribution of Weeden Island Period Sites in North Florida.* New School for Social Research, Ann Arbor, MI.

Spike, Tamara

2006    To Make Graver This Sin: Conceptions of Purity and Pollution Among the Timucua of Spanish Florida. PhD dissertation, Department of History, Florida State University, Tallahassee.

Stephenson, Keith, Judith A. Bense, and Frankie Snow

2002    Aspects of Deptford and Swift Creek on the South Atlantic and Gulf Coastal Plains. In *The Woodland Southeast,* edited by David G. Anderson and Robert C. Mainfort, 318–51. University of Alabama Press, Tuscaloosa.

Turner, Bethany L., John D. Kingston, and Jerald T. Milanich

2005    Isotopic Evidence of Immigration Linked to Status during the Weeden Island and Suwannee Valley Periods in North Florida. *Southeastern Archaeology* 24: 121–36.

Vanpool, Christine S., and Elizabeth Newsome

2012    The Spirit in the Material: A Case Study of Animism in the American Southwest. *American Antiquity* 77: 243–62.

Weisman, Brent R.

1992    *Excavations of the Franciscan Frontier: Archaeology of the Fig Springs Mission.* University Press of Florida, Gainesville.

Worth, John E.

2012    An Overview of the Suwannee Valley Culture. In *Late Prehistoric Florida: Archaeology at the Edge of the Mississippian World,* edited by Keith H. Ashley and Nancy M. White, 149–71. University Press of Florida, Gainesville.

Zedeño, Maria Nieves

2009    Animating by Association: Index Objects and Relational Taxonomies. *Cambridge Archaeological Journal* 19: 407–17.

# Ritual at the Mill Cove Complex

## Realms beyond the River

KEITH ASHLEY AND VICKI ROLLAND

Copper plates, long-nosed god earpieces, and spatulate celts are not often thought of as the material possessions of foragers, particularly ones living at the edge of the early Mississippian world. But in northeastern Florida, St. Johns II (AD 900–1250) fisher-hunter-gatherers acquired appreciable quantities of stone, metal, and other mineral artifacts from far-off lands. The majority of these nonlocal items appear to have been consumed at the community level through mortuary ritual at two ceremonial centers: Mill Cove Complex and Mt. Royal. What is rarely mentioned, however, is the fact that these St. Johns II societies also interred artifacts from much earlier periods of manufacture in these same mortuary mounds. Early Mississippi period inhabitants of Mill Cove were fully aware of the antiquity of these objects and their associated mounds and middens. We propose herein that their acquisition, use, and burial in St. Johns II mounds helped forge a connection to a deep and sacred past. In this chapter we explore the use of exotica and pieces of the ancient past as a fundamental part of St. Johns mortuary ritual from the vantage point of Kinzey's Knoll at the Mill Cove Complex.

## The Mythical Past

Evidence of past cultures is present everywhere across the landscape, and throughout time and place societies have been guided in the present by their past (Lowenthal 1985; Gosden and Lock 1998, 2). As a product of human action, culture is incontrovertibly historical in that it is continually negotiated and passed down from generation to generation. Because of the ongoing process of its construction, culture is not reproduced in its exact form, although human actions are certainly constrained by the structural context from which they derive. In fact, it is history that bestows the structural possibilities for human agency or any action that can conceivably run contrary to the norms, practices, and rules of society. Thus, all human action builds upon what came before. In this chapter, we are concerned more with the deep past, a time that existed beyond the lifetime or memory of any one person in a society.

Memory allows us to recall stored information and bring it forth into the present. It works at both individual and group scales, which means that a vast array of memories can coexist in any given community. Here, our interest centers on social memory or "a collective notion . . . about the way things were in the past" (Van Dyke and Alcock 2003, 2). Memories are not static or fixed reflections of the past; their meanings are continually subject to negotiation, contestation, and redefinition (Lowenthal 1985, 210; Wilson 2010, 3). As the gap between the past and present widens, the past is reconstituted using whatever evidence is available. In Florida, material clues of primordial times would have existed in the form of mounds, middens, and durable artifacts as well as natural landscape features such as rivers, creeks, and distinct landforms. With this in mind, a distinction can be made between genealogical history and mythical history, although the two are not necessarily mutually exclusive. In the former, the past is constructed through ties to known ancestors, whereas in the latter deeper descent lines and "a less well-known past is evoked" (Gosden and Lock 1998, 3). A mythical history constitutes a peoples' notion of what happened before the known past.

In Native American societies, history is recounted through kinship rendering and the repeated oral telling of stories and events associated with those individuals. The memory of the living is recreated through various physical and verbal mnemonics that serve to restate the past and keep the memory alive within a society (Gosden and Lock 1998, 3). Social memory is retrieved through a variety of means such as song, story, dance, and art, and it is often collectively embodied in the landscape, in architecture, and in portable objects. But what about the ancient past, the long ago that has faded from everyone's memory? This is a past that is open to interpretation; it is a mythical history that is constructed to serve the needs of those in the present. As Lowenthal (1985, 210) states, "the prime function of memory . . . is not to preserve the past but to adapt it so as to enrich and manipulate the present." In the following we explore how St. Johns II societies of northeastern Florida may have used mortuary ritual and "pieces of the past" to authenticate what they perceived as tangible connections to mythical ancestors.

## Mill Cove Complex

The Mill Cove Complex is the largest early St. Johns II settlement in northeastern Florida. Mapped onto rolling relict dune fields along the south bank of the St. Johns River, Mill Cove consists of a complex of residential shell middens, special event or ritual middens, earthen causeways, and sand burial mounds. Many of the sacred features are grafted onto natural rises that allow the monuments to change shape and height depending on one's viewpoint on the landscape. The site's inhabitants were afforded ready access to daily life-sustaining resources in the form of fish, shellfish, reptiles, and land mammals. Wild plants, nuts, and fruits were procured, but farming was not practiced. Far-reaching social relationships ensured a flow of ideas and nonlocal materials, which meant that St. Johns II societies were never isolated from events and developments of the early Mississippian world (Ashley 2002, 2012).

The most salient features of the Mill Cove Complex are the Grant (8DU14) and Shields (8DU12) mounds, situated approximately 750 meters from one another (Ashley 2005a; Thunen 2005). Much of what we know about the two mounds comes from the late-nineteenth-century excavations of C. B. Moore (1894a, 1894b, 1895). Away from the two sand monuments, grid-based, shovel testing and the excavation of a limited number of larger investigative units have taken place over the past 25 years (see Ashley 2005a, 157–65 for a review). Radiometric assays date St. Johns II occupations at Mill Cove to ca. AD 900–1250.

The Grant and Shields mounds were erected atop the two highest points of the site (figure 13.1). Grant Mound was built at the edge of a 10-meter bluff fronting the St. Johns River, whereas Shields was situated along the top of a natural dune ridge about 100 meters from the river. Moore (1895, 30) described the shape of Grant Mound as "the usual truncated cone" and recorded its height at about eight meters. Shields Mound was different: "a great platform mound entirely unlike in form any aboriginal earthwork on the [St. Johns] river" (ibid., 11). Although not as tall as Grant Mound, at six meters in height, Shields Mound was long and narrow with a platform summit at one end (northeast) and a fishhook-like feature at the other end (southwest). Figure 13.2 shows Moore's diagram of Shields next to a recent LiDAR-derived topographic map. The latter reveals the flat-topped northern end, described by Moore, but it depicts a more conical mound at the opposite end of what appears to be a linear relict dune. At this point it is unclear whether the discrepancy is due to landform changes since Moore's visit or to cartographic errors on the part of Moore's mapper. The architecture of Shields and Grant mounds was quite different, which means that they were not twin pillars bracketing the site.

Each mound was an accretionary cemetery with a long history of soil addition and reconfiguration as new burials were added. Moore's notes and stratigraphic profile maps of Grant Mound drawn by Thunen (2005) in the 1980s reveal that distinct episodes of burial were marked by colored sands, particularly zones that were intentionally tinted with varying shades of red, depending on the amount of hematite added to white or pale yellow sand. This artificial coloring would have entailed thorough grinding of fine-grade, nonlocal iron oxide. Local ferruginous nod-

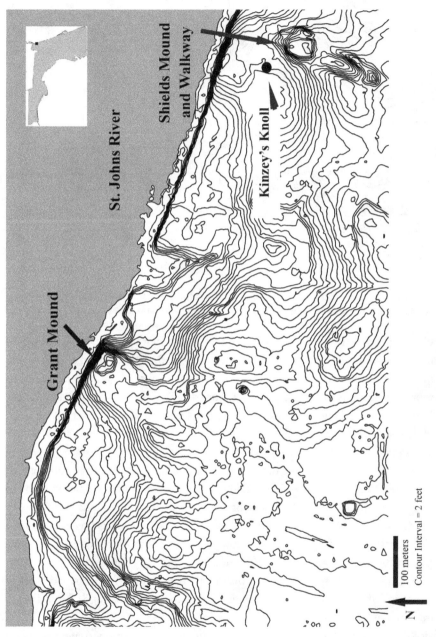

St. Johns River

Grant Mound

Shields Mound
and Walkway

Kinzey's Knoll

N

100 meters

Contour Interval = 2 feet

Figure 13.1. The Mill Cove Complex showing the location of Grant Mound, Shields Mound, and Kinzey's Knoll.

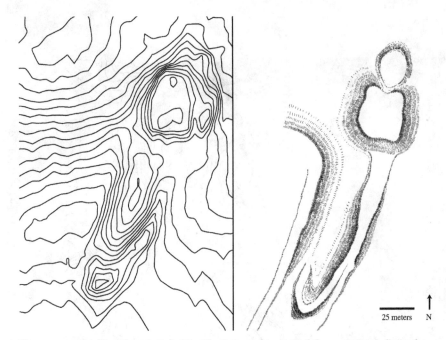

Figure 13.2. Shields Mound. *Left*: Florida Geographic Data Library LiDAR-derived topographic map with 2-foot contour intervals. *Right*: Map from Moore 1895, 10.

ules consist of little more than loosely concreted sand with ferric staining that would not have produced the impressive volume of silt-sized particles of red dust observed in mound profiles. The ritual acts of processing the red sands and layering them in mortuary mounds can be traced back to the early Woodland times in northeastern Florida (see also White this volume). The basal portion of both mounds consisted of deposits of pure white and black organic sands, natural soils that are readily available in the Mill Cove area.

Acts of monumentality at the Mill Cove Complex appear to have commenced with the accumulation of a shell midden; a practice that contrasts sharply with the premound surface preparations associated with earlier sand mounds in the region. The building of local Woodland period Swift Creek mounds was preceded by land clearing and the removal of topsoil followed by the deposition of a layer of charcoal-laden white sand. Wallis (2008, 252) interprets this as a conscious act of purification that symbolically marked "new historical beginnings." In contrast, portions of Grant and Shields mounds were built directly on top of preexisting St. Johns II shell middens, and rather thick middens at that (Moore 1895, 24; Thunen 2005). This is also the case at the Grand (8DU1) and Goodman (8DU66) mound sites (Ashley et al. 2007; Jordan 1963; Recourt 1975). If St. Johns II groups were new to far northeastern Florida, as has been previously suggested on the basis of settlement distribution and ceramic evidence (Ashley 2003, 298–301; Ashley 2005b, 295–96), the creation of refuse deposits may have served as a way for the new arrivals to establish a community connection to the territory.

These underlying shell middens clearly predate the onset of mound construction but perhaps only by weeks, months, or a few years. A question arises about the circumstances of their deposition: Is it refuse related to founding events, the by-product of feasting, or merely trash just lying around? In light of what has been recovered at Kinzey's Knoll (see below), we see no reason to discount the possibility that each mound began with commemorative feasting. We need to consider the possibility that the juxtaposition of the two mounds and shell middens was a culturally informed choice and not simply a coincidence. In effect, they preset the landscape for a cemetery they knew they would eventually need. Although inspirations for mound building may have derived from elsewhere in time and/or space, the actual social practice of constructing the mound and processing and interring the dead was enacted locally at a specific moment in history (Wallis 2008, 237–38).

Mound artifacts at the Mill Cove Complex are highlighted by elaborate foreign goods such as the two ground stone spatulate celts from Shields Mound and a set of copper long-nosed god maskettes from Grant Mound (Moore 1895, 18, 43). Other nonlocal items in both mounds included mica, galena, faceted and globular quartz crystals, ground stone celts, steatite pipes, variously shaped small copper plates, and other copper-covered items made of stone, bone, wood, and shell. These materials came from far-flung areas of eastern North America; cultural centers such as Macon Plateau, Georgia, and Cahokia, Illinois, are strongly implicated in their movement (Ashley 2012, 113–14).

A curious aspect of both Grant and Shields mounds, and one that has received little if any attention, is the inclusion of artifacts whose period of manufacture greatly predates St. Johns II mound construction and use. These include Archaic bannerstones (figure 13.3), polished stone beads, and projectile points (e.g., Benton, Turkey Tail; see Johnson and Brookes 1989) as well as possible Woodland period (Hopewell-related) ground stone plummets, quartz crystals, and steatite elbow pipes (figure 13.4). It also is possible that some of the many ground stone celts from Grant Mound were manufactured before the St. Johns II period. Wilcox (2010, 81–82) notes that the Archaic projectile points from the Grant and Shields mounds display highly symmetrical shapes with minimal evidence of retouching, perhaps suggesting a preference for idealized biface forms in ritual use. The lithic materials from the Mill Cove Complex are nonlocal because the site lacks an Archaic component and the closest known chert sources are about 100 kilometers away.

Although they are separated by 130 kilometers, Shields and Grant mounds are remarkably similar to Mt. Royal in terms of placement on the landscape, construction, material content, and modes of human interment. Mt. Royal, located upriver (south) of Mill Cove in the middle section of the St. Johns River valley, is another

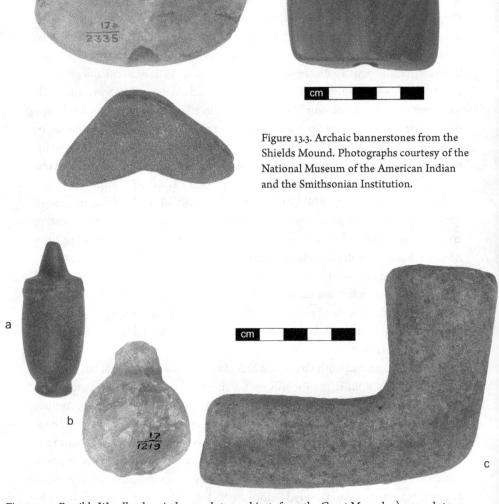

Figure 13.3. Archaic bannerstones from the Shields Mound. Photographs courtesy of the National Museum of the American Indian and the Smithsonian Institution.

Figure 13.4. Possible Woodland period ground stone objects from the Grant Mound: a) ground stone pendant; b) quartz pendant; c) steatite elbow pipe. Photographs courtesy of the National Museum of the American Indian and the Smithsonian Institution.

major St. Johns II mound center with strong ties to the early Mississippian world (Ashley 2005c). Access to and departure from each mound was guided by walkways in the form of raised earthen berms (Ashley 2002, 169). Anyone who stands at the edge of the steep bluff fronting each of these three mounds cannot help but recognize that each provides a similar panoramic view. At the base of the bluff wall lay a broad section of the St. Johns River that separated sacred high ground on the mound side from the broad shallow marshes and web of wetland islands and creeks that spread out from the opposite bank. These sacred spaces were specifically located and laid out with processional approaches and public viewing in mind.

## Kinzey's Knoll

Beyond the Grant and Shields mounds is a widespread yet variable distribution of household garbage was accentuated by several impressive shell middens (Ashley 2005a, 157–65). One lies near the Grant Mound and another (Reeves Rise) is located about 100 meters north of the Shields Mound. The most intensively tested to date, however, is Kinzey's Knoll. This dense shell midden, positioned on a low rise about 50 meters northwest of the Shields Mound, measures about 30 meters in diameter and has a distinctly mounded core approximately 15 meters in diameter and 80 centimeters thick. Two contiguous but staggered 2-meter squares were excavated in 1999 and 2000 (Ashley 2005a, 161), and another 2-meter square and a 1-x-2-meter unit were excavated in 2012. Although analysis of the latter units is ongoing, preliminary statements about what was recovered are provided in the following discussion.

Kinzey's Knoll has yielded a striking inventory of artifacts and raw materials that are more indicative of a mortuary mound than a shell midden. Among its varied contents are whole and fragmented items of both local and exotic material that seem far too precious to have been discarded in a common trash heap. To date, no domestic context at Mill Cove or anywhere else in the region has yielded similar foreign materials, although Ocmulgee pottery and occasional chert points and flakes occur in household middens throughout northeastern Florida (Ashley 2012, 118). Elsewhere it has been argued that Kinzey's Knoll is the material manifestation of mortuary ritual and feasting associated with the nearby Shields Mound (Ashley 2005b, 291–92; Marrinan 2005; Rolland 2005). Several lines of evidence have been brought to bear on this claim.

First, many of the same kinds of materials were recovered from both contexts. More than 5,000 pottery fragments have been recovered from Kinzey's Knoll. On the basis of rim sherd data (i.e., orifice size, paste, and rim and surface treatments), a minimum of 400 separate vessels are represented. In the 1999–2000 assemblage, roughly 75 percent of the pottery was St. Johns (mostly check-stamped and plain), and six variations of sponge spiculate paste were represented. Grit- and grit-grog-tempered Ocmulgee Cord-Marked wares composed 22 percent of the assemblage. Neutron activation analysis combined with sherd refiring points to the presence of both nonlocal Ocmulgee Cord-Marked pottery from south-central Georgia and locally produced copies at Kinzey's Knoll (Ashley 2003, 104–27; Rolland 2004, 132–50). In fact, refiring experiments using samples from various stratigraphic levels reveal higher frequencies of Ocmulgee pottery made of local clays in the upper levels (Rolland 2005, 230). Burnished and red-filmed wares also occurred in greater than expected numbers, particularly compared to other domestic contexts across the site.

A much higher percentage of large-mouthed and small-mouthed bowls are represented at Kinzey's Knoll compared to other areas of the site and other domestic contexts in the region. Both St. Johns and Ocmulgee wares exhibited minimal to no surface attrition, abrasion, or heavy sooting. Rather, their nearly pristine surfaces suggest limited or perhaps first-time use prior to discard. As a result, Kinzey's Knoll ceramics have been interpreted as a special event assemblage (Rolland 2005, 220–22).

Kinzey's Knoll was also marked by a high concentration of bone and shell tools (Penders 2005). More than 90 formal bone tool fragments—most of which were still usable—have been recovered (including the 2012 excavations), many of which are ornaments. Bone pins dominate the assemblage, and several display intricately engraved designs that were enhanced by working fine iron-oxide powder into the incisions (figure 13.5). Other modified animal bone includes awls, pendants, shark centrum beads, dolphin teeth gravers, an antler flaker, a drilled turtle plastron, and fossilized and nonfossilized shark teeth gravers and drills (Penders 2005). Shell artifacts consist of discoidal, tube, and barrel-shaped beads; pendants; a scraper; a gouge; and an abrader.

Figure 13.5. Incised bone pendant, Kinzey's Knoll.

Stone and mineral items also were recovered in atypical numbers and include nonlocal sandstone abraders, chert points and debitage, and ground stone fragments (Bland 2001). Among the latter is a basalt grinder, which appears to represent a broken and reused celt fragment embedded with iron oxide powder in one rounded end. It likely was used to crush iron-oxide nodules into powder. Diagnostic hafted bifaces consist of seven Mississippi period Pinellas points, two Cahokia Side-Notched points (figure 13.6), one Citrus point, and one Santa Fe projectile point; the latter two date to the Archaic period. Except for one of the Cahokia points, which is reworked, all are in nearly pristine condition. Iron-oxide or hematite nodules were present throughout Kinzey's Knoll, and red pigment or dust was displayed on a variety of artifacts and occasionally on discarded oyster and clam shells. Moore (1894a, 1894b, 1895) encountered layers and deposits of hematite-laden sands throughout the Shields and Grant mounds, often in association with human burials.

Fragments of sheet copper and a rolled bead further distinguish Kinzey's Knoll from other areas of the site. It is generally assumed that copper artifacts arrived in northeastern Florida in finished form. While this is apparently the case for long-nosed god maskettes and other items with a broad geographical distribution, copper-covered bone, wood, and shell artifacts and rolled beads were likely crafted locally from previously hammered pieces of sheet copper. We interpret the pres-

Figure 13.6. Cahokia Side-Notched points, Kinzey's Knoll.

ence of copper scraps along with utilized shark teeth (with evidence of bi-rotational wear), teeth gravers, shell scrapers, bone needles, sandstone abraders, and modified deer antler tines as the material traces of mortuary craft production.

The quality and quantity of animal bone from Kinzey's Knoll suggest a deposit that was distinct from the deposits of quotidian life (Marrinan 2005). The ethnographic literature is rife with evidence of feasting in the context of ritual or religious events in middle-range societies (see Dietler and Hayden 2001). In a recent faunal study, Parsons and Marrinan (2013) calculated vertebrate faunal density (total estimated biomass divided by number of cubic centimeters excavated) for nine sites along the Georgia Bight. In their sample, Kinzey's Knoll yielded 26,000 grams of biomass per cubic meter, which was slightly more than twice the biomass of the closest context, a Late Archaic shell ring along the Georgia coast. Moreover, this calculation does not consider the dietary contribution of oysters and other shellfish species.

Fish and shellfish dominate the biomass, but deer remains are more prevalent than at other known St. Johns II contexts or in local refuse deposits dating to both earlier and later time periods. Avian remains are well represented, and all but five of the 20 species of birds identified were local or migrating waterfowl. Also documented were several unusual marine or predatory mammal species such as dolphin, bear, gray fox, and bobcat (Marrinan 2005). Unique to this midden, by mere presence and frequency, were unmodified vertebrae and teeth representing eight large cartilaginous fish. Though they tend to support the idea that the faunal assemblage is the result of ritual feasting, Parsons and Marrinan (2013, 58) conclude that "comparisons with other feasting assemblages are needed to evaluate whether faunal density can be linked to ritual behavior and feasting."

Finally, human bone was present in the shell midden at Kinzey's Knoll, which implicates this locus as part of the prolonged mortuary program practiced by the residents of Mill Cove. A large piece of an innominate bone was identified during the 2000 field season, and a heavily modified right femur from a robust adult and several permanent and deciduous teeth were found in 2012. The former is a shaft fragment 36 centimeters long from an athletic and muscular individual (David Steadman, personal communication 2012); the proximal and distal ends were removed before the bone was deposited in the midden. A narrow U-shaped, drilled or punched-out channel was made to remove the lesser trochanter. The edges of the channel (maximum length of 8.5 centimeters) are slightly beveled to the interior and display four cut marks on the surface of the unsmoothed, bumpy beveled edge. Evidence of battering is also evident, as is a lump of charcoal (5.4 × 6.7 millimeters) that is embedded in the exposed spongy bone at the very proximal tip. However, the bone was not thermally altered. Sections of the diaphysis are well polished, and at least six short cut marks are visible along the shaft. None of the cut marks were deep. While the teeth and smaller remains might have been lost during handling and transport of skeletal remains in the final stages of mortuary ritual, the femur is clearly a piece of worked human bone. Regardless of the specific manner and sequencing of the postmortem processing of bodies, this processing involved Kinzey's Knoll.

What appears to be another similar event midden is situated 25 meters to the north at Reeves Rise. To date, only limited testing has been done at this location in the form of a single one meter square unit and a 50-centimeter shovel test dug in 1988. Excavations have yielded abundant bone and pottery, a ceramic effigy adorno (canid), and a soapstone fragment. An oyster shell from Reeve's Rise has been radiometrically dated to the twelfth century, which suggests that it postdates the Kinzey's Knoll shell midden (Ashley 2005b, 293).

## Mortuary Patterns

At present, no St. Johns II burials have been recovered from nonmound contexts at Mill Cove, although some human bone clearly ended up in the Kinzey's Knoll shell midden. Current evidence indicates that all deceased members of early St. Johns II society ended a potentially lengthy mortuary process in a sand mound. Although Moore (1894a, 1894b, 1895) failed to provide any estimate of the total number of burials he encountered, his excavation summaries hint at the presence of hundreds of burials (including single skeletal elements) in each mound. Coeval mounds in the region are much smaller and held the remains of far fewer individuals (Ashley 2003, 182–207). Moore's description of the Shields and Grant mounds indicates that interments displayed differing degrees of completeness and articulation, which suggest both primary and single and multiple individual secondary interments. According to Moore (1895), interments of "unnatural juxtaposition" dominated at Shields. Mixed and disarticulated skeletal remains are common in most St. Johns mounds.

Little is currently known about St. Johns II handling of corpses prior to final mound interment, but defleshing, storage, and other forms of secondary manipulation evidently took place. It is unclear where bodies and bundled bones were stored after death—in charnel houses, on scaffoldings, or in the mounds themselves. The presence of different burial modes could reflect group/status differentiation or maybe the existence of a culturally prescribed time or season for mound burial. While it seems unlikely that burial diversity reflects mobility patterns, as has been modeled for earlier Woodland mounds (Wallis 2008, 249), the large numbers of burials in the Grant and Shields mounds may indicate that individuals living in outlying settlements were eventually interred there sometime after death.

Hutchinson and Aragon (2002, 42) remind us that "many mounds [in eastern

North America] contain a mixture of fairly isolated primary supine or flexed burials and secondary bundle burials[,] often with a few cremations." This is exactly what we see in the Grant and Shields mounds. Their interpretation of such situations points to the possibility that primary and secondary burials represent different phases in a multiphase mortuary process (Hutchinson and Aragon 2002). Some corpses might have been placed in a sand mound only to be exhumed and reinterred at a later date during a commemorative event. Although we currently lack complete knowledge of the St. Johns II mortuary program, there is little doubt that a lengthy liminal stage was required before a recently deceased individual transitioned into a venerated ancestor.

## Trying to Tie It All Together

The Shields and Grant mounds were corporate cemeteries situated in the midst of everyday happenings. The consignment of the dead to human-made monuments of sand has a long history along the St. Johns River that extends back to the Middle Archaic (Sassaman 2010, 70). But mounds were far more than a pile of sand used to store bodies. Shields and Grant mounds were storehouses of social memory and identity. Their physicality projected visual and conceptual constructs that allowed the living and the dead to share time and space through recurring ritual. The episodic nature of their creation allowed a myriad of relationships and identities to be reaffirmed, negotiated, or even contested. The mounds were daily reminders of community and common history, and their sacredness and physical presence further evoked memories of the various outcomes of social interactions played out during past mortuary events.

The same can be said of Kinzey's Knoll, which represents an accretional special-event midden. Its positioning on a distinct rise in the shadow of the Shields Mound was not inconsequential; it was a culturally negotiated use of space. Two radiocarbon assays, separated vertically by 50 centimeters, produced one-sigma calibrated dates of AD 865–1035 (lower midden) and AD 990–1070 (upper midden), which suggests that the shell midden accrued rapidly during the late tenth or early eleventh century (Ashley 2005a, 164). Much of Kinzey's Knoll consists of thick deposits of clean, unconsolidated shells and little soil that appear to have been piled quickly, as is common in Late Archaic shell rings that some interpret as the "result of feasting" (Russo 2004, 43). Other sections of the midden, however, exhibit loosely consolidated shell with more soil, hinting at less rapid buildup at times. Based on the density distributions of shellfish, finfish, and pottery remains, Rolland (2005, 229) suggests that the sampled section of Kinzey's Knoll accumulated as a result of at least two episodes of more intensive use.

The details that led to the formation of Kinzey's Knoll may never be known with certainty, but on the basis of available data it seems reasonable to conclude that activities included graveside feasting, preparation and purification of corpses or skeletons, and ritual acts involving the crafting and use of specific mortuary items associated with activities centered on the adjacent Shields Mound (Ashley 2005b). The current absence of evidence for any kind of wall, screen, or barrier suggests that the events at Kinzey's Knoll were spectacles that were open (visually and audibly) to the public. This locus fostered a complex interaction between the living, the recently deceased, and immemorial ancestors. Such rituals may have been a drawing card and a source of power for Mill Cove, operating on one scale to negotiate the community's local and regional identities. It is likely that a similar locus existed near the Grant Mound; the presence of the two coeval mounds in such close proximity suggests some form of duality or social division at the Mill Cove.

A conspicuous component of both Kinzey's Knoll and the Shields and Grant mounds is items of a foreign nature. These include objects of both the contemporary Mississippian world and the deep past, most of which ended their use lives in mortuary or ritual contexts. We contend that these materials (and the social relationships they engendered) were necessary for St. Johns social reproduction; these items were material evidence of the connection of St. Johns groups to people and places from far away and in days of old (Ashley 2012, 121). By the eleventh century, in the wake of or perhaps shortly before the emergence of the Mississippian megacenter at Cahokia, Illinois, St. Johns II communities became entrenched in widespread interaction and exchange networks that reached across the greater Southeast. It has been suggested that the copper long-nosed god maskettes were "gifts handed out to people who would have forever after been affiliated with Cahokia" (Pauketat 2009, 145). Other items at Mill Cove from the American Bottom include a copper-covered biconical earpiece (Grant), two Cahokia points (Kinzey's Knoll), and perhaps some copper plates from Shields and Grant mounds. These and other similar items might have been gifted to St. Johns groups to win them over as important suppliers of marine shell and other Atlantic coastal materials such as yaupon holly and bird feathers (Ashley 2002, 167; 2012, 116–17).

Gifting engages partners in a recurring sequence of giving and receiving that has the potential to forge prolonged social relationships over great distances; it keeps bonds alive between individuals and groups (Mauss 1967; Sahlins 1972). Such social actions may have been part of adoption or alliance ceremonies that transformed strangers into allies, friends, or even fictive kin. Based on the quantities of exotica at Mill Cove, the community appears to have been quite successful at securing social relations with a variety of early Mississippian communities. Once acquired, the foreign materials might have served as specific referents to successful social networking (Wallis 2008, 259). Unfortunately, with the data at hand, it is difficult to gauge whether the appreciable quantities of nonlocal metal, stone, and other minerals in these St. Johns

II mounds were the result of relatively stable, low-intensity exchange over a long span of time (AD 900–1250) or higher-intensity interactions over a shorter interval.

What about the pieces of the past that are present at Mill Cove? These consist mostly of durable lithic artifacts, both chipped (projectile points) and ground stone (e.g., bannerstones, elbow pipes, steatite cooking stones) implements, that were originally manufactured during the earlier Woodland or Archaic periods. In early St. Johns II societies, these objects likely helped establish a cultural continuum that brought the past to the present and provided a tangible link to the immemorial roots of St. Johns II society (sensu Lillios 1999; Gosden and Lock 1999). These historical referents embodied the ancestors and mythical events that formed the basis of their origin stories and cosmologies. A periodic display of potent objects or material symbols that communicated incontrovertible ties to the ancestral past was needed for relationships with remote ancestors to be preserved effectively over consecutive generations (Lillios 1999, 237).

All of the pre–St. Johns II foreign artifacts at Mill Cove conceivably could have come from mounds in northeastern Florida. We see no reason to dismiss the notion that St. Johns people dug into centuries- or even millennia-old sand mounds to retrieve these artifacts of the mythical past. Such endeavors undoubtedly would have brought them into contact with human skeletal remains, linking in their minds the artifacts, the human bones, and the mound construction to ancient peoples. It was the histories of these people that they appropriated and made their own. Actual consanguinity was irrelevant; these were their ancestors.

By salvaging these items directly from ancient monuments, St. Johns II societies may have helped bolster assertions of an imagined genealogical history that extended back to the days of the original mound builders. Moreover, it reinforced their claims to the land and its resources. Perhaps recovery of ancient exotica played a part in the reawakening of local involvement in long-distance interactions networks during the tenth century as St. Johns II communities tried to emulate the accomplishments of their ancestors.

Mortuary ritual, whether at Grant Mound, Shields Mound, or Kinzey's Knoll, drew together dispersed community members in solidarity-avowing social gatherings at which assertions of ancestry and identity were renewed or transformed. The invocation of ties to ancestors is most critical during rites of passage, particularly the liminal phase between life and death. Summoning ancestral and otherworldly spirits through the public display of exotica derived from the both the contemporary and primordial worlds was essential to these rituals. But objects manifest no intrinsic meaning; that quality is inscribed upon them by people. Around the world, ritual has provided a powerful context for imbuing objects and symbols with meaning. These endowed objects, in turn, enabled people to actively construct social memory, identity, and history among the living.

In fact, pieces of the past have "no ancestral identity or cosmological authentication"; these qualities are ascribed to them by the living (Lillios 1999; 247). Mortuary rituals are authored by the living, not the dead (Barrett 1990, 182), and it was the living who carried out funeral ceremonies to create and recreate life at Mill Cove. New practices and beliefs that were enacted to engender connections to deep time and far-flung areas of the contemporary world were likely rendered traditional or ancient in order to validate community identity and extant sociopolitical relations. Through time, as the community's web of social connections began to disintegrate, some members of the society may have tried to use these rituals to tout new ideologies and create more exclusive fictive genealogical ties to important ancestors in order to legitimate social inequalities and exclusive rights to power. But such attempts by elites to hijack ideology do not appear to have taken hold at Mill Cove during early St. Johns II times (Ashley 2002, 172; 2012, 123–24).

Because gifting among the living produced and reproduced social relationships, gifts to the ancestors or the spirit realm may have achieved a similar goal. Although placing these symbolically charged items in the mound would have alienated them from the living and hidden them from public view, their importance was not lost. Through this ritualized act, the Mill Cove community gifted the materials to the spirit/ancestor world and in the process secured their placement in a sacred arena that objectified social history, identity and memory, in effect keeping-while-giving (Weiner 1992). Out of sight was not out of mind.

A final question to consider with respect to the material remains from Kinzey's Knoll is this: Why were complete projectile points, scraps of copper, and modified and unmodified fragments of human bone discarded there? Why were these hard-to-obtain materials not recycled or placed in the nearby burial mound? Perhaps social convention dictated that such symbolically charged materials could not leave designated areas of sacred space and thus had to be ritually discarded at designated times during or at the conclusion of the event. Maybe these objects were confined to a liminal state in which they could not associate with the living or the ancestors. Instead of keeping the objects, it seems that what was most important was keeping active the shared acts and social links of obligation attained through acquiring these objects via gifting, exchange, or questing. Being "St. Johns" at this time may have rested partly on a community's ability to sustain linkages that spanned long distances and extended deep in time, and success may have been materialized through the acquisition of foreign objects. Sand mounds and the ancestral bones and sacred objects they held referenced not only the present and past but also future relations that communities aspired to sustain or secure through far-reaching social networks (Thomas 1993; Wallis 2008, 259). The memories created through public ritual and other commemorative performances were as much, if not more, an invention of the social realities of early Mississippian times as they were an accurate representation of the past.

The broken bone and shell artifacts and copious amounts of fragmented pottery at Kinzey's Knoll also are interesting, particularly because the broken objects were still usable. Is this also merely ritual trash that was deposited there because it was the socially required thing to do? Or was there more to their fragmented condition? It is worth noting that while many of the sherds from Kinzey's Knoll are quite large and number more than 5,000, not one vessel has been reconstructed (wholly or partly) from lip to base, despite extensive attempts at cross-mending. The concept of enchainment offers a compelling possible explanation for why, in certain contexts, special artifacts occur in broken or unmendable conditions (Chapman 2008, 188). Enchainment links people, places, and things through the deliberate breakage of objects and the subsequent distribution of their parts among various households across a potentially broad landscape. In mortuary contexts, fragmentation and enchainment act to cement an ideological link among the living, their ancestors, and the not-yet born (Ashmore 2008; Casey 2008; Chapman 2008; Strang 2008, Taçon 2008). The fragments become mnemonic or metaphorical references to people (living and dead), places, and events. It is another case of keeping-while-giving.

During culturally meaningful gatherings, Mill Cove residents and other participants may have been allowed to contribute food and other craft items. Those used during these events, or merely those belonging to attendees, may have been broken or fragmented and a portion deposited in the shell midden at Kinzey's Knoll, with the remainder retained by the crafter and/or family members as a symbolic token of a shared community experience (Chapman 2008, 187; Strang 2008, 51). Might the basal sections or "hearts" of "killed" vessels deposited in the many mounds along the St. Johns serve the same function, enchaining the individual potter (family or other social group) to the ancestral past? Kinzey's Knoll cannot be simply dismissed as trash or an accumulation of rubbish associated with a particular gathering. Continued and expanded refitting attempts in conjunction with additional excavations at Kinzey's Knoll are needed to eliminate sampling bias as the cause of incomplete object recovery.

## Conclusions

Five centuries before the invasion from Europe, the Mill Cove Complex was one of the premier mound centers in Florida. The St. Johns II communities at Mill Cove and those to the south at Mt. Royal were in the vanguard of incipient and early Mississippian interactions during the late tenth through twelfth centuries. They were able to establish social relations with distant peoples and bring exotic raw materials and finished products to northeastern Florida. In this chapter we argue that at Mill Cove these items assumed mortuary and ritual significance, eventually terminating their use life in the Shields or Grant mound or in special-event middens such as

Kinzey's Knoll. These exotic materials were not used for utilitarian purposes. Not only did Mill Cove residents acquire objects from distant lands, they also secured items from the deep past. Through ritual, these items created a community connection to ancestors and the cosmos.

Excavations at Kinzey's Knoll have produced a tremendous number of ceramic vessel fragments; a diverse range of modified bone, shell, and lithic artifacts; pieces of copper; and an incredibly high density of faunal material. The amount of animal bone per cubic meter of midden matrix is simply staggering. These material residues spotlight ritual behavior during the eleventh century that involved preparation and consumption of food, burial preparation, and crafting and discard of highly specialized materials. At sacred locations such as Kinzey's Knoll, memories of the recent past and deeper histories were authenticated and made public. Sand monuments clearly were not the only arenas of ceremony at the Mill Cove Complex.

## Acknowledgment

We would like to thank Kinzey and John Reeves as well as the entire Reeves family for allowing us to work on their property. Their continued support of our research is greatly appreciated. We thank Michael Boyles for his help with figures 13.1 and 13.2, Buzz Thunen for figure 13.5, and Ray Eslinger for the LiDAR images. Figures 13.3 and 13.4 were used with the permission of the National Museum of the American Indian at the Smithsonian Institution. Thanks also to Neill and Asa for putting together the symposium and marshaling the volume through the publication process.

## References

Ashley, Keith H.
2002    On the Periphery of the Early Mississippian World: Looking Within and Beyond Northeastern Florida. *Southeastern Archaeology* 21: 162–77.
2003    Interaction, Population Movement, and Political Economy: The Changing Social Landscape of Northeastern Florida (A.D. 900–1500). PhD dissertation, Department of Anthropology, University of Florida, Gainesville.
2005a   Introducing Shields Mound (8DU12) and the Mill Cove Complex. *Florida Anthropologist* 58: 151–73.
2005b   Toward an Interpretation of at the Shields Mound (8DU12) and Mill Cove Complex. *Florida Anthropologist* 58: 287–301.
2005c   An Archaeological Overview of Mt. Royal. *Florida Anthropologist* 58: 265–87.
2012    Early St. Johns II Interaction, Exchange, and Politics: A View from Northeastern Florida. In *Late Prehistoric Florida: Archaeology at the Edge of the Mississippian World*, edited by Keith Ashley and Nancy M. White, 100–125. University Press of Florida, Gainesville.
Ashley, Keith, Vicki Rolland, and Rochelle Marrinan
2007    A Grand Site: Testing of the Grand Shell Ring. Report on file, Division of Historical Resources, Tallahassee.

Ashmore, Wendy

2008    Visions of the Cosmos: Ceremonial Landscapes and Civic Plans. In *Handbook of Landscape Archaeology*, edited by Bruno David and Julian Thomas, 167–76. Left Coast Press, Walnut Creek, CA.

Barrett, John C.

1990    The Monumentality of Death: The Character of Early Bronze Age Mortuary Mounds in Southern Britain. *World Archaeology* 22: 179–89.

Bland, Myles C. P.

2001    Moore to the Point. Paper presented at the 58th Annual Southeastern Archaeological Conference, Chattanooga, TN.

Casey, Edward S.

2008    Place in Landscape Archaeology: A Western Philosophical Prelude. In *Handbook of Landscape Archaeology*, edited by Bruno David and Julian Thomas, 44–51. Left Coast Press, Walnut Creek, CA.

Chapman, John

2008    Object Fragmentation and Past Landscapes. In *Handbook of Landscape Archaeology*, edited by Bruno David and Julian Thomas, 187–202. Left Coast Press, Walnut Creek, CA.

Dietler, Michael, and Brian Hayden (editors)

2001    *Feasts: Archaeological and Ethnographic Perspectives on Food, Politics, and Power*. Smithsonian Institution Press, Washington, DC.

Gosden, Chris, and Gary Lock

1998    Prehistoric Histories. *World Archaeology* 30: 2–12.

Gosden, Chris, and Yvonne Marshall

1999    Cultural Biography of Objects. *World Archaeology* 31: 169–78.

Hutchinson, Dale L., and Lorraine V. Aragon

2002    Collective Burials and Community Memories: Interpreting the Placement of the Dead in the Southeastern and Mid-Atlantic United States with Reference to Ethnographic Cases from Indonesia. In *The Place and Space of Death*, edited by Helaine Silverman and David Small, 27–54. Archeological Papers of the American Anthropological Association vol. 11. American Archaeological Association, Arlington, VA.

Johnson, Jay K., and Samuel O. Brookes

1989    Benton Points, Turkey Tails, and Cache Blades: Middle Archaic Exchange in the Midsouth. *Southeastern Archaeology* 8: 134–45.

Jordan, Douglas F.

1963    The Goodman Mound. In *Papers on the Jungerman and Goodman Sites, Florida*, edited by D. F. Jordan, E. S. Wing, and A. Bullen, 24–50. Contributions of the Florida State Museum Social Sciences no. 10. University Press of Florida, Gainesville.

Lillios, Katina T.

1999    Objects of Memory: The Ethnography and Archaeology of Heirlooms. *Journal of Archaeological Method and Theory* 6: 235–62.

Lowenthal, David

1985    *The Past Is a Foreign Country*. Cambridge University Press, Cambridge, UK.

Marrinan, Rochelle

2005    Early Mississippian Faunal Remains from the Shields Mound (8DU12). *Florida Anthropologist* 58: 173–208.

Mauss, Marcel

1967    *The Gift: Forms and Functions of Exchange in Archaic Societies.* W. W. Norton, New York.

Moore, Clarence B.

1894a    Certain Sand Mounds of the St. Johns River, Florida. Part I. *Journal of the Academy of Natural Sciences of Philadelphia* 10: 5–103.

1894b    Certain Sand Mounds of the St. Johns River, Florida. Part II. *Journal of the Academy of Natural Sciences of Philadelphia* 10: 129–246.

1895    Certain Sand Mounds of Duval County, Florida. *Journal of the Academy of Natural Sciences of Philadelphia* 10: 448–502.

Parsons, Alexandra, and Rochelle Marrinan

2013    An Assessment of Coastal Faunal Data. In *Life Among the Tides: Recent Archaeology on the Georgia Bight,* edited by Victor Thompson and David Hurst Thomas, 47–74. Anthropological Papers of the American Museum of Natural History no. 98. American Museum of Natural History, Washington, DC.

Pauketat, Timothy R.

2009    *Cahokia: Ancient America's Great City of the Mississippi.* Penguin Books, New York.

Penders, Thomas E.

2005    Bone, Antler, Dentary, and Shell Artifacts from the Shields Site (8DU12). *The Florida Anthropologist* 58: 237–51.

Recourt, Peter

1975    Final Notes on the Goodman Mound. *Florida Anthropologist* 28: 85–95.

Rolland, Vicki

2004    Measuring Tradition and Variation: A St. Johns II Pottery Assemblage from the Shields Site (8DU12). MS thesis, Department of Anthropology, Florida State University, Tallahassee.

2005    An Investigation of St. Johns and Ocmulgee Series Pottery from the Shields Site (8DU12). *Florida Anthropologist* 58: 209–35.

Russo, Michael

2004    Measuring Shell Rings for Social Inequality. In *Signs of Power: The Rise of Cultural Complexity in the Southeast,* edited by Jon L. Gibson and Philip J. Carr, 26–70. University of Alabama Press, Tuscaloosa.

Sahlins, Marshall

1972    *Stone Age Economics.* Aldine de Gruyter, New York.

Sassaman, Kenneth E.

2010    *The Eastern Archaic, Historicized.* AltaMira Press, Lanham, MD.

Strang, Veronica

2008    Uncommon Ground: Landscapes as Social Geography. In *Handbook of Landscape Archaeology,* edited by Bruno David and Julian Thomas, 51–60. Left Coast Press, Walnut Creek, CA.

Taçon, Paul

2008    Marks of Possession: The Archaeology of Territory and Cross-Cultural Encounter in Australia and South Africa. In *Handbook of Landscape Archaeology,* edited by Bruno David and Julian Thomas, 218–28. Left Coast Press, Walnut Creek, CA.

Thomas, Julian

1993    The Politics of Vision and the Archaeologies of Landscape. In *Landscape: Politics and Perspectives,* edited by Barbara Bender, 19–48. Berg, Providence, RI.

Thunen, Robert L.

2005    Grant Mound: Past and Present. *Florida Anthropologist* 58: 253–61.

Van Dyke, Ruth M., and Susan E. Alcock

2003   Archaeologies of Memory: An Introduction. In *Archaeologies of Memory*, edited by Ruth M. Van Dyke and Susan E. Alcock, 1–14. Blackwell, Oxford.

Wallis, Neill J.

2008   Networks of History and Memory: Creating a Nexus of Social Identities in Woodland Period Mounds on the Lower St. Johns River, Florida. *Journal of Social Archaeology* 8: 236–71.

Weiner, Annette B.

1992   *Inalienable Possessions: The Paradox of Keeping-While-Giving.* University of California Press, Berkeley.

Wilcox, Jennifer R.

2012   An Assessment of Archaic Hafted Biface Use in Mississippian Burial Contexts. MA thesis, Department of Anthropology, State University of New York, Albany.

Wilson, Gregory D.

2010   Community, Identity, and Social Memory at Moundville. *American Antiquity* 75: 3–18.

# Contributors

Keith Ashley is coordinator of archaeological research and instructor of anthropology in the Department of Sociology and Anthropology at the University of North Florida.

Robert J. Austin is vice president and principal investigator at Southeastern Archaeological Research, Inc. He received a PhD in anthropology from the University of Florida in 1997.

Meggan E. Blessing is a PhD candidate at the University of Florida. Her research interests are centered on the Archaic Southeast, zooarchaeology, and animism.

Robert S. Carr co-founded the Archaeological and Historical Conservancy in 1985 and has served as its executive director since 1999. He has worked with the State of Florida's Division of Historic Resources, the National Park Service, and Miami-Dade County. He received a MA in Anthropology from Florida State University, is former editor of *The Florida Anthropologist*, a former president of the Florida Archaeological Council, and the recipient of the Bullen Award and Florida's Historic Preservation Award.

Craig Dengel is a PhD student at Louisiana State University. For the past five years he has investigated Woodland period settlement patterns along the Florida Gulf coast as an Oak Ridge Institute for Science and Education fellow at Tyndall Air Force Base near Panama City.

Zackary I. Gilmore is a PhD candidate in the Department of Anthropology at the University of Florida. He received his BA in 2007 from Texas A&M University and MA from Southern Illinois University, both in anthropology. He is interested in the types and scales of social interaction engaged in by Archaic Period hunter-gatherers in the southeastern United States. His current work focuses on the spread of early pottery technology and the development of large-scale gathering places in northeast Florida during the Late Archaic.

George M. Luer holds a PhD in archaeology from the University of Florida. His research specialties include ceramics, shell tools, metal ornaments, canoe canals, shell middens, radiocarbon dating, zooarchaeology, and geomorphology, especially as they relate to American Indians such as the Calusa, Tocobaga, and their predecessors.

Paulette S. McFadden is a PhD candidate at the University of Florida. Her research uses geoarchaeological methods to focus on environmental change in coastal environments, particularly as it relates to human-landscape relationships.

Jeffrey M. Mitchem is associate archeologist for the Arkansas Archeological Survey and research associate professor of anthropology at the University of Arkansas. He directs ongoing research at the Parkin site in Parkin Archeological State Park in northeast Arkansas. His research in Florida centers on the Woodland and Mississippian cultures on the peninsular Gulf coast, early Spanish contact, ceramic analysis, and the history of Florida archaeology.

Micah P. Monés is a PhD candidate at the University of Florida. His research examines Woodland shell works on Florida's northern Gulf coast.

Jason M. O'Donoughue is a PhD student at the University of Florida. His research focuses on the archaeology, history, and paleohydrology of Florida's freshwater springs.

Andrea Palmiotto is a PhD student at the University of Florida. Her research centers on seasonality and mobility patterns among coastal populations on the northern Gulf coast of Florida.

Thomas J. Pluckhahn is associate professor of anthropology at the University of South Florida. His work focuses on the archaeology of the southeastern United States, particularly the societies of the Woodland period (ca. 1000 BC to AD 1000) on the Gulf coast.

Asa R. Randall is assistant professor of anthropology at the University of Oklahoma. His research examines the origins and significance of shell mounds in the Middle St. Johns valley.

Vicki Rolland is research assistant in the Archaeology Laboratory at the University of North Florida.

Michael Russo focused on subsistence and seasonality studies of Late Archaic and Woodland wetland sites in Florida in his MA and PhD work at the University of Florida. Since 1994 he has worked at the National Park Service Southeastern Archeological Center, where he has investigated state and federally owned coastal Late Archaic shell rings and mounds and Woodland ring middens and mounds from South Carolina to Louisiana.

Kenneth E. Sassaman is Hyatt and Cici Brown Professor of Florida Archaeology at the University of Florida. His research in Florida centers on the ancient people of the middle St. Johns River valley and the northern Gulf coast.

Rebecca Saunders, a University of Florida graduate, has done work on prehistoric and early historic sites on the lower Atlantic and Gulf coasts for almost 40 years. She is interested in the development and sustainability of coastal cultures and in the utilitarian and social uses of pottery.

Theresa Schober is an archaeologist and museum consultant in southwest Florida, where she directed restoration and exhibit development to provide a public museum at Mound House on Fort Myers Beach. Her research focuses on human adaptations to coastal environments, the impact of culture contact on patterns of diet and health, and public education in archaeology.

Jeffrey Shanks is an archaeologist with the National Park Service, stationed at the Southeast Archeological Center in Tallahassee, Florida. He received his MA in classical archaeology from Florida State University and has worked on archaeological projects in Europe, Asia, and North America. Over the last decade he has conducted fieldwork at a number of historic and prehistoric sites in the Southeastern United States and the Caribbean. In recent years his primary research has focused on Woodland period sites in northwest Florida.

Victor D. Thompson, assistant professor at the University of Georgia, has been involved in field- and museum-based work in Mexico, the Caribbean, the Midwest, and the Southeast, especially in Veracruz, Kentucky, Georgia, and Florida. His research interests include the archaeology of islands and coasts, regional analysis, shallow geophysics, historical ecology, hunter-gatherers, ritual, and monumentality.

Neill J. Wallis is assistant curator in archaeology at the Florida Museum of Natural History, University of Florida. His research is focused on the archaeology of the lower southeastern United States, particularly the histories of ancient communities in northern Florida and their interactions with each other over the past 3,000 years.

Brent R. Weisman is professor of anthropology at the University of South Florida, where he specializes in Florida archaeology, historical archaeology, and North American Indians. His publications with the University Press of Florida include *Unconquered People: Florida's Seminole and Miccosukee Indians* (1999) and *Pioneer in Space and Time: John Mann Goggin and the Development of Florida Archaeology* (2002).

Ryan J. Wheeler grew up in Fort Lauderdale, where he developed a lifelong interest in all things related to Florida, including its history and environment. He has graduate degrees from the University of Florida and worked for many years as an archaeologist for the Florida Division of Historical Resources. He is director of the Robert S. Peabody Museum of Archaeology at Phillips Academy in Andover, Massachusetts.

Nancy Marie White is professor of anthropology and registered professional archaeologist at the University of South Florida. She conducts an ongoing research program in the archaeology of the Apalachicola/lower Chattahoochee Valley region of northwest Florida.

Margaret K. Wrenn is a recent graduate of the Department of Geography and Anthropology at Louisiana State University. Her graduate research focus was a comparative analysis of the motifs and designs found on Late Archaic Orange Pottery from Northeastern Florida. In the future she hopes to pursue an interest in archaeological illustration and artistic reconstruction of archaeological sites.

# Index

Page numbers in *italics* refer to illustrations.

acorn nutshell and nutmeat, *45*, 49

Aftandilian, Dave, 216

agricultural production, 135. *See also* maize agriculture

Alligator Lake, *244*

alligators, 83, 210, *211*, 212, 214, 217

Alligood site, *244*, 249

Almy, Marion, 94, 103

alternative futures past: conceptualization, 145–46; emplacements, 152–53, *154*, 155–56; relocation and resettlement, 148–49, *150*, 151–52; resilience, 156–58; summary and further questions, 158–59. *See also* archaeology: of the here and now

AMS assays: Chattahoochee Landing, 229; development of, 95; Estero Island, 42–43, *45*, 48, 49; Parnell Mound, 255; SGSW, 28; Shell Mound, 153; Suwannee Delta sites, 149; Suwannee Valley, 248. *See also* radiocarbon dating

ancient urban planning: concept, 63, 64–65; messages of, 69–70. *See also* elaboration

Anderson site (Pinellas County), 96, *96*, 102, 103, 104

Andrus, C. F. T., 63

animal interments: as "ceremonial trash," 213–14, 217; dog burials, 211–12; Miami Circle, 203, 204, *204*, *205*, 206, 210, 212, 213–14, 217–18; rare examples of, 209–11, *211*; reconsidered, 9; summary and further questions, 216–18

animals: human connections with, 83, 212, 214, 216, 217; imagery on artifacts, 172, *215*; modified bones in special event assemblage, 270, 272–73; as persons, 9; preparation and consumption for feasting, 246, 253–57. *See also specific animals*

Apalachicola/Lower Chattahoochee Valley: approach to, 223, 225; archaeological and environmental background, 225–26; Chattahoochee Landing site, 228–30, *230*, 235, 237–38; continuities in design, 232–33; cultural chronology summarized, 225; exotic objects, 233–34; Late Woodland less visible in, 234–35; map, *224*; misunderstanding of Middle Woodland pottery, 231–32; mound building, 227–28; proposed pottery classification, 230–31; shell middens, 227; summary, 239. *See also* Fort Walton culture

—CHRONOLOGY: before Woodland, 226–27; early Woodland, 227–28; middle Woodland, 231–34; late Woodland, 234–35; Mississippi, 235–38

aquatic resources: benefits of access to, 53; increased exploitation, 24; mobility, fishing economies, and, 82–84; significance downplayed, 20; site typology linked to, 50–51; weirs or ponds constructed for, 41, 51, 53, 55. *See also* coastal archaeology; fishing; marine environments; shell fishing

Aqui Esta Mound site (Punta Gorda), *4*, 75, 78, 87

Aragon, Lorraine V., 273–74

archaeology: correcting classifications in, 228; field schools, 21, 65; of the here and now, conceptualized, 144–48; valuation, 13–14. *See also* coastal archaeology

*Archaeology* magazine, 212

Archaic period: migratory evidence, 20; radiocarbon assays (SGSW), 24–26, *25*, 27, 28–29, 32

—EARLY ARCHAIC: Apalachicola/Lower Chattahoochee Valley settlements, 226; living away from shell depositions, 30–32; water sources, 24

—MIDDLE ARCHAIC: aquatic resources, 24

—LATE ARCHAIC: Apalachicola/Lower Chattahoochee Valley ceramics, 226, 227; exotic goods in burials, 78; mound construction with clean shell, 110; shell rings, 8–9, 127, 137n1, 137–38n3 (*see also* Guana Shell Ring; Rollins Shell Ring); skeletal material dating and, 111–12; social organization, 187; Suwannee Delta sites, 147–48, 149, *150*, 151. *See also* Orange culture

## Ripley P. Bullen Series

FLORIDA MUSEUM OF NATURAL HISTORY

*Tacachale: Essays on the Indians of Florida and Southeastern Georgia during the Historic Period*, edited by Jerald T. Milanich and Samuel Proctor (1978)

*Aboriginal Subsistence Technology on the Southeastern Coastal Plain during the Late Prehistoric Period*, by Lewis H. Larson (1980)

*Cemochechobee: Archaeology of a Mississippian Ceremonial Center on the Chattahoochee River*, by Frank T. Schnell, Vernon J. Knight Jr., and Gail S. Schnell (1981)

*Fort Center: An Archaeological Site in the Lake Okeechobee Basin*, by William H. Sears, with contributions by Elsie O'R. Sears and Karl T. Steinen (1982)

*Perspectives on Gulf Coast Prehistory*, edited by Dave D. Davis (1984)

*Archaeology of Aboriginal Culture Change in the Interior Southeast: Depopulation during the Early Historic Period*, by Marvin T. Smith (1987)

*Apalachee: The Land between the Rivers*, by John H. Hann (1988)

*Key Marco's Buried Treasure: Archaeology and Adventure in the Nineteenth Century*, by Marion Spjut Gilliland (1989)

*First Encounters: Spanish Explorations in the Caribbean and the United States, 1492–1570*, edited by Jerald T. Milanich and Susan Milbrath (1989)

*Missions to the Calusa*, edited and translated by John H. Hann, with an introduction by William H. Marquardt (1991)

*Excavations on the Franciscan Frontier: Archaeology at the Fig Springs Mission*, by Brent Richards Weisman (1992)

*The People Who Discovered Columbus: The Prehistory of the Bahamas*, by William F. Keegan (1992)

*Hernando de Soto and the Indians of Florida*, by Jerald T. Milanich and Charles Hudson (1993)

*Foraging and Farming in the Eastern Woodlands*, edited by C. Margaret Scarry (1993)

*Puerto Real: The Archaeology of a Sixteenth-Century Spanish Town in Hispaniola*, edited by Kathleen Deagan (1995)

*Political Structure and Change in the Prehistoric Southeastern United States*, edited by John F. Scarry (1996)

*Bioarchaeology of Native Americans in the Spanish Borderlands*, edited by Brenda J. Baker and Lisa Kealhofer (1996)

*A History of the Timucua Indians and Missions*, by John H. Hann (1996)

*Archaeology of the Mid Holocene Southeast*, edited by Kenneth E. Sassaman and David G. Anderson (1996)

*The Indigenous People of the Caribbean*, edited by Samuel M. Wilson (1997; first paperback edition, 1999)

*Hernando de Soto among the Apalachee: The Archaeology of the First Winter Encampment*, by Charles R. Ewen and John H. Hann (1998)

*The Timucuan Chiefdoms of Spanish Florida*, by John E. Worth: vol. 1, *Assimilation*; vol. 2, *Resistance and Destruction* (1998)

*Ancient Earthen Enclosures of the Eastern Woodlands*, edited by Robert C. Mainfort Jr. and Lynne P. Sullivan (1998)

*An Environmental History of Northeast Florida*, by James J. Miller (1998)

*Precolumbian Architecture in Eastern North America*, by William N. Morgan (1999)

*Archaeology of Colonial Pensacola*, edited by Judith A. Bense (1999)

*Grit-Tempered: Early Women Archaeologists in the Southeastern United States*, edited by Nancy Marie White, Lynne P. Sullivan, and Rochelle A. Marrinan (1999)

*Coosa: The Rise and Fall of a Southeastern Mississippian Chiefdom*, by Marvin T. Smith (2000)

*Religion, Power, and Politics in Colonial St. Augustine*, by Robert L. Kapitzke (2001)

*Bioarchaeology of Spanish Florida: The Impact of Colonialism*, edited by Clark Spencer Larsen (2001)

*Archaeological Studies of Gender in the Southeastern United States*, edited by Jane M. Eastman and Christopher B. Rodning (2001)

*The Archaeology of Traditions: Agency and History Before and After Columbus*, edited by Timothy R. Pauketat (2001)

*Foraging, Farming, and Coastal Biocultural Adaptation in Late Prehistoric North Carolina*, by Dale L. Hutchinson (2002)

*Windover: Multidisciplinary Investigations of an Early Archaic Florida Cemetery*, edited by Glen H. Doran (2002)

*Archaeology of the Everglades*, by John W. Griffin (2002)

*Pioneer in Space and Time: John Mann Goggin and the Development of Florida Archaeology*, by Brent Richards Weisman (2002)

*Indians of Central and South Florida, 1513–1763*, by John H. Hann (2003)

*Presidio Santa Maria de Galve: A Struggle for Survival in Colonial Spanish Pensacola*, edited by Judith A. Bense (2003)

*Bioarchaeology of the Florida Gulf Coast: Adaptation, Conflict, and Change*, by Dale L. Hutchinson (2004)

*The Myth of Syphilis: The Natural History of Treponematosis in North America*, edited by Mary Lucas Powell and Della Collins Cook (2005)

*The Florida Journals of Frank Hamilton Cushing*, edited by Phyllis E. Kolianos and Brent R. Weisman (2005)

*The Lost Florida Manuscript of Frank Hamilton Cushing*, edited by Phyllis E. Kolianos and Brent R. Weisman (2005)

*The Native American World Beyond Apalachee: West Florida and the Chattahoochee Valley*, by John H. Hann (2006)

*Tatham Mound and the Bioarchaeology of European Contact: Disease and Depopulation in Central Gulf Coast Florida*, by Dale L. Hutchinson (2006)

*Taino Indian Myth and Practice: The Arrival of the Stranger King*, by William F. Keegan (2007)

*An Archaeology of Black Markets: Local Ceramics and Economies in Eighteenth-Century Jamaica*, by Mark W. Hauser (2008; first paperback edition, 2013)

*Mississippian Mortuary Practices: Beyond Hierarchy and the Representationist Perspective*, edited by Lynne P. Sullivan and Robert C. Mainfort Jr. (2010; first paperback edition, 2012)

*Bioarchaeology of Ethnogenesis in the Colonial Southeast*, by Christopher M. Stojanowski (2010; first paperback edition, 2013)

*French Colonial Archaeology in the Southeast and Caribbean*, edited by Kenneth G. Kelly and Meredith D. Hardy (2011; first paperback edition, 2015)

*Late Prehistoric Florida: Archaeology at the Edge of the Mississippian World*, edited by Keith Ashley and Nancy Marie White (2012; first paperback edition, 2015)

*Early and Middle Woodland Landscapes of the Southeast*, edited by Alice P. Wright and Edward R. Henry (2013)

*Trends and Traditions in Southeastern Zooarchaeology*, edited by Tanya M. Peres (2014)

*New Histories of Pre-Columbian Florida*, edited by Neill J. Wallis and Asa R. Randall (2014; first paperback edition, 2016)

*Discovering Florida: First-Contact Narratives from Spanish Expeditions along the Lower Gulf Coast*, edited and translated by John E. Worth (2014; first paperback edition, 2015)

*Constructing Histories: Archaic Freshwater Shell Mounds and Social Landscapes of the St. Johns River, Florida* by Asa R. Randall (2015)

*Archaeology of Early Colonial Interaction at El Chorro de Maíta, Cuba*, by Roberto Valcárcel Rojas (2016)

*Fort San Juan and the Limits of Empire: Colonialism and Household Practice at the Berry Site*, edited by Robin A. Beck, Christopher B. Rodning, and David G. Moore (2016)

*Rethinking Moundville and its Hinterland*, edited by Vincas P. Steponaitis and C. Margaret Scarry (2016)